PASSION FOR ISLAM

SHAPING THE MODERN MIDDLE EAST:
THE EGYPTIAN EXPERIENCE

CARYLE MURPHY

A LISA DREW BOOK

SCRIBNER

NEW YORK   LONDON   TORONTO   SYDNEY   SINGAPORE

SCRIBNER
1230 Avenue of the Americas
New York, NY 10020

SCRIBNER and design are trademarks of Macmillan Library Reference USA, Inc.,
used under license by Simon & Schuster, the publisher of this work.

A LISA DREW BOOK is a trademark of Simon & Schuster, Inc.

For information about special discounts for bulk purchases,
please contact Simon & Schuster Special Sales:
1-800-456-6798 or business@simonandschuster.com

Text set in Janson

Manufactured in the United States of America

1   3   5   7   9   10   8   6   4   2

Library of Congress Cataloging-in-Publication Data
Murphy, Caryle.
Passion for Islam : shaping the modern Middle East : the Egyptian experience / Caryle Murphy.
p. cm.
1. Islam and state—Egypt—20th century. 2. Islam and politics–Egypt—20th century. 3. Islam—
Social aspects—Egypt—29th century. 4. Egypt—Politics and government—1981– 5. Egypt—
Social conditions—1981– 6. Religious awakening—Islam. I. Title.
BP64.E3 M866 2002
297'.0962—dc21   2002030290

ISBN 0-7432-3578-9

This book is dedicated with love to my parents,
Muriel K. Murphy and the late Thomas J. Murphy

And to the memory of Richard M. Keane and Francis E. Grogan,
who lost their lives September 11, 2001,
at New York's World Trade Center

CONTENTS

FAITH AND MODERNITY

PEOPLE OF THE BOOK

THE PATH AHEAD

INTRODUCTION

1

First Verses

"Thee do we worship, And Thine aid we seek. Show us the Straight Way."
— OPENING PRAYER OF THE QUR'AN, VERSES 5–6

"Someone exclaimed in a voice hoarse with pain, 'God exists!' . . .The mention of God's name was like a magnet attracting and assembling around it their roving thoughts which had been scattered by despair."
— NAGUIB MAHFOUZ, *Palace Walk*

The minivan was cruising steadily down the bumpy, two-lane blacktop that runs through the luxuriant Nile Valley. "South Sinai Travel" was emblazoned on its hood and the roof was piled high with suitcases and camping gear. Cramped inside were nine tourists, including Sharon Hill, a British nurse on her first trip to Egypt. The Egyptian driver and guide were seated up front. The group had just eaten lunch and was marveling at scenes unchanged for centuries: solitary farmers bent over their fields, slender palm trees bowing to the land, and wobbly-wheeled donkey carts poking down the road. Beyond the flat farmland, chalky pockmarked cliffs stood as sentries before vast reaches of desert. The town of Assiut lay ahead, and beyond it, the travelers' destination: the ancient city of Luxor with its majestic Temple of Karnak and one of the world's most fabled monuments to female ambition, Pharaoh Hatshepsut's colonnaded mortuary temple.

But as the van passed, a boy on the side of the road whistled. It was, it now seems, a cue. Suddenly, a hail of gunfire erupted from both sides of the road. Windows split and passengers screamed, blood gushing from their bodies. With one of the tires blown out, the van sped up and then jammed to a halt.

The attackers fled into a dense, green sea of sugar cane and corn. Sharon's white T-shirt bore a sickening, widening stain of red. Hit in the stomach, she died a few hours later at a nearby hospital. She was twenty-eight.

A claim of responsibility came swiftly in a handwritten Arabic statement delivered to Egyptian reporters in Assiut. It said that Islamic Group, an underground rebel movement fighting to install an orthodox Islamic state in Egypt, had mounted the October 1992 attack—the ninth violent assault on foreigners that year, but the first fatal one. "Tourism," the statement declared dryly, "is our second target after high-level political leaders in the bid to implement Islamic law in Egypt."

A few weeks later, a bus carrying twenty-two German tourists was fired on as it neared the weedy central plaza in Qena, another town in southern Egypt. Six Germans and the Egyptian bus driver were wounded in the mid-day attack, which left more than twenty bullet holes in the bus. In Qena's marketplace furious townspeople quickly tackled one of the assailants. He was dressed in blue jeans and toting a machine gun. Bestawi Abdel Meguid was a high school drop-out from a small nearby village called Hujairat. He confessed, Egyptian papers reported, to being a member of Islamic Group. In the front-page photos showing him being led away by police, he looked terrified.

Tried before a military tribunal in Cairo, Abdel Meguid was convicted and sentenced to death. His mother, Harissa Al Soghaiar, visited him in prison. "His hands were tied behind him and I couldn't touch him," she recalled, rubbing her hands in desperation. "What can I say? We were separated by a screen. He cried. I cried. I had no chance to hug or kiss him. I saw unjust days, incredibly unjust, since the 'event.' Now they are telling me that my son is going to be killed."

At dawn on a warm July morning in 1993, Abdel Meguid was hanged in Cairo's Central Prison near Bab Al Khalq, which means "Gate of the People." If he ever fully understood why, no one knew. He was eighteen.

Seated at my desk in Cairo as a correspondent for *The Washington Post*, I read the wire reports of Sharon's death and a few months later of Abdel Meguid's execution. What, I wondered, was going on here? For centuries, Egypt had embraced foreigners with suffocating affection and been renowned for its tolerant brand of Islam. Usually, the natives' idea of murder was talking you to death. This gentle land was now siring youths who gunned down tourists?

In another autumn eight years later, under crisp blue skies oblivious to disaster, three hijacked airliners rammed into New York's World Trade Center and the Pentagon. A fourth, diverted from its intended target by passengers, crashed in Pennsylvania. It was the worst terrorist attack in

American history, and quite possibly the single worst act of terrorism outside the context of a mutually declared war in modern times.

This time I watched the catastrophe on television in my living room in Washington. This time I was personally affected, losing a close family friend and an in-law in the fiery carnage in New York. And this time I felt I knew much more about Islam and the Middle East.

Like most Americans, I first became aware of Islam's new power in the Middle East on a winter day in 1979 when our television screens showed a frail, scowling man dressed in a black turban and flowing gray robe emerge from an Air France jet at Tehran International Airport. At the unrevolutionary age of seventy-seven, the exiled Ayatollah Ruhollah Khomeini had come home to lead Iran's Islamic revolution. The white-bearded ayatollah's dour demeanor was as ominous as the frenzied clamor of the crowds greeting him.

In the years to come, those stirrings of fear proved valid. The Islamic Republic of Iran meted out vengeful "justice" to officials of the ancien régime and allowed religious vigilantes to beat up women wearing lipstick or showing their hair. Its clergymen-turned-politicians claimed to rule in the name of God and Khomeini issued a death sentence on British author Salman Rushdie. For Americans, a painful tableau unfolded: In Tehran, the humiliating 444-day seizure of the U.S. embassy; in Beirut, bombings that killed over 300 Americans and the years-long holding of Western hostages.

For better or for worse, the early days of Iran's Islamic revolution shaped our perceptions of Islam in the Middle East. To many Americans, Islam became synonymous with theocracy, intolerance, and violence.

Watching these events from afar, I was part perplexed, part intrigued. For most of my life Islam, a faith that springs from the same monotheistic tradition as Judaism and Christianity, was something exotic to me. I grew up in an Irish Catholic family in Boston, the eldest of six children. We did not know, as far I recall, any Muslims. After graduating from college, I taught in Kenya for two years. I eventually decided that I wanted to be a journalist and that a good place to start would be Africa. I ended up in Angola, where I worked as a freelance reporter covering the civil war that followed Angola's 1975 independence from Portugal. Hired by *The Washington Post* in 1976, I had many different assignments in the years that followed. At home, I covered schools, immigration, and the federal courts. In the late 1970s, I was the *Post*'s correspondent in South Africa for four years.

Then, in late 1989, ten years after Iran's 1979 upheaval, I became the *Post*'s correspondent in Cairo, covering the Arab world. The next five years were adventurous. I found myself in Kuwait the day Iraq invaded, which offered me a unique chance to see the early days of the occupation. After twenty-seven days, some of them in hiding, I fled to Saudi Arabia with a group of Kuwaitis. I helped a large contingent of *Post* reporters cover the Persian Gulf War of 1990–1991 that followed. Both before and after the war, I was fortunate to be able to travel widely for my newspaper, visiting, among other countries, Iraq, Syria, and Iran. I spent the last four months of my tour in Jerusalem, covering Israel and the Palestinians.

But for most of the time, my home was Cairo. It was the first time I made my home in a Muslim country, and I soon found that in Egypt, religion is ever present. A casual "How are you?" is answered with "Fine, thanks be to Allah." Cabdrivers, upon being told the desired destination, invariably reply "If Allah wills it." At the small vegetable stall where I shopped, the owner kept his produce tightly stacked on shelves lining the walls from top to bottom. One day, I saw that he'd lovingly interspersed a packed shelf of white turnips with deep purple eggplants to spell "Allah." He smiled proudly when I noticed. He would find it preposterous that his display of religious devotion might offend a customer.

Just a century ago, the slender minarets of Cairo's mosques stood like erect pickets over the city's hunched skyline, soaring symbols of its religious identity. Nowadays, those minarets are surrounded by a forest of boxy high-rises, gaudy with neon, in a sign of the growth of the twenty-first century secular city. But even hidden among skyscrapers, Cairo's minarets are very well heard. Five times a day, their scratchy loudspeakers pierce the urban din in echoing waves with the muezzins' reminder that "God is most Great. I testify that there is no god but God. I testify that Muhammad is the messenger of God. Come to prayer. Come to well-being. God is most Great. There is no god but God." Borne on the air, it is a message that defies escape. And for those who hear it proclaimed throughout the land every single day of their lives, it offers comfort and reassurance.

I knew the Arabic word *Islam* means "submission." But seeing it was another thing. Standing shoulder to shoulder in mosques, thousands of Muslims form straight and orderly rows—a configuration notably absent in Egyptian bus stops and post offices. Kneeling in unison, they press their foreheads to the ground in a sign of submission to God. At this silent moment, worshipers differ from each other no more than peas in a pod, and individuality very visibly gives way to community, something highly valued in Islam.

But my tour in Cairo also saw a different face of Islam. In the early 1990s, a brutal Islamist insurgency erupted that was unlike anything before in modern Egypt. It was longer, more pervasive, and more deadly than earlier spikes of Islamist violence. The rebels were younger, more numerous, and more daring than in the past. They came close to killing President Hosni Mubarak, three cabinet ministers, and the Arab world's only Nobel Laureate in literature. For a while, they eviscerated Egypt's tourist industry.

Before the government subdued the rebellion, at times using methods as brutal as those of the rebels, more than thirteen hundred people, including terrorists, policemen, and innocent civilians, had been killed. Among the dead were nearly a hundred foreigners, of whom Sharon Hill was the first. Of those, fifty-eight were slain in one horrific day in a November 1997 attack at Hatshepsut's Temple in Luxor, the very place Sharon had been headed. The insurgency also led to the hanging of close to ninety Egyptians, the largest number of executions for political crimes in Egypt's modern history. Despite their determination, the rebels had been no match for the stolid Egyptian state.[1]

By the end of my five-year stay in Cairo, two things were clear to me. First, the Islamist rebellion had not settled many big questions about Egypt's future. Second, the religious extremism it typified was only part of a much bigger movement sweeping the country. Egyptians of all ages and social ranks were looking at Islam in new ways, and this religious revival was transforming their country. Egypt was not becoming "another Iran," but it was becoming a different Egypt. I saw the same heightened interest in Islam as I traveled throughout the Middle East, from the Arabian peninsula to Algeria.

The underlying theme of this book is that the religious terrorism emanating from the Middle East has to be understood—not excused, but understood—in the context of three historical forces. They include Islam's reawakening and subsequent internal turmoil, the enduring presence of authoritarian governments, and the failure to resolve the Israeli-Palestinian conflict. Over decades, these forces have combined to create a combustible environment in the Middle East. It is not an environment that turns every Muslim into a kamikaze terrorist. But it has allowed a fanatical minority to gain a foothold.

Set in Egypt, this book explains the interaction of these three forces. It begins with Islam's reawakening, which has been building for decades and will be a major influence on the world's 1.3 billion Muslims for years to come. The best way to grasp this historical drama, I believe, is by observing how it unfolds on four separate but overlapping levels.

First, *Pious Islam*. Beset by temptations and traffic jams in Cairo's teeming shantytowns, Egyptians have turned to their religion with increased devotion. With more women donning headscarves, more men shunning alcohol, and everyone more observant of religious rituals, personal piety has seen a grassroots groundswell. The upshot has been an increasingly Islamicized society, which provides the backdrop for the second level of Islam's revival.

Political Islam. In Egypt as elsewhere in the region, Islamist activists are seeking to wrest power from secular-oriented governments in order to implement a religious-based vision of an Islamic state and society. They are seeking to redefine Islam's role in the public arena.

Among these Islamists, a radical minority has taken up arms to spread a puritanical, xenophobic, and intolerant version of Islam. Their eventual aim is to unify all Muslims and strengthen Islam as a global force. Their violence and terrorism, which scarred Egypt, Algeria, and Israel in the 1990s and the United States in 2001, has pushed what is sometimes called "Radical Islam" to the forefront of Western consciousness and to the top of policymakers' agendas. Its dangers are real and it is reprehensible, victimizing mostly innocent civilians.

But to see Islamist terrorism inflicted by a Muslim fringe as the sum total of Political Islam is misguided. Violent extremists like those in Osama Bin Laden's Al Qaeda are only one manifestation of Political Islam, which is a broad spectrum of Islamists, most of whom reject violence. Some are driven by personal ambition. Others aim to build a more just and moral social order. Some are unreconstructed fundamentalists unable to shed outdated interpretations of their scriptures. Still others seek to blend Islam with democratic principles and the demands of modernity—an endeavor in which they still have a long way to go. But to dismiss them or fail to distinguish them from radical Islamists is to misunderstand Political Islam, a multifaceted, dynamic force that will influence Middle East politics for decades to come and one that is closely allied to the third aspect of Islam's revival.

Cultural Islam. Amid a globalizing world, many Muslims feel threatened by a "cultural invasion" from the West. In response, they are reasserting their existential cultural guidepost, Islam. They are returning to their Islamic "roots" because they see Islam as a protective armor against a humiliating loss of identity.

American pop culture, particularly its obsessive flaunting of sex, is the first target of Cultural Islam. But Muslims are also challenging Western cultural values often associated with modernity, such as individualism, secularism, and feminism. In their search for cultural and psychological independence from the West, they reject the assumption that as people around the world modernize, they inevitably will think and act like Westerners.

The fourth layer of Islam's renewal is theological. I call it *New Thinking* in Islam. To a degree unprecedented in modern times, Muslim men and women are reexamining Islam's sacred scriptures, even challenging traditional methods of interpreting those texts, in order to make their religion more relevant to the realities of modern life. Propelled by an imperative to revitalize their ancient faith, these Muslims have set out on a communal journey with many miles still to go. But the theological ferment within Islam, with its promise of dynamic and creative "new thinking," is likely to be the most important and lasting legacy of the complex historical juncture through which the faith is now passing.

There is, however, a downside to such intellectual introspection in a faith with no central authority. Scores of divergent voices within Islam are claiming that they hold the only true version of their faith. These voices are engaged in a raging, intramural battle for the Islamic soul. In many parts of the world, particularly in the West, moderate Muslims who are taking modernity into account in their theological reassessments are gaining advantage. But in other regions, and in particular the Middle East, the opposing forces of orthodoxy, traditionalism, and extremism, which resist new thinking in Islam, remain powerful.

Islam's multilayered revival has been accompanied by two other historical forces that have shaped the prevailing climate in the Middle East. One is authoritarian Arab governments that for decades have choked civil society, public debate, a free press, and democracy. The result has been an infantile, authoritarian political culture and few legitimate outlets for dissent—in short, a breeding ground for underground extremists.

Finally, there is the long-festering wound of the Israeli-Palestinian conflict. Viewed through the eyes of Arabs, who are overwhelmingly Muslim, it is a conflict prolonged far too long by American bias toward Israel. For years, Arabs have watched Israel radically alter the demography of Jerusalem, confiscating Arab property to build Jewish neighborhoods even as it demolished Palestinian homes. They have fumed as Israeli occupation forces subjected Palestinians to humiliating bureaucratic rules just to travel or work. They have bristled to hear Israel call Jerusalem, a city with Islam's third holiest site, the "eternal capital" of the Jewish state. They have watched in despair as over 200,000 Jewish settlers, half of them since the 1993 Oslo peace agreement, moved into the West Bank and Gaza to live on the very land that Palestinians have long envisioned as their future national state.

At every turn, Muslims were bewildered, unable to comprehend how the United States, which gives Israel $3 billion annually, could not stop these Israeli activities. The emotions aroused in Muslims by the Israeli-Palestinian conflict have poured fuel on a regional climate already smoldering with political dissatisfaction and the conflicts inherent in the revival of a faith.

Some 230 million Arabs live in a score of countries that span five time zones and stretch from Iraq's snowcapped mountains to Arabia's oil-rich deserts to Morocco's Atlantic coastline. All have an interest in the resolution of the Israeli-Palestinian conflict. Most lack democracy. The history, customs, and temperament of each nation affect how Islam's renewal is expressed, but people throughout the region are responding to the revival in similar ways. In this book, Egypt is the paradigm, the boilerplate if you will, for understanding the bigger picture of Islam's power in today's Middle East.

It is an appropriate choice for several reasons. Except perhaps for the petroleum powerhouse of Saudi Arabia, there is no Arab country whose internal stability is more important to the United States than Egypt. It was the first Arab state to make peace with Israel by signing the Camp David Accords in 1979, the same year as Iran's Islamic revolution. Since then, it has been a cornerstone of U.S. diplomacy in the Middle East and the second largest recipient, after Israel, of U.S. financial and military assistance, receiving a total of $55.8 billion since 1948. The country's 358,000-strong military is the largest and most effective in the Arab world since the demise of Iraq's military strength. With nearly seventy million people, Egypt is the most populous Arab nation and its Christian minority is the largest in any Middle Eastern country.[2]

Egypt provides the ballast in Arab politics and diplomacy. It likes to talk first, last, and longest. And there is no other Arab capital with the magnetism of Cairo, the "Mother of the World" as the city modestly calls itself. A rendezvous for East and West since time began, it once produced some of Islam's most influential scholars and is the seat of thousand-year-old Al Azhar University, the religion's oldest center of learning.

For all these reasons, Egypt is center stage in the drama of Islam's contemporary revival. How it unfolds there will have widespread repercussions, affecting Saudi Arabia's internal stability, Muslim-Christian relations, Israel's security and integration into the region, as well as American interests in the Arab world.

Finally, at least three Egyptians were implicated in perpetrating our national tragedy in September 2001. The presumed ringleader of the nineteen suicide hijackers was Mohammed Atta of Cairo, who grew up in a middle-class neighborhood I passed many times on my way to the pyramids on the edge of the city. He reportedly left Cairo to study urban planning in Germany in 1993, while I was in Egypt. Two of Bin Laden's right-hand men, Ayman Zawahiri and Mohammed Atef, were also first radicalized in their native land of Egypt. Their names were already familiar to me when they surfaced in connection with the 2001 attacks. I'd heard about them many times as I reported on the Islamist insurgency. In addition, seven of the FBI's twenty-two "most wanted" terrorists are Egypt-ian—the most from any single country. If these men could emerge from the land along the Nile, a country with close ties to the United States, it is imperative to ask why. I left Egypt with a better understanding of that question and this book is the fruit of that journey.[3]

Sharon Hill and Bestawi Abdel Meguid never met. But these two ordinary people from very different worlds were both victims of a powerful storm blowing out of the Middle East associated with Islam's renewed power. Understanding this religious resurgence is vital as global integration brings different cultures into ever-closer contact and as America itself experiences growing religious diversity, including an expanding population of Muslims.

Also vital is clarity on words. In this book, I use *Islamic* to describe something that arises from the religion of Islam, such as Islamic prayer, Islamic art, and Islamic scripture. The word *Islamist* is a controversial term, partly because it sometimes carries negative connotations and partly because there is no universal agreement on its meaning. For me, *Islamist* is a useful, neutral term that can be applied to a wide range of thought and opinion. I use *Islamist* to describe those Muslims who take Islam and its corollary, *shari'a*, or Islamic law, as their principal reference points, and seek to restore them to the center of Muslim life through social, political, economic, or educational activities. In this book then, the *Islamist* canopy covers violent extremists as well as moderate political activists who reject violence. It encompasses people whose attitudes vary widely on such issues as culture, intellectual freedom, relations with non-Muslims, the role of women in modern society, and relations with the West.

Some say Islam's contemporary revival is already a spent force. But that assessment comes from an impaired vision equating Islam's renewed vigor with Radical Islam, the religious extremism that is now the focus of the U.S. war on terrorism. That vision ignores how Islam's revival is reshaping Egypt and other Arab countries in ways beyond violent politics. The yearning for personal solace, a just political system, indigenous lifestyles, and relevant theology all await satisfaction.

Just as the Nile runs through Egypt for almost eight hundred miles, giving it life, so also the Straight Way, the way of Allah, runs through it, beckoning its people. The search by Egypt's Muslims for a modern understanding of the Straight Way is the essence of today's passion for Islam.

Our story begins in the place Bestawi Abdel Meguid called home.

2

Withered Dreams and "Zucchini" by the Bushel

"O ye who believe! Stand out firmly for justice, as witnesses to Allah, even as against yourselves, or your parents, or your kin, and whether it be [against] rich or poor: For Allah can best protect both."

—QUR'AN 4:135

"How great is the luck of one whose uncle is chairman."

—EGYPTIAN PROVERB

Hujairat sits beneath a lush parasol of leafy trees at the end of a dirt path four hundred miles upriver from Cairo. I went to the hamlet of mud-brick homes in search of why Bestawi Abdel Meguid landed in a military court-room to face death so far from home. Hujairat was not on the tourist circuit. Take away the overhead electrical wires and there were few signs that it had been touched by modern times. Credit cards, flush toilets, and air-conditioning did not come up in conversations. Televisions were more common than refrigerators, which were rare. The nearest telephone was a mile away and there was one elementary school. The village's barefoot women wore the traditional loose black gown and kerchiefs of black gauze. They baked bread in clay ovens, raised pigeons in rooftop coops, and drew water from outdoor hand-pumps. Donkeys and camels lumbered along dusty passageways, ferrying sacks of harvested wheat, corn, and barley to market. Mournful-faced *gamussas*, the black water buffaloes so beloved by Egyptian farmers, loitered in the shade as slender-necked egrets preened on their beefy backs. Sultry breezes from the Nile drifted through

12

Hujairat, built around an irrigation canal jutting from the river. But when the soft winds slept, flies and mosquitoes attacked every patch of bare skin. Here, time passed in a dreary sloth. Here, I began to discover why Islam's promise of justice has led so many Egyptians to cling ever more closely to their faith.

Abdel Meguid's family lived in a two-story mud-brick house. Their beds were straw mats on the floor. The living room was lit by one bare bulb and a television. Its only furniture was a few wooden benches shoved against the walls. The scent of cow manure wafted through the open window. His family apologized for not turning on the fan. It was damaged, they said, when police rammed their dwelling with bulldozers as punishment after Abdel Meguid's arrest.

The house, larger than others in Hujairat, was built largely with money that Abdel Meguid's father earned in Saudi Arabia, where he was a migrant worker who came home once or twice a year. Abdel Meguid, the second of five children, was only fourteen when his father became an absentee parent, and maybe this helps explain why his son, a good student in his primary grades, failed high school.

The state-run, outpatient clinic serving Hujairat was located in an empty, two-story hospital built in the 1960s. A decade later it stopped taking patients because funding dried up, said clinic director Dr. Shahata Mohammed Mostafa, who used a few rooms of the run-down complex to see patients.

"This is the 'Administration,' " Mostafa joked, showing me a small room with a folding card table, a few bottles of medicine, and some ledger books. In the nearby examining room, paint was peeling from the walls and the sink was stained with grime. On a table, a few medical utensils lay in a cardboard box next to a bottle of disinfectant, its cap askew. The bedsheets were brown from repeated use. In addition to Mostafa, two nurses and a dentist staffed the clinic. It had no phone.

The young doctor saw about fifteen patients a day, mostly children with diarrhea and adults with bilharzia, a river-borne parasite. He had no problem getting medicine from the government supply office to treat bilharzia. But securing other medicines was less certain. "It's fifty-fifty," he said. When Mostafa asked for paint for the examining room, he was told there was no money. "Troubles increase," he said, "when you have many children and little money."

The deprivations of Hujairat did not go unnoticed by it residents. A twenty-three-year-old woman who'd only give her first name, Mahrussa, was pumping water outside her home. "Yes," she said, she had known Abdel Meguid. I asked her why he'd been attracted to Islamic Group.

"Look at our village!" she snapped. "You wouldn't know it's part of

Egypt! We have no services. The people who rule Egypt are taking all the money!"

It wasn't supposed to turn out like this. A generation before Abdel Meguid was born, Egyptians had high hopes for their future. Gamal Abdel Nasser, who helped engineer the 1952 coup that overthrew the monarchy, declared Egypt a revolutionary republic. The handsome, mustachioed army colonel raised the banner of "Arab socialism," promising everyone a free education and every university graduate a job. He took land from rich farmers and parceled it out to poor ones. He built the Aswan Dam and created a huge public sector charged with producing, as the slogan of the day went, everything "from the needle to the rocket." Nasser, the son of peasants from southern Egypt, told his twenty-two million countrymen that the government was on the side of the struggling poor.

But those promises wilted away. By the time Abdel Meguid was born in 1975, Nasser had been dead five years and his successor had set about dismantling the socialist state. Aiming to energize the economy, Anwar Sadat embarked on a carefully calibrated return to capitalism. His "Open Door" policy retained the bloated public sector while encouraging the rebirth of the private sector, mainly through import monopolies for well-connected Egyptians. These entrepreneurs rushed through Sadat's "open door" and have been amassing private fortunes ever since.[1]

The new wealth is evident in Cairo's crowded nightclubs and chauffeured cars. Egypt imported five hundred Mercedes Benzes in the first five months of 1994, the second-highest number of any Arab country. By 1997, eight new golf courses, surrounded by $1.5 million luxury villas, were under construction, and the choicest beach spots along Egypt's Mediterranean and Red Sea coastlines had sprouted thousands of high-priced condominiums. Blocks of boutiques bathed in megawatts of light beckoned the affluent with big-name brands: Bally, Panasonic, and Jaguar Egypt.[2]

For the vast majority of Egyptians, such luxuries might as well be on the moon. The poor and the middle class bore the brunt as their state abandoned Nasser's promises and then abandoned its people. The rich few got richer while everybody else, including the Egyptian state, got poorer.

Hundreds of rural villages like Hujairat are the flash cards of Egypt's underdevelopment. An estimated sixteen million Egyptians live below the poverty line, over half of them in the countryside. Nearly 50 percent of the country's population is illiterate. With 500,000 new jobseekers entering the job market annually, unemployment has long been a national catastrophe; some estimates place it at 15 percent. Government salaries in Egypt, where GDP per capita in 2000 was $1,420, are such pittances that civil servants have to hold down two or three other jobs.

Part of Egypt's problem is its expanding population. Its annual population growth rate in 2000 was 1.69 percent—down from an average of 2.3 percent during 1975–1999. Even so, the country's nearly seventy million people are expected to swell to eighty-four million by 2015. And more than one-third of the population—34.5 percent—is under the age of fifteen.[3]

Like Abdel Meguid's father, millions of Egyptians sought a better life by taking jobs in oil-rich countries such as Iraq and Saudi Arabia starting in the 1970s. Though the bonanzas they once made in those countries are no longer possible, nearly two million Egyptians still hire themselves out to their richer Arab brethren, particularly in the Gulf.[4]

But the biggest escape valve for Egypt's rural poor has always been Cairo. They have streamed into the capital at such a pace in recent decades that its sixteen million residents account for almost a quarter of the country's entire population. The first casualty of this vast migration was decent housing. Graveyards and garages filled up with permanent residents long ago. The city's army of *bo'aabs*, the ubiquitous, eagle-eyed doormen who guard the entrances of every building, spend their off-hours sleeping in broom closets and under staircases. Alleys are lined with shacks made of cardboard and scrap metal.

Most newcomers to Cairo have squeezed into the nooks and crannies of shantytowns such as Al Zawya Al Hamra. This sprawling area in northeast Cairo, whose name means "Little Red Mosque," was still semirural in the 1960s when Nasser built several blocks of square apartment buildings for families of government workers. Since then, Zawya has expanded with an urban design perhaps best called "Haphazard Eclectic." No zoning regs here. Walk-up tenements stand cheek by jowl with car-repair shops, cobblers, and coffeehouses. Outside the Pepsi bottling plant, street vendors hawk vegetables piled beneath faded beach umbrellas. Kids tugging at homemade kites skip around old women selling watermelons. In the streets, impatient drivers honk without pity at pokey donkey carts. Buses belching black fumes and listing at precarious angles, hurtle past with passengers riding alfresco, like flies on sticky paper.

People of Zawya do just about anything to make a buck. On one stretch of sidewalk, I saw a barber giving haircuts and shaves on a plastic tarpaulin, a man sharpening knives, and a third selling TV antennas he'd made from aluminum plates and plastic tubing. Here, recycling is less a civic duty than a matter of survival. A toothless man was touting filthy secondhand clothes. Another held out cigarette butts. Indeed, recycling seems a national obsession. On several occasions I opened a newly purchased copy of the *International Herald Tribune* to find the crossword puzzle already filled out. In most countries, airline cleaning crews discard the crumpled newspapers left by passengers. Not in Egypt. The papers are carefully refolded, taxied downtown, and delivered to sidewalk newsstands.

In Zawya, the word I heard most often was *ta'baan*, which means tired or worn-out.

"To be honest, life is tiring and everything is very expensive," said Yousef Alwan as he sat outside Galal's Coffee Shop hoping to get hired for a day's work in construction. Alwan said he was forty-five but looked ten years older. His white turban was loosely wound and one end of it hung rakishly by his right ear. He pulled down the collar of his galabia, the ankle-length robe worn by Egyptian farmers, to show me a purple, pus-filled blister on his shoulder. It was a souvenir of yesterday's job.

Alwan used to run a small sundry shop in Iraq. But since returning to his hometown of Fayoum, about an hour's drive south of Cairo, he had not been able to find steady work. In debt to a relative and with five children to support, he'd come to Zawya.

Alwan slept on the dirt floor of a hut. "It's dirty and has cockroaches," he said disgustedly, leading me to a warren of pint-sized shacks near a textile factory and a vacant lot with open pits of burning garbage. The windowless hovel was made of blobs of cement stuck with large rocks. I peered inside and saw a pair of dirty boxer shorts drying on a string. Two rumpled blankets lay on the eight-by-eight-foot floor.

"It should be for two people, but they put five to six people in each," Alwan said. A stout woman waddled over to listen. Without speaking, she confirmed what Alwan said by moving her index finger along her forearm in short lines side by side. Like sardines in a tin. For this, Alwan paid $1.77 a month.

If he got hired in the morning and worked all day, he earned about $6. He scrimped on meals to save money. "Sometimes," he said, "one saves oneself to have a late lunch and no dinner. I wouldn't come to Cairo except for the fact that I'm in such despair."

I could see Alwan was not exaggerating, as people sometimes do in the hope of getting a small tip. What I saw before me without question was a man at his wit's end. But I was moved even more by his final comment as we parted. "We think somebody from the government should go to the rural areas and see what life is like," he said. "Like the president visits abroad and the ministers who go abroad, they should come and visit our rural areas. They never do. All these people come from Fayoum and there is despair."

Mahmoud Metwalli, a professional ironer who presses clothes with his left foot, is more than tired. "Many people like myself are . . . exhausted," he said. "What makes us weak is the limited income. We're rapidly becoming worn out. We have our eyes on many things we desire but we can't get them."

Metwalli is a wiry, blunt-speaking man of forty-three who cannot read. Dressed in pajama bottoms and a T-shirt, he kept working as he answered my questions. First, he neatly laid out a pair of trousers on a low bench about a foot off the floor. Then he took a gulp of water from an aluminum cup and spit it out in a perfectly formed spray over the trousers. Grabbing the long handle of a large, triangular iron warming on a gas stove, Metwalli placed his left foot on its wooden lid and slid it over the pants.

If he pressed sixty pieces of clothing a day, he took home about $2.40. He does this backbreaking work six days a month when off-duty from his regular job as a government messenger in Menufiyah, a ninety-minute train ride from Cairo. That job pays $34 a month and about one-third of that pays the rent on the house he shares with his wife and four children. Metwalli calculated that he needs $135 a month for his family's basic needs, but said he never makes that much.

Even Zawya's permanent residents were struggling. I met Ahmed Sadek standing by his truck, waiting for an order. For each load of sand he delivered, he earned $10. Sadek is a tall, thin man with gaunt cheeks; dark, recessed eyes; and thinning black hair. "I'm a living example of the crisis," he said. "I'm thirty-four years old and I'm not married. And this is one of the problems. I could have gotten married some time ago but every time I found more and more problems. To get an apartment means you have to have large sums of money."

Sadek's father moved his family from central Cairo to Zawya in 1963 and built a three-story tenement on a narrow alley called Algiers Street. The building is now home for thirty-five members of Sadek's extended family and he invited me to see it. The entryway held a heap of truck tires and a workbench covered with paint cans. The concrete staircase was just wide enough for one person, which gives a pretty good idea of the scale of the rooms.

The tiny living room held a mirrored armoire, a coffee table, and several cane-backed chairs. It had a carpet, a clock, and artificial flowers in a vase. A bare bulb hung on a cord beneath a glass chandelier. Sadek said that after getting his high school degree, he did a stint as a graphic designer in an ad agency and then took off for Saudi Arabia because the money was better. He returned some years later with about $3,000 in savings.

"I had two choices," he explained. "Either to get married, which means my monetary situation would be very difficult all the time, or to get this truck. And so, God help me, I got the truck. And I'm waiting for it to pay a return. I tell you, if I had this income ten years ago, I would have been married by now. And I would have had a son who is nine years old," he said ruefully.

He leaned back in his chair, as if saying all this had drained his energy.

Sadek's trucking venture gave him a monthly income of about $200, but he still felt his life was pinched. "The problem we face is that now one cannot get his basic needs and so we have no luxury in our lives," he said. "Recreation is nonexistent, except for watching television or a video. Going to the cinema or to a casino? You only do it if you are engaged. A long time ago, we used to have parties in an area like this, birthday parties. Now, they don't do this. And weddings used to be feasts. Now people don't have this. Instead they have boxes of sandwiches because they are cheaper, even though feasts are something characteristic of the Islamic religion."

Egyptians no longer expect much in the way of services from their government, having given up on Nasser's cradle-to-grave promises long ago. What riles them more is having the playing field tilted against them by zucchini.

"Zucchini?" I repeated to the man who'd painted my office and was standing by the door waiting to be paid. He was in his mid-fifties, had white hair, and wore his glasses on the tip of his nose. We'd been chatting awhile when the floodgates opened.

"We want everyone to have enough to live. But that's not how it is," he said. "You find the rich here have so much money. And they get it by corrupt methods. For example, I have a shop for twenty years and I make enough to move my life. But you find others who open a shop and then buy Mercedes and then build big buildings and they do this in a corrupt way. But me, since I do things the way God wants, I don't. These are sensitive matters. And the rich don't care about the rest of us. As long as we have this zucchini, we won't all have full stomachs."

Zucchini or *kossa*, I learned that day, is Egyptian slang for corruption. No one seemed to know how this staple of the Egyptian diet got so maligned. The best explanation I heard was that zucchini grows very fast. So if something happens unnaturally fast or easily, it's zucchini.

Egyptians believe that zucchini—meaning favoritism, bribe taking, and nepotism—has reached epidemic proportions in their country. They often cite the so-called Gang of Sons as an example, referring to the children of top state officials who somehow always land lucrative government contracts and manage to have homes and lifestyles way beyond their fathers' official salaries.[5]

Just as annoying to Egyptians is zucchini's sidekick, known as *wasta*. A *wasta* is a "connection" in high places who can blowtorch the bureaucracy in order to help you get whatever you need, be it a job, a permit, or a meeting with a key official. More broadly, *wasta* means working those connections to your advantage. It is a souped-up version of networking uninhibited by conflict-of-interest laws or press scrutiny.

All Middle Eastern countries work to some degree on *wasta*—in Kuwait, they call it "Taking vitamin 'W.' " But many Egyptians feel their system is overloaded with zucchini and *wasta*, making it manifestly unjust. "If a rich person enters a police station it's blatantly clear the difference in treatment between him and a poor person," said trucker Sadek. "You find a poor person being treated horribly whereas a rich person is treated well. A rich person often has more than one *wasta*. He knows highly placed people like police officers. It's all *wasta* and zucchini. And it proves the old Egyptian proverb that says 'How great is the luck of one whose uncle is chairman.' "

Usually, cultivating your *wastas* and harvesting zucchini is done privately. But occasionally, Egyptians get a peek into how it's done at high levels. It happened once while I was in Cairo. Samir Ragab is editor of the government newspaper *Al Gomhuria*, a post that is a presidential appointment. Ragab was also a member of the Sun Sporting Club, a private gathering place for Cairo's well-to-do, and had tossed his name in the ring to be elected club president. As the election approached, Ragab dispatched a note to the minister of new communities asking him to set aside five hundred new state-built apartments for members of his club. The minister was apparently afflicted with temporary amnesia about the millions of Cairenes who can't find affordable apartments. And in what was a record response time for a cabinet minister, he wrote back *that same day* agreeing to "brother" Ragab's request.

Ragab also requested favors for his private club from other senior officials, including the installation of seven pay phones at the club grounds, free tutoring for its members' children, and fifteen slots on government-subsidized pilgrimages to Mecca, Islam's most holy site in Saudi Arabia.

Unfortunately for Ragab, his correspondence with the ministers was leaked to Al Badri Farghali, an opposition member of parliament. Farghali promptly raised the matter on the floor of the legislature. That night, the TV nightly news showed the prime minister soberly telling parliament that "mistakes were made," without elaborating on exactly what the "mistakes" were. The mystery deepened for viewers when officials at the state-run television station tried to contain the government's embarrassment with some creative editing: They aired a clip of Farghali denouncing the favoritism given Ragab without sound! "It came on television like an old silent movie," Farghali moaned.[6]

In the end, Egyptians got details of the "mistakes" from their newspapers, Ragab's *wastas* hastily canceled their favors and he dropped out of the club's presidential campaign. But he kept his job as editor.

For most Egyptians, the harder they scramble to get ahead, the more they feel they are standing still. Their lives are a burlesque of what matters most to any nation: The belief that tomorrow will be better. On top of that, they feel that the state, which Nasser promised would be the *wasta* of the poor, has become instead a partner to the rich.

The result is a sullen, embittered apathy among many toward those in power. Attorney Ahmed Sharaf Al Din, who works out of a shoe-box office in Wilad Al Aalem, a tiny oasis of gimcrack shanties surrounded by upscale apartment buildings, said he could sum up Egyptians' attitude toward their government with one word: Animosity. They believe "that this country is not their country but the country of rich people and thieves," he added. "They love Egypt. But they hate the government."

Mohammed Atta, the thirty-three-year-old Egyptian who is believed to have flown American Airlines flight 11 into New York's World Trade Center on September 11, 2001, apparently shared those sentiments. The Cairo University graduate, who studied architecture, used to call his country's ruling elite the Fat Cats, classmates reported. He was angry, they explained, at the government's coziness with the rich.[7]

I'd heard such sentiments often, but didn't realize how intense they were until the prime minister was nearly blown to bits by an Islamist rebel car bomb in late 1993. Afterward, Egyptians could be heard murmuring among themselves. The lament was sotto voce but unmistakable: "Too bad they missed."

When nations feel something has gone terribly wrong in their midst and citizens feel they have lost control of their lives, they take refuge in the familiar and fundamental. In Egypt, and in other Arab countries, that refuge is Islam. For ordinary people, Islam is their lodestar and deepest certainty. It has cradled them for thirteen centuries and is more enduring than the snazzy modern ideas they have recently tried—socialism, capitalism, and Arab nationalism. For millions of Egyptians transplanted from villages to places like Al Zawya Al Hamra, Islam remains the abiding anchor in their lives. It is enough to know that tiny Hujairat had four mosques.

Familiarity, however, is not Islam's only attraction. Equally important is its insistence on justice as the gold standard of society, the first principle on which nations and rulers are judged. Prophet Muhammad is revered not just as a religious leader but also as a social reformer who stressed justice. The Qur'an, Islam's holy book, emphasizes the necessity of a just and ethical social order.

Justice, wrote the nineteenth-century Egyptian historian Abd Al Rahman Al Jabarti, "is the most perfect virtue, its effect being all-inclusive and its usefulness permeating all things." If it is asked, he added, " 'What is the definition of a just king?' we say, according to the saying of those who know God, 'He is the one who deals justly with God's people and keeps himself from oppression and corruption.' "[8]

When citizens are disenchanted with their rulers, and have no means of redress, their hearts and minds incline to subversion. And in Islam's insistence on justice they find a powerful weapon. Thirsting for social justice, Egyptians and millions of others living on the edge throughout the Middle East are drawn to Islam because its message of justice indicts the authoritarian regimes under which they live. Algerian families whose apartment is so crowded they sleep in shifts, Saudi men who find no jobs yet know of the luxury in royal palaces, and Iraqis enduring the maniacal rule of Saddam Hussein are all unhappy with societies that revolve around the lucky few whose uncle is chairman. In response, many are grasping Islam ever more firmly.

This is the backdrop for understanding the first two levels of Islam's new power, the pious and the political. We turn first to Pious Islam.

PIOUS ISLAM

3

Personal Awakenings

"As to the righteous . . . they perform their vows, and they fear a day whose evil flies far and wide. And they feed, for the love of Allah, the indigent, the orphan, and the captive—saying, 'We feed you for the sake of Allah alone; No reward do we desire from you, nor thanks.'"

—QUR'AN 76:5–9

"We left God, so he left us."
—GASSER SHADI,
HONDA SALESMAN IN CAIRO

As the afternoon dwindles during Ramadan, Cairo slowly winds down like a tired watch. By five o'clock it is a ghost of itself. Tahrir Square, the massive merry-go-round of traffic that pumps cars into the city's main arteries, like a heart pumping blood, is deserted. Its garish neon signs touting Coca-Cola and Saudi Airlines beam into an ethereal hush. Policemen are nowhere to be seen. The last bus has run and clots of stragglers scurry home on foot, toting dirty work clothes in plastic bags. In the gathering dusk, the steel bridges that span the Nile like giant safety pins, binding the city's swelling half-moon flanks, no longer trill with traffic.

Hunger has becalmed this rambunctious city. Behind hunger is spiritual fealty. Cairenes observe their holy month of penitence by fasting all day—not even a sip of water. Now, invaded by the silence of its desert hinterland, the city waits. In homes, families crowd around tables. In streets, the poor gather outside mosques. Patiently, they listen for the ancient Krupps artillery cannon that sits on a bluff overlooking the capital. Its muffled boom officially decrees sundown and, with it, God's permission for his people to eat their first meal of the day. At this precise moment, all of Cairo, indeed all of Egypt—from Aswan to Alexandria—unites in savoring *iftar*, Ramadan's fast-breaking dinner.

Ramadan fasting, which is intended as an exercise in self-discipline, is one of Islam's five "pillars," or religious duties, for Muslims. The others are sincerely saying the *shahada*, or profession of faith that "There is no god but God, and Muhammad is His messenger"; praying five times a day; giving alms; and, when financially possible, performing the hajj, or pilgrimage, to Islam's holiest city of Mecca in Saudi Arabia. I'd been in Cairo awhile, however, before discovering how differently Ramadan is observed now compared to, say, thirty years ago. A generation or two ago, many Egyptians had become lackadaisical about the fast. This was especially true among those who came of age after World War II, when adopting the West's secular lifestyle and leftist political theories was fashionable in Egypt and other developing countries.

In the 1960s and 1970s, many Cairo restaurants stayed open all day during Ramadan. People smoked in public, even though this, too, is forbidden during the daylight fasting period. For many young Egyptians, Ramadan was less a religious duty than a traditional practice better observed by their less-sophisticated rural cousins. "We are moving into modern times, we are educated and religion is not our concern," this worldly wise generation thought.

But nowadays, most coffee bars and restaurants open only at *iftar*. If smokers must take a drag, they do so behind closed doors, and few Egyptians are willing to risk the dirty looks and verbal darts flung at those observed eating before sundown. Shirkers, in fact, could face more than public disapproval. In 1996, the head sheikh of Al Azhar University demanded "punishment for those who eat and drink in public during Ramadan," calling them "sinners" who "are bad examples and . . . influence others to follow suit."[1]

The shift in Ramadan observance is one of the most obvious signs of the grassroots revival of Islam that has taken place in Egypt and other Arab countries in the last quarter century. Egyptians of all economic and social classes have become more attentive to the role of religion in their personal lives and more observant of Islamic rituals. They are not so much returning to something they'd left as they are seeing it with new eyes and renewed devotion. This surge in personal piety, or Pious Islam, is the ground level of Islam's contemporary revival.

No Egyptian religious leader or politician orchestrated this movement, which is the fruit of personal awakenings by millions of individual Muslims. Like so many other revivals in history, it is a response to several factors. The grinding poverty of villages like Hujairat, the "tired" lives of Al Zawya Al Hamra, and a frustration with "zucchini" and *wasta*, have all nudged Egyptians closer to their religion. So has the need for spiritual purpose and meaning. In addition, the psychological upset to Egyptians sparked by their 1967 military defeat by Israel played a major role in nurturing Pious Islam.

By touching the inner lives of Egyptians, Pious Islam has altered the outer face of Egypt. But unlike Iran, where the 1979 revolution imposed religion onto public life overnight, the Islamicizing of Egyptian society has been more like the slow, almost imperceptible swivel of a sunflower as it turns toward the beams of a moving sun. Gradually, Egypt has leaned ever closer to Islam, overtly displaying practices and attitudes traditionally associated with the faith.

Hussein Amin, a retired Egyptian ambassador in his sixties, recalled when the new piety of his countrymen first struck him. It was one evening in the early 1990s. Amin was attending a dinner with professional colleagues at Cairo's Diplomatic Club, a spacious villa of the 1920s that now serves as a quiet if threadbare gathering spot for Egypt's diplomatic fraternity. During the meal, the minarets of Cairo sang out the call to prayer and "two-thirds of those around the table went out to pray," Amin recounted. "This was unheard of before! They were all ambassadors, they'd been exposed to Western civilization, had traveled and seen a lot.

"Thirty five years ago, I wouldn't be able to name a single diplomat who prayed or fasted," Amin confided. "Now it is the exact opposite. Now you have ambassadors who aren't a member of a religious group. But they have religious feelings."

Other evidence of Pious Islam is all around. An Arab journalist friend, who was a committed Marxist during his university years in Baghdad, confided that he has taken his son to visit Mecca, given up alcohol, and "is doing a lot of reading about Islam." Stand outside any mosque on Fridays, the Muslim day of rest, and see its overflow crowd of worshipers at the midday prayer service. Of those mosques, far more were built in recent years by individuals and community groups than by the government. And there is hardly an office building or bank without a small corner for employees to lay out their rectangular prayer mats in the direction of Mecca.

One elderly Egyptian recalled that when answering the telephone, "we used to say 'Hello.' Now, it is '*As Salaamu 'Alaikum!*' " a greeting meaning "Peace be with you." At public beaches, the bikinis and bathing suits that were commonplace twenty-five years ago are now the exception among Egyptians, and many women swim in the sea fully clothed. At Cairo's upscale Gezira Sports Club, men and women shared its swimming pool for years. Now there are special hours for women-only bathers who want to splash around unseen by men. In the club coffee shop, someone will as likely be reading the Qur'an as a magazine.

In Egyptian films of the 1950s women wore Western-style dresses with plunging necklines. Both sexes were shown drinking, smoking, dancing, and kissing. Nowadays, if screen stars kiss or drink, they are usually portraying characters of ill repute, such as prostitutes. Egyptian newspapers regularly carry stories of once-saucy belly dancers and actresses who abandoned their careers and donned the veil because they "returned" to their religion.

Many men have taken to wearing silver wedding rings instead of gold because Prophet Muhammad called gold unseemly on men. Bookshop owners say requests for books on Islam have never been greater. On weeknights, people gather for Qur'an study groups. And Al Salam department store, a three-story fashion emporium devoted to "Islamic"-style clothing, does a brisk business in long skirts with matching headscarves.

Perhaps the most visible sign of Egypt's Islamicization has been the ever-growing number of women who have chosen to veil, or wear *hijab*. Wearing the Islamic veil is not a "pillar" of Islam, and Muslims differ, depending on their interpretation of the Qur'an, as to whether it is optional or required for women. The veil takes a variety of forms in different countries and may involve partially or fully covering one's face. In Egypt, it most commonly means covering only one's hair in public. Just a couple of generations ago, most middle- and upper-class Egyptian women adamantly refused to veil as a sign of their emancipation from a traditional way of life that they, as "modern" women, were leaving behind. They were following in the footsteps of Hoda Sharawi, founder of Egypt's first Feminist Union in the 1920s, who tore off the tiny, white face veil then worn by upper-crust women like herself in a public display of female liberation.

Today, that attitude has almost totally disappeared. More than ever, the veil is taken as a sign that its wearer is a pious woman dutifully obeying Islamic notions of modesty. The veiling trend has been spurred by a host of reasons ranging from mere convenience (fewer trips to the hairdresser) to fashion consciousness to family pressure. Some young girls even say they wear a headscarf to heighten their chances of snagging a mate. Boys, they say, believe pious girls will make better wives and mothers. Whatever explanations women give for wearing the veil, however, the primary impulse for this trend has been a heightened consciousness of religion that has modified perceptions of female modesty.[2]

The same inclination toward piety is evident in other Arab countries. During one of my visits to Baghdad, I had dinner with an Iraqi woman and her family. She told me that during the previous Ramadan, "everyone in

Iraq was fasting. We even did it here in this family, and we hadn't done that before." When I asked why, she replied, "To feel good about ourselves."

The populist reassertion of Islam has also been visible in expanding charity networks. The ideal Muslim community has always been described as one displaying not only personal piety but also communal responsibility for the less fortunate. As people began to take their faith more seriously, this command nurtured a growth in neighborhood groups devoted to assisting the poor, the sick and the orphaned.

In Al Zawya Al Hamra, the Mohammedi Benefit Society is run by Ibrahim Mohammed Al Ataban, a retired fifty-three-year-old traffic cop. "Here in Egypt, we have people who are very relaxed and some people who are on the floor. The people who are tired, of course, are more," said Ataban, a rotund man with dark skin and large, droopy eyes who has lived in Zawya more than thirty years. "We give to people who are tired."

Started in 1975, the charity distributes rice, beans, and cooking oil to families without breadwinners. "On the day of giving aid, we get an unbelievable number of people . . . over five hundred families," said Ataban. It gives poor families a small monthly stipend and assists them with funerals, providing the coffin, body wrapping, and portable chairs so the family can receive mourners. It offers classes "to memorize the Qur'an," Ataban added, and depends mostly on donations "from good people" in the community. When I asked if it got financial help from the government, he replied, "We get no help from the government and from the government we don't request anything."

Renewed enthusiasm for ritual and charity are not the only evidence of Pious Islam. It is also manifested in the intellectual journey of many Egyptians. Mustafa Mahmoud's story is a common one. Now in his late seventies, Mahmoud is a tall, thin man with a large, square brow and tinted, reddish-brown hair. He has an intense demeanor that is accentuated by large, tortoiseshell glasses. He lives in the middle-class neighborhood of Mohandseen amid a complex that includes a large mosque, a health clinic, a library, an aquarium, and a small geological museum. Mahmoud raised the money for all these projects, and for a nearby sixty-bed private hospital. He is a familiar face around Egypt because he has a television program called "Science and Faith" on which he discusses how, in his belief, the Qur'an forecast many of modern science's discoveries. He talks of Islam as "a religion of mercy and love."[3]

But it was not always so. If you'd visited Cairo in the 1950s and found Mahmoud, then a young physician fresh out of medical school, he would have droned on about the virtues of "dialectical materialism."

"I was not exactly a Marxist, but a materialist thinker," explained Mahmoud, as we sat in his living room. Decorated in hues of rust that matched his dyed hair color, the room held a television, VCR, and lots of books. A prayer mat was draped over the back of the sofa. His first book, *God and Man*, was controversial when it came out in 1956 because it showed, Mahmoud said, that although raised a Muslim, "I was skeptical about religion."

But as he studied the works of Kant, Buddha, Aristotle, William James, and others, "a slow evolution began in my thinking," he said. "It was a long trip and I began to doubt this materialist philosophy, dialectical materialism, and all this nonsense." By 1988, he was converted to a worldview whose keystone was Islam. He called his next book *The Fall of the Left*.

"This trip took twenty years. It was not only reading books. It was suffering inside. It was an existential crisis," said Mahmoud, who'd given up medicine to write books full-time. "I have a deep belief in Islam. But it's a pity Islam is misunderstood in the West. They understand Islam through Khomeini and extremist groups. They remember the hostages and car bombs. Islam is a religion of mercy and love and beliefs. And it is also realistic. You find everything in this book," he said, touching the Qur'an. "You find the last word on everything."

As with Mahmoud, a spiritual restlessness set many Egyptians on a personal journey toward Islam. But there is still another reason, many Egyptians will tell you, for their country's deepened attachment to the faith. It was, they say, the psychic shock of six days in 1967.

After toppling King Farouk in 1952, Gamal Abdel Nasser lifted his people to dizzying heights on the world stage. While still in his thirties, he forced the last British troops out of Egypt. When the United States backed away from an offer to finance construction of the High Dam at Aswan, Nasser nationalized the British and French–run Suez Canal Company. In retaliation, the two European powers and Israel invaded Egypt in 1956. But even that crisis gilded Nasser's image as the three later withdrew under U.S. pressure. In the Third World, the dashing Egyptian leader shared celebrity status with India's Jawaharlal Nehru, Ghana's Kwame Nkrumah, and Yugoslavia's Josip Broz Tito. With them, he founded the Non-Aligned Movement, the Third World's response to the Cold War's bipolar world. Nasser's refusal to kowtow to the West and his fiery nationalist rhetoric made him a hero. From Morocco to Iraq, Arabs hunched over radios in bazaars, coffee shops, and offices to catch every last word of his static-encrusted declamations. And they wept for joy. Egyptians preened.

But then, when they least expected it, disaster struck. In June 1967, war broke out between Israel and its neighbors. The Arabs presumed that victory would be theirs because Israel was one small country against many. Arab airwaves and coffeehouses were filled with talk of "driving Israel into the sea." But in the space of only six days, Egypt's army was vanquished by the young Jewish state.

In the Six-Day War, as it came to be called, Israel captured huge swaths of territory from Egypt, Jordan, and Syria. Even worse for the Arabs, Israel wrested East Jerusalem and its ancient, walled "Old City" from Jordanian troops, putting one of Islam's holy sites in Israeli hands. The Dome of the Rock, whose sparkling gold dome is visible for miles around Jerusalem and is the city's most famous icon, is where Muslims believe Prophet Muhammad ascended into heaven for one night. Now their shrine was in the hands of non-Muslims.

The military rout psychologically devastated the Arab world. Arabs were haunted by profound questions: Why is this happening? What went wrong? It was a trauma similar in some ways to the one Americans experienced with the terrorist attacks of September 11, 2001. Even now Arabs refer to their defeat in shorthand. They call it Al Nakba, The Catastrophe. Egyptians were perhaps the most shattered, having fallen from such heights. But they chose to put a more optimistic spin on their military defeat, calling it Al Naqsa, The Setback.[4]

"People came out of this defeat of '67 morally shattered," recalled Ambassador Amin, then Egypt's ambassador in Moscow. "I came back immediately. Some people told me 'When we wake up in the morning we don't have the energy or desire to get out of bed. Why should we?' "

The military defeat set off years of anguished soul-searching. With their illusions of greatness that Nasser had so ably nurtured now broken to pieces, many Egyptians turned to religion for consolation and explanation. "They tried to look for an accommodation with life. Something to bring back the will to live," said Amin. "And many found it in religion, understandably. It's not the first time in history. And it grew . . . Whenever I came back from abroad, I found more and more veils and beards, and in the best of families, not only among the lower classes. People searched for a meaning in their lives and found it in religion."

Not a few Egyptians interpreted their disgrace as divine "punishment" for straying from God. "The loss of June 1967 lives inside all of us," said Egyptian novelist Mohammed Yusuf Al Qa'id. "It's interpreted as God's wrath on us since we drifted away from Islam."

As Egyptians absorbed the aftershock of their military defeat, a new and powerful force arrived on the scene that would fuel Pious Islam: oil.

In the 1970s, Saudi Arabia was awash in petroleum dollars. Schools, bridges, roads, hospitals, apartments, and refineries were carpeting the desert kingdom and this development spree needed workers. Egyptians left their villages in droves to work as laborers, teachers, doctors, and office help.

For many, working in Saudi Arabia was a dream. Not only were they earning more money than they could ever make at home, but they were also living in the Prophet's land, the birthplace of Islam.

These migrant workers, who were mostly men but included some women, too, were also exposed to Saudi Arabia's brand of Islam, which is far more conservative, rigid, and puritanical than Egypt's. Initiated by the eighteenth-century Saudi religious reformer Muhammad Ibn 'Abd Al Wahhab, this version of Islam is sometimes called Wahhabism. In Saudi Arabia, women are banned from driving cars and cannot travel without a male chaperone. Most are forbidden to leave their homes unless their husbands permit. The country has no cinemas or theaters since acting, dancing, and singing are deemed un-Islamic by Saudi religious authorities. Unlike in Egypt, government offices and shopping malls shut down during daily prayer times. "Religious police" roam the streets looking for slackers not praying at the appointed times or women talking to men who are not their relatives. There are no churches in Saudi Arabia and Christians have been arrested for holding religious services in their own homes.

Many Egyptian workers absorbed the severe religiosity of Saudi Arabia, returning home not just more pious but also more religiously conservative. Some of their new wealth went into building small neighborhood mosques to demonstrate gratitude to God for their new prosperity.

At the same time, Saudi Arabia used its oil windfall to spread its austere interpretation of Islam, sometimes derisively referred to by other Arabs as "Petrol Islam." Donations from both the government and Saudi multimillionaires poured into Egypt, benefiting those who were most religiously devout. Some Saudi money went to mosques and charities, like Mustafa Mahmoud's hospital. Some went to journalists and academics. Some also went to Al Azhar University for constructing satellite campuses all around Egypt whose curriculum reflected the Saudi tradition-bound approach to Islam. Many graduates of these schools, who emerged with an inordinate attachment to religious dogma, went on to become government civil servants, many of them teachers.

The Saudi variant of Islam, transferred through migrant workers and money, had a major effect on the reawakening to Islam in Egypt. In many quarters, Pious Islam acquired a distinctly conservative and intolerant character.

From Gasser Shadi's dress, I could see that the thirty-two-year-old Honda car dealer did not wrestle with the economic travails that exhaust Al Zawya Al Hamra's "tired" people. The day we met, he was wearing a tailored suit, pink shirt, soft leather shoes, and a diamond-studded watch. He drove a BMW.

"I speak to you as an Islamic man," he said as we sat in the trailer that served as his car lot office. His large, brown eyes had the piercing fix of the newly converted. He seemed eager to win another soul for Islam in the Roman Catholic newspaper reporter seated across from him. A soft-covered Qur'an lay among the papers on his desk.

Shadi grew up in a "rich family" with Muslim parents who "didn't know how to give me an Islamic education," he said. "Most Islamic people didn't get an Islamic education. So they grow up and say they are Muslims but they are so far from Islam. They say 'There is no God but God' but they don't know what it means. They are Muslims only by ID card. My father is a businessman. He doesn't have time to know God. I didn't pray to God until I was twenty-five years old, and my family is Islamic!"

Shadi explained that his life changed when, out of curiosity, he dropped into a mosque near his car lot. "They explained to me," he said, "the meaning of 'There is no God but God.' When the early Muslims said 'There is no God but God,' God lifted up Muslims and the nonbelievers went down. So Islamic people got all of Europe. . . . This is real history."

The born-again Muslim had firm views. He condemned *mulids*, the carnival-like celebrations with music, dancing, and outdoor performances that Egyptians have staged for centuries to honor saints and holy people. These celebrations, Shadi said, are "against Islam." He called veiling "an order from God," though Islamic scholars differ on whether it is mandatory or voluntary. "Many people speak about many different ways in Islam," added Shadi. "It's rubbish. There is only one way in Islam."

The mosque that influenced Shadi was located a stone's throw from Cairo's central railway station. Its worshipers were mostly young people drawn by the fiery sermons of its imam, or prayer leader. The women who attended services there dressed in a style seen in parts of Saudi Arabia: covered from head to toe in black, they wore black gloves and full-face veils with small slits for their eyes. Shadi said he listened to audiotapes of sermons by preachers in Saudi Arabia, where "seventy percent" of the religious leaders are "good."

A recurring theme in Shadi's conversation was that Muslims are weak and disunited because they do not love God enough. "We left God, so He left us," he said. Once Muslims truly love God, he added, all their problems will be solved. "Our problem is to be deep in love with Allah. If we fit soul with body right, we can control all the world by Allah. We say victory is through God."

The influence of Saudi orthodoxy on Egypt's resurgence of piety disturbs some Egyptians, especially those whose formative years in the 1960s were shaped by Nasser's secularist-oriented socialism. They are not upset that people are more pious or more active in community service. Rather, they fear that Pious Islam, when swayed by Saudi notions of Islamic propriety, fosters an intolerant atmosphere of conservative religiosity that can lead to more profound changes in culture and politics. On the fringes of Pious Islam, they see an Islamic Moral Majority trying to impose its Saudi-like standards on Egyptian society.

These Egyptians regard themselves as good Muslims and believe it is nobody's business whether or not they pray, fast, drink wine, read racy novels, swim in a pool with bathers of both sexes, or even quietly conclude that God does not exist at all. "Sure I'm afraid. It's the social pressure. It's making my life more difficult," said sociologist Soha Abdel Kader. "Usually I go to middle-class beaches. Last year, I went to the beach on a Friday. It was a lower-class beach. My sister and I were the only ones in bathing suits.

"I'm starting to wear longer sleeves. If I dress like I dressed ten years ago, I don't think I could talk to anyone or walk in the street. It's making me uncomfortable," Abdel Kader added. In her youth, she did not think twice about going out in jeans, miniskirts, and halter tops. "I never did it to be sexy, but because it was so hot and therefore practical."

We were talking in her Cairo office a few hours before one of her field trips to a town about an hour's drive north of the capital. "I don't go in the veil but I have a feeling I'll be the only one unveiled," Abdel Kader said. "I will feel they will not feel comfortable with me. Lately, every time I sit in a group I find the conversation somehow moves over to a discussion of Islam. You cannot avoid talking about Islam. This is the thing which is happening to Egypt. To both men and women. Men are also becoming more religious. And they are trying to make women live according to the dictates of Islam as they interpret them—that is, seeing the woman principally as mother and wife.

"I think it's a bit like quicksand," she added. "Once you put your foot in it, you just go down. The way people are interested in religion now, I don't think of it as a spiritual thing. It's ritualistic. They start by praying . . . then they become fanatic . . . they are impressed by very conservative interpretations of Islam."

Nabil Al Din was also bothered. At the time we met, he was in his early thirties and desperate to find an affordable apartment so he could marry his fiancée. He wore a black faux leather jacket and a nice-looking watch but he was by no means well off. Unlike many of his peers, however, Al Din had a steady, secure job. He worked for the security police, hunting down Islamist extremists.

We had been talking for a couple of hours over lunch when he suddenly burst into a tirade—not against the extremists, then mounting almost daily terrorist attacks, but against the puritanism he saw seeping into all areas of Egyptian life.

"The way you're dressed is *haraam*," he said, using the Arabic word for "religiously forbidden" as he pointed to my clothes and uncovered hair.

"Drinking wine is *haraam*! Wearing a watch is *haraam*! Wearing a gold ring is *haraam*! Smoking is *haraam*! The color red is *haraam*! Life in general has become *haraam*!" he cried, throwing his hands higher in the air with each "*haraam.*"

"So we'll die. We're better off!"

Puffing on his cigarette to calm his secular nerves, Al Din paused. "The real danger is not radical Islamists," he added. "It's this 'Petrol Islam.' "

The gradual Islamicizing of Egyptian society is a distinct movement of its own, separate and apart from politics. My grocer was not making a political statement when he arranged his turnips and eggplants to write "Allah." The rows upon rows of men kneeling in prayer at mosques every Friday are not the shock troops of an Islamist political movement. Some devout Muslims even claim to scorn politics. "This center has nothing to do with politics," Mustafa Mahmoud said of his medical and scientific complex. "It's a purely religious center, we are in fact against politics. I have one value here: goodness. To try and help the poor, those who are ignorant."

Still, Pious Islam no doubt has influenced Egypt's political life, first of all by providing a congenial backdrop. "Political Islam," one journalist said, "is encircled by Pious Islam, which is wider of course." An increasingly devout populace has meant a more sympathetic ear for Islamist activists and a more hospitable environment for Political Islam.[5]

Second, although charities like Zawya's Mohammedi Benefit Society usually have no political agenda, their social services inadvertently highlight the state's inability to provide such assistance. Thus, they chip away at the government's credibility.

"Trying to get something out of the government is like trying to get milk from a bull," said a widow who gave her name only as Aisha. The mother of four, whose husband was a cart driver before his death, told Fatemah Al Farag, an Egyptian reporter who worked for me in Cairo, that she was very happy with the assistance she got from Shareya Association, a private Muslim charity for fatherless children founded in 1981 by Shareya Mosque. "This is the best place . . . it is the people from my area who are good Muslims and on every fifteenth of the month I come and stand in line and get my monthly sum," said Aisha. "There are no problems. I have a friend who has to go through many problems to get her husband's pension from the government."

Such charity organizations, usually affiliated with a neighborhood mosque, offer a model of community service based on shared religious values rather than loyalty to the state or to a secular political party. As such, they are tangible examples of how Pious Islam has created community bonding outside the political arena.[6]

There is one more way that Pious Islam has affected Egyptian politics. As in all Arab countries, any politician who seeks the favor of his people must be seen as an observant Muslim devoted to Islam. So as Egyptians slipped into a more religiously conservative mind-set, their leaders felt compelled to follow suit. In the late 1970s, President Anwar Sadat began calling himself "The Believer President" and signing his name "Mohammad Anwar Sadat." He ordered Egypt's state-run television to interrupt programs with the call to prayer on the screen five times a day and to increase religious programming. Both the government and ruling National Democratic Party launched religiously conservative publications, including *Akidati*, which means "My Belief," and a newspaper called *Islamic Banner*. In more than half of Egypt's twenty-six governorates, local officials banned the sale of alcohol except at places catering to foreign tourists. And in the mid-1980s, Egypt Air flights stopped serving alcohol.

All these moves were meant to demonstrate the government's religious credentials and its participation in people's renewed devotion to Islam. As a result, the government abetted the Islamicizing of Egyptian life, which some interpret as a ploy to buttress its hold on power. "This government is here to stay and if staying means becoming Islamist, they will become Islamist," said Egyptian film director Yousry Nasrallah. "What does it take? Ban beer? Then they will ban beer. No women on TV? Then they will take women off TV. They will stay in power at any cost."

Government efforts to appear "religiously correct" were hilariously satirized in the Egyptian film *Terrorism and Kebab*. It tells the story of a hapless Egyptian so frustrated by the state bureaucracy that he spontaneously leads a rebellion to seize a huge government office building in downtown Cairo. But the hundreds of civil servants and ordinary people in the building who become his hostages are so similarly fed-up that they join his impromptu uprising. Marching through the building's corridors, they chant "We want justice!" and "A government that lies must resign!"

Outside, nervous government officials mistakenly conclude that Islamist "terrorists" have commandeered the building. When the call to prayer sounds from a nearby mosque and a senior police official negotiating with the "terrorists" declares himself too busy to pray, an alarmed aide whispers that the "terrorists" might "misunderstand" if he doesn't pray. Cursing to himself, the police official bows his head in worship.

Despite Al Din's long list of "forbiddens," Egypt's swell of piety has not turned the country into a bastion of straitlaced severity. When the late Um Kulthum's rapturous voice sings of love's pain on car radios, men swoon at the wheel. The couples in cars parked late into the night under the willow trees on the airport road are not discussing religion. Take a walk any weekend afternoon and watch the boys and girls sitting along the Nile side by side. Very side by side. More often than not, the girl is wearing her Islamic headscarf.

"While there is this apparent rise in Islamic conservative feelings, if you just scratch the surface, you find this immorality," observed Omayma Abdel Latif, a young Egyptian journalist. "There are a lot of young men and women who sleep together now without their parents knowing. There is a lot of indecent socialization between boys and girls."

In some cases, Egyptians are conforming to their society's conservative religious drift merely on the surface, as they would any fad. For them, Islamic-style clothing is a matter of "designer piety." And one Arab journalist discovered that outward piety is sometimes only skin deep when he went to get his official work permit after arriving in Cairo.

"First, I had to wait until the guy who signs the papers had finished his prayers in the hallway," he recounted. "Then the guy began hemming and hawing and being slow to sign the papers. I didn't understand at first, but then I finally realized that this guy wanted a bribe. So I gave it to him and when he'd signed the papers, I said, 'You just finished your prayers and now you are taking a bribe. How come?' He replied that it wasn't 'a bribe,' that it was 'just . . . a sweetener.'"[7]

These contradictions, however, do not diminish the reality of Pious Islam and the changes it has brought to Egyptian society. There has been a growing awareness among millions of Egyptians in recent years of what Islam can do for them personally. Islam's profile has acquired a larger dimension in Egyptian society. These forces will likely endure no matter what happens in the other arena of Islam's contemporary revival, Political Islam.

POLITICAL ISLAM

4

What Kind of Country Are We Going to Be?

"Justice is the basis of governance."
— SIGN, IN ARABIC,
HANGING BEHIND JUDGES
IN EGYPTIAN MILITARY COURTROOM

"Islam is coming!"
— SIGN, IN ENGLISH,
UNFURLED BY DEFENDANTS
IN EGYPTIAN MILITARY COURTROOM

The black steel cage riveted my eyes. It was ten feet high and bolted to the sloping floor of the small auditorium. A holding pen for fifty men. Most were in their twenties, many had beards. Some lifted dirty, bloodstained galabias to show legs and backs bruised by blows from prison guards. Others pressed the Qur'an through the bars of the cage and demanded to be tried under *shari'a*, Islamic law. Sometimes they prayed, sometimes they raged.

"I expect no justice from you!" one defendant shouted.

"I remind you that you will be judged by God!" another yelled.

Dressed in brown serge uniforms, the stiff-necked military officers on the stage did their best to ignore the threats of divine vengeance. Behind them, a red velvet curtain was pinned with an Egyptian flag. Two large fans riffled their papers.

But occasionally, Major General Mohammad Wagdi Al Leithi, the chief judge, felt compelled to assert his own credentials as a good Muslim. This he did by quoting a well-known passage from the same holy book brandished by the boxed-up rebels.

41

"It was not we that wronged them," Leithi intoned, "they wronged their own souls."[1]

Below the judges, on the auditorium floor, a puddle of suits was in constant motion, chattering and passing documents back and forth. These were the defense lawyers, civilians who had only a smidgen more regard than their clients for the military tribunal. Some supported the political cause of the caged defendants, though not their violent methods.

Like other reporters observing the proceedings in this makeshift court-room, located on an Egyptian military base twenty miles north of Cairo, I sat among relatives of the defendants. The women, draped in swaths of black material and face veils revealing only their eyes, fussed over toddlers, murmured prayers, and sobbed into tissues. Uncles and fathers sat immobile, hands folded on their laps, eyes staring straight ahead. In full view of everyone, Egyptian security agents videotaped the proceedings from the stage wings.

Scenes like this were repeated dozens of times during Egypt's violent Islamist insurgency in the early 1990s after President Mubarak, frustrated with the slow-moving civilian courts, ordered captured extremists tried before military tribunals. Over protests from human rights groups and lawyers, the tribunals prosecuted more than a thousand defendants and handed down at least ninety death sentences, most of which were carried out, from 1992 to 1998.[2]

Never before in modern memory had Egypt sent so many of its own sons to the gallows for insurrection. Never before had this reverently Islamic country hanged scores of its own people for disputing the kind of government it should have. And never before had so many of its youth used violence in pursuit of an orthodox Islamist state.

How did it come to this? From what deep river of dissent had these rebels sprung?

Understanding modern Political Islam, with all its various currents, requires knowing the past. A good place to start is in the year 1882. In America, Chester Arthur was president and John D. Rockefeller was forming Standard Oil Trust. Bell's telephone and Edison's lightbulb had just been invented. Malted milk was the food fad of the year. The rails of the "Iron Horse" stretched from sea to shining sea and the Wild West was being tamed. Fortunes were amassing and America was spinning like a top in its "Gilded Age."

But thousands of miles away, Egypt's own "Gilded Age" had turned to ashes. Thousands of Queen Victoria's imperial troops patrolled Cairo's streets. They'd come on the pretext of helping Egyptian ruler Tawfiq Ali

Pasha quash an army revolt. In reality, Egypt had succumbed to British colonial rule.

This turning point in Egypt's modern history had been preceded by eight decades of unprecedented economic and social change launched by Tawfiq's great-grandfather, Muhammad Ali Pasha. Egypt was technically a vassal state of the Turkish sultan in Istanbul, capital of the Ottoman Empire. But Ali governed his country as if it were a sovereign state. His reforms were aimed at making Egypt a great world power and they touched nearly every aspect of Egyptian life. The country acquired five thousand miles of telegraph lines, four hundred bridges over the Nile, scores of new canals, and hundreds of miles of railroad tracks. Agriculture was revolutionized as Egypt became one huge cotton plantation for the English market. The government imported Egypt's first printing presses, began publishing newspapers, opened the first government school for girls, started a national postal system, created a salaried civil service, and reorganized the army along European lines.[3]

British, French, and Italian citizens crossed the Mediterranean to settle in Egypt. Christian missionaries and schoolteachers followed. With its new, tree-lined boulevards, Cairo became a "must see" for well-heeled Europeans "doing the Orient." One of them, a tall, blond Frenchman of twenty-eight years named Gustave Flaubert installed himself at Cairo's Hôtel du Nil in the fall of 1849.[4]

But if Egypt was pollinating Europe's romantic imagination, the reverse was also true. Hundreds of young Egyptians sent on government scholarships to study in Europe returned with new ideas that were setting the Continent aflame: freedom, constitution, and liberty. In the 1860s, Egypt's ruler appointed an advisory Consultative Assembly, whose members came from "notable" families. It was the country's first executive cabinet. By the 1880s, Egyptian commercial courts were applying France's Napoleonic Code. Egyptians listened to European music in Cairo's parks. Government workers and the upper class began wearing European-style clothes. When the Suez Canal was inaugurated in 1869, the festivities included a performance of Verdi's *Rigoletto* at Cairo's first opera house, known as the Italian Theater.

In the midst of the Suez celebrations, Muhammad Ali's grandson, Ismail Ali Pasha, made a boast that laid bare the dream behind Egypt's dramatic transformation. It was a dream in which imitation defeats geography.

"Egypt," Ismail declared, "is henceforth part of Europe, not Africa!"

Unfortunately, Egypt's development cost money, and Ismail had so mismanaged his country's finances, borrowing ever more from European creditors, that his government was forced into bankruptcy in 1876. For the first time, British and French bankers took direct control of Egypt's finances. When the 1882 army rebellion broke out under Ismail's successor Tawfiq, Britain sent in troops to secure its investment.

Suddenly, Egyptians discovered that at the end of all their "progress," their economy was in hock to outsiders and their land occupied by foreign troops. The foreigners they so diligently emulated were now their overlords. Worse still, they were not Muslims.

Just as the waters of the Nile seep relentlessly into its rich, loamy banks, troubling questions seeped into Egypt's national psyche. In their hearts, people believed that Islam was the final and perfect revelation of God's word, completing and surpassing what He had earlier revealed to Jews and Christians. And because Islam was perfect and final, it was destined to spread to the entire world.

So why, they wondered, is Europe colonizing us, and not the other way around? How come Christian Europe has a higher standard of living, more vibrant universities, more books, better hospitals, bigger guns, and stronger armies? What had gone wrong? *What on earth was God doing?* Where was Islam headed? And most important—Ismail's boast notwithstanding—*what kind of country was Egypt becoming?*

The Scholar

"We see no reason for [Europe's] position of wealth and power except their progress in education and the sciences. Our first duty, then, is to endeavor with all our might and main to spread these sciences in our country."[5]

—Muhammad Abduh, 1876

A square, compactly built man of average build with a thick beard, Muhammad Abduh was known for his piercing glance, quick temper, and sometimes biting tongue. He was also a man of extraordinary intellect, exuberant curiosity, and deep religious commitment. First as a teacher and later as a writer, newspaper editor, theologian, and judge, he sought an explanation for his countrymen's nagging questions. In doing so, he laid the foundation for a profound rethinking of Islam and its role in a modern society. At its heart, Abduh's answer was simple: Unless Islam was reformed, Egypt and other Muslim countries had no hope of coping with the demands of modern times.

Abduh was born in 1849, the same year Flaubert arrived in Cairo to indulge his bohemian spirit. The Egyptian grew up in Mahallat Nasr, a hamlet in the Nile Delta north of Cairo where his father was a farmer. As a teenager, he attended a school run by Islamic religious scholars, or *ulama*, where he displayed the independence that would mark his intellectual life. Annoyed by his teachers' refusal to explain difficult terms they used in class, he ran away and hid with relatives in another village.[6]

At Al Azhar University in Cairo he was equally frustrated. Students were expected to memorize the Qur'an, the sayings of Prophet Muhammad, and the writings of medieval Islamic jurists but not analyze or challenge these texts. Nor were they to dispute or debate their teachers, who regarded themselves as the sole custodians of Islamic doctrine and interpreters of Islam's scriptures. Abduh relapsed into truancy, sometimes skipping lectures to read books on logic, mathematics, geometry, and philosophy that he borrowed from friends.

Not one to mince words or suffer fools gladly, he once vented his disdain for the *ulama* in an article for a new Cairo newspaper called *Al Ahram*. These religious scholars, the young student wrote, are supposed to be "the spirit of the nation," but instead they are dragging Egypt down by "not realizing the fact that we are living in a new world."[7]

Though some of his incensed teachers tried to block his diploma, Abduh graduated from Al Azhar and promptly joined the faculty to teach theology and Arabic. In 1880, he was appointed editor of the government's official newspaper, *Egyptian Events*, and used its pages to condemn bribery, urge improvements in Arabic instruction, and discourage polygamy. He wrote that veiling of women is not a religious duty but merely a custom and that representative government is consistent with Islam.[8]

An outspoken nationalist, Abduh also used his paper to promote the aims of the Egyptian army officers then agitating against British and Turkish interference in Egypt, though he warned against resorting to arms. Rejecting his counsel, the officers went ahead with their revolt against Tawfiq. After their defeat by the British expeditionary force, Abduh was arrested as an accomplice and in September 1882, convicted of having supported the failed rebellion. His punishment was exile for at least three years.[9]

Abduh spent a year in Beirut and then went to Paris. There he joined Jamal Al Din Al Afghani, an old teacher and friend from Cairo who was a prominent Muslim intellectual. The two launched an Arabic newsletter called *Al'Urwa Al Wuthqa*, "The Unbreakable Bond." Warning of the dangers of Western colonialism, they urged Muslims to unite, return to the basic principles of their faith, and initiate religious reform. Though it had only eighteen issues, the newsletter was enthusiastically received in Middle East mosques and coffeehouses.[10]

While in exile, Abduh acquired an ambivalence to the West that was to last his whole life. He openly admired Europe's scientific advances, voraciously read its books—he was a fan of Leo Tolstoy—and became fast friends with Herbert Spencer.[11] But Abduh detested European interference in Egypt and lambasted the "foreign devils" who established Christian schools in his homeland, fearing they would lure Muslims away from their religion. He also criticized Europeans for belittling Islam and failing to live up to their Christian principles.

In 1888, Abduh was permitted to return home, where his intellect, enhanced reputation, and personal piety won him new respect with both British and Egyptian authorities. Appointed a judge, he oversaw a reorganization of the courts, promoted educational reform, and wrote his most important theological work, "Treatise on the Unity of God." In 1899, he was named Egypt's grand mufti, which made him the state's most senior interpreter of Islamic law. In July 1905, as he prepared to embark from Alexandria on a trip to Europe, he died of kidney cancer at the age of fifty-six.

Abduh's greatest legacy was to reopen something mostly everyone else of his day viewed as a closed matter. The learned sheikh wanted to rejuvenate a practice that had marked Islam's early days but had fallen into widespread disuse, that of *ijtihad*. This refers to the intellectual endeavor of "exerting one's utmost to understand" Islamic scriptures by using all relevant resources. In order to apply Islam to contemporary times, Abduh insisted, Muslims must perform *ijtihad* on their holy texts using the tools that had midwived Europe's material success: reason and science. Europeans had extended their influence throughout the world and developed a sophisticated society not because they were Christian or superior beings, Abduh realized, but because they were mastering modern science.

Muslims could do the same because Islam recognizes the role of human intellect in knowing God and the world. "Islam declares openly that man was not created to be led by a halter," Abduh wrote, "but that it is his nature to be guided by science and by signs of the universe and the indications of events." Moreover, Abduh taught, when reason conflicts with a "literal meaning of the Divine Law," reason takes precedence.[12]

Abduh's call for a renewal of *ijtihad* was a direct attack on *taqlid*, the approach to Islamic scriptures that had so frustrated him as a student, first in his village and then at Al Azhar. *Taqlid* means blindly imitating the conclusions and analyses of earlier Islamic authorities, no matter how convoluted, incomprehensible or irrelevant they are to modern circumstances. Because of *taqlid*, Islamic theology in Abduh's time was weighed down by tradition and the past. Slavish imitation of earlier authorities had brought an overemphasis on legalistic, outmoded regulations at the expense of Islam's larger, moral message. Critical analysis, innovation, and independent thinking were discouraged and even suspect.

Abduh believed that a centuries-long aversion to *ijtihad* among Islam's *ulama* had led to *taqlid*'s strong hold over Muslims, depriving them of a true understanding of their faith. It had cut off Muslims from science and modern knowledge and made them resigned to unjust rulers. So strong were his feelings on this matter that he once accused the *ulama* of having "infected" the people with "the disease" of *taqlid.*

For Abduh, more than just Muslims' understanding of their faith was at stake. Islam itself, he believed, was threatened by *taqlid.* "[N]othing else but this has vitiated the religion; and if we continue to follow this method of blind acceptance, no one will be left who holds this religion," he wrote. "But if we return to that reason to which God directs us . . . there is hope that we can revive our religion."[13]

Abduh wanted Muslims to understand Islam as a call to be coworkers with God in building the ideal Islamic society. They should regard themselves, in his word, as God's "agents" on earth. This could not happen if they saw Islam as a fossilized set of rules and rituals. It could only happen with a revitalized Islam that recruited reason and science as allies and that valued *ijtihad.*[14]

Abduh's reformist ideas were resisted by the orthodox *ulama* who saw them as a threat to their privileged position. But the sheikhs were not Abduh's only ideological rivals. Many young nationalists believed that Egypt's best bet for becoming a modern state and escaping British colonial rule was to adopt European nationalism, liberalism, and secularism. They joined Abduh in embracing science and reason. But for them, any religion, even his reformed Islam, would have to play a secondary role in nation building.

By contrast, Abduh stressed Islam's utmost relevance to modern development. All his life, he echoed the theme of his exile writings in Paris: Development of a modern society in Egypt would be hollow and, worse, lead to tragedy, if it were not firmly grounded in a reformed Islam. With his intuitive grasp of Egyptian society, Abduh saw that the vast majority of his countrymen would never totally accept or understand the social, political, and cultural changes coming with modernity unless they were adapted to an Islamic framework and shown to be consistent with the moral values of Islam. Ordinary Muslims, he believed, had to see these changes as consistent with their Muslim identity and the divinely revealed Qur'an.

Knowing this, Abduh was concerned that importing European ideologies with no regard for the Islamic worldview of Egypt's peasantry would lead to a dangerous rift. On one side would be an elite with Western lifestyles who thought in Western, secular terms; on the other would be the conservative majority of ordinary people untouched by foreign ideas and in thrall to *taqlid*-loving *ulama*. Abduh feared that the gap between the state, supported by the elite, and the rest of Egypt's people would grow unbearably wide. On this score, he was uncannily prescient, as anyone visiting Egypt a century later can easily see.[15]

Abduh was not the only Muslim thinker searching for exits from the dilemma of Egypt and other Muslim states as they confronted Europe's more advanced societies in the late 1800s. But he was among the most influential. His work paved the way for Islamist political ideologies of the twentieth century. In a very real sense, he is the intellectual grandfather of Egypt's contemporary Islamists who are still grappling with the same questions that pricked Egypt's pride more than a hundred years ago. If the eloquent and dignified sheikh were alive today, he would be proud of some of his intellectual heirs. Of others, he would be profoundly ashamed.

In the end, Egypt's secular-inclined nationalists won the day with help from World War I. Young people had taken note of U.S. president Woodrow Wilson's wartime Fourteen Points, which included a promise of "autonomy for the subject peoples of the Ottoman Empire." After the war, that empire was dismembered by the Allied victors as punishment for siding with Germany.

When anti-British riots broke out in Cairo, London bent with the winds of change. In 1922, Egypt became an independent state as a limited monarchy with a Westminster-style government and a constitution modeled on Belgium's. With this step, Egypt became a modern, twentieth-century nation-state. It was a huge break with its past.

For the first time in four hundred years, Egypt was no longer part of the wider Muslim community embodied in the Ottoman Empire. Stretching from Baghdad to the Balkans, Ottoman rule had allowed ordinary Muslims to feel the faded glory of early Islam when the young religion's authority had extended across the Middle East and into southern Spain. The Ottoman royal court had given the Muslim imagination a concrete, historical connection back to the Prophet Muhammad because the sultan was regarded as the caliph, the political successor to the Prophet. Known as the "Commander of the Faithful," he united Islam's far-flung community of believers, the *umma*, and was at once their highest political and religious leader. Even if the British were meddling in Cairo, the people still saw the sultan's face on their coins and Egyptian rulers still tipped their turbans to him, averring that they ruled in his name.

After World War I, all this cultural, religious, and emotional symbolism attached to Ottoman rule was swept away. Now, for the first time since Islam's beginning, Muslims of the Middle East did not have a ruler whose raison d'être was to unite them and defend their faith.[16]

For the young nationalists of Egypt and other Arab states, the Ottoman's demise was something to celebrate. They saw its splintering as an opportunity for the birth of Arab nation-states modeled on the West that would bring them progress, prosperity, and respect. Egypt's new constitution declared Islam the official religion of the state. But secular nationalism became the operative ideology of its new politicians. Many of them were not overly concerned about how their Western-derived outlook would mesh with the religiously dominated worldview of ordinary folk who, for thirteen centuries, had taken their political, social, and personal cues from Islam.[17]

Even after independence, however, Britain continued to govern Egypt by remote control. British expatriates ran the state bureaucracy and police. London's ambassador whispered instructions into the king's ear. Britain's hated troops occupied the Suez Canal. And a large expatriate community of Westerners enjoyed lavish living conditions compared to those of most Egyptians. An obsession to get rid of this foreign presence was a major impetus for the next phase of Political Islam in Egypt. The man who would lead it entered the world fifteen months after Abduh left it.

THE ACTIVIST

"Eject imperialism from your souls and it will leave your lands."
— HASAN AL BANNA[18]

Hasan Al Banna was born in October 1906 in the palm-fringed town of Mahmudiyya, about ninety miles northwest of Cairo. The eldest of five boys, he was a devout child who joined local religious groups promoting moral behavior in the village. According to his father, a watch-repairer and an imam, or prayer leader, ten-year-old Banna once demanded that police remove an "obscene" statue of a seminaked woman from a riverboat.

After graduating in 1927 from Dar Al Ulum, Cairo's first teacher-training college, Banna was assigned to teach Arabic at a primary school in the Suez town of Ismailiyya. The town symbolized all that Egyptians hated about the British presence in their country: a large British military camp, offices of the British-controlled Suez Canal Company, and spacious housing compounds for foreigners.

Teaching soon took a backseat to Banna's religious and nationalist zeal. On evenings and weekends, the bearded, full-cheeked teacher, wearing the boxy Turkish fez then fashionable in Egypt, turned up in local mosques, schools, and coffeehouses. He would preach to whoever would listen about the dangers to Egypt and Islam from the non-Muslim foreigners.

Banna's two goals were to evacuate the British from Egypt and set up an

"Islamic system" in which government and society would first and foremost be guided by religion. *Shari'a* would be implemented and the Qur'an would be Egypt's "constitution." With these goals in mind, the twenty-one-year-old schoolteacher founded the Society of Muslim Brothers in March 1928. His cofounders were six Egyptian laborers from the British military camp in Ismailiyya.

From these humble beginnings, the Muslim Brotherhood became the first urban mass movement of Islamist political dissent in modern history. At its peak in the late 1940s, it had about half a million members in two thousand branches around the country and inspired similar movements in other Muslim countries.[19]

Banna believed the key to Islamic reform was changing Muslims' mentality through example and education. As more and more individuals underwent a "spiritual awakening" and began living according to the Qur'an, society would become more Islamicized and an "Islamic system" would come into being. "You are not a benevolent society, nor a political party, nor a local organization having limited purposes," Banna once wrote his followers. "Rather, you are a new soul in the heart of this nation to give it life by means of the Qur'an.

"When asked what it is for which you call, reply that it is Islam, the message of Muhammad, the religion that contains within it government, and has as one of its obligations, freedom. If you are told that you are political, answer that Islam admits no such distinction. If you are accused of being revolutionaries, say, 'We are voices for right and for peace in which we dearly believe, and of which we are proud. If you rise against us or stand in the path of our message, then we are permitted by God to defend ourselves against your injustice.' "[20]

Banna was the first political activist in a modern state to demonstrate Islam's power to galvanize large numbers of people. In creating his Brotherhood, he dragged Islam's revival out of its ivory towers and into the streets. Abduh and his fellow scholar-reformers had a tremendous impact on how Muslims thought about their religion. But they were intellectuals who reached a limited, highly educated audience. Banna by contrast was populism personified. He mobilized the masses and sent his message of an "Islamic system" into the nooks and crannies of Egypt's dusty alleyways. By doing so, he went beyond the intellectual and theological concerns of the scholarly Abduh and elevated the *political dimension* of Islam's revival into its most prominent feature, a situation that prevails even today.

Banna also illustrated another important development. Unlike Abduh, Banna did not belong to the *ulama* class and did not aspire to it. He was educated at a secular college, started out as an Arabic teacher, and became the consummate preacher-politician. And yet he was accepted by thousands of ordinary Muslims as an authoritative spokesman on Islam. His career was evidence that the circle of those who would be accepted as legitimate religious authorities had widened beyond the exalted *ulama* community. In the years to come, this circle would widen as an increasing number of groups used Islam as a vehicle for political dissent. And as the circle expanded, it contributed to what remains a burning issue in Islam today: Who holds authority?

Banna also criticized *taqlid*, saying the Qur'an and other Islamic texts had to be reinterpreted, using reason and science, for modern times. But in contrast to Abduh's openness and flexibility, Banna followed some of Abduh's disciples into a more rigid and moralistic approach to the scriptures. His Brotherhood also acquired a tendency to regard itself as the authorized instrument through which Egyptians should receive the meaning of their scriptures and instructions on how to put that into practice. This same attitude would show up in later Islamist movements, contributing to an intolerant atmosphere in what had been for centuries a very pluralistic faith.[21]

If television had existed, Banna would have rocketed to stardom. He was a spellbinding orator with a magnetic personality and a gift for connecting with people from all walks of life. His charisma was stoked by traits that he assiduously projected in public: sincerity and selflessness on behalf of his followers. He had a sparkling genius for organizing.[22]

Banna was also secretive and authoritarian, tolerating no dissent and requiring members to take an "oath of obedience." One Egyptian newspaper took the measure of Banna's hold on his flock by observing: "If Banna sneezed in Cairo, the Brothers in Aswan would say 'God Bless you.' " His totalitarian style led to regular dismissals of Brotherhood officials who disagreed with him and sometimes gave the Brotherhood the aura of a cult.

Like some contemporary American Christian preachers, Banna urged a return to conservative values. This "moral rearmament" aspect of his preaching, as well as his rigid, austere personality, infused the Brotherhood with a righteous arrogance that did not sit well with nonmembers and marks the organization even today.[23]

Members were organized in locally based groups called "families" and instructed to recite "There is no God but God" a hundred times a day as well as read from the Qur'an. This was in addition to the customary prayers said five times a day by most devout Muslims. Members were also urged to memorize sayings of Prophet Muhammad. They were to take care of their health by not smoking or overindulging in coffee and tea. Cleanliness was considered a high virtue along with truthfulness and not wasting time. Brothers were told to avoid people who drank alcohol or had immoral ways, to shun revealing, Western-style clothes and to buy goods made in Muslim countries.[24]

The movement made its biggest inroads among Egypt's emerging urban middle class of craftsmen, teachers, small businessmen, students, civil servants, engineers, lawyers, carpenters, and grocers. Even a future president became enamored of the Brotherhood. "I was in the Brotherhood as a youngster," Hasni Mubarak once told an interviewer.[25]

Its growth was due to several reasons. Widespread disillusionment with the ineptitude, infighting, and corruption of the monarchy and secular politicians in the 1940s drove Egyptians into the Brotherhood pipeline. The economic hardships and overt British interference in Egyptian politics during World War II added to its appeal. In addition, the Brotherhood paid attention to the needs of working people, seeing community service as a part of its Islamic mission as well as an avenue for recruitment.

The movement set up its own schools—separate ones for boys and girls—and organized religious study groups. It also organized health clinics, night literacy courses, and workers' insurance funds. It employed people in its own publishing house and textile company, formed labor unions in the transportation and oil refining industries, built mosques and put out newspapers and magazines. Athletic activities were organized for young people, who were drafted into the movement's youth wing, the "Rovers."

Banna's use of the traditional idiom of Islam also added to the Brotherhood's appeal. Unlike his secular opponents, Banna did not talk about "democracy" and "constitutionalism" and "liberalism." When he said Egypt should have an "Islamic system" ruled by *shari'a*, his listeners knew exactly what he meant, for even simple peasants know from childhood that *shari'a* is God's law.

Banna's "Islamic system" included an Islamic state to defend and protect Islam. But he did not envision a theocracy run by clergy. Like Abduh, who saw no conflict between Islam and representative government, Banna believed that a Muslim ruler's authority and legitimacy came not from God but from the *umma*, the community of believers. Moreover, an Islamic ruler was required to consult with his people. So while Islam would guide and inspire the state, it did not give the ruler divine sanction or license. Beyond these generalities, however, the Brotherhood failed, even up to now, to lay out the nitty-gritty of how an Islamic state would actually work or deal with modern problems.[26]

Banna's demand for an Islamic state may seem curious given that Abduh and other earlier Muslim reformers were not preoccupied with the concept. This contrast underscores the new political terrain Egypt entered when it left behind the Ottoman Empire and joined the ranks of independent nation-states. As it began transplanting Western political institutions into the Nile Valley under British tutelage, Egypt confronted Banna with a concrete political reality Abduh had never faced: a secular-oriented, Western-style government that he considered alien to Muslim Egypt. Thus, Banna felt a more urgent need than Abduh to offer an Islamic alternative.

Unlike Abduh who had seen a mixed bag of good and evil in the West, Banna saw only perfidy, forever seeing Western "plots" against Islam and Muslim countries. Moreover, he and his followers saw moral rot all around them. They abhorred the Egyptian upper crust's adoption of Western lifestyles and dress. They castigated Egyptians for mingling with foreigners in restaurants, nightclubs, theaters, and literary salons. They were repulsed by the brothels serving British "Tommies" and by Cairo's social circuit where alcohol flowed and men and women intermingled.

These practices were further proof for Banna and his congregation that Egypt was leaving behind its Islamic values, becoming an appendage of the "imperialist" West and its materialistic civilization. In their eyes, Muslim society, and even Islam itself, were in danger of becoming extinct because of where Egypt was headed under a Western-oriented elite and a king in cahoots with the British.[27] Essentially, they were contesting the very identity of the Egypt that was emerging in the first part of the twentieth century. They were saying that Islam, not the West, should be Egypt's point of reference for its sojourn into modern times. So while most of Egypt's postindependence politicians thought religion best confined to the sphere of personal conscience and kept out of politics, Banna was constructing an alternative political mural in which Islam was the keystone.

"Islam is a faith and a ritual, a nation and a nationality, a religion and a state, spirit and deed, holy text and sword," declared Banna. All these are "the core of Islam and its essence."[28]

The Brotherhood also had a darker side. The former schoolteacher's stress on gradual reform through education was complemented by a decidedly militant tone in both public speeches and private meetings. He spoke of the need for *jihad* in the sense of an active, physical struggle that entailed the possibility of death. He told his followers they were the "troops of God" and that martyrdom in the fight to reach their "Islamic system" was an honor. "Victory," he wrote, "can only come with the mastery of the 'art of death.' "[29]

Not surprisingly, these rhetorical flirtations with violence inspired some of Banna's followers to move beyond educational and self-help endeavors. Rising tensions and violence in Egyptian politics persuaded Banna of the necessity for a clandestine, paramilitary branch of the Brotherhood, which he set up in the early 1940s. His justification was to defend his movement from the British-influenced Egyptian government and its secret police, as well as from the Communist Party, which the anticommunist Banna viewed as a mortal enemy.

The Brotherhood was not alone in resorting to violence. Several other political parties also had paramilitary wings. All of them were responding to the combustible political scene caused by the unstable combination of a despotic king, interfering British officials, and inept, dictatorial secular politicians. In the eyes of the government and its British patrons, however, the Brotherhood's underground wing was the most threatening.[30]

Known as the Secret Apparatus, it was composed of highly motivated, well-indoctrinated Brothers whose induction ceremony took place in a darkened room and turned on an oath of "obedience and silence" sworn before a Qur'an and a pistol. Estimates of Apparatus militants, who included some army officers, range from four hundred to three thousand. Even the high estimate was a tiny fraction of the Brotherhood's total membership, most of whom knew nothing about the secret unit. But the activities of this minority would spell doom for the movement and Banna.[31]

The unit's operations included bombings and armed attacks on politicians, judges, and British soldiers. On December 28, 1948, as he entered a government building, Prime Minister Mahmud Fahmi Nuqrashi was gunned down by a man in a police officer's uniform. Evidence at the assassin's trial disclosed that he was a veterinary student who had belonged to the Brotherhood for four years and that an Apparatus member had planned the operation. A month later, another Apparatus member was captured after a failed attempt to bomb a Cairo courthouse.

Banna publicly repudiated Nuqrashi's murder and openly condemned the violence, saying that its perpetrators "are neither Brothers, nor are they Muslims." Privately, he lamented that he'd lost control of his paramilitary wing.[32]

But it was too late. The violence boomeranged on the Brotherhood with a vengeance.

As Banna entered a taxi in downtown Cairo early on the evening of February 12, 1949, he was shot at close range. He died shortly afterward at a nearby hospital at the age of forty-two. The government's security police had exacted their revenge.[33]

All mourners except immediate family were barred from attending Banna's funeral and the cortege escorting his body to a dusty cemetery off Al Kordi Street in Basateen was flanked by tanks and armored cars. Five decades later, Basateen is a run-down pocket of Cairo oozing people from every crevice. As customary in Egyptian cemeteries, Banna's grave is surrounded by a walled enclosure with an iron gate. The site has no trappings of a shrine and is unremarkable from others around it except for the inscription over the padlocked gate: "This is the Temple of Martyr Hasan Al Banna."

As with most movements of charismatic leaders, the Brotherhood lost its bearings after Banna's death and was riven by internal divisions. Still, it remained powerful enough to be courted by the young army officers secretly plotting to topple King Farouk in the early 1950s.[34] The Brotherhood joined the conspiracy because it shared the officers' vision of greater social justice and their nationalist yearnings to expel the British. But the collaborators had very different agendas and soon after the 1952 coup their partnership unraveled. In 1954, the revolutionary junta, now led by Nasser, outlawed the Brotherhood. A few months later, a Cairo tinsmith who was a Brotherhood member fired eight shots at Nasser as he addressed a huge crowd in Alexandria. He missed eight times.

Nasser brought down his sledgehammer. To the shock of many Egyptians, six Muslim Brothers, including several prominent figures in the movement, were hanged less than a month later after being convicted of participating in the attempted assassination. Nearly one thousand others were put on trial and sent for long stays in desert camps. Scores more scampered into exile.

Just five years after his death, Banna's "new soul" in the heart of his nation had passed into limbo. It would stay there until the 1970s.

For the next twenty years, debate over Islam's role in public life was only a little more vigorous than the embalmed cadaver of a pharaoh. Once again, just as after Egypt's 1922 independence, a national ideology that drew heavily on Western ideas was fashioned at the top and imposed on the people, this time by the junta that overthrew the monarchy. Its program of Arab socialism was a mix of Egyptian nationalism, pan-Arabism and socialism. In this medley, Islam was an important but minor chord.

Like many of his contemporaries, Nasser saw a clear divide between politics and religion, with the latter largely a personal matter. He performed his prayers in private, where he also occasionally sipped a whiskey on ice. For him, Islam was a broad, cultural force that could reinforce the dominant ideas of his worldview: nationalism and Arab unity. These were the yardsticks of his policies, and he believed that Islam and its institutions were to serve the state, not the other way around.

To that end, Nasser sprinkled his speeches with Islamic phrases. Pitching his economic policies, he described Islam as "a religion that is 100 percent socialist." He signed off on a new republican constitution declaring *shari'a* "one of the principal sources" of Egyptian laws.

He also brought Al Azhar University, which had been an independent center of Islamic learning for almost a millennium, directly under the control of the president's office. Al Azhar's grand sheikh, chosen by his peers for centuries, would henceforth be appointed by Egypt's president. Its religious scholars became civil servants paid out of the state budget.[35]

Then came the Catastrophe. The Arabs' humiliating 1967 defeat by Israel not only helped spark the grassroots regeneration of personal faith, or Pious Islam. It would also deeply affect political life. Three years after Egypt's military debacle, Nasser collapsed with a fatal heart attack. The fifty-two-year-old leader was buried with a massive outpouring of grief. His people absolved his faults and failures because, for a while, he had shown them what heights their nation could reach on the world's stage.

But the luster was off Nasser's Camelot. Bitter soul-searching set off by the Catastrophe raised doubts about his legacy of Arab socialism. One conclusion many drew from their military defeat was this: Egypt and other Arab states were weak because they had not built their nations on religion as the Zionist Jews had. Never mind that many of Israel's Zionist leaders had secular lifestyles and were not particularly observant Jews. What was important, many Egyptians concluded, was that they had built a state founded on religion. It was a Jewish state.[36]

So Egyptians began anew their quest for girders to hold up their society, for timbers that wouldn't give. And as with Abduh and Banna, that search led many back to their religion and, eventually, to a new blossoming of Political Islam in the mid-1970s.

The Islamist dissent that reemerged from hibernation, however, was affected by changes in Egypt. For one, the country's population had skyrocketed from 22 million shortly after the 1952 coup to 37 million by 1975. In the same time span, Cairo had gone from 2.5 million to 6 million. Its shantytowns were swollen with rural newcomers torn from traditional roots and with university graduates unable to find jobs for which they had been educated.

In addition, Egyptian society had been deeply penetrated by Nasser's socialist dictatorship. Far more than Egypt's kings or British occupiers had ever done, the Nasserist state had tried to control Egypt's people. It promised them security from birth to death and absconded with their freedom. Land, factories, newspapers, schools, professional associations, charities, student unions—indeed, any group beyond the family—were nationalized. Under the infamous Law 32, every community, social, artistic, or educational organization had to be licensed by the military government. Assisted by a vast police apparatus, Nasser drove the state's spike very deep into Egyptian society.

Finally, the withdrawal of the last of Britain's colonial troops from Egypt in 1955 deprived political activists of their longtime enemy and scapegoat: the foreigner. The British had been Banna's number-one bogeyman. But for the new generation of Islamist dissidents in the 1970s, the enemy was not the foreigner. It was the all-controlling, secular state at home.[37]

The Ideologue

"Setting up the kingdom of God on earth, and eliminating the king- dom of man, means taking power from the hands of its human usurpers and restoring it to God alone."[38]

—Sayyid Qutb

The man who responded to all these changes with a new theory of Islamist political action was Sayyid Qutb. In 1964, he published *Signposts on the Road*, a book of enormous influence on radical Islamists even today.

Qutb was born one month before Banna in September 1906. He grew up in the bucolic, broad-minded village of Musha, a serene and beautiful place surrounded by acres of rich, black soil in southern Egypt. After grad- uating from Cairo's Dar Al Ulum in 1933, Qutb joined the Ministry of Edu- cation and worked for sixteen years as a teacher and school inspector. He joined a secular nationalist party for a time but grew disenchanted with pol- itics. He was more interested in writing, producing poetry, novels, short sto- ries, literary criticism, and numerous newspaper articles. A lifelong bachelor, Qutb was sensitive, reticent, and intense to the point of being humorless. In midlife, he experienced a religious awakening that ripened in an improba- ble place: the United States.

In 1948, the ministry sent Qutb to America to study education. He first went to Washington, D.C., where he attended Wilson's Teaching College, which later became part of the University of the District of Columbia. He then went to the University of Northern Colorado Teachers' College, getting a master's degree in education, and also briefly attended Stanford University. Qutb's new piety deepened in the United States, where he was shocked by its sexual permissiveness, racism, and pro-Israel sentiments. When he headed home two years later, he was relieved to be leaving what he considered a godless, amoral society doomed to decline.[39]

Back in Egypt, Qutb quit his ministry job, authored a thirty-volume inter- pretation of the Qur'an, and joined the Muslim Brotherhood, becoming one of its top theorists. When Nasser cracked down on the Brotherhood in 1954, Qutb was arrested, tortured, and sentenced to a fifteen-year prison term. Suffering from tuberculosis and the aftereffects of torture, he spent much of his time writing in the prison infirmary.

He was granted clemency by Nasser in 1964, only to be rearrested a year later after the government got wind of another purported Brotherhood conspiracy to seize power. He was brought before a military court on charges of attempting to overthrow the state by force. Despite little evidence of his direct involvement in the alleged conspiracy, he was found guilty and sentenced to death in August 1966. Eight days later, he was hanged with two other Brothers.

But Qutb lived on in *Signposts on the Road,* which made him an icon in the ideological pantheon of radical Islamists. Written in prison, it reflected Qutb's experiences with two key aspects of the Nasserist state: its emasculation of independent civil society and cruel torture of Muslim Brothers, including Qutb.[40]

Unlike Nasser, Qutb believed in the necessity of an Islamic state. "If Islam is to be effective, it is inevitable that it must rule," Qutb wrote. "This religion did not come . . . merely to find a place in the hearts and consciences of men. It has come that it may govern life and administer it and mold society according to its total image of life, not by preaching or guidance alone but also by the setting of laws and regulations."[41]

Qutb argued that Egyptian leaders and society were living in a "pagan" state, like the one in the Arabian peninsula before Islam arrived, because they were living under laws created by human beings instead of God's law. By using the word *jahiliyya* for "pagan," or "barbarian," Qutb was saying that Egyptians and their rulers were not Muslims at all but atheists, one of the worst accusations one Muslim can make against another.

A "pagan" society, Qutb wrote, allowed "the recognition of the existence of God while limiting the domain of his power to the heavens, to the exclusion of the here and now. . . ." Such a society, he argued, "does not regulate its existence on the basis of divine law nor on the eternal values that He established as its foundation. Although it permits people to worship God in synagogues, churches, and mosques, it prevents them from demanding that divine law govern their existence. . . ."

It didn't take a genius to see that Qutb was describing Nasser's regime.

True Muslims, Qutb wrote, had a duty to wage *jihad* against "pagan" rulers in order to establish "God's reign on earth." This *jihad* was double-barreled: a spiritual struggle for personal growth and physical action against "pagan" rulers. For this, Egypt needed a "vanguard" of believers modeled on Prophet Muhammad's companions in the first Islamic community. They would mentally withdraw from the "barbarian" society rather than compromise with it. Eventually, the "vanguard" would become a "movement," overthrow Egypt's "pagan" rulers and establish a new community of true Muslims who recognized God's sovereignty in all aspects of life.[42]

Signposts never mentioned guns or bombs or explicitly called for armed rebellion. But its assertion that Muslims have a religious obligation to act against a "pagan" state clearly implied insurrection.

Qutb shunted the locomotive of Islamist political dissent that Banna had set in motion onto a brand new set of rails. For one, Banna would never have thought to call his fellow citizens "pagan," even though he thought many had strayed from Islam.[43] Qutb also brought the Brotherhood's concept of an Islamic state much closer to a theocracy.

Finally, there was the matter of method. Banna did speak of *jihad* but his Secret Apparatus was a small part of his larger, lifelong effort to build a mass movement that would gradually reform society by education and example. Some influential Brotherhood members believed their organization should be a vehicle for armed revolution, but this never became the consensus view of its leadership. The Brotherhood, which would later publicly disown Qutb's views, never officially advocated that its members abandon their reformist approach in favor of overthrowing the state.[44]

Qutb, in essence, was history's juncture for a fork in the road of modern Islamist dissent. After him, two competing trends would dominate Political Islam in Egypt and other Arab states: one reformist and nonviolent, the other revolutionary and violent. In retrospect, the Brotherhood's Secret Apparatus merely foreshadowed this great divide.

Revolutionary Youth

Nasser's successor Anwar Al Sadat wanted to set Egypt on a new course. He partially redeemed his country's pride by orchestrating Egypt's surprise attack on Israeli military positions at the Suez Canal in October 1973, sparking a war that ended in a cease-fire three weeks later. But his efforts to revive Egypt's shabby economy and mend its broken relationship with the United States were met with vocal left-wing opposition. Clinging to Nasser's socialist ideals and the mantra of Arab unity, leftists hounded Sadat for betraying these values and selling out to "Western capitalism."

Sadat saw Islam as a counterpoint to the ideology of his noisy, secular-minded left. He responded to the rising wave of Pious Islam by instructing the press to call him "The Believer President" and to use his full name of *Muhammad* Anwar Al Sadat. He also tipped his hat to *shari'a* by amending Egypt's constitution, which since Nasser's time had described Islamic law as "*one* of the principal sources" of Egyptian law. Sadat amended it to say *shari'a* is "*the* principal source of legislation."

But he still needed political help. Calculating that a "tame" Islamist opposition could tip the balance in his favor, Sadat made a pact with the aging leadership of the fiercely anticommunist Muslim Brotherhood: He would release them from prison and allow them to quietly resume their work if they promised to spurn violence. By now, these leaders were a far cry from the militants they had once been. Older, many in ill health from torture and long years in detention, they had no problem agreeing to Sadat's terms. Still believers in Banna's emphasis on education and gradual reform to reach their desired "Islamic system," they were now more than ever committed to working within the political system.

Between 1971 and 1975 they were released from prison in batches. Officially, the Brotherhood remained banned, but its leaders opened an office, published their magazine, and quietly recommenced proselytizing.

Meanwhile, student groups known as Islamic Associations began appearing on university campuses, exhorting fellow students to read the Qur'an and live "pure" Muslim lives modeled on Prophet Muhammad. To help students from poor, rural families, they sold photocopies of textbooks at discount prices, offered tutoring, provided "Islamic" outfits for female students, and organized minibuses to transport students from off-campus living quarters to classes. They also attacked their leftist peers for their "atheistic" ideas and secular lifestyles, which initially endeared the Islamic groups to Sadat.

Just as the lay preacher Banna had expanded the circle of religious authority compared to Abduh's time, this generation of Islamist students enlarged it further. Among the first Egyptians to benefit from Nasser's universal education policy, they could read the Qur'an themselves. Unlike their illiterate peasant parents, they felt confident enough to interpret it without help from Al Azhar's government-employed *ulama*.

But the Islamic student groups grew increasingly more aggressive. On some campuses, they demanded sexual segregation in lecture halls and cafeterias, prayers before classes, and an end to the teaching of un-Islamic topics such as Darwinian evolution. They harassed female students who did not wear headscarves and broke up, sometimes violently, student recreational outings, film shows, and theater productions.

They also began publishing extracts of banned radical Islamist writers like Qutb and demanding that the government implement *shari'a*. Gradually they took their activities off-campus and into poor neighborhoods where they preached in mosques and organized open-air prayer services on Muslim feast days, drawing huge crowds. In southern Egypt, they whipped up sectarian hostility by verbally attacking Christians.

In 1977, Islamic Association candidates were elected to top positions in the state-sponsored national student association, long used by the government to manipulate campus politics in its favor. Sadat meanwhile was losing patience with the Islamist students. His historic 1977 visit to Jerusalem and Egypt's peace treaty with Israel two years later further provoked his critics. Leftists accused him of betraying Nasser and "the Arab cause." Islamists accused him of betraying Islam. In June 1979, he moved against the Islamist students by banning the national student association.[45]

Political Islam under Sadat was also marked by the appearance of small bands of militants bent on overthrowing the state by force. These loosely organized, fragmented groups had no commanding, overall leader, coalescing instead around individuals who represented a certain geographical area or theological viewpoint. Most of these groups were heavily influenced by Qutb's ideas and believed that they were his "vanguard of the *umma*." None had the disciplined unity of the Brotherhood or the intellectual depth of Abduh. Their members were mostly disenchanted, impatient young men hopelessly out of touch with Egyptian political realities. Police quickly smashed their violent operations, which included the 1976 kidnapping and murder of a former cabinet minister. Not until 1981 did one of these clandestine groups put an irrevocable stamp on Egyptian history. Its name was Jihad.

A central figure of Jihad was twenty-seven-year-old Mohammad Abd al-Salam Faraj, an electrician employed at Cairo University. A former Brotherhood member, he'd turned against the organization for its perceived timidity in pursuing an Islamic revolution. Faraj put down his ideas on how to conduct such a revolution in a booklet, and then printed five hundred copies. Entitled "The Neglected Duty," it was an ode to *jihad*. Borrowing heavily from Qutb, Faraj pushed the envelope of the master's ideas, arguing that the first step in creating a true Islamic society was to assassinate the main enemy, or Egypt's "pagan" rulers. The next step was to foment a national uprising.

Faraj developed a small following in Cairo, preaching his ideas in a neighborhood mosque. In 1980, he met some like-minded Islamist radicals from southern Egypt also intent on hastening an Islamic revolution. Mostly in their late twenties, these southerners included activists from Islamic Associations in the towns of Minya and Assiut. Unlike most of their campus peers, these young men had moved from student politics to hard-core, violent militancy.

Sometime in 1980 a loose alliance was formed between these two tiny clusters of would-be Islamist putschists, one based in Cairo under Faraj and the other based in southern Egypt. Members of the two groups collaborated but never united into one, cohesive organization. In this, Jihad reflected the fragmented character of Islamist militancy in the 1970s as well as the north-south rivalry that even today marks Egyptian politics.

The conspirators held several meetings to discuss a coup d'état but did little to actually execute one. Until fate intervened.

Though lionized in the West for his 1979 peace treaty with Israel, Sadat was dangerously out-of-touch at home, where both leftists and Islamists were trashing his peacemaking. His economic policies were unpopular and in the summer of 1981, terrible street clashes erupted between Muslims and Christians in Cairo.

The president's response was a wide-ranging crackdown. On September 3, 1981, his police arrested 1,536 people, including prominent journalists, opposition politicians, religious leaders, student activists, and civic figures. The most senior Christian leader in Egypt, Coptic Pope Shenouda III, was confined to a monastery. The detainees spanned Egypt's political spectrum from right to left but most were Islamist activists. In a speech two days later, Sadat accused the detainees of contributing, directly or indirectly, to religious strife. "There is no religion in politics," he declared, "and no politics in religion."[46]

Among those arrested was Mohammed Islambouli, an Islamic Association leader at Assiut University who was pulled from his bed at his parents' home in the middle of the night. As it happened, Islambouli had a younger brother serving in an artillery unit of the army who was also a secret member of Faraj's branch of Jihad. When twenty-four-year-old Lieutenant Khalid Islambouli learned of his brother's arrest, he vowed to take revenge. At the time, he didn't know exactly how he would accomplish that.

A few days later, Khalid Islambouli was assigned to participate in an upcoming military parade commemorating Egypt's 1973 stealth attack on Israel. He went to Faraj and convinced him that this was the opportunity they had been waiting for—a chance to kill Egypt's "pagan" president. Three days later, Jihad leaders convened in Cairo for an urgent meeting to hear Islambouli out. After some debate, they approved the assassination plan. Most of the conspirators naively believed Sadat's death would spark a popular insurrection and usher in their utopian Islamic state. In order to nudge the uprising along, the southern-based Jihad members undertook to stage an armed rebellion in Assiut soon after Sadat was killed.

So much could have gone wrong with this amateurish concoction. Nothing did.

On the brilliant, blue-sky day of October 6, 1981, the "Believer President" was chauffeured to a reviewing stand on a broad Cairo avenue. There, he joined cabinet ministers, military officers, prominent sheikhs, and much of Cairo's diplomatic corps to watch the celebratory parade. Television viewers watching a live broadcast of the event saw the president, wearing his blue field marshal uniform with a green military sash, proudly salute his marching men. More tanks and gunnery lumbered past.

Suddenly, a military truck slammed on its brakes directly in front of the reviewing stand. Islambouli and three accomplices jumped from the vehicle, tossed grenades onto the stand, and raced toward Sadat, all the while machine-gunning his bemedaled chest. As panic-stricken security guards drew their guns, the sixty-two-year-old Egyptian leader crumpled to the floor in a pool of blood, his horrified guests overturning chairs as they scattered like rabbits.

"I am Khalid Al Islambouli," the head assassin shouted after opening fire. "I have killed pharaoh and I do not fear death!"[47]

With Sadat's murder, another chapter in the saga of Political Islam in modern Egypt had come to a close. The story had begun with Abduh, the intellectual reformer who preached a new approach to understanding Islam. It continued with Banna, who created a mass movement of reform in the Muslim Brotherhood. It was followed by the radical, Qutb-influenced campus activists and revolutionaries of the 1970s.

This saga was the historical lineage of the next chapter of Political Islam in Egypt, which played out in the early 1990s. It was to be a chapter marked by the country's most brutal insurgency in modern times, a widening of the divide between moderate and radical Islamists and massive repression of all kinds of Islamist activity by the government.

It was a chapter that featured the angry young men raging from their locked steel cage in the military tribunal of Major General Leithi.

5

The Ghost

"Where I come from they are known as the 'Sons of the Night,' those who hold sway in the night-time and kill anybody who gets in their way. At that age they held a great attraction for me: I dreamed of joining the ranks of those who made ordinary mortals, happy with their miserable lot, tremble at the mention of their name. For me, the 'Sons of the Night' embodied the ideals of manhood, a concept linked in my mind with extraordinary acts performed by extraordinary men, and I wanted to be identified with them because it was the men of our village whose mundane calm they disturbed.

"In short, I wanted to become a hero, since that's what being a real man meant to me, and so I was continually following the movements of my idols, my own heroes, down to the most trivial detail, with the same passionate ardor that the youth of today reserve for the doings of film stars and rock singers. I dreamt of getting to know them, or any one of them, and in my dreams we would make friends and he would teach me his trade, show me how to kill, and I would come out of the experience a man."

YUSUF IDRIS, "THE STRANGER"[1]

I never met Bestawi Abdel Meguid. By the time I visited his home in Hujairat, he was already on death row. But I'm sure I saw him in "The Stranger," Yusuf Idris's short story set in rural Egypt of the 1940s. Looking back on his youth, the narrator recalls how an encounter with one of his "heroes," a local bandit and murderer, changed his life. His teenage fascination with that outlaw eerily foreshadowed, I believe, the beguiling allure that Abdel Meguid and his peers felt for very different "Sons of the Night" fifty years later.

Abdel Meguid's "heroes" were the Islamist rebels of the early 1990s. Militant and more educated than their fathers, these young outlaws had the righteous swagger of those convinced they do God's work. They had "attitude" and an itch to disturb the "mundane calm" of their village men. Some were already notorious because of their involvement in events surrounding Egypt's most shocking event of recent times, President Anwar Sadat's 1981 assassination. One, in particular, stood out. His name was Talaat Mohammad Yassin Hammam. But the police called him "The Ghost" because every time they thought they were closing in on him, they ended up looking at an empty room. "Hammam," one reporter noted, "always seems to have a premonition to leave his abode just before the police force arrives to arrest him."[2]

Hammam was a senior leader in the militant Islamic Group, a partly clandestine, partly overt movement spawned by anger and a deep yearning for change. Its ranks embraced the genuinely devout, the religiously confused, as well as rogues and riffraff. It was a magnet for thousands of young Egyptians who looked at their future and saw only a brick wall.

Islamic Group had no offices or membership rolls. Usually centered in mosques, its local branches draped over Egypt like a beaded necklace. Each of its loosely affiliated cells was led by an emir, or commander. Emirs had a high degree of autonomy but also answered to a hierarchy of superiors who shifted in and out of the shadows and whose lines of authority were never totally clear. They often contradicted one another. For an outsider, watching Islamic Group was like observing a football game played in a blinding snowstorm. It was easy to tell when a touchdown was scored. But the plays in between were indecipherable.

No one knew for sure how many members and sympathizers Islamic Group had. Estimates ranged from 10,000 to 100,000. But at its peak in 1991–1993, it seemed to have a presence everywhere in Egypt, especially in Cairo and the southern part of the country. When it came to antigovernment groups, its popular support was second only to that of the older and more sedate Muslim Brotherhood.

Eventually, however, Islamic Group shed all of its many faces but one. In a fateful mix that was equal parts design, default, and destiny, it became a violent terrorist movement, generating Egypt's most brutal and sustained insurgency in modern times. In the end, Islamic Group became Egypt's 1990s version of Radical Islam. And "The Ghost" played a central role in that transformation.

Details of Hammam's early life are sketchy. He was born in 1963 in Sohag, a town about three hundred miles south of Cairo. His father worked in the government tax office. Fairly well off, his family lived in a four-story house across from Sohag's fire station on Al Girgawiah Street, which means "Those who come from Girga," a smaller nearby town. When Hammam was ten, one of his older brothers died in the 1973 Arab-Israeli war.

In his late teens, Hammam went to Assiut University, about fifty miles north of Sohag, to study engineering. He was active in the campus Islamic Association but not a prominent leader. Apparently uninterested in studying, he flunked out. He first made a name for himself—and caught the eye of the Egyptian authorities—in the tumultuous days following Sadat's assassination.

On October 8, 1981, with the country still in shock over Sadat's murder, a group of armed Islamist rebels stormed Assiut's central police station hoping to spark a national uprising. For the next two days, this placid city on the banks of the Nile was convulsed with bloody fighting between the rebels and elite paratroopers flown in from Cairo. When it was over, scores of policemen had been killed.

Eighteen-year-old Hammam participated in the rebellion, which the Islamists called "the uprising against the tyrant," though his exact role is unclear. After the rebels' defeat, he went into hiding and eluded capture for several days. "He was the only one able to escape to Sohag," said the late Hisham Mubarak, who was an Egyptian human rights activist and expert on Islamic Group. "The security police spotted him three times, but he was still able to escape. He was a person the police had great difficulty in arresting at that time."[3]

And so the legend of "The Ghost" was born in the days after the pharaoh's slaying. At the time, Bestawi Abdel Meguid was living eighty miles up the Nile in Hujairat. Only six years old, he was far too young to know how the man behind the legend would one day change his life.

Eventually, Hammam was captured and charged as defendant #70 in the Sadat conspiracy trial of about 300 Islamist militants. He was accused of joining an illegal group and participating in the assault on Assiut's police headquarters. But when the verdict came in September 1984, he "escaped" again. He was one of 174 defendants acquitted for lack of evidence.

Though cleared, however, Hammam was not immediately released. And his prolonged incarceration with hundreds of other militants in the early 1980s amounted to an extended jailhouse seminar on Islamist revolution. With not much else to do, the prisoners debated Islamist doctrines, argued about strategies for bringing down the government, and penned political screeds that were smuggled out to their followers. These were the birthing days for Egypt's new "Sons of the Night."

Eventually, the prisoners jelled into two competing factions. Some congregated around Abud Zumour, a onetime army intelligence officer serving a life sentence for his part in the plot to kill Sadat. This faction, which later came to be known as Islamic Jihad, was small and tightly disciplined. Its leadership was heavily weighted with Egyptians from the northern part of the country. Among its members was a thirty-year-old Cairo physician named Ayman Zawahiri, who was given a three-year sentence for his participation in the conspiracy to murder Sadat. Years later, Americans would hear much of Zawahiri as Osama Bin Laden's senior deputy.

A second cluster of detainees, which included Hammam, were predominantly from southern Egypt. They had been active in the campus-based Islamic Associations of the late 1970s. Their group was less elitist and less organized than Islamic Jihad and they chose a fellow inmate, the roly-poly, blind sheikh Omar Abdel Rahman, as their spiritual leader. This contingent would become the core leadership of Islamic Group.

The gray-whiskered Abdel Rahman, who would later receive a life sentence in an American court for conspiring to blow up New York City landmarks, had made a name for himself in the 1970s by publicly lambasting the Egyptian government and its religious allies at Al Azhar University, his alma mater. In early 1981, he agreed to act as spiritual guide for a loose-knit, clandestine group of Islamist militants determined to install an Islamic state in Egypt. Several months later, some members of this group in alliance with Faraj's Cairo-based cell of Jihad secretly plotted to murder Sadat. In the aftermath of his assassination, Abdel Rahman was among those arrested. He was twice tried—and acquitted—on charges of sanctioning the president's killing in a *fatwa*, which is an authoritative religious opinion by someone learned in Islam's sacred texts.

By most accounts, Abdel Rahman did not meet that qualification. His 1972 graduate dissertation at Al Azhar was a rambling analysis of one chapter in the Qur'an entitled "Repentance." Other Islamic scholars found it unimpressive. "He is not an authority on Islamic jurisprudence. He is not even a good orator. I think he has no philosophy," said Fahmy Shinawy, a Cairo author and student of Islamist movements who was once briefly detained with Abdel Rahman. "He is a very ordinary man."[4]

This, however, did not stop Abdel Rahman from issuing *fatawa*, or religious opinions. In any event, his popularity with imprisoned militants like Hammam had nothing to do with his scholarship, brilliance, or integrity. Nor his self-control. A diabetic, he often made himself sick by succumbing to cravings for chocolate. And the married sheikh enjoyed conjugal visits in prison, a privilege denied his jailed devotees.[5]

Rather, what made the forty-something Abdel Rahman attractive was his undying devotion to *jihad*, which he called "the fountainhead of everything."[6] Jihad comes from the Arabic root word *jhd*, meaning to struggle or strive. It can mean an individual's personal struggle to overcome short-comings and sin or a society's communal effort against some evil, like America's war on drugs. It can also mean a military campaign or "holy war." This was the definition of *jihad* that Abdel Rahman elevated to heroic pro-portions.

The turbaned sheikh, who lost his sight as an infant and wore dark glasses, elucidated his single-minded conception of *jihad* during his two tri-als. Speaking in his own defense, he noted that government prosecutors had argued to the court that the correct meaning of *jihad* is a "spiritual *jihad* against evil, against poverty, sickness and ignorance" and that any idea of *jihad* involving actual fighting "is alien to Islam."

"From which branch of Islamic theology or Islamic tradition or thought does the prosecution derive its knowledge?" Abdel Rahman sarcastically asked the judges. "Is there any verse in the Qur'an . . . confining *jihad* to a struggle against sickness, poverty and ignorance? It may be that a divine spirit, of which we Muslims know nothing, has endowed the prosecution with its unique knowledge. . . . Let the whole world listen and observe the prosecution distorting the law of God.

"Those who have a minimum of religious knowledge know that *jihad* means fighting for God's sake, so that His word should rise and prevail among us. *Jihad* is the duty of every Muslim, for doesn't the Qur'anic verse order us to fight?" Abdel Rahman declared, quoting the verse that says, "And they fought until there was no dissension and religion was only for God."[7]

Like his militant forebears Qutb and Faraj, Abdel Rahman preached that Egyptian rulers were heretics because they applied man-made laws instead of God's law, *shari'a*. Since Muslims cannot be ruled by heretics, who are by definition non-Muslims, good Muslims have a religious duty to oust them through "holy war" in order to make way for a true Islamic state ruled by *shari'a*.

As Islamic Group's spiritual guru, Abdel Rahman's role was to give reli-gious legitimacy to decisions of the young militants like Hammam who actually ran the movement. Just as the Egyptian army officers who led the 1882 nationalist uprising turned to Muhammad Abduh for counsel, and just as Egyptian governments today turn to Al Azhar for religious sanction of their policies, Egypt's "Sons of the Night" turned to Abdel Rahman.

The two groups of jailed militants also disagreed over the best way to reach their shared goal of an Islamic state. Imbued with missionary zeal, Islamic Group believed in having an open, visible presence in the commu-nity and in publicly taking responsibility for its actions. Far more secretive,

Islamic Jihad had no interest in building a mass movement. It favored creating covert networks within the army and security forces that would, in due time, execute a coup d'état to install an orthodox Islamic state.

Personal rivalries also played a part in the split among the militants, which became apparent in discussions of their spiritual leaders. Those gathered around Zumour said they couldn't accept Abdel Rahman because, as a blind man, he was physically "incapacitated." Abdel Rahman's followers countered that they could not accept Zumour because he would be in prison for the rest of his life. This rivalry, of course, amused Egyptian security police who called it "the great struggle between the captive and the blind."[8]

While the militants debated revolutionary strategies behind bars, another face of the movement that would come to be known as Islamic Group was taking shape in Cairo's shantytowns and rural villages. Up and down the Nile, young men and women were coalescing into groups dedicated to the idea of what might be summed up as "better living through Islam." Largely spontaneous in origin, they arose, writer Shinawy observed, "autonomously, automatically . . . like grass which grows in the ground."

To accentuate their rejection of a society they regarded as insufficiently pious, these young people adopted a new style of dress. The women's full-face veils, gloves, and long black dresses set them apart from most Egyptian women, who cover their hair but not their faces. The men grew beards, eschewed gold jewelry, and wore white robes several inches shorter than the ankle-length, colored galabias traditionally worn by Egyptian men. Some members tossed aside their toothbrushes, cleaning their teeth instead with small twigs, just as Prophet Muhammad is said to have done.

Many cultivated a small brown spot on their foreheads by vigorously pressing their brows to the ground during prayer. Egyptians call this spot "a raisin," or *zabiba*. For centuries, it had been the mark of simple, pious men who conscientiously performed their daily prayers. But for these young Egyptians, the "raisin" had become something else as well. It was a visual alert that its owner had transferred his loyalty from the government to a higher authority.

All these practices were intended as pious imitations of Prophet Muhammad's lifestyle as described in texts attributed to his early disciples, which are known as hadith. These anecdotal stories of the Prophet's deeds and sayings are somewhat like the gospel accounts of Christ's life. Hadith are part of the Sunna, the vast collection of customs, precedents, and traditions passed down through generations of Muslims. The zeal of the young Islamists to comply with every jot-and-tittle of the Sunna led other Egyptians to nickname them *suniyeen*.[9]

The *suniyeen* spent hours in prayer and Qur'an study groups at their mosques. They performed good works for the community such as tutoring students and selling meat to the poor at discount prices. But because they took literally the Qur'an's description of Muslims as those who "do what is good and forbid what is wrong," they also believed that they had a religious duty to bring their fellow Muslims more into line with Islamic Group's version of piety. Thus, they encouraged people to pray and fast but also to avoid dancing, singing, and mixed social outings. One year, some *suniyeen* in Minya distributed a pamphlet with suggestions on how to observe Ramadan. "Don't Watch Television" topped the list. Television, one young man told me, "corrupts our religion."

In southern Egypt, where Islam is like the air that people breathe, the *suniyeens'* piety inspired widespread admiration. And their community service was a tonic to this rural, poverty-stricken part of the country long neglected by the central government in Cairo. In the drowsy town of Aswan, which lies six hundred miles upriver from Cairo, for example, tourists can enjoy a Stella beer on the verandah of the Cataract Hotel while gazing at an ancient Nile landscape. It is the same view that enthralled mystery writer Agatha Christie, whose long stays at the hotel are commemorated in a suite bearing her name.

Most tourists, however, do not see Aswan's ramshackle neighborhoods where in the early 1990s the local *suniyeen* leader taught business in a high school. Several residents, who were not *suniyeen*, told me that he had "very high morals and education" and was "loved in Aswan." As for his followers, "anyone who had been treated badly they would defend them. Anybody who was sick, they would help them. Anybody who needed material assistance, they would give it," said a local lawyer. "They were slaves of God."

But even these admirers complained that the *suniyeen* sometimes went too far in their moral revival campaign. In Aswan, they had been known to break up wedding parties and rough up people caught drinking. In other villages, they'd ransacked shops selling alcohol, firebombed video stores, and harassed Christians, charging that they were anti-Muslim and tied to "crusader" foreigners. This zealotry did not sit well with most Egyptians, who have a strong bent for tolerance. "They're good," said a hotel manager in Aswan. "But I wouldn't want them to come to power because they will forbid many things, like tourism."

The lawyer was more expansive. "Their ideas are different," he said. "I don't want to call them extremists. . . . They take the harder side. . . . For example, if they see a sinner, they try to make him reform. If I see a sinner, I say 'It's not my problem. He will have to deal with God.' The difference is that they undertake God's work in their hands."

Reactions were similarly divided in Bestawi Abdel Meguid's home village of Hujairat. Like many rural places in Egypt, Hujairat was riven by murderous family feuds that made the Hatfield-McCoy row seem like mild bickering. "This place used to be terrorized by fights between families," said Mahrussa, the young woman at the water pump. But the *suniyeen* "reconciled these people and had them walking hand in hand from the day they came here. They made right many things that were wrong. They were the best thing to happen to our village in a long time."

Khodari Masloob had a more ambivalent view. Short and hardy, Masloob was a devout man in his early sixties who had built Al Salaam Mosque in Hujairat and served as its caretaker and prayer leader. When the *suniyeen* began organizing in the village, they took to gathering in Al Salaam. They installed fans in the mud-brick building, raised the thatched roof so it shaded the entire prayer area, and spruced up the wooden door with orange and green paint. At first, Masloob appreciated the improvements. But later, his traditional view of Islam clashed with the ideas of the younger men. "They were against the way we used to do things," Masloob said, "so I left."

No doubt one of their disagreements was over the Qur'anic verse that the *suniyeen* had written over the mosque's newly painted front door: "Whoever does not allow one to pray is a tyrant."

Everyone knew the *suniyeen* boys had not selected this verse by accident. Everyone also knew who the "tyrant" was. He lived in the presidential palace in Cairo. But village people like Masloob were not used to making political statements in their mosques. Still, no one in Hujairat, and certainly none of the police or government officials who dropped by, could complain about a verse from the Qur'an. After all, it *was* the Holy Book and they, too, were good Muslims!

The government men and the *suniyeen* boys may have been alike in religion, but they were worlds apart in age. As in other Arab countries, Egypt's ship of state is commanded by a top-heavy gerontocracy too long in power, too stubborn to leave, and too unimaginative to lead in a fast-changing world. In a country where a third of the population is under fifteen, the average age of cabinet ministers in 1994 was sixty-three. That same year, the cabinet acquired the distinction of being the longest serving ever in Egypt's modern history.[10] This sclerotic body politic was out of sync with a society whose center of gravity was a younger, larger generation dangerously disenfranchised from political power and for whom the emerging Islamic Group was a lifeboat. "Young people join because it gives them an identity," observed Ahmed Sadek, the trucker from Zawya Al Hamra. "They feel like they are somebody."

The movement's loose structure of semiautonomous cells offered young people a chance to feel useful, wanted, and part of something bigger than themselves. Political analyst Nabil Abdel Fattah put it this way: "On the one hand you have old men hanging on to the reins of power and wealth, yet offering no vision or solutions to the various crises facing the Egyptian political system. On the other hand you have the radical Islamist tendency giving the younger generation plenty of opportunities to take on leadership roles . . . leading cell-groups and taking local initiatives."[11]

Meanwhile, as the *suniyeen* movement gathered steam in Egyptian slums and villages, a siren song wafted in from the East. It was a ballad of adventure, camaraderie, and, most seductive of all, "victory" for Islam. It was a call to *jihad* in Afghanistan.

The origins of this "holy war" lay in one of modern history's most peculiar twists: The decision by the United States to covertly finance and arm radical Islamist guerrillas battling the Soviet troops that had occupied Afghanistan in 1979. Egypt and other Islamic states enthusiastically endorsed this American project because they, too, wanted to liberate Muslim Afghanistan from the clutches of "godless" communists. In Cairo, government officials and religious sheikhs at Al Azhar openly encouraged young Egyptian men to join the *jihad*. Defense Minister Kamal Hassan Ali even announced that volunteers could train in Egyptian army camps.

The Muslim Brotherhood, for once in agreement with the government, actively recruited volunteers and arranged their travel to Peshawar, the Pakistani mountain redoubt near the Khyber Pass that served as the *jihad*'s nerve center. Before setting off, new recruits were handed a booklet with phone numbers and addresses offering temporary lodging in Peshawar. This handy guide, entitled "Catch Up with the Caravan," was issued by a Brotherhood-owned publishing house.[12]

Arabs from across the Middle East, including several hundred Egyptians, responded to the call. "Any self-respecting Islamist or adventurer had to get off to the *jihad* at that time," recalled a U.S. official involved in the Afghan operation.[13] In Peshawar, the Arabs were unfamiliar with the language and culture of the Afghan guerrillas they'd come to assist. But someone understood them. Abdurrab Al Rasul Sayyaf led one of the smaller Afghan guerrilla factions. A former university professor, he spoke fluent Arabic and knew Egypt well, having studied at Al Azhar. Then in his forties, Sayyaf was also renowned for his personal courage. And he had money.

Sayyaf was well connected in Saudi Arabia because he followed that country's brand of strict, puritanical Islam. The Saudi government, which bankrolled the Afghan *jihad*, donated heavily to Sayyaf's religious crusade, as did wealthy Saudi individuals.

In Peshawar, the guerrilla leader took care of his Arab protégés. While some Egyptians were content to work in Peshawar as medics or clerks, others wanted to see action. So Sayyaf set up a training camp at Gagi in Afghanistan's Paktia province a few miles from the Pakistan border.[14] Here, in a valley surrounded by spectacular mountain peaks, the Egyptians were trained in rudimentary guerrilla warfare and explosives. They named their camp Al Khilafa, which means "The Caliphate." It was an important clue to their dreams. The caliphate is a government ruled by Islamic law and led by someone considered a political successor of Prophet Muhammad—that is, the caliph, or in Arabic, *al khalifa*. For five centuries, the Ottoman Empire, whose writ extended over much of the Arab world, was seen by Muslims as the Caliphate. That empire came to an inglorious end, however, when the Allied powers carved it up into colonized nation-states after World War I.

Many contemporary Islamist radicals are seized with the notion of reviving the caliphate as a way of uniting Muslims all over the world. Such unity, they believe, will bring Muslims the power and influence they enjoyed during Islam's golden age in the eighth to tenth centuries. This seems fanciful in today's world of nation-states, but Islamist radicals cling to the idea. And many Egyptians who shivered through Afghan winters learning the intricacies of bomb making at Camp Al Khilafa believed they were helping to restore the caliphate by restoring Muslim rule to Afghanistan.

The early 1980s, then, were years of rekindling militant Islam in Egypt. The rigors of prison forged new leaders in scores of radicals like Hammam who were detained after Sadat's slaying. A grassroots movement of politicized religiosity spread from village to village along the Nile. And an international *jihad* offered militants an opportunity to expand their horizons and fight for their faith.[15]

In 1984, the Egyptian government began releasing militants who had completed their sentences or been acquitted. Some, including Islamic Jihad's Zawahiri, immediately left for Peshawar. Others remained in Egypt. Sheikh Abdel Rahman settled with his extended family in Fayoum, a farming center an hour's drive south of Cairo, and resumed his denunciations of Egypt's "heretical" government. He also traveled abroad to drum up support for the *jihad* in Afghanistan, visiting Peshawar several times in the late 1980s and at least twice visiting the United States for Islamic conferences. At the time, the U.S. government and Abdel Rahman were on the same side: Though for different reasons, both wanted the Afghan *jihad* to succeed.

Hammam also stayed in Egypt after his release from prison in 1986, two years after his acquittal. He and other freed militants emerged as heroes to the *suniyeen* for surviving Egyptian prison. Capitalizing on their new stature, they moved swiftly to give more structure to the religiously inspired youth groups that had sprung up. They wrote articles in newspapers, evangelized for new members and sought to raise the movement's profile in the crucial political battlefield of Cairo.

Sometime in 1987, they also formed a policy-making committee to give the movement greater leadership. Some members of this executive committee, called a *shura*, were still in prison, some worked openly in the community, and others lived in Peshawar. If not a formal member of this inner circle, Hammam certainly was close to it and had a say in its deliberations.[16]

But unlike other leaders, Hammam did not pursue a public profile. His taciturn personality was better suited for the more discreet task of running the movement's security network. Composed of underground cells that operated separately from the movement's overt groups, Hammam's network supervised the *suniyeens'* "moral patrols" and provided security at their public meetings, seminars, and demonstrations. At such events, Hammam's men provided marshals, complete with badges, for crowd control and posted lookouts for police spies and provocateurs.

Montassir Al Zayat, a rotund defense lawyer who had close ties to Islamic Group, knew Hammam in those days. "My impression was that he was courageous and very intelligent," Zayat recalled in his bustling law office near Cairo's Opera Square. "He followed orders, was very disciplined and extreme in believing in his cause. He believed in the Islamic cause. He said he wanted to implement Islamic *shari'a*."

"His character was that of a military guy," added the human rights activist Hisham Mubarak. "He was very serious, professional, secretive and strict. He wouldn't meet anyone, even the [security] groups he formed. He wouldn't appear in public. He never gave a public speech, unlike all the other Islamic Group leaders. He had a strong sense of security." Another writer, who had good police sources, wrote of Hammam: "He never lost his temper whenever he was arrested."[17]

Increasingly, what had been an amorphous movement acquired a more discernible identity. It began calling itself Islamic Group and even adopted an official logo: an upright sword standing on an open Qur'an with an orange sun rising in the background. Encircling this scene was the same Qur'anic verse that Abdel Rahman had quoted at his trials while trying to explain *jihad* to the judges: "And they fought until there was no dissension and religion was only for God."

It had become Islamic Group's official motto.[18]

By the late 1980s, Islamic Group had succeeded in establishing a visible presence in some Cairo neighborhoods, particularly those like Imbaba that were home to recent arrivals from southern Egypt. Under large, colorful reproductions of its logo, the movement held open-air meetings as the ever-watchful police looked on. Denouncing financial corruption, suppression of free speech, and the torture of detainees, speakers railed at government "tyrants" and warned they would be "punished" for defying God's law.

In between rallies, Islamic Group members listened to Abdel Rahman's fiery sermons on audiocassettes. "I say these words mixed with tears and I wish my blood will carve out these words," he declared on one tape. "Say 'No' to injustice. You strugglers of Egypt, say 'No' to dictatorship, to one-party rule . . . military trials, arbitrary and unjust arrests. . . . We are not the silent majority, but the revolutionary majority, God willing!"

The movement's sassiness delighted the millions of Egyptians leading "tired" lives. Finally, someone was voicing their frustration and anger. Finally, somebody was speaking on behalf of those who had no *wasta*, saying out loud what they really thought of their neglectful and uncaring leaders. No other group so brazenly attacked the government's failings. Not the Muslim Brotherhood and certainly not the weak-kneed secular opposition parties. "People don't sympathize with Islamic Group because they love it, but because they hate the government," said trucker Sadek. "Despair is the reason for Islamic Group. Despair."

Still, I sensed that "tired" lives and Islamic Group's antigovernment tirades did not entirely explain its appeal. There was something else going on here and I couldn't quite put my finger on it. I finally grasped the elusive ingredient on a trip to Aswan. I had boarded a clunky wooden boat with my interpreter James Martone to visit the ancient Temple of Isis that sits on an island in the Nile. Ali was at the outboard motor, his galabia flapping in the breeze as he steered across the broad river. For a few minutes, this young twenty-seven-year-old knew he could speak without fear of betrayal. His two foreign passengers, the only ones within earshot, were unlikely to be police informers. "For myself, I support Islamic Group one hundred percent because they teach well," he shouted over the buzz of the engine. "They teach the true sayings of Islam."

A few days later, I heard something similar in the cramped living room of a hotel manager when I pressed him for an explanation of the movement's appeal. "It can all be summed up by saying that Islamic Group is working in a religious context," said the clean-shaven man in his late twenties. "Essentially, it is made up of the profound principles of Islam, which is an honor to us. The government doesn't want the Group to stand so strongly by their religion because if they have too much support, they will come to power."

And so it dawned on me. Islamic Group supporters were not bothered by its paucity of practical economic and political policies. What drew them was its religious message. "Talking Islam" made all the sense in the world to Ali and the hotel manager. For them, Islam was the most emotionally comfortable and comprehensible reference point for political protest. It resonated with their deep sense of injustice. It spoke of how their world should be ordered.

Many of the movement's supporters believed that devout attachment to Islam would bring its own reward. I glimpsed this one day as I chatted with Ali Hassan Al Abassi, a young, dark-bearded lawyer in Cairo. Like many others, Abassi believed that if Egypt only had an Islamic government ruled by *shari'a*, God would reciprocate by solving its problems. We were sitting on rickety aluminum chairs in the garden of the Egyptian Lawyers' Association and I asked him to explain how Egypt's economic miseries would end if tourists and foreign investment were chased away. He smiled sheepishly, seemingly torn between religious faith and worldly logic. It was the shank of the evening and the dipping sun was dragging dusk over Cairo like a blanket. Amid the bleating horns of rush-hour traffic, a muezzin began his singsong call to prayer from a nearby mosque.

Finally, Abassi spoke. In a quiet voice he said, "We hope that God will not abandon us."

Initially, President Hosni Mubarak and his security police tolerated Islamic Group's proselytizing and "moral patrols" largely because the movement was most active in southern Egypt. But the police took more notice as the militants grew increasingly violent. They attacked video stores, alcohol sellers, and theater productions for promoting sinful behavior. Local thugs began using the movement as a cover to lord it over other Muslims and intimidate Christians. And Sheikh Abdel Rahman's drumbeat of antigovernment rhetoric grew more insistent. But most menacing for the government was Islamic Group's growing presence in Cairo, where it was winning hundreds of supporters.

By the late 1980s, the uneasy truce between Mubarak's security barons, who'd been badly burned by Sadat's assassination, and Islamic Group started unraveling and an increasingly nervous government began squeezing the movement. Members were detained without charges for long periods, tortured in police custody, harassed at their mosques, and sometimes mortally dispatched under murky circumstances.[19]

Even Hammam was caught up in these dragnets. In 1986, he was detained twice for short periods. Feeling the pressure, he snuck out of Egypt sometime in 1989 and headed for Peshawar. By then, the "holy war" was over. Superpower politics and discontent in the Soviet military had much to do with Moscow's decision to retreat from Afghanistan. But elated Afghan rebels and their Arab comrades saw it differently. They were celebrating Islam's first "victory" over an "infidel" army in centuries.

Eager for a new military campaign, Hammam and his Egyptian compatriots at Camp Al Khilafa turned their sights on a battleground much dearer to their hearts: the land along the Nile. In 1989, Islamic Group leaders took a fateful step that moved the organization closer to the violent revolutionary outfit it would ultimately become. They formed a military wing.

Like the movement's policy-making committee, its military branch was to be collectively run by a widely scattered network whose leaders included veterans of the Afghan *jihad* in Peshawar, militants still serving sentences in Egyptian prisons, and others operating clandestinely in Egypt. To run operations on the ground, these leaders turned to one of their most skillful and secretive warriors, someone eminently qualified for the job. They chose "The Ghost." The formation of Islamic Group's military wing was a milestone for Islamist opposition in Egypt. For the first time, an antigovernment movement with significant popular support at home also had an organized, external branch of mobile operatives with funding, foreign assistance, and an ability to communicate back home by telephone, fax, and jet-setting couriers.[20] One of history's ironies is that Islamic Group acquired these assets largely as a result of the last major U.S. covert operation of the Cold War. The U.S.-supported *jihad* in Afghanistan had given Islamist militants from Egypt, and other Arab countries, self-confidence, expertise in guerrilla tactics, and connections to an international network of like-minded, well-financed militants, including wealthy Saudi Arabians like Osama Bin Laden.

Hammam initially drafted his military men from the security network he had established in Egypt before leaving for Afghanistan. To avoid detection, they held regular jobs, shaved their beards, and steered clear of Islamic Group mosques and public rallies. This firewall between the military wing and the rest of the movement, its leaders hoped, would allow Islamic Group to continue its overt "missionary" work. According to some former members of the movement, those selected for military missions were illiterate, destitute, "brainwashed," and known for "blind obedience" to their commanders. That may have been true for some. But others were influenced by Abdel Rahman's theology of *jihad* and believed they were fulfilling a religious duty by taking up arms.[21]

In interviews, Islamic Group militants sometimes argued that the military wing had been formed in response to police brutality, and that its purpose was to "protect" and "defend" members of the movement. Its military operations were mainly in places where police had been especially tough on Group activists, they asserted, and were meant to deter police harassment.

Many rank-and-file members no doubt believed this. But self-defense was not the entire story. The attachment to *jihad* among the movement's more hardline leaders guaranteed that Islamic Group's military operations would inevitably expand beyond self-defense. This was clear when the first issue of Islamic Group's official magazine, edited by Hammam's friend Talaat Fouad Kassim, hit the streets. Not the streets of Cairo, but those of Peshawar. Called *Al Murabitoon,* "The Steadfast Ones," the magazine's February 1990 cover showed a gun with the headline, "Terror Is a Means to Confront God's Enemies."[22]

Even before *Al Murabitoon* appeared, Hammam had slipped back into Egypt to organize the military wing's first major attack, which came early one Saturday morning in December 1989. The target was Interior Minister Zaki Badr, whom Islamic Group held responsible for the intensifying police attacks on its activists. A tough cop who favored blunderbuss tactics and stated his views with unvarnished candor, Badr was Egypt's "Bull" Connor, the police official who turned fire hoses against civil rights demonstrators in Birmingham, Alabama. Only worse. When upbraided by critics for saying he wanted to kill all Islamist activists, Badr, sixty-one, shot back, "I only want to kill one percent of the population."

This particular morning, Badr was in the back of a chauffeured car heading for his regular tennis game. As his motorcade zoomed under a highway overpass, a Suzuki pickup truck loaded with gunpowder exploded. But there was more noise than damage, and the driver, a twenty-four-year-old medical student burned by the blast, was arrested fleeing the scene.[23]

It was a callow attempt at guerrilla warfare. "The Ghost" still had a lot to learn. But as before, Hammam's legend waxed even in failure. Evading an intensive manhunt, he slipped away.

Islamic Group's public antigovernment protests continued. Just a month after the botched attack on Badr, the movement's official spokesman, Ala'a Mohieddin, led a peaceful march of about three hundred members in Cairo's sprawling shantytown of Imbaba. The militants demanded the release of fifty-two prisoners, some of whom Badr had detained without charges for eighteen months. Mohieddin declared that the movement was willing to start "a free and balanced dialogue with the government. . . . We want a new era with no torture or humiliation." He then ordered the demonstrators to disperse peacefully, which they did.[24]

But other Islamic Group militants were more confrontational. A few months after Mohieddin's march, anti-Christian riots broke out in several southern cities. Churches were burned and desecrated. Once again, the movement was sending mixed messages. In April 1990, a fed-up government ordered Abdel Rahman out of his own country. They didn't care where he went; he just had to leave Egypt. Rousted from his home in Fayoum, he was given a police escort to the airport and placed on a five A.M. flight to Sudan. Weeks later, he obtained a visa from the U.S. embassy in Sudan. By July, he was settled in his new home: Jersey City, N.J.[25]

Some weeks later, Islamic Group's spokesman Mohieddin, one of the movement's brightest and most articulate leaders, was gunned down in broad daylight on a Cairo sidewalk. Islamic Group leaders concluded that he had been killed by security police for ignoring their earlier orders to leave Cairo. Human rights activists who investigated Mohieddin's slaying agreed. His death was a huge loss for the movement.[26]

If government counterinsurgency officials thought that eliminating Mohieddin would take the wind out of Islamic Group, they were badly mistaken. The proof surfaced one month later as the limousine of parliamentary speaker Rifaat Mahgoub neared the entrance of a swank, downtown Cairo hotel. Riding two motorbikes, four of Hammam's men bore down on the car and opened fire with machine guns. Mahgoub and four bodyguards were killed. The choice of victim seemed puzzling. But it later turned out that Islamic Group's military leadership, reportedly meeting in Saudi Arabia, had ordered the assassination of Egypt's interior minister in retaliation for Mohieddin's slaying. Hammam's gunmen had attacked the wrong limousine.

The assassination made clear that Islamic Group had dropped any pretense that their military wing was meant for reactive self-defense. From now on, their intention would be all-out frontal assault on the enemy state. In other words, total *jihad*.[27]

For more than a year, however, "The Ghost" and his forces were quiet as the world's attention focused on Iraq's invasion of Kuwait and the subsequent U.S.-led military campaign, Operation Desert Storm. Then, in January 1992, an event thousands of miles away gave Egypt's Islamic Group militants another reason to believe that *jihad* was the only way they would attain their goal of an Islamic state.

In Algeria, a militant Islamist movement called Islamic Salvation Front, which had openly accepted the rules of a democratic political process, was poised to win a parliamentary majority in that country's first, truly free national elections. The Front's electoral victory would have been the first time that a populist Islamist movement was voted into power in the Middle East. (In Iran, Islamists came to power by revolution.) But the prospect of an Islamist movement ruling Algeria proved too much for its powerful, corrupt military establishment. In a bloodless coup d'état, the army canceled the election, banned the Islamic Salvation Front, and jailed thousands of its members.[28]

Most Arab states praised the move, which also was welcomed by many nervous Algerians. Western capitals were mostly silent. "Pro-democracy" Washington offered a muted response, saying it "regretted" the move. Overall, the reactions seemed to approve the Algerian army's illegal actions. For most Islamists across the region, the message was loud and clear: Even if you play by democratic rules you will never be allowed to come to power.

A few months later in May 1992 Egypt's Islamist insurgency began in earnest in the village of Manshiet Nasser when Islamic Group terrorists massacred thirteen unarmed Christians. By all accounts, the killings were not the work of Hammam's underground military wing. Rather, they arose from a dispute between a local Islamic Group leader and Christian residents of Manshiet Nasser.

It seems that a former government employee named Gamal Farghali Haridi had taken it upon himself to run Manshiet Nasser's affairs in the name of Islamic Group.[29] Haridi, who was in his early thirties, declared that he was "the government" in Manshiet Nasser and ordered Christians to pay him a "tax" whenever they bought or sold property, according to one of the village's Christian farmers, Abdullah Massoud. "He started to wear a white galabia . . . and underneath the galabia he would wear a sweat suit. He was in conflict with the government. He used to come with large numbers of motorcycles and cars. They all had beards. They began to build a mosque. And they used to sleep in our fields," Massoud told me.

A month after the massacre, Islamic Group struck again. This time it was an operation planned by "The Ghost." And it was where the government feared it most—in Cairo.

Farag Foda was an agronomist, author, and politician who recently had launched a new political party called The Future. He also had written passionate defenses of secularism to rebut Islamists' demands for an orthodox Islamic state and demanded harsher criminal penalties for Islamic Group extremists. Not one to mince words, he did not conceal his contempt for Islamists, whom he labeled "forces of darkness." On a June evening in 1992, Foda was machine-gunned to death by two masked men on a motorcycle as he left his Cairo office with his fifteen-year-old son. Islamic Group publicly boasted of killing the forty-nine-year-old secularist, saying he was "an apostate" because he opposed the application of Islamic law. His murder was a signal that Islamic Group's *jihad* now extended beyond government officials to ordinary citizens who supported a secular society.

But it was a strategy declared just weeks later that led the rebels' into full-blown war with the government. Henceforth, they told Egyptian reporters, foreign tourists were legitimate targets for its military operations. Some spokesmen for the movement justified the decision by complaining that tourists were a moral "abomination" because of their immodest dress, alcohol consumption, and alleged efforts to contaminate Egyptians with drugs and AIDS. No one took such nonsense seriously. Most Egyptians have little time for sexual trysts or pub crawls with tourists. They are far more interested in persuading foreigners to part with a few dollars in exchange for a bumpy camel ride or an "ancient" papyrus scroll just delivered from the factory.

Islamic Group's new strategy had nothing to do with tourists' alleged moral laxity and everything to do with depriving the government of its single largest source of foreign currency—$3.3 billion annually from tourism. *Al Murabitoon* editor Kassim once described Islamic Group's attacks on tourists as "one of our strategies for destroying the government," adding that "it does not cost us much." He then bragged that he had come up with the idea.[30]

The initial attacks on tourists were minor and mostly ineffectual with no serious injuries. But in October 1992, Sharon Hill, the British nurse, became the first victim of Islamic Group's new terror strategy. The well-planned attack bore the indelible imprint of "The Ghost."

By this time, Bestawi Abdel Meguid had fallen in with the Islamic Group crowd in Hujairat and was hanging out at Al Salaam Mosque. He was primed to do whatever his "heroes" and their more secretive friends asked. A few weeks after Sharon's murder, Abdel Meguid was recruited for an operation that, he was told, was revenge for a recent police raid on an Islamic Group mosque. He was given a machine gun and, police later claimed, a down payment of 5,000 Egyptian pounds, about $1,500. The next day, he and four accomplices opened fire on a busload of German tourists in Qena.

"The Ghost" had struck again. And Abdel Meguid, who had been only six years old when Hamman launched his renegade life, had been captured by the legend.

Shortly after the bus attack, Abdel Meguid was promptly captured by police.[31]

Over the next eighteen months, Hammam's anti-tourism campaign involved attacks on cruise boats, trains, and minivans. Bombs exploded outside banks and Molotov cocktails burst under buses outside the Egyptian Museum in the heart of Cairo. Besides Sharon, eleven other foreigners and twenty-four Egyptians were killed in tourist-related incidents, which also injured sixty-seven foreigners and thirty-four Egyptians. The killings had a devastating impact.

Restaurant doors were fortified with metal detectors and armed guards. Once-bustling hotel lobbies became hushed caverns. Lateen-rigged feluccas, which normally scud across the Nile laden with tourists on sunset sails, bobbed idly at wooden piers. And shopkeepers in the ancient bazaar of Khan Al Khalili bemoaned the loss of customers.

In some southern towns, where tourism is the primary industry, the situation was even more desperate. Souvenir hawkers, antiquity guides, and taxi drivers had nothing to do. In Luxor, a young man sitting on the curb jumped up, his face aglow with hope, as I came out of my hotel.

"Can I get you anything, madam?" he asked, joining my stride down the sidewalk.

"No thank you."

"You need ride in taxi?"

"No."

"You need tour guide?"

"No."

"Ride in boat to see Nile?"

"No."

I waited for one last try.

"Ride in helicopter?"

We laughed. But in a country where the average annual income then was less than $700 and one out of every fifteen jobs was directly linked to tourism, the fallout from Islamic Group's antitourism campaign was a catastrophe. In 1993, government earnings from tourism plummeted to $1.5 billion, half the amount it had earned each year prior to the attacks.[32]

Hammam's network also escalated its attacks on police officers and citizens cooperating with them. Several senior police officials and their bodyguards were shot dead in daylight ambushes. Scores of low-ranking policemen were picked off as they left home for work in the morning. One survey found that in 1993, more cops than terrorists were killed—the score was 120 police and 111 militants. Officials asserted that they were maintaining "law and order" against "criminals." The rebels claimed they were fighting a "holy war" against "tyrants." The mutual rhetoric obscured the fact that revenge ruled the day. Tit-for-tat became the tempo of the insurgency, inevitably escalating the conflict.

Blazing firefights between rebels and police in densely packed neighborhoods and public roads added to the casualties, killing scores of innocent bystanders, including children. In 1993, 1,106 persons were killed or wounded, a huge leap over the 322 casualties of 1992.[33]

Meanwhile, Islamic Group acquired new notoriety in the United States when the World Trade Center was bombed in February 1993, killing six people and injuring several hundred. There was no evidence that any of the Group's Egyptian-based operatives was involved in the bombing. But Abdel Rahman, who had been living in the New York area since his forced departure from Egypt three years earlier, came under suspicion and was arrested a few months later. In 1995 he was convicted of conspiring to blow up other New York landmarks and given a life sentence.

Back home, Hammam's operations, which had included an unsuccessful attempt to assassinate Egypt's information minister in April 1993, began drawing the highest form of flattery: imitation. Islamic Jihad, Egypt's other radical Islamist group, had always favored covert organization rather than open confrontation with the state. It belittled Islamic Group's attacks on policemen, Christians, and tourists as juvenile and counterproductive. But Islamic Group's activities drew Islamic Jihad out of its hole. Aiming for bigger fish, it pulled off two spectacular assassination attempts. In August, two men seated on an explosives-laden motorcycle blew themselves up as Interior Minister Hassan Al Alfi's car entered the gates of his ministerial office in central Cairo. Alfi was badly hurt. In November, a car bomb detonated seconds after Prime Minister Atef Sedky passed by in his limousine. The blast missed Sedky but killed a schoolgirl. Within the space of seven months, three cabinet ministers had barely escaped death in broad daylight.

Amid these unnerving events, faxed press releases from Islamic Group regularly surfed over the electronic transom of Western news offices in Cairo. The messages always began with the opening words of the Qur'an, "In the name of God, Most Merciful and Most Compassionate." Usually they were claiming responsibility for a recent attack. Sometimes they warned foreigners to leave Egypt "for their own good" or ordered foreign banks and investors to pull out their money. (At this time, 60 percent of all new investments in Egypt was going into tourist-related projects.) One of my personal favorites was a fax entitled "God Is Great and May Usury Fall." Egyptian banks, the statement said, were "usurious monuments which have become huge treasuries for the loot plundered by senior officials from the toiling masses." I imagined the author as a formerly devout Marxist who'd become a devout Islamist without retooling his political slogans.

This "revolution by fax" was a deft psychological weapon. It allowed the rebels to get their message across to journalists while also making the police look incompetent. The faxes were difficult to trace because they could be sent from any number of different telephones by simply moving the fax machine. (One arrived from the government post office in Peshawar.)

By the end of 1993, "The Ghost" was on a deadly roll. His "Sons of the Night" had police cartwheeling from one brushfire of violence to another and were roiling the "mundane calm" of the men of their country. Even the enemy camp grudgingly acknowledged the skill of Hammam's men in a rare departure from the scorn officials normally poured on them. "In terms of number, the militants are not that powerful," Brigadier General Baheddine Ibrahim, a senior police official, told a reporter. "But in view of their good organization, strong belief, dedication and readiness to sacrifice their lives, they form a force to be reckoned with. They are dedicated fighters."[34]

At its peak, Hammam's underground network involved perhaps two to three thousand men, a small portion of Islamic Group's sympathizers. Not all his fighters were directly involved in violence; some did logistics, surveillance, and message carrying. These rebels differed from their predecessors of the late 1970s in two significant aspects. Back then, 80 percent of the militants charged with violence were university students or graduates and their average age was twenty-seven. But a dozen or so years later, only 20 percent of rebels charged with violent crimes had attended university, and their average age was twenty-one. Clearly, radical Islamists had become younger and less-educated—a worrisome trend in a country with such a youthful population.[35]

Meanwhile, Hammam's myth grew. He was said to be in three different places at once. He was in Sudan. No, he was in Peshawar. No, he'd been seen in Cairo. Egyptians began saying that Hammam "had a better sense of smell than dogs," noted rights activist Mubarak. "They were saying that he could smell when police were near."

Hammam reportedly slipped in and out of Egypt in the early days of the military wing's operations. But during the height of its activities in 1993–1994, he is believed to have remained inside the country. With no mountain redoubts, no forest retreats, and a police informer on every block, where in hell, the police were silently screaming to themselves, was he hiding?

He was, they would eventually discover, right under their noses.

In fact, Hammam was so close that if the police had tried, *they* could have smelled *him*. As it turned out, he was living only yards from one of their heavily fortified headquarters.

*   *   *

But for the moment, tour cancellations were pouring in, Egypt's woes were making world headlines and Hammam's operations were causing Egyptian officials to sputter in rage. Several times, they proclaimed "victory" only to be embarrassed by another high-profile attack. And their invective matched the rebels' as they vowed to "decapitate" the "terrorists" and "liquidate" the "nests" and "dens" of the "miserable bullies."

Press speculation that Egypt was on its way to becoming a fundamentalist Islamic state was way off base. But it left government officials unhinged. Egypt had weathered Islamist militancy before, they sternly reminded reporters. A few "bandits" and "terrorists" were not going to shake "a country with 5,000 years of civilization!" Sometimes, patriotic frisson stretched this historical pedigree to "7,000 years of civilization."[36]

Officials were also incensed by the rebels' claim to be acting in the name of Islam. "These terrorists," officials insisted, "had nothing to do with Islam, a religion of peace, and would we reporters *please* stop calling them 'Islamic' rebels?" A military judge, moved to exasperation, declared from the bench that he didn't need religious lessons from defendants half his age. "We were saying 'There is no God but God' before these defendants were born," sniffed army general Ahmed Abdullah. "And we, like them, say 'God alone is our judge.' We are Muslims, too!"[37]

Government officials had a point when they pleaded with the press to stop calling the extremists "Islamic," for nowhere does Islam justify the slaughter of innocents, even in a "holy war." Centuries of Islamic legal writings had banned harming noncombatants and counseled Muslims to respect the sanctity of human life. The Qur'an itself teaches that anyone who kills another person outside certain allowed conditions "it would be as if he killed all mankind." And "if anyone saved a life, it would be as if he saved the life of all mankind."[38]

By the same token, corruption, unaccountability, lying, and torture are not "Islamic" by anyone's interpretation of the religion. And the more the rebels' harped on these official vices, the more they chipped away at the government's pretension to being a paragon of Islamic virtue and the legitimate purveyor of "true Islam."

The insurgency was well under way before authorities fully realized the impact of veterans returning from the Afghan *jihad*, the very crusade Egypt had once so heartily endorsed. The chickens they had encouraged to fly the coop were coming home to roost with a vengeance. Hoping to pen them up, military tribunals began judging the "Afghan Returnees," as the veterans were dubbed by the press, even before they had been arrested. Hammam was in the first group of "returnees" tried in absentia by a military court at the end of 1992. Convicted of belonging to an illegal organization and attempting to overthrow the state, he and seven others were condemned to death. It was the first time the government publicly connected Hammam to the insurgency. His death sentence, no doubt, gave him added incentive to avoid capture.

The government liked military courts because the judges, with an eye on their next promotion, were more "reliable" than their civilian counterparts, who were known for their independence. Military officers were not inclined, for example, to question the circumstances of "confessions" elicited from defendants or be overly concerned about fair procedure.

In Bestawi Abdel Meguid's case, he and more than forty codefendants were tried in forty-five days on charges that included murder, attempted murder, "damaging the national economy by attacking tourism," and "damaging national unity and social peace by calling for a change in the system of government." Defense attorneys routinely received hundreds of documents from military prosecutors with pages out of order and so badly Xeroxed they were barely readable. Government witnesses were often detained incommunicado until testifying. And there was no appeal from military courts, even for death sentences. Verdicts were widely regarded as foregone conclusions, which one defendant seemed to confirm when asked his name in court.

"My name is 'Dead!' " he shouted.

Besides military courts and mass detentions of suspects, the government took a number of other measures to break the insurgency. It toughened the penalties for terrorism and broadened that term to include "spreading panic" and "obstructing the work of authorities." The national telephone company suspended direct dial to Pakistan, Iran, Sudan, and Afghanistan in order to hinder communication between the exiled leadership of Islamic Group and their peers inside Egypt, but also inconveniencing everyone else. Police agents were trained to infiltrate Hammam's network. Pakistan was persuaded to expel Egyptians from Peshawar and use its influence to shut down the Al Khilafa training camp.[39]

The government also began working on its people. Conferences on "true" Islam were given high-profile coverage in the state-run press. An editorial in *Al Akhbar* newspaper reminded readers that "informing the police about the terrorists is a sacred duty." To encourage compliance, cash rewards were offered for information. Famous movie stars were drafted to make antiterrorist films. Television soap operas began portraying the extremists as stupid and misguided. And in an appeal to Egyptians' deep-seated nationalism, officials portrayed the insurgents as "mercenaries" of foreign paymasters. "They are far removed from any religion," President Mubarak thundered, "and willing to sell their country for a few pounds."

Cairo repeatedly accused Iran of backing Islamic Group but the insurgents got very little, if any, financial help from Tehran. Instead, most of Islamic Group's external funding seemed to come from government-sponsored charities in Saudi Arabia or wealthy Saudi businessmen. Though embarrassed and angry by this, Cairo was loath to complain publicly for fear of offending its purported ally, which hosted thousands of Egyptian migrant workers. The assistance from government sources was scaled back after Mubarak privately complained to the Saudis but some continued to flow from private Saudi charities and individuals.[40]

Other sources of income for Islamic Group included membership dues; contributions from Egyptians living overseas and "donations" from Islamic foundations and banks located in Europe and the Middle East. Egyptian police claimed that some of the rebels were drug running, and for a while they were robbing Christian jewelers to get funds. In addition, according to Interior Minister Alfi, Sheikh Abdel Rahman sent Islamic Group "hundreds of thousands of dollars" he'd collected in the United States.

One option the government adamantly rejected in its battle with Islamic Group was a negotiated truce. Islamic Group offered to discuss a cease-fire on several occasions and its conditions were always the same: the release of detainees not charged with crimes; a halt to torture and to the practice of detaining family members of fugitive terrorists until they surrendered. It also demanded freedom to openly resume proselytizing, since police had closed most of its mosques. The conditions never included political demands, such as implementation of *shari'a* or creation of an Islamic state. Rather, they were aimed at restoring the status quo of the mid-1980s.

The subtext of these cease-fire offers was clear to anyone who cared to listen. Islamic Group wanted to be taken seriously and treated as a worthy interlocutor. In this, it was expressing young Egyptians' desire for a political voice. The yearning for a role in how their nation was governed was evident as far back as 1990 when Islamic Group spokesman Mohieddin, a few months before his assassination, declared during the protest march in Imbaba that Islamic Group wanted "a free and balanced dialogue with the government."

But the government always dismissed the rebels' cease-fire offers, taking them as evidence that they were buckling under pressure. "Now that they've taken up arms, we cannot have any dialogue with them," Mubarak declared. "We will never legalize their parties. I will make no concessions to the Islamists. We will fight with arms those who take up arms against us."[41]

The government also made no effort to exploit the movement's internal divisions. Even at the height of the violence, statements issued in the name of Islamic Group both claimed and denied responsibility for tourist attacks. Some Islamic Group spokesmen warned that U.S. interests in Egypt would be hit. Others said such actions would never take place. (None ever did.) Some leaders wanted to talk to the U.S. government to explain their ideas. Others in the movement viewed this as consorting with the enemy. And while some rebel leaders inside Egypt, aware of the terrible price ordinary people were paying for their *jihad*, were willing to sue for a truce, their exiled comrades pushed for greater violence, contemptuously rejecting any negotiations with the state. One of these hard-liners was Hammam's friend, magazine editor Kassim, who told an interviewer: "There will be no dialogue until one side is victorious over the other. . . . After coming to power perhaps we will enter into a dialogue with the leaders about how they can leave the country."[42]

Some Egyptians argued that the government further radicalized the movement by refusing a cease-fire and closing most of its mosques, which forced its nonmilitary supporters underground. "These people are thinking that God will vote for them and that everything will be simplified. They know nothing about the world. They are working in the dark," said writer Fahmy Howeidy. "As long as they are talking to themselves, they are not talking to society."

The police did permit Islamic Group to continue operating a handful of mosques, presumably as peepholes into its activities. And each Friday, hundreds of worshipers converged on Al Rahma Mosque in downtown Assiut for prayers. A couple of police squad cars were always discreetly parked a block away.

"They have good sermons," Fettah Al Fadil, twenty-one, said as he headed into Al Rahma. The tall, clean-shaven pharmacology student wore Western clothes and thick, tinted glasses. "Their politics are a bit extremist. But they are not bad. There are some things I agree with and some I don't," he said. He liked, for instance, Islamic Group's insistence that women cover their faces in public. He did not agree with "the use of violence," which he knew about because "sometimes they send out announcements that they are responsible for certain acts of violence. We hear it on the Voice of America."

After Islamic Group rebels shifted their gun barrels from little-loved government officials and policemen to tour bus drivers, church watchmen, and innocent bystanders, the movement began suffering a massive hemorrhage of support. Particularly loathsome to Egyptians were the attacks on tourists, which offended their sense of hospitality and drained their pocketbooks.

The antitourism onslaught was controversial even among Islamic Group supporters. Former member Gamil Hussein Metwalli recalled in an interview with Egyptian reporters that after hearing of Sharon Hill's death, he "could not believe" that Islamic Group was responsible. "People at work argued with me . . . and I assured them that [the movement] would not do such a thing. Then I found out that they had claimed responsibility," Metwalli said.

He went to discuss the matter with his comrades in the movement. "I was pleading with them to stop killing tourists, who are visitors and guests in our country. We are destroying the economy and making people lose their jobs." To Metwalli's dismay, he recalled, one of them "matter-of-factly replied 'hitting tourism is nothing but pressure on the government.' "[43]

On a trip south in mid-1993, I found plenty of disillusionment. "They were good in the beginning. They wanted *shari'a*. That's good," said an Assiut taxi driver. "Then they were infiltrated by thieves and drug addicts. And these people don't want *shari'a*. They grow beards and hide behind them."

The elderly driver of a horse-drawn buggy in the village of Qusiya was equally unimpressed: "Their brains are messed up," he snarled. And at Qusiya's police station, I found an exhausted Mahmoud Hussein seated at his desk at nine o'clock in the morning. The police officer had been up all night. He was in no mood to talk about the "Sons of the Night" who had just gunned down a church guard and policeman a few blocks from the station.

"They're this group of lost people," Hussein said, shaking his head. "We don't know what they want."

The government took comfort in growing public anger with Islamic Group. Officials made much of how passersby were aggressively pursuing terrorists at the scene of attacks, often beating them to a pulp before surrendering them to police. But in urban slums and rural hamlets, people's disgust with the militants' violence did not fluently translate into enthusiasm for the government and its counterinsurgency methods. In one breath, Egyptians would sneer at the rebels' "messed up" brains, and in the next, they would denounce mass detentions, torture, and death sentences as overly harsh and unjust.

Sometimes, the government's tactics were wildly counterproductive. After police stormed an Islamic Group mosque in Aswan during a prayer service, killing seven people, residents accused the government of an unprovoked "terrorist" attack. "It makes people dislike the government even more," said one lawyer.

Occasionally, a whole village was put under curfew, its crops burned and homes demolished as punishment for allegedly harboring terrorists. After

Bestawi Abdel Meguid and his friends attacked the German tour bus, police bulldozed seven homes in Hujairat and arrested about a hundred people. "It was haphazard arrests," said Abdel Meguid's mother, Harissa Al Soghaiar, who was held for thirteen days. "We were taken just for being relatives. They took all the mothers."

Abdel Meguid's uncle, Abdullah Ahmad Al Soghaiar, added, "The government is terrifying us. They detain and destroy houses at will. Human rights are thrown into the dust. If we were in Israel, they wouldn't treat us like they do here."[44]

Egyptians like the Soghaiars are far more numerous than Cairo's coddled elite. And it was this larger mass of citizens—disenchanted with both the government and Islamic Group—that security cop Nabil Al Din had in mind when I asked him where the insurgency was headed. He answered by shaking his head and shrugging his shoulders.

"What I know is the people are spectators," he finally said. "They are waiting to see who wins. That's the only thing I know for sure."

On February 16, 1994, Hammam's picture ran on the front page of *Al Akhbar* newspaper with an appeal for help in hunting him down. A reward was offered. With his picture peppered over sidewalk kiosks, coffeehouses, and doorsteps, his security was severely compromised. Perhaps this unnerved Hammam. Perhaps it amused him. By now, he might be forgiven for believing he really was as hard to catch as a ghost. All we know for certain is that it didn't slow him down. He was in the midst of planning his most dangerous operation.

Major General Raouf Khayrat was the son of a Cairo police chief who had followed in his father's footsteps. He joined the much-feared General Directorate of State Security Investigations (SSI), the agency responsible for internal security, and after twenty-three years had risen to the position of deputy chief. As Egypt's second-highest counterterrorism official, he oversaw SSI's department of Extremist Religious Activities, whose mandate is to eradicate Islamist militancy. For the rebels, Khayrat was a lush target.

Like his ghostly prey, however, the forty-eight-year-old police official had acquired a sense of invincibility. He refused to post guards outside his residence in a neighborhood near the pyramids. He also dispensed with a government chauffeur, preferring to drive himself back and forth to work in his Peugeot 504. Khayrat believed, a police official said, that he was "secure from the terrorists."[45]

On a Saturday night two months after Hammam's picture was plastered all over Cairo, Khayrat went to the garage of the apartment building where he lived with his wife and children, got into his car and headed for the office.

It was shortly before ten P.M. but this was not unusual. SSI does a lot of its work at night. Khayrat guided his car into Maharan Street and as it slowed near the intersection with Lotfi Al Sayid Street, just five hundred meters from his home, another Peugeot with three passengers drew up on Khayrat's right and blocked the front of his car. The vehicles were no more than six feet apart.

A passenger in the backseat of the blocking car opened fire on Khayrat with a machine gun. Simultaneously, two men on a Suzuki motorcycle bore down on the general from the rear and hurled a firebomb into his Peugeot. It burst into flames so intense that the tires ruptured. "The body of the general turned into coal in front of shocked pedestrians," one newspaper reported. The attackers took off into Cairo's farrago of traffic, an Egyptian terrorist's equivalent of the jungle hideout.

A doctor later noted that Khayrat's body had no bullet wounds. He'd burned to death and his features were so severely scorched they were unrecognizable. His wristwatch was stopped at five minutes to ten.

Two days later, Islamic Group gloated over Khayrat's murder in a fax. "Our trap resulted in his death and the burning of his corpse in less than a minute," it bragged. His killing, it added, was revenge for the brutality inflicted on detainees by his policemen. He "died and burned the way they fight the youth: unjustly. But we are not alike. Our martyrs are in heaven and their dead are in hell."[46]

To say the assassination stunned the government is an understatement. Islamic Group had previously slain three of Khayrat's top aides in ambushes. The ease of those killings and the rebels' knowledge of Khayrat's routine and route to work, which helped them locate their victim despite his use of an unmarked car, led some to wonder if Islamic Group was getting inside help. When Interior Minister Alfi was asked at a press conference if perhaps the rebels had "penetrated" Egypt's vaunted antiterrorist agency, the mere thought of such incompetence, with its treasonous overtones, provoked him to declare, "It is not they who have penetrated us, but we who have penetrated them!"[47]

The minister may have revealed more than he'd meant to. And Hammam would have done well to take his outburst to heart.

Even as he pulled off Khayrat's killing, Hammam was finding it more difficult to work. The public had soured on Islamic Group, mass arrests had depleted his networks, and some recent successes had given the police a second wind. Two months before the attack on Khayrat, seven rebels were shot dead in a police raid on their apartment hideout in Zawya Al Hamra, which was discovered with the help of an informant. In early March, police arrested twenty-five militants who'd been planting bombs outside Cairo banks. An official statement noted that they had received military training "during the Afghan war." These were all Hammam's people.

In an unusual indication that the rebel leader was aware of the dangers, Hammam attached a cryptic message, apparently intended for members of his network, to an Islamic Group fax received by news agencies around this time. The movement, it said, was temporarily suspending violent acts in Cairo "for reasons particular to the Group." The fax requested members to cancel all meetings and movements for a week "for the sake of the supreme interests of the Group."[48]

With his network facing increased pressures, Hammam was forced to do things he had always avoided, such as meeting face-to-face with front-line operatives rather than sending intermediaries. These security breaches were godsends for the police, who were drawing ever-smaller circles about their prey. Two weeks after Khayrat's fiery death, their noose finally closed on a fifteen-story apartment building in Cairo's northern neighborhood of Hada'ak Al Kubbah.

In its heyday, Hada'ak Al Kubbah was a fashionable neighborhood of tree-lined boulevards and huge villas. Now it also sports high-rise apartment complexes that shelter engineers, teachers, doctors, and computer technicians. While not wealthy, these middle-class Egyptians led comfortable lives far removed from the "tired" ones of so many fellow Cairenes and had little sympathy for Islamic Group.

Building 532, like the others in its complex, was landscaped with tiny flowerbeds and squares of grass. Each of its fifteen floors held two spacious apartments with balconies. Nearby, were some high-caliber neighbors. Across the street from one side of the complex sat Kubbah Palace, one of Mubarak's presidential offices. Another flank of the compound faced the headquarters of Egypt's General Intelligence Services (GSI). Even more than Khayrat's SSI, the GIS is the state's most powerful spy agency. Responsible for both external espionage and internal security, it is the FBI and CIA wrapped into one and headed by a military general who reports directly to the president. Its headquarters in Hada'ak Al Kubbah is surrounded by a tall, whitewashed wall dotted with armed guards in watchtowers.

Right here, Hammam was living his double life. Indeed, he had ensconced himself so close to the government's security behemoth that he'd become impossible to see, invisible as a ghost.

Invisible, that is, until sometime after two A.M. on April 25, 1994, when a small army of camouflaged antiterrorist and special operations police converged on building 532. Bristling with automatic rifles, walkie-talkies and batons, they raced to the twelfth floor and straight to the slatted, wooden door of apartment 1. Backups lined the narrow staircase and still others blocked the tiny elevator on the landing. A man living three floors above recalled being awakened by what sounded like "a small bomb" as police blew open the door of apartment 1. He heard a woman screaming, then silence for "about fifteen minutes," and then "shooting for five to ten minutes."

When the commotion ended, police photographers entered the three-bedroom apartment, furnished with heavy drapes, faux French provincial furniture, and glass-doored china cabinets, to catch their prize on film. The color snapshots show thirty-one-year-old Hammam sprawled on his back on a thick, ornately patterned carpet of beige and brown. Blood was streaming from bullet holes in the top of his head, which was turned to his left. His black hair was cut very short. His round, high-cheekboned face was clean-shaven except for a black mustache. His right eye was open. The left one, blackened and swollen shut. His mouth was smeared with blood. His left arm stretched out straight from his shoulder and his right arm was raised above his head. Both hands were stained with blood, as if he'd tried to stanch his wounds before losing consciousness. He wore a bright red shirt that looked like a pajama top. A black German-made pistol lay just to the right of his chest on the floor. And about six inches to the left of his head, a bloody shoeprint stained the carpet, as if someone had stopped to look down and contemplate, at last, the long-sought corporeal presence of "The Ghost."

The pictures were distributed to the media.

Hammam's death was on the international news wires by eleven o'clock that morning. A few hours later, the Interior Ministry faxed to the news media its account of how police had exorcised "The Ghost." "The accused shot at the forces and they returned fire, leading to his death," the statement said, adding that there were no police casualties. The ministry asserted that police had tailed Hammam for four days and had moved in after discovering that he planned to leave Egypt "at noon" on the day of the raid.[49]

The ministry also broke its long radio silence on Hammam's crucial role in the Islamist insurgency. He was "the most dangerous of the terrorists because he alone occupied the strategic position of having experience in all elements of the terrorist organization including the military wing." He had been "the primary source of funds . . . and the highest organizational leader on the domestic front, representing the main link between the internal and external units" of the rebels' movement, the ministry said. He had distributed money from abroad to militants in Egypt—possibly as much as $480,000—and had "issued all the declarations representing the terrorist movements" sent to international news agencies. In other words, we journalists should not expect any more rebel faxes.[50]

The police also said Hammam had been "the driving force behind" Khayrat's killing and listed items found in his apartment as proof. These included a map of Khayrat's home and his route to work, a hand-drawn map of what police termed "the execution place," and a draft in longhand of the communiqué faxed to news media after Khayrat was burned to a crisp.

Newspapers quoted police sources as saying Hammam was implicated in more than twenty terrorist crimes, including the murder of Sharon Hill, attacks on Nile cruise boats, and the bombings of Cairo banks. The leading government paper, *Al Ahram*, lavishly praised the police officer in charge of hunting down Hammam, referring to the unnamed official only by his sobriquet, "The Confrontation Fox."[51]

Hammam had actually been using two apartments in two different buildings within the complex. He had rented them from a female relative working in Italy, reportedly as a belly dancer. According to press reports, he had used one flat as his residence and the other as an "operations room," where police found a fax machine, computer, telephone, typewriter, books and "extremist tapes."[52]

The police also seized forged passports and fake identification papers showing Hammam wearing eyeglasses. A bonanza of documents, some very detailed, helped police arrest 120 of Hammam's confederates in the weeks following his death. By one press account, police "stormed 36 dens" of the rebels, finding at least seven cars, including one used in Khayrat's assassination.[53]

The government and its official press also quickly cashed in their winning ticket in the propaganda lottery. Articles noted that Hammam's apartments were not exactly shrines to Islamic piety, describing how police had found $12,000 in cash, a videotape recorder, three televisions, "pornographic" tapes, and "photographs of naked women," according to *Al Ahram*. Some of these items likely belonged to the female relative from whom Hammam had rented the apartments, but the state-run media overlooked this detail, portraying the lusty paraphernalia as evidence of a decidedly un-Islamic lifestyle on the part of a man who had waged "holy war" in the name of Islam. The caption beneath a photograph of one apartment read, "His flat from inside showing the luxury in which he was living with the terrorism money sent to him." Another picture of a bathroom and its large tub was entitled: "Massive Hugeness."

"It is enough to say that he lived like a sultan with cars, apartments and large amounts of money coming to him from everywhere," an unnamed senior security official told *Al Ahram*. "He gave small amounts to those who committed the crimes while he stayed away from the scene of events and didn't put his life in danger. . . . This 'Grand Struggler,' as they call him in

[Islamist] groups, left university and started leading his terrorist organization because it made more money. . . . Where is the conviction? Where is the Islam they are talking about?"[54]

None of the police statements or press reports on Hammam's death mentioned the arrest of his wife, Ragaa Yousef, and their two small children, Ahmad and Khaled, who were in the apartment when Hammam was killed. Despite his busy, clandestine life, Hammam had acquired a family. Yousef and her children were detained in Cairo for about two months and then released to Hammam's relatives in his hometown of Sohag.[55]

The official version of Hammam's death also did not mention his clever deception. Here was a fugitive who, according to Egyptian security officials, coolly cashed money orders sent from overseas at six different banks in the capital city even as he was running a terrorist operation to bomb Cairo banks![56] But what better disguise could there be for a terrorist than tooling around in a late-model red Mitsubishi as part of a bourgeois lifestyle far removed from Cairo's teeming slums? What better place to hide than a stone's throw from the state's all-powerful spy headquarters?

After Hammam's death, neighbors told reporters that he and his wife had lived in the flat for about ten months. Meeting Hammam in the elevator or in the street, they called him "Abu Ahmad," or "Father of Ahmad," the traditional Arab greeting for a man, using the name of his child. "He was decent, polite to the neighbors," said an Egyptian journalist whose relatives live three floors above Hammam's flat. "He looked rich because he had a car. The surprise was being in a place like that, so close to the police."

So how did police find Hammam, at last, living under their noses?

No official explanation was ever given. Security officials, speaking off the record with Egyptian journalists, were quick to claim that they had successfully infiltrated agents into Hammam's faltering network. Several independent observers believed this was the most likely explanation. For them, Minister Alfi's claim of having "penetrated" the rebels' network had not been an idle boast. The government also had mounted electronic surveillance on suspected militants overseas, anticipating they would return to Egypt and contact Hammam. This monitoring, one source told me, helped lead police to the rebel commander.

Was the police version of Hammam's death how it really happened? Did he open fire first? It's probable, even likely, that he did. Hammam knew only too well the physical horrors in store for him if he were captured alive. And if his professed piety was not a sham, he believed that dying from a police bullet meant instant passage to paradise as a "martyr" of jihad. He was also in a bind. His only escape route was over a twelfth-floor balcony.

"I don't think Hammam was expecting to be arrested," said Hisham Mubarak. "He was probably thinking that he was beyond the police catching him."[57]

Logically, the police should have wanted to take him alive. He already had a death sentence, so his end was assured. And his head was full of information they desperately wanted. Who was sending him money? Who were his associates? Where were their safe houses? Where were his arms stashes? Tear gas and negotiations, however, were apparently not tried. Logic is not always the way in Egypt.

Two days after Hammam's killing, his men also broke radio silence on their commander. Using his name for the first time in one of their faxed press releases, they vowed that "Talaat Yassin's pure blood will let loose a sea of blood and none of the angels of punishment will be safe from now. . . . His blood has doubled our willpower. As for you, Mubarak, your head will not satisfy us as revenge for Talaat Yassin, take our word for it."

Using the little propaganda leverage they had left, the rebels tweaked the police by noting how their deceased commmander had planned his operations "a few meters from the general intelligence offices." And in the months that followed, the rebels defiantly signed their faxes with a new nom de guerre: "Battalions of Martyr Hammam."

But nothing could change the reality that Hammam's death was a devastating blow to Islamic Group. Rebel attacks dropped off significantly and were limited to certain areas of southern Egypt. Over the next few years, the insurgents mounted several spectacular attacks, including a 1995 assassination attempt against President Mubarak in the Ethiopian capital of Addis Ababa. The most gruesome assault of all came in November 1997, when fifty-eight mostly Swiss tourists and four Egyptians were slaughtered at Hatshepsut's mortuary temple in Luxor. If Egyptians had any sympathy left for Islamic Group, it evaporated in this ghastly act.[58]

Even before Luxor, however, imprisoned leaders of the movement urged their followers to halt all violence in a unilateral, unconditional cease-fire. From his American prison cell, Sheikh Abdel Rahman endorsed that call a year later, and in early 1999, the hard-line exiled leadership of Islamic Group also gave its assent.[59]

By then, some of these exiled leaders had found a new crusade: Osama Bin Laden's international *jihad* against America. His 1998 decree urging Muslims to kill Americans everywhere was signed by two Egyptians: Islamic Group leader Rifa'i Ahmed Taha and Islamic Jihad's Ayman Zawahiri. Several others who'd helped direct Egypt's insurgency from abroad turned up as linchpins in Bin Laden's terrorist network. Their failed effort in Egypt had been a prelude to a new and larger *jihad*.[60]

In the end, Islamic Group degenerated from a religiously inspired, somewhat idealistic movement into a nihilistic terrorist organization. The movement's youthful leaders had not understood their own people. They had underestimated Egyptians' distaste for violence and their rejection of radical Islam's intolerance. Islamic Group also had not understood its foe. An authoritarian regime backed up by a 360,000-man army, a 600,000-strong internal police force, and a powerful, wealthy business elite is not an easily raided estate. To believe it would succumb because of attacks on tourists, Christians, and policemen was dangerously delusional.

The rebels, finally, became victims of their misguided revolutionary enthusiasm, which Mubarak, the human rights activist, described with an image drawn from warm Cairo nights. "They remind me," he said, "of a big wave of moths flying toward the light just to get burned."

Islamic Group's stalled passage over Egypt, however, carried a perilous omen for the victorious state. To be sure, it had triumphed over the outlaws of the early 1990s. But to see this victory as final is a snapshot perspective, mistaking a moment in time for a much broader historical process: the unfolding drama of Political Islam in Egypt. In this drama, whose roots go back a century, the Islamist rebellion was just one act. But Hammam's men had broken new ground. Theirs was Egypt's first populist insurgency fought in the name of Islam. For a while, it had the government on the run and the nation's economy staggering under body blows. Their challenge led to more deaths than any previous political conflict in modern Egypt as more than thirteen hundred Egyptians, including almost a hundred foreigners, were killed. It also sent almost ninety Egyptians to the gallows. Clearly, the pattern is not encouraging. With each new phase, the struggle over the country's Islamic soul seems to be getting more violent.

In "The Stranger," the narrator relates how he decided to prove his manhood to his "hero" by killing someone. And so it came to pass that the cutthroat outlaw and his ingenue protégé hunkered down by a village road one night to await their unsuspecting victim—that is, whoever next came down the road. Hours passed before a farmer appeared in the moonlight astride his donkey. Dressed in a turban and white galabia, the farmer was singing sweetly to himself, blissfully unaware of the lurking danger. As he drew nearer, singing ever more passionately, the youth followed him with the muzzle of his Italian submachine gun. His sweating fingers rested on the trigger as he took better aim. But at the last moment, he could not squeeze it. He could not kill. Jumping to his feet, he threw down the gun and ran home, leaving his "hero" behind forever.

In real life, Bestawi Abdel Meguid and thousands of others made a different choice. They did not flee "The Ghost." They joined his "Sons of the Night."

For Egypt, that made all the difference.

6

Death of a Lawyer

"O Prophet! Say to those who are captives in your hands: 'If Allah findeth any good in your hearts, He will . . . forgive you: for Allah is Oft-forgiving, most Merciful.'"
—QUR'AN 8:70

"Do you understand how terrorism is born? It is born in the womb of the state . . . Torture is the only producer of terrorism."
—MOUKHTAR NOUH,
ISLAMIST LAWYER AND ACTIVIST

Springtime arrives in Cairo on the wings of gentle, perfumed nights. Dust-weary vines of jasmine, clinging to crumbling city walls all year long, suddenly sprout soft, popcorn-white blossoms. Their sweet fragrance falls into the arms of the evening breeze from the Nile and together they dance over darkened streets and alleys until dawn. Intoxicated by this urban eau de cologne, Cairo leaves behind the hard, taut edges of nervous days, quickens to the pulse of a new season and begins to dream of love. On a springtime night like this, Abdel Harith Madani met his Black Policeman.

It was not the first time lawyer had met torturer. They had jousted before, usually on Madani's terrain—that is, in a court of law, where the weapons are legal documents and verbal thrusts. Madani had won some of those contests. But on this sweetly scented night in 1994, the two foes met on Black Policeman territory, which is to say in a room wired, plugged and lit to achieve maximum terror. The weapons here were fists, feet, batons, ropes, burning cigarettes, electric shocks, and something terrible, something still unknown that left seventeen dark bruises on Madani's smooth, coffee-colored skin. On this night, the jasmine smell of spring was drowned in the stink of blood, sweat, and urine. And at the age of thirty, Madani was no longer an attorney, a father of two girls, and an Islamist militant. He was a corpse.

We are not dealing here with the death of a saint.

Madani, who had jet-black eyes, a high, wide forehead; and a tightly coiled, dark beard, had not concealed his association with Islamic Group. He briefly served as its official spokesman. He'd been with the movement, he told me, since 1981 and was serenely confident that Egypt's destiny was to become an Islamic state ruled by *shari'a*. He defended Islamist extremists in court and did not condemn their violence in public. Like other apologists for Islamic Group, he argued that the movement had been forced into violence as a means of self-defense. Besides, what was going on in Egypt was, in his words, "a war."

Still, he had misgivings. He knew the violence was dividing Egyptians and hurting the rebels' cause. Looking for a way out of the spiraling feud of revenge between Islamist extremists and police, he approached a member of parliament with a truce proposal from the rebels.

The government, however, saw no nuances in Madani. After his death, officials accused him of being a "dangerous terrorist" and a key link between "The Ghost" and other Islamic Group members. They asserted that he had carried messages from imprisoned rebel leaders to extremists on the street and distributed money to them. President Mubarak called him "a criminal." His death only hours after being arrested, officials said, was due to a "severe asthma attack."[1]

No, the death of Madani was not the slaughter of an angel. Just the cold-blooded slaying of a human being.

Madani died because the Egyptian government succumbed to one of power's most corrosive temptations: Moving the battle with its opposition from open courtrooms to hidden torture chambers. Torture has never been completely out of fashion in Egypt, and different governments have relied on it to some measure. But in the early 1990s, torture became the state's weapon of choice as it moved to excise what officials called "the cancer" of Radical Islam.

In doing so, the state forgot its own history. Torture, which works marvelously in the short term, had not stopped Islamist extremism from reappearing. Torture of Muslim Brothers by the Nasser regime in the 1960s led some of them to a more radical vision of their mission, which showed up in the ideology of Sayyid Qutb, who himself was tortured. Torture of detainees rounded up after Sadat's assassination so embittered some of its victims that they went on to join Osama Bin Laden's Al Qaeda.[2]

Egypt is not unique among Middle Eastern countries in its addiction to torture. Practically all of them, including Israel, use it in varying degrees of degradation and viciousness. Egypt also is not the worst. Syria, Iraq, Iran, and Turkey are Islamic countries whose record on torture is far more horrific than Cairo's. But that is hardly something to boast about.[3] People accustomed to a political culture in which torture is a tool, albeit a hidden one, often have a hard time letting go of it. Egyptian-born officials of Osama Bin Laden's Al Qaeda network reportedly authorized and used torture on their prisoners in Afghanistan.[4]

Torture is toxic to the moral and spiritual fiber of those who administer it and states that allow it. A year before Madani was born, Egyptian writer Yusuf Idris warned his country of these perils in his 1962 short story "The Black Policeman." It is the tale of a torturer who comes to a sad end but who, in his heyday, was "notorious" for "what he did to prisoners and detainees . . . His job had been to beat them up, some of them to make them confess and others just for the sake of it, to break their spirits. [A]mong all those entrusted with beating up the political prisoners he was the most brutal. . . . People who had watched him working on his victims said that he did not look human."[5]

> "Any person arrested, detained . . . shall be treated in the manner concomitant with the preservation of his dignity. No physical or moral harm is to be inflicted upon him. . . . If a confession is proved to have been made by a person under . . . duress or coercion, it shall be considered invalid."
>
> Egyptian Constitution, Article 42

In Egypt, the handling of politically suspect prisoners is the domain of the General Directorate of State Security Investigations (SSI), which is in charge of internal security. Its military-like chain of command reports to the interior minister. Like security policemen around the globe, SSI personnel are night owls who prefer to roust suspects from their beds in the predawn hours. Handcuffed and blindfolded, detainees are usually taken direct to SSI offices and only later delivered to a prison or police station for paperwork on their arrest. In other instances, detainees are removed from prison cells to SSI offices for interrogation with no documentation of the transfer.[6]

A principal torture site is SSI headquarters at Lazoghly Square in downtown Cairo, so named for its imposing statue of a man in puffy pantaloons identified as "Laz Ogli Muhammed Bey 1828." The stony visage of this nineteenth-century politician faces SSI Central, located in a multistory building with a soaring radio antenna and a huge satellite dish on its roof. The building, which stands next to the Justice and Interior Ministries, is surrounded by a high, thick wall with palm trees peeking over its top.

Since 1985, the Egyptian Organization for Human Rights (EOHR) has published numerous sad catalogs of human abuse carried out by SSI. Based on EOHR's investigations and its interviews with released detainees, the menu includes:

Beatings with wooden sticks or wires

Being forced to stand naked outside in cold weather and then doused with cold water

Beatings on the soles of feet

Electric shocks to all parts of the body, including genitals

Being forced to stand in a pool of water through which an electric current is sent, forcing the detainee to hop until he falls down from exhaustion

Being hung from a door for hours

Being hung by the wrists for long periods of time in various contortions, variously known as "the phantom," "the slab of meat" or "roasted lamb"

Being burned by cigarettes

Having beard and pubic hair pulled out

Being tied to a wet mattress through which an electric current is passed, this being called the "electric mattress"

Stripping females and putting them in the same room with naked male detainees

Sticking metal rods or wooden sticks up anuses

Victims of torture in Egypt have included farmers, fishmongers, carpenters, street vendors, doctors, lawyers, students, engineers, housewives, computer technicians, psychologists, journalists, clerics, and poets. They have been male and female and have ranged from teenagers to people in their sixties.[7]

Torture has two purposes for the government. One is to instill terror in the population to render it passive, which it certainly does. This type of torture "has limits," said the late Hisham Mubarak, one of EOHR's first investigators. The second kind of torture seeks to elicit information and has "no limits," Mubarak said. Sometimes it kills.[8]

In addition to investigations by human rights groups, there were other clues about what was happening in the rooms of Egypt's Black Policemen during Islamic Group's insurgency. First, there was the inevitable "singing." As if by magic, detainees began ratting on friends and "confessing" to horrible crimes within hours of arriving at SSI offices. The mafia code of *omerta* was unknown. Officials blithely reported "breakthroughs" in the fight against terrorism because of "confessions." But there was never any elaboration by them or by the press on how these "confessions" emerged, why they were so rapid, or whether they were voluntary. To judge from the Egyptian media, "confessing" was as natural to Egyptians as their passion for soccer.[9]

Another pointer to the terror going on behind SSI's closed doors could be found in the filing cabinets of the Justice Ministry. If a detainee claims he was tortured or if he dies in custody, his attorney has the right under the law to demand an examination by a Justice Ministry physician. Government prosecutors often procrastinate before approving such examinations, biding time until telltale wounds have healed. But in the end, they usually get done.

For the most part, however, those in authority maintain a studied blindness to these medical reports. Even those who bravely document the physical abuses inflicted on prisoners stand mute, lest they lose their jobs. One year, the EOHR was so impressed with the honesty of these examiners that it gave its annual human rights award to the Justice Ministry's forensic medicine department. But a day before the public ceremony, a representative of the department called to say that no one would be able to attend to accept the award.[10]

A 1992 report by Human Rights Watch/Middle East concluded that "the methods of torture in Egypt are rigorous yet predictable, indicating that a system appears to be in place to train SSI personnel in torture techniques and that the use of torture is directed and supervised by officers in the SSI." A similar conclusion was reached by Amnesty International, the United Nations, and the U.S. State Department.[11]

The Egyptian government denies that it has a deliberate policy of torture. During the insurgency of the early 1990s, Interior Minister Hassan Al Alfi asserted that detainees hurt themselves in order to bring the police into disrepute. "These people are professional criminals," he said. "They beat themselves with metal chains to make fake wounds." Another time, the minister called reports of torture "mere lies" from "offenders, weirdos and people who have a vested interest."[12]

Officials from President Mubarak on down also attacked Western human rights groups for publicizing instances of torture. These groups, Mubarak once declared, "interfere in the internal affairs of the country" and "are just defending terrorists and criminals." On occasion, Egyptian officials admitted that "undisciplined" SSI interrogators and other policemen may have gone to extremes and promised to punish them. Usually, nothing happened.[13]

The resort to torture, some Egyptians say, has been facilitated by two decades of rule under emergency laws. In exceptional times of national crisis, the Egyptian constitution allows the president to temporarily invoke a state of emergency. Sadat's 1981 assassination was such a crisis, and his successor, President Mubarak, dutifully declared an emergency. Contrary to what everyone expected, however, the emergency laws have been in place ever since. Temporary became permanent.[14]

By suspending civil liberties and procedures normally guaranteed by the constitution, the emergency laws affect such rights as free assembly as well as how arrests and detentions are carried out. Emergency laws also deprive the judiciary of some of its constitutional prerogatives.

Yehia Al Refai was one of the few judges who spoke out against the emergency laws, urging Mubarak on several occasions to lift them. Refai was a dignified, silver-haired man who served more than forty years on the bench before he retired. When we met, he was a vice president of the Court of Cassation, the second-highest appeals court. As a lover of the law, he was deeply concerned about the erosion of respect for Egypt's constitution and its courts, which he blamed on the long-running emergency laws.

These laws "make it easier for torture to happen," said Refai, leaning forward in his chair with one elbow resting on his knee. We were sitting in his apartment, situated above a row of boutiques on a noisy street in the Cairo neighborhood of Zamalek. He was dressed in a dark suit. Sunshine streamed through the room's large windows. Refai explained that emergency laws, among other things, suspend the constitutional procedures governing arrest and detention and permit police to pick up suspects without a court order. As such, the emergency laws provide SSI with greater opportunities to torture, intimidate, and abuse.

Torture has a boon companion: indefinite incarceration without formal charges or trial. This, too, is expedited by the long tenure of emergency laws in Egypt. Regulations allow detainees held without charge for thirty days to petition the Supreme State Security Court for their release. The police then have fifteen days to tell the court why the detainee should not be released. If the court disagrees with the police, the detainee is freed. But when such releases are ordered by the courts, SSI frequently resorts to a blatant ruse to get around them. Instead of freeing the prisoner, it takes him to a police station and has a brand-new detention order issued. This starts the rigamarole over again, forcing the detainee to wait another thirty days before again petitioning the court to be freed. In this way, hundreds of persons have been held for long periods, sometimes for years, without ever being charged or convicted of a crime.[15]

"What I care about is that justice prevails in my country and that all the people have trust in the court system," Refai said. If emergency laws were lifted, he added, "the present security forces would lose their powers and their duties would increase. Instead of obtaining security by force, they would need to get security by their minds, which is obviously very difficult." He did not smile at his sarcastic put-down of SSI's competence. Instead, he slumped back in his chair with a pained look on his face.[16]

Judge Refai's anxiety is not misplaced. Egyptian courts have long been respected for probity and independence and enjoy far more autonomy and power than courts in other Arab countries. Judges in Iraq, Syria, and Saudi Arabia don't even dream of ordering security police to free detainees. But Egypt's courts have been increasingly hamstrung by the emergency laws and the security establishment's cavalier disdain for the constitution and judicial orders.[17]

In a curious way, SSI became a mirror image of its radical Islamist foes. The militants rejected democracy because its Western provenance supposedly made it alien to an Islamic state. SSI rejected habeas corpus, a hallowed pillar of Western law, because it did not suit their state of "emergency."

Abdel Harith Madani was born more than four hundred miles upriver from Cairo near the town of Isna in 1963, just a few months after Talaat Yassin Hammam, the "Ghost" with whom Madani would become fatally entwined. He was the son of a government civil servant in the office of land reform. Like many bright students in the hinterland, he went to Cairo after high school and in 1985 graduated from the law school at Ain Shams University.[18]

Returning home, Madani began proselytizing for Islamic Group and founded its first chapter in Isna around 1986. As tension between Islamic Group and the police grew, he was twice arrested for minor infractions. He moved back to Cairo, where he joined the law offices of Montassir Al Zayat. The two friends were a study in opposites. Zayat's large girth and silk-smooth style were offset by Madani's doll-like physique and an obvious effort to choose the right words to express himself. He came across as confident but not arrogant. "He was very quiet, very skillful. And God seemed to be satisfied with him," recalled attorney Fatima Al Zahra Ghoneim. "He was one of the few lawyers you liked even before you met him."[19]

After a few years with Zayat, Madani opened his own office. He married Wafaa Mohammed Ahmed, a cousin who also was a committed Islamic Group member. They soon had two daughters, whose pictures Madani proudly extracted from his wallet to show friends. In one snapshot, two-year-old Miriam wore an Islamic headscarf.

I first met Madani in 1993 at the trial of two dozen Islamic Group members charged in connection with the 1990 assassination of Egyptian parliamentary speaker Rifaat Mahgoub. During a recess, I was interviewing a defendant through the bars of his courtroom cage when a voice behind me asked, "So, is America trying to find out who is stronger, Mubarak or the Islamic movement?" Turning around, I saw Madani smiling at his question.

In subsequent conversations he defended Islamic Group's violence, claiming that it was "forced to use violence to defend itself from dangers through which it is passing, such as repeated detentions, torture and family hostage-taking," he said. I questioned him once about the murder of a policeman by the extremists. "What's the problem?" he snapped. "That's the response to the death of dozens!

"Don't blame me. . . . What I say is that the government is responsible for this situation. . . . What's the big deal? Why can't they let go of two thousand detainees? Someone is accused [of a crime] and they arrest his mother, his family. Why?"

Madani argued that attacks on tourists were "an attempt to strike at the economy. The tourist is not the one aimed at." This, of course, was a distinction without a difference. It meant nothing to the grieving families of slain tourists like Sharon Hill.

Since torture was usually an issue in trials of Islamist defendants, Madani was often toe-to-toe with Egypt's Black Policemen. On occasion, he won. In the Mahgoub trial, the three civilian judges acquitted all twenty-four defendants of murder after ruling their "confessions" inadmissible because they had been subjected to "the ugliest forms of torture." Demonstrating that judicial independence had not been totally hobbled by emergency laws, the judges cited the Justice Ministry's own medical reports as evidence of the abuse, which included electric shocks. The torture, wrote Chief Judge Wahid Mahmoud Ibrahim, was "proof of the failure and incapacity of the police to discover the truth."[20]

Despite Madani's spirited defense of Islamic Group rebels, he was troubled by the attacks on tourists and groping for an exit from the escalating strife that was tearing Egypt apart. In April 1994, his search led him up the creaky stairs of a decaying, colonial-era building near the Hotel Omayad in downtown Cairo and into the law offices of Kamal Khalid, an iconoclastic lawyer and political loner then in his late sixties.

Some of Khalid's countrymen regarded him as quixotic; others called him "nutty." But until his death in 1998, this short, round-faced man with a black mustache was a rarity in Egypt's fiercely conformist society: An independent thinker who openly challenged the status quo. On several occasions, he took the government to court over its election rules, arguing that they were unconstitutional. He prevailed each time, twice forcing the government to dissolve parliament and hold new elections.[21]

Egypt's top officials, Khalid told me when I visited him, were like "tailors" because of their penchant for snipping the constitution to suit their political interests. We were sitting in his wood-paneled office, which looked as though a sandstorm had passed through. Disheveled and dusty, it was crammed with knickknacks, memorabilia, and stacks of papers in profound disarray. A portrait of his journalist father, wearing a red fez, hung on the wall. Sitting at his elbow was a black telephone with no dial and a receiver shaped like a large, curlicue *C*. It was heavy enough to be a doorstop and of an age to once have rung with news about the advance of German panzers across the North African desert. Amazingly, it still worked.

Khalid was eager to talk about Madani's 1994 visit and drew a small, pink notepad out of his top drawer. "When Madani came to me," he explained, "I was taking some notes." The two men had not previously met when Madani arrived alone around 8:30 P.M.

"He told me he was coming as a representative of the leaders of the Islamic trend," Khalid related. They had decided to approach Khalid, Madani told him, because he had been part of the defense team in the Sadat assassination trials. In 1994, Khalid was also a member of parliament.

According to Khalid, Madani told him that Islamic Group leaders could "issue a general order to stop acts of revenge and violence inside Egypt" but preferred not to issue a public appeal to their militants because people "will say that there has been an agreement between Islamic Group and the Egyptian government."

To avoid this, the leaders wanted to tell their followers to halt the violence "in their own way," Madani told Khalid. He also said Islamic Group leaders did not control all the rebels and promised to inform the police if they learned about attacks planned by rebels beyond their control.

In return, Islamic Group was asking for the same things that it had requested in past cease-fire offers: that the police halt torture, release detainees ordered freed by the courts, and stop taking family members of militants as hostages. Madani did not refer to these as "conditions," Khalid said, but as "measures that would help members of Islamic Group to obey their leaders when they asked them to stop the violence."

Madani made it clear that he wanted Khalid to convey his message to President Mubarak and asked Khalid not reveal his name when doing so. Khalid said he met one of Mubarak's top aides, Zakaria Azmi, and conveyed Madani's message. Azmi promised to relay it to Mubarak. Before Azmi could get back to Khalid, however, Madani was dead.

Having reached the end of his story, Khalid's composure evaporated. "The methods the government is using definitely increases the phenomenon of terrorism in Egypt," he shouted. "When the police go to a city in Upper Egypt they are looking for one or two terrorists. But they arrest four hundred people and take them to the central security camps and torture them. This means that two terrorists becomes four hundred. . . . This is a laboratory to produce terrorism! The police in Egypt need more preciseness and scientific methods in searching for criminals, not arresting four hundred in order to find two!"[22]

I left Khalid's time-warped office wondering why nobody in Egypt was listening to a man who did not seem "nutty" to me.

Less than a week after Madani's secret visit to Khalid, Egyptians celebrated the holiday that heralds the arrival of spring. Appropriately, the day is called "Smell the Breeze," and families spend it picnicking along the Nile and taking leisurely walks. Amid the festivities, news of "The Ghost's" death earlier that morning shot through Cairo newsrooms like a bullet.

Madani, however, did not hear it until late that evening when, according to his wife, Wafaa, he went out to get the early edition of the next day's papers. The story was on every front page. When Madani returned to their apartment, "he was crying" and "in a very bad condition," Wafaa recalled in an interview. "I asked him to tell me what's wrong. And he told me 'This is the fate of Muslims in Egypt. In Egypt, they choose the best youth and kill them.' "[23]

Madani began to pray in the apartment. "When he was putting his head to the ground, he was staying for a long time," Wafaa said. "This is time [during prayer] when you ask God for help in problems. He was asking God for something. He was making petitions so loud that I could hear him. He was praying, asking God 'to accept me as a martyr.' Afterwards, he started crying, he was devastated."

Madani's emotional reaction to Hammam's death clearly showed that the dead terrorist had been someone special to the young lawyer. And the reference to martyrdom during his prayers suggested that Madani saw Hammam's death as a bad omen for himself.

The next day, Wafaa begged her husband to stay home but he told her that "this day in particular, I have to go."

If Madani believed he was in greater peril now, he pretended otherwise. Zayat, his former law partner, recalled that they attended court together that morning. "We talked about the killing of Hamman and Madani was normal," he said. "We laughed together despite the very difficult circumstances we were passing through at that time. It was his nature, he was lighthearted even in the worst conditions."

That night Madani went to his office as he usually did to work with his three associates. Around 9:30 P.M., three SSI officers in civilian clothes walked in. They were accompanied by four special forces policemen in black uniforms and about ten others in military-style fatigues. The SSI agents ordered the four attorneys to raise their arms and stand against the wall as they searched their pockets and took their identification cards. The officers, who were communicating with their head office by walkie-talkie, searched the office. When the phone rang, one of the officers answered it, pretending to be Madani's secretary.

"They were careful not to talk to each other at all. When they found a book or document, they would take it to their chief," recalled Moshir Ahmed, one of Madani's associate lawyers. "When we asked why they were doing this they told us to shut up."

Sometime after eleven P.M., the security men hustled Madani into a waiting Peugeot and let the three other attorneys go. Madani and his escorts arrived at his apartment around 11:30 P.M., according to Wafaa. "There were lots of policemen spread all over the flat. . . . They searched every bit of the house, they even took out the dirty laundry and searched it. They searched the bedroom and even the holy book of the Qur'an, they looked into its pages."

Looking at a shopping list of items including sugar and cooking oil that had been written by Madani's aunt, the SSI officers "thought the numbers beside each item were some kind of code," said Wafaa. "They actually took the piece of paper and told Madani to give the code. They pressured him very much on this piece of paper and he swore it didn't mean anything, that it was his aunt's paper, and they told him they were going to discuss this business."

They seized a bag of files, another bag Madani used for traveling, and a wallet with 1,500 Egyptian pounds, or about $450.

As they finished up, Wafaa said she overheard the SSI man in charge tell his supervisor by walkie-talkie that Madani "has nothing in his house."

A scratchy voice replied, "Okay, bring him in and we'll deal with it."

Their daughter Miriam, whose picture Madani kept in his wallet, had slept through the commotion. When Madani asked if he could kiss her good-bye, his escorts said no. From the apartment balcony, Wafaa watched her husband get into a police car. He was not ill at the time, she said, and had never suffered from asthma.

What happened next is in dispute.

Madani's friends and wife say he was taken to the SSI office in Giza, the closest one to his home. A few hours later, he was carried into a special ward reserved for SSI detainees on the top floor of Qasr Al 'Aini Hospital.

Attorney Ali Ismail Hussein, a close friend of Madani, said that one of his clients was also in the hospital ward that night. Massoud Al Arif Ibrahim was an Islamist insurgent awaiting trial on murder charges. He was later sentenced to death by a military court and executed in August 1994. But before his hanging, "he told me a serious secret," Hussein said. "This secret is that he saw Madani and he saw him in a serious state because of torture."[24]

Hussein said Ibrahim told him that he overheard a doctor in the ward telling the SSI officer who brought Madani in that his prisoner was dying and that "if he wanted Madani admitted to the hospital, he had to write a report documenting the wounds in his body."

This conversation "was around two A.M. on the twenty-seventh of April and it was only one or two hours afterwards that Madani died," Hussein said. His client, he added, had not previously known Madani but he asked the dying prisoner his name and Madani told him.

It is impossible to verify what Ibrahim told Hussein. But, as later events would strongly indicate, something terrible happened to Madani during those first hours in SSI custody. Something that killed him.

"Madani was like a box," said human rights activist Mahmoud Kandil. "They wanted the information in this box. He died while they were opening the box."[25]

For ten days after Madani's death, the government said nothing. Except for some terrified hospital personnel, no one outside the closed, secretive loop of Egypt's Black Policemen knew he was dead.

On May 7, the bell on the Reuters teletype in my office began jangling, the alert to an urgent story. I went over and read the bulletin as it jerked out of the machine line by line. News of Madani's death was out because his family had been called to the local police station the previous night. There, Wafaa's father and a cousin of Madani were handed a note from SSI ordering them to pick up his body at the morgue. The family called attorney Hussein for advice and he told them not to accept the body until he tried to get approval for an independent autopsy. And so began an unseemly, surreal battle of nerves between Madani's family, who refused to take his body without an independent autopsy, and the SSI, who demanded they accept it without further ado.

While Hussein and other attorneys negotiated with the attorney general to get approval for the autopsy, Madani's uncle and two cousins were again summoned to the police station and verbally pressured to take custody of the corpse. Officials threatened to bury Madani in a secret, unmarked grave if they refused.

By the end of the second day, the police had worn the family down. One of Madani's brothers signed the paperwork to accept the body without an autopsy and the closed casket was swiftly loaded into an ambulance. It was near midnight. The family was ordered to leave Cairo immediately.

Wafaa stayed behind, but Madani's mother, sisters, father-in-law, and cousins accompanied the ambulance as it took Madani on his last journey home. The traveling coffin was escorted all the way by several police cars. Throughout the night and early morning, the macabre procession trundled down the asphalt ribbon along the Nile, deeper and deeper into southern Egypt, reaching Isna late in the morning of May 9.

At noon, Madani was buried with only his immediate family members and police in attendance. Perhaps because he was the most senior official present, Isna's chief of police led the traditional Islamic prayers over Madani's body as it was lowered into his grave. When the ceremony was over, he promptly posted a police guard at the burial site. The SSI was being thorough to the end, making absolutely sure that this troublesome corpse would stay entombed in the earth, where they hoped it would no longer be a bother.[26]

The government made no comment on Madani's death until May 11. Its explanation was incredible. Interior Minister Alfi told reporters that "the man died of an attack of asthma and it has nothing to do with torture and I am not going to say any more about it."[27]

But Alfi would be forced to say more. Madani's death was reported around the world. In Europe and the United States, legal and human rights groups were outraged. Foreign embassies in Cairo, including that of the United States, officially requested information on how Madani died. A delegation of American lawyers left New York for Cairo to do its own investigation.

Confounded by this unexpected reaction, Egyptian officials grew defensive and angry. More than two weeks after Madani's death, the Interior Ministry finally released a six-page statement on May 14 with its account of his death. "Security forces arrested the terrorist Abdel Harith Madani on the evening of April 26 . . . in his office," it said. "He was taken to search his house . . . where a large amount of papers and important organizational documents were found. While he was being taken to search his other house in the Warrak Al Arab area he had difficulty breathing and fainted."

He was taken to the hospital, the statement added, and on "the afternoon of the next day, April 27, the hospital gave notice that he had died from a serious collapse of the respiratory system and a failure of the lungs as a result of a severe attack of asthma."

The ministry then proceeded to lay out the case for why Madani did not merit all this attention. In their "confessions," detainees who belonged to Islamic Group had "confirmed" that Madani "was the direct link" to Hammam, the statement said. He had transmitted "organizational directives" between imprisoned Islamic Group leaders and clandestine cells led by Hammam, "abusing the nature of his profession as a lawyer to facilitate this terrorist activity."

The ministry also asserted that Madani was responsible for "financing this organization by distributing money which came from outside" Egypt. He had received more than $16,000 "in seven installments . . . all of which he spent on terrorist acts of the terrorist groups." Based on this information, a warrant had been issued for Madani's arrest, the ministry said.[28]

Far from calming the situation, the government's account fanned the anger at Madani's death. It was the first time in anyone's memory that an attorney had died in police custody and lawyers staged a one-day national strike that closed down the courts. The Egyptian Bar Association was draped with a cloth banner demanding "retribution" and a group of attorneys attempting to march on a nearby presidential palace were met with tear gas and rubber bullets. "Are we in a state or in a jungle?" the lawyers shouted. "Are we led by a government or a gang?"

Meanwhile, information discrediting the official version of Madani's death leaked out bit by bit. A doctor at the hospital told the Associated Press that Madani had suffered a fatal heart attack. An unnamed coroner at the morgue told *The New York Times* that the body had several "puncture wounds" surrounded by large blue bruises, adding, "I consider this was due to torture." A bar association spokesman told *The Washington Post* that lawyers "were told by doctors . . . that he died of electric shocks and a wound in the head twelve hours after his arrest." The doctors, he added, "are afraid to say this openly."[29]

In June, the New York–based Lawyers' Committee for Human Rights, reporting on its fact-finding visit to Egypt, disclosed that Egypt's attorney general had told the chairman of the Bar Association that the preliminary postmortem, as well as an inspection of the body by the attorney general's staff, had revealed "marks of torture." A few weeks later, the bar chairman elaborated, telling a reporter that he was informed that the postmortem report listed "seventeen injury marks" on Madani's body.

In fact, government prosecutors had evidence contradicting the Interior Ministry's asthma explanation soon after Madani's death. An official postmortem conducted by the Justice Ministry's forensic division on April 28 found bruises on Madani's chest, abdomen, and limbs, as well as bleeding on the surface of his brain. These findings were summarized in an official internal memorandum dated May 7, the same day that Madani's death became public.[30]

Although these sordid details were not public knowledge at the time, the government's behavior suggested a cover-up. The ten-day delay in notifying the family of Madani's death, the hasty burial under police guard, the police picket at the gravesite, the refusal to allow an independent autopsy and the failure to release the official postmortem report all pointed to something other than "asthma" as the cause of Madani's "breathing difficulties." In addition, the official death certificate was not filled out until June 12, 1994, and was left incomplete. The "date of death" is recorded as April 27, 1994, but the box for "time of death" is empty. A line is drawn through the space under "cause of death."[31]

In time, the government began backing away from significant aspects of its original story. In a letter sent to Amnesty International six months after Madani's death, it stated that the arrest warrant for Madani was based on information that "implied" that he was a "prominent" member of Hammam's network. This is far cry from the "confirmed" information based on "confessions" cited by the Interior Ministry's initial statement. The letter also noted that among the documents seized in Madani's apartment was "correspondence between himself and imprisoned members of the organization." This is hardly surprising, since many of these people were Madani's clients. Finally, the letter made no mention of asthma. While it still maintained Madani had "difficulty in breathing," it said a postmortem was done "to determine the cause of death." The letter did not state the cause.

Two years after Madani's death, the government indicated that it had completed its investigation but declined to publish its findings. No criminal charges were filed in connection with his death, at least not as far as the Egyptian public knows. And the Black Policemen who met Madani that springtime night remain faceless and, presumably, unpunished.[32]

Not everyone in Egypt was outraged by Madani's death. Many Egyptians have no qualms about torture and long-term detention without trial of alleged terrorists. "It's natural. How else can the police get to these people?" asked dentist Mawoud Hassanein. "It takes a long time for these people to understand. So you have to deal roughly with them. If you deal leniently with them, they'll never shut up. Before, they used to have the government on the run. Now the government is stronger."

I used to imagine the reaction of people like Hassanein if torture and detention without trial were being carried out by an Islamist government in Egypt rather than by its present-day secular regime. What would these proponents of "a strong hand" say then? I think I know. They would be hollering from hotel rooms in London and New York, to which they had fled, about the "barbarity" of it all. And they would do so because the victims would be people like themselves.

As the American lawyers who investigated Madani's death noted,

"Many in Egypt have already jumped to one of two conclusions. They either hold the government to blame for a death by torture . . . or they accept that Mr. Madani was a terrorist and . . . therefore the government's actions may have been regrettable, but were justified.

"The second of these conclusions . . . is the more damaging to the long-term prospects for the rule of law and political stability in Egypt," the lawyers added. "Whatever the provocation presented by terrorism, if the Egyptian government, like other governments in similar situations, neglects to abide by the law when dealing with its opponents, it cannot credibly expect its citizens to respect the law."[33]

Torture was an effective state weapon in stamping out the Islamist insurgency of the 1990s because torture is always effective for a time. But it exacts a price. Torture made Islamic Group more vindictive and may have prolonged the rebellion. The movement's faxed communiqués routinely cited torture of its detained members as justification for its deadly attacks on senior police officers, as happened in the scorching of Khayrat.

It also heightened the extremists' conviction that they were being persecuted for their religious beliefs. "There is a saying by Prophet Muhammad that 'There will come a day for my people in which those who are holding to religion are holding on to a piece of fire, like coal,' " Madani's wife, Wafaa, said. "And there's another where he says 'The day will come when you will be attacked like beasts.' "

Certainly, torture would not necessarily disappear if Egypt were to become the orthodox Islamist state sought by the rebels. Recent history has given ample proof—in Iran and Sudan—that governments claiming to rule in the name of God are not immune from the same temptation of power to which Egypt's secular government yielded. No government, whether it calls itself secular or Islamic, is truly following Islam if it practices torture. For torture mocks Islam's demand that Muslim rulers be just.

In Idris's fable, the Black Policeman was a symbol of what the writer feared for his country. Shunted out of his post by a change in government, the torturer fell into an abyss of depression, and finally, madness.

Over his bed, a framed certificate hung on the wall under dirty glass. It was a government "service award" issued to the Black Policeman years before. It cited "his self-sacrifice in the service of the highest interests of the nation."[34]

7

Education, Not Revolution

"Help one another to piety and godfearing; do not help each other to sin and enmity."

— Qur'an 5:2

"We will always have an Islamic opposition because we are an Islamic country."

— Saad Eddin Ibrahim,
Egyptian sociologist

On this particular day, it's safe to say that Amani Kandil looked distinctly out of place. To begin with, she was the only female speaker at the conference of Islamist activists, men with very traditional views of a woman's place. In addition, Kandil is not one to favor the subdued, suited look of power-dressing. When I met her, she had on gobs of makeup, gargantuan-framed glasses, earrings as big as grasshoppers, and a bulky necklace. Her brown, wavy hair cavorted wildly around her head except for a few strands coquettishly anchored by a barrette over one ear. A plume of smoke drifted upward from the cigarette permanently attached to her hand.

Contrary to the bubblehead her looks might suggest, Kandil is a highly respected, no-nonsense political scientist, which is why she was asked to address the conference. When she had finished, someone in the audience passed her a note. Unfolding it, she read, "Dr. Kandil, I give you my compliments and I support you with all my heart. You are very good, but please try to veil."

Kandil began boiling inside. Whether she wore a headscarf or not was nobody's business but her own, and she said so. "I read the note and I said to them, 'This is not acceptable,'" she recalled. "'I don't give anyone the right to talk to me about the way I dress. It's a special relation between me and God. I am a Muslim and I respect my Islam very much and I'm not expecting anybody to give me such comments.' "

As an embarrassed silence filled the room one of the younger men quickly approached Kandil. "He was very nice, very intelligent," she recounted. "He said, 'Our colleague who did this admires you very much and he just wanted to say that you are a good lady and that everything is well in you. But that if you put on the veil it might be better for you because you are very attractive.' "

Essam El Erian's diplomatic intervention was the start of an enduring friendship between the young Muslim Brother and Kandil, despite their very different politics. Over the years, "his behavior revealed high respect for me as a woman and as a career woman in particular," she said. "He believes in something, in some principles. He's fighting for these principles. And he could accept part of what I am doing, though the other part he does not accept. He can deal with me."[1]

Erian's ability to connect with people across political divides has been a hallmark of his career. From Islamist student leader in the 1970s, to member of parliament in the 1980s, to political prisoner in the 1990s, it is a career spanning the Muslim Brotherhood's emergence as Egypt's best-organized, best-financed, and most popular opposition force.[2] Erian's is the story of moderate Political Islam in Egypt. It is the tale of Islamists who, though they shun violence for grassroots organizing and electoral politics, are repressed by Egypt's secular-oriented government.

It is also a story about how a younger generation of activists brought new energy and political success to the Brotherhood but then clashed with its older leaders, who find it difficult to adapt new ideas. Some, including Erian, chose to stay with the Brotherhood. Others left to set up their own groups and preach on the need for pluralism in the Islamist political movement. These young activists want a role in governing their country and a voice in setting its national agenda. They are smart, seasoned, and eager for power. And they scare the government of President Hosni Mubarak to death.

A physician by training, Erian's thick glasses and black mustache give him a nerdy look. To call his sartorial taste "mix 'n' match" would be kind. Had he been born Christian in the United States instead of Muslim in Egypt, he might well have been part of the band of conservative Republicans who stormed Congress in the early 1990s waving a Contract with America to restore its civilization. He no doubt would have embraced the Christian Coalition's religious-based family values.

Like the faith-oriented American politicians, Erian is a true believer anxious to turn his country around, get it back on the right track, resurrect its heritage. The difference, of course, is that for him this means making Islam his country's one and only lodestar. Erian has pursued that goal for twenty-five years with the approach favored by Western reformers: peaceful political activities. He has tried to change the system from inside, obeying its rules and waging, as he put it, a *"jihad* of the tongue."

Erian was born April 28, 1954, in the rural village of Nahia just beyond the pyramids of Cairo. Six months later, Nasser launched his bonecrunching crackdown on the Brotherhood and set out to mold Egypt into a socialist state, a project that formed the backdrop of Erian's childhood. His father, an Arabic teacher and elementary school principal, died when Erian was six. His mother shaped the four Erian boys. "She was not educated, but she had a very strong personality and she was very smart with a big smile on her face," recalled Erian's wife, Fatma Fadl Sayed. "She brought them up to be independent, to go to the city to get an education and put in them the seed of good morals and good religion."[3]

After primary school in Nahia, Erian attended Orman Model School in Dokki, a leafy neighborhood in central Cairo. He was an assiduous student who got top grades. When he entered Cairo University's faculty of medicine in 1972, five years after the Arabs' stinging military defeat by Israel, the campus was vibrating with student activism.

Erian helped found the first Islamic Association in the medical faculty and expand it campus-wide. He wrote articles for the Islamist student newsletter, "Voice of Truth," and was elected head of the committee liaising with Islamic Associations on other campuses. He helped organize the 1977 student elections in which Islamists gained control of the government-financed national student union.

After graduating in 1977, Erian signed up for his compulsory, one-year military service. But his Islamist orientation made him suspect and he was honorably discharged two months early. In 1979, twenty-five-year-old Erian married Fatma. He also joined the Muslim Brotherhood, which was emerging after two decades of forced inactivity.

Following Sadat's decision in the mid-1970s to let the Brotherhood resume its work as long as it renounced violence, the movement set up shop in "Star of Tawfikia." The building sits amid Tawfikia market—a narrow lane clogged with vegetable peddlers, donkeys, and cars. It was perhaps once worthy of its glittery name, but now its wooden floors groan under foot and its walls are caked with dust and grime. Only the antique, phone booth–sized Otis elevator, with its glazed windows and red leather seat, still hint at the decrepit building's long-ago elegance.

Here, above the racket of the sidewalk vegetable stalls, the Brotherhood hung out its shingle: a red Qur'an with two crossed swords of white against a background of green, the universal color of Islam. Beneath these symbols were the words "Be Prepared!" which come from a verse in the Qur'an cautioning Muslims to be wary of enemies even after making peace with them.

The Brotherhood set out to revamp its image from a revolutionary group to a legitimate political force that obeyed the rules of the game. On the books, it was, and still is, a banned organization. But in Egypt, such laws are enforced at the discretion of the president. For the moment, "The Believer President" was in need of allies against his left-wing critics. The Brotherhood's resurrection was precarious and ambiguous, for it depended on pharaoh's whim. But precarious was better than nothing.

The revived Brotherhood was very different in some respects from the one that Nasser had crushed. Its elderly leaders had formally denounced the radical ideas of their foremost ideologue, Sayyid Qutb.[4] Many had also become successful businessmen and bankers during exile in places like Germany, Switzerland, Kuwait, and Saudi Arabia. Returning to Egypt under Sadat's amnesty, they took advantage of the country's new pro-capitalist climate and invested in department stores, banks, construction firms, and publishing houses. By the time the Brotherhood resurfaced, its leadership had gone bourgeois.[5]

As a result, the Brotherhood did not favor upending Egypt's existing economic system for anything as radical as land reform. Nor did it want to drastically alter the political structure. Its desire was to gild these structures with Islamic symbolism and load them up with Muslim Brothers. As one scholar wrote, the organization's inclination was "to repaint existing structures in Islamic green without any great upheaval."[6]

It still hoped to reach Banna's goal of an "Islamic system" ruled by *shari'a* through education and good example. As its spokesman Maamoun Hodeiby once told me, "Islam cannot be applied by force and by punishing people, but by elevating them and bringing them up in the correct way and giving them a good example."[7] As in its earlier years, the Brotherhood stressed community service, running tutoring courses, schools, hospitals, outpatient clinics, and summer camps.

Another key aspect in which the Brotherhood had not changed was its high self-regard. It still saw itself as the sole trustee of Islamist reform in Egypt.

The movement easily reconnected with its middle-class constituency of doctors, lawyers, businessmen, civil servants, and tradesmen. Pious Islam, after all, had been priming the pump for years. Thousands of returned

Egyptian migrant workers who had been exposed to Saudi Arabia's Islamically conservative atmosphere also warmed to the Brotherhood.

University students were another matter altogether. When the Brotherhood reached out to campus Islamic Associations hoping to bring them under its wing, reaction was decidedly mixed. Brimming with the radical views of their martyred hero Qutb, many students regarded Brotherhood leaders as mildewed moderates lacking the requisite fire in their bellies to confront the state. These students were already spinning toward the confrontation that would climax in the murder of Egypt's "Believer President."[8]

But other students had concluded that education was a better way than revolution to reach their goal of an orthodox Islamic state ruled by *shari'a*. These students, who included Erian, welcomed the Brotherhood's mentoring. "I belonged in practice and in intellectual orientation to the Muslim Brothers' school," Erian once wrote. "I was guided by it, profited from its expertise and was a disciple of its sheikhs and men of thought. So there was no decision by me . . . to break from the Islamic Associations we had founded to join the Muslim Brotherhood." In other words, for Erian and his friends, it was a seamless shift from their campus activism into the Brotherhood.

Students who rejected the Brotherhood as too moderate were "a small group," according to Erian. They "took an absolutely different path in terms of their understanding of Islam and . . . on the use of violence." For Erian, *jihad* "means to spend your energy and all your efforts, all that you can, to reach the truth. Therefore, *jihad* includes many meanings starting with fighting yourself to obey Allah, up to the *jihad* of the tongue to spread the call to Islam as well as political *jihad* to reform political affairs."[9]

As a new Brother, Erian cautioned against extremism. In an article for *The Call*, the group's magazine, he wrote that it was harmful to give too much attention to rituals not essential to Islam, like cleaning one's teeth with twigs just because Prophet Muhammad was said to have done so. He criticized those who rejected interpretations of the Qur'an other than their own.

Erian also lamented his countrymen's infatuation with foreign ideas, particularly the notion of separating religion from other spheres of life. As a result, he wrote, "Muslim peoples have experimented with Western-style democracy and Communist socialism: the fruits have been bitter!" But he was confident that "an Islamic awakening" was on the way.[10]

Two years after joining the Brotherhood, Erian got his first taste of the risks associated with opposition politics when he was arrested in Sadat's sweeping crackdown of September 1981. The president was murdered weeks later and Erian was among the detainees targeted as police sought to uncover the extent of the assassination conspiracy. "The ways of torture included severe beating, applying electric shocks, being hung by the shoulders from doors, being left in the open air for long periods and being kept in solitary confinement for very long periods," Erian recalled. After one session, Erian "couldn't lift up his arms when he was brought back to the rest of the group," recounted his friend and fellow prisoner Ahmad Omar.[11]

Erian's thinking was affected by another experience in prison. He saw that some of his secular political rivals endured the pressures and torture more courageously than some Islamists. For the first time, he saw his opponents "as human beings," said sociologist Saad Eddin Ibrahim, a longtime acquaintance of Erian. "He realized that Islamists were not the only patriots and tough guys."[12]

Seeing how his fellow detainees represented "all types of political and ideological trends in Egypt," Erian said, "I came to believe that different views must be respected, allowed to coexist and function freely." He saw more clearly the need for coalition building with "all sincere people" in order "to save Egypt from political dictatorship." At the same time, however, his prison stay strengthened his belief in the "moderate Islamist approach."

Erian had nothing to do with Sadat's killing and was never charged with a crime. But he was detained for almost a year. During his incarceration, Fatma gave birth to their second child, a son named Youssef. The infant died a month later without Erian ever seeing him.[13]

Over the next few years, Erian worked at a government hospital by day and at a Brotherhood-run community health clinic in the evenings. He also got a master's degree in clinical pathology. His thesis topic was how fasting during Ramadan affects the body's metabolism.

But for Erian, medicine was a job. Politics was his vocation. He and other young Muslim Brothers began applying the organizing experience of their student days to new terrain, the country's professional associations. These organizations provide a variety of services to doctors, lawyers, engineers, teachers, pharmacists, and others. In some ways, they function like a union, promoting their members' concerns and offering low-cost insurance, medical and pension plans. Partly funded by members' fees and partly by the government, associations also advise the government on state regulations for various occupations and issue certificates of professional competency to their members.

Most associations had long been docile partners of the government. But that began to change in the 1980s as Islamists, most of them affiliated with the Brotherhood, saw associations as a way to advance their political agenda. Their first success came in the Egyptian Medical Association, with 130,000 physician members. In 1984, Islamist candidates won seven of the executive board's twenty-five seats. In each succeeding election they did better, and by 1990 they controlled twenty seats. A similar process occurred in other associations. The most politically significant Islamist victory came in September 1992 when they won nineteen of the twenty-five seats on the executive board of the Egyptian Bar Association, which had been a bastion of secular liberalism since its founding in the early 1900s. Eventually, Islamists controlled the boards in six of the country's twenty-four professional associations.

These gains did not mean that the majority of Egyptian doctors, pharmacists, engineers, and lawyers had suddenly become Brotherhood supporters or wanted an Islamic state governed by *shari'a*. In fact, Islamists only accounted for about 20 percent of the membership in these associations. Rather, the Islamist gains were mainly the result of old-fashioned, plain vanilla politicking. Aware that turnout in association elections was usually low, the Islamists made sure their supporters got to the polls on voting day. During campaigns, they had plenty of "walking around" money contributed by wealthy Brotherhood members. Plus, the Islamists were far more motivated, energetic, and organized than their government-backed opponents.[14]

I once asked Erian how he and other Islamists got along with members of the ruling National Democratic Party in the medical association. "We work well with the NDP because the NDP is not a real party," he replied with a wry smile. "It's a collection of people who serve their own interests."

Perhaps the biggest reason for the Islamists' advances was something every politician knows is crucial: constituency service. Once elected, Islamists worked hard to address the needs of members. In the medical association, for example, they organized exhibitions of medical equipment members could purchase on installment plans. "They understood that doctors of today are not the doctors of yesterday," political scientist Kandil explained. "Yesterday, doctors in Egypt were very wealthy. But nowadays, we have about 130,000 doctors and . . . their income is very low. I mean, 50 percent of them, their income is about $100 a month for a long time.

"If you address my needs, and then you say 'Elect me,' I will elect you because you understand my needs," she said. "This is what Erian and others were doing."

Looking through her huge eyeglasses, Kandil added, "It's very dangerous for the government."[15]

Building on its successes in the professional associations, the Brotherhood turned next to national parliamentary elections. But it had a problem. Not only was it not a legal political party, it was also still a banned group. The only way it could field candidates would be to piggyback on the slate of a legally registered political party. So in 1984 the Brotherhood formed an electoral alliance with the largest opposition party in parliament, the Wafd.

Though a shadow of its old self, the Wafd is Egypt's most venerable party. It led the independence movement after World War I and professes the ideal of liberal, secular democracy. But like all parties, Wafd felt the breeze of Pious Islam blowing through Egypt and reasoned that in such a climate, a friendly working relationship with the Brotherhood would be a vote-getter. It desperately wanted to enlarge the opposition's tiny presence in Egypt's 444-seat parliament.

Erian, whose prison experience had left him comfortable working with secular partners, was assigned to run the campaign of Wafd candidates—three of whom were Muslim Brothers—in Giza, the district that included his birthplace of Nahia. Nine Muslim Brothers were elected to parliament. But political differences between the Islamists and the secular-oriented Wafd proved hard to reconcile. Their alliance was never popular with the Wafd's rank and file and had soured by the time new elections were called three years later. This time, the Brotherhood joined two smaller parties to form the Islamic Alliance. Its campaign slogan was "Islam Is the Solution."[16]

By one count, the tripartite coalition collected over 1.1 million votes, with half going to Brotherhood candidates. Of the alliance's fifty-six parliamentary seats, thirty-eight were held by Muslim Brothers, who now occupied the largest number of opposition seats in parliament, having won three more than its former partner, the Wafd.[17]

The youngest member of the new legislature represented his home village of Nahia. At thirty-three, Erian the Islamist had made his way into the heart of Egypt's political establishment.

As a new deputy, he submitted written questions to cabinet ministers on human rights violations. He joined committees dealing with youth, Arab affairs, and environmental health. He also enrolled in Cairo University's law school, he said, to be "better informed about everything which had to do with my activities at parliament."

"Erian was the one who communicated the most with the government," recalled Moukhtar Nouh, a Muslim Brother also elected to parliament in 1987. "He smiled and joked with them."

Hamdi Sayed, a member of parliament from the ruling National Democratic Party and chairman of the medical association, recalled how Erian rejected a government attempt to interfere in the internal affairs of the association as a violation of the group's charter. "Of course, most Islamists think that our charter is not Islamic," Sayed said. "But Essam El Erian was insisting that this charter should be followed and that the government should not do anything against it.

"I'm just giving this example to show you how shrewd a politician he was. . . . He was trying to keep within the political framework," added Sayed. "This showed me that . . . he's not rigid in his thinking. He's ready to make compromises. He's a man with such a wide vision that he could very easily . . . bridge the gap between the Islamist movement in this country and the other political movements."[18]

But Erian was still a Muslim Brother with an Islamist agenda, and "implementing *shari'a*" was still his Holy Grail. He and his fellow Brothers in parliament lobbied to revise Article 2 of Egypt's constitution. Since 1980, that article had stated that the principles of *shari'a* are "the principal source" of Egyptian legislation. The Brotherhood wanted it rewritten to say that *shari'a* was "the *only* source" of legislation. They also introduced legislation that they claimed was mandated by *shari'a*, including a ban on alcohol and male hairdressers in beauty salons.[19]

These efforts were unsuccessful but they demonstrated that the Brotherhood's core mission of "implementing *shari'a*" had not changed from Banna's time. What accounted for this mantralike focus? An explanation requires an understanding of some fundamental concepts in Islam.

For all Muslims, not just Islamist activists, Islam is not a religion in the Western sense—that is, a matter of personal belief and private devotion existing apart from the secular domain. Rather, Muslims regard Islam as a complete way of life that governs not only individual belief but also politics, economics, culture, marriage, commerce, and family matters.

This all-encompassing nature of Islam stems from the religion's bedrock tenet of *tawhid*, which means "unifying." *Tawhid* expresses a Muslim's conviction, intuitively grasped since childhood, that God is One and that all of life is unified in Him. So when Muslims profess belief in God, they regard everything in their lives as part of their relationship with God. For them, *tawhid* is fundamental.[20]

People of all faiths, however, act imperfectly on their beliefs when confronted by everyday realities. This is no less true of Muslims. Despite their belief in *tawhid*, many Muslims accept a de facto separation of Islam from a wide range of ordinary, daily activities. They do all sorts of things—sing love songs, cheer soccer teams, perform heart surgery, and build highways—without making explicit, conscious connections to Islam or consulting the Qur'an.

In addition, millions of devout Muslims live under governments that have tacitly delinked religion from politics. In Egypt, for example, the government considers itself Islamic. It uses state funds to employ religious officials and build mosques. It operates under a constitution that asserts that Islam is the "religion of the state." But the government does not make decisions or adopt foreign policy positions on theological grounds. It does not go to the Qur'an or consult religious officials to determine its actions. Instead, most of its decisions are based on secular rationales, such as how to meet public expectations for free public education, how to please foreign investors, and, above all, how to stay in power. In other words, like most other Arab Muslim nations, Egypt has a hybrid government best described as "semi-secular."[21]

Most Muslims are not bothered by this de facto, if unspoken, separation of Islam from some aspects of their lives. But Islamists regard the cleavage, especially between religion and politics, as a spiritual flaw. For them, it violates *tawhid*. Moreover, they believe this separation is the root cause of problems in Muslim societies.

Their remedy for this un-Islamic situation is to make society visibly and openly reflect *tawhid* by "implementing *shari'a*." Not only that, they believe it is every Muslim's religious duty to strive for the formal reestablishment of *shari'a* as the sole guide for all aspects of modern life. The Muslim Brotherhood calls it "an Islamic obligation."

Indeed, restoring *shari'a*, or God's law, to a place of primacy in Muslim societies in order to respect *tawhid* has been at the core of Islamist politics for decades. "Every aspect of the 'renaissance' of Islam in the twentieth century," wrote one scholar, "focused on this central problem of the *shari'a* and its corollary, the 'unity of life.' "[22]

But the demand to "implement *shari'a*" raises the crucial question: Exactly *what* is *shari'a*?

Shari'a comes from the Arabic root, *shara'a*, meaning to set a path or way. It is the same root from which comes *shariah*, the Arabic word for "street." The most common translation of *shari'a* as "Islamic law" is correct but inadequate.

In its broadest sense, *shari'a* means the principles revealed by God in the Qur'an that lead to a good, ethical, noble, and virtuous life. These principles make up "the path" or "the way" that God intended humans to follow and that will lead them to just, prosperous, and successful societies as well as happiness in the afterlife. In this sense, *shari'a* refers to the Qur'an's progressive moral message stressing the worth, dignity, and freedom of human beings.[23]

In Prophet Muhammad's time, women were more or less treated like chattel, easily divorced and ignored in the matter of family inheritance. Girl infants were commonly killed at birth because they were not boys. But the Qur'an forbade infanticide and said women are entitled to a share of their late father's wealth. Since these injunctions elevated women's status from what it had been, the "path" or *shari'a* of the Qur'an was seen as an advance over prevailing moral norms.

As Islam spread through the Middle East and southern Europe, its religious scholars faced the task of applying the Qur'an's moral message to everyday life in a variety of local circumstances. Using the texts of the Qur'an and the Sunna, the written record of Prophet Mohammad's deeds and sayings, the scholars wrote volume after volume explaining how *shari'a* governs every aspect of Muslim life, both personal and communal. Their writings covered prayer rituals, marriage, divorce, business contracts, women's dress, war and peace, cleanliness, child custody, inheritance, government, and the duties of an Islamic leader. The "oneness of God," or *tawhid*, propelled them to make the path set down by God in the Qur'an relevant to all of life.

This vast ocean of Islamic legal opinions and writings produced over centuries is collectively known as *fiqh*, or Islamic jurisprudence, which today has five major schools of thought. In a way, *fiqh* is similar to the corpus of prior legal rulings and precedents used by U.S. judges as guidelines when deciding a case. Because *fiqh* rulings were written by human beings in different lands with varied customs and biases, they are not uniform and sometimes contradictory.[24]

Even today, the world's 1.3 billion Muslims, who have no pope to enforce doctrinal conformity, do not agree on what *shari'a* mandates on many different issues. In Egypt, for example, senior religious scholars have issued conflicting rulings on artificial birth control, female genital mutilation, and the payment of interest.[25]

Obviously, there is a big difference between *shari'a*, understood as the Qur'an's "path" of divinely revealed moral principles, and *fiqh*, the corpus of legal rulings developed by human beings who were influenced by their times and circumstances. Very often, however, Islamist activists fail to distinguish between the two. Asked for a definition of *shari'a*, they recite or list various legal opinions. For them, the profound meaning of *shari'a* as God's moral message is reduced to legalistic, often anachronistic, *fiqh* rulings.

The upshot has been widespread confusion over what is meant by "implementing *shari'a*."[26] The confusion gets worse because Muslims don't agree on exactly how to read the words of the Qur'an. Should they be read literally, without regard for linguistic nuances and the cultural and social attitudes of Prophet Mohammad's time? Or should they be read in a more symbolic way, keeping the historical context in mind?

This debate is not unlike the disagreement among American Christians over how to read the Bible. In 1998, the Southern Baptist Convention resolved that a wife should "submit herself graciously" to her husband and cited numerous biblical passages to support its contention that women cannot have authority over men. Millions of other Baptists disputed the Convention's interpretation. They argued that the Bible cannot be properly read without considering the cultural environment in which it was written, the original meaning of its words, as well as Christ's overall message on the equality of all human beings.

Three problems, then, complicate the Muslim Brotherhood's demand to "implement *shari'a*." First, there is the multiplicity of views on how to apply the broad moral principles of *shari'a* in any given situation. Then there is the tendency to equate *shari'a* with specific *fiqh* rulings. Finally, there is the disagreement on how to read the Qur'an.

When I would ask a Muslim Brother what "implementing *shari'a*" in Egypt would mean, I was usually told that there would be bans on gambling, alcohol, and interest on loans. Women, including Christians, would have to cover their hair in public. And punishments listed in the Qur'an, such as amputating a hand for theft and stoning to death for adultery, would be applied. (They would quickly add that these punishments would be rare because *shari'a* sets rigorous preconditions before they can be imposed.)[27]

The Brotherhood's vision of *shari'a* came across as a narrow, legalistic catalog of "dos" and "don'ts." It gave the false impression that Islamic jurisprudence, or *fiqh*, is the essence of *shari'a* and of Islam. It also appeared to reduce the broad moral message of the Qur'an to concerns over alcohol, gambling, interest-bearing bank accounts, women's dress, and punishments for adultery and theft. These are not crucial matters to the future of a Muslim nation. And yet many Brotherhood officials, especially of the older generation, would repeat these items over and over, even insist on them, to the alarm of many Egyptians. Stoning in the twenty-first century? Forced veiling on all women? Hands cut off for theft? No interest on the money I've put into my bank account? No beer while I watch my soccer game?

To be sure, this rendition of *shari'a* had its appeal. I met a taxi driver in Aswan who said he favored running the government according to *shari'a* "like in Saudi Arabia." When I asked why, he replied, "There are people in the government who are corrupt and who steal money. But under *shari'a* there isn't anything like this because the person who steals has his hand cut off. And someone who murders has his head cut off."

Brotherhood leaders seemed to have little interest in elucidating how *shari'a* should address such matters as the accountability of rulers, social justice, poverty, freedom of speech, freedom of worship, treatment of minorities, war and peace, the role of women in public life, the right to a just wage, and the conflict between intellectual freedom and religious orthodoxy. Some individuals associated with the Brotherhood did wrestle with how *shari'a* should regulate these matters. But as an organization, the Brotherhood did not.

One of the big reasons for this failure was its leadership. Some senior officials had been intimates of Banna and had suffered deeply for their beliefs, spending years in prison under Nasser. But in a mirror image of the government they opposed, they tightly controlled decision making and were reluctant to share power with a younger generation. They also showed little interest in updating their ideology to fit new times.

The dean of this Old Guard is Mustafa Mashur, a bearded, elflike man who had been a meteorologist at Egypt's National Weather Forecasting Center. Mashur joined the Brotherhood in 1938 when he was seventeen. He knew Banna personally and was a member of the Secret Apparatus in the 1940s. He spent at least eighteen years in prison for his Brotherhood activities. Released in the early 1970s, Mashur hovered in the upper echelons of the Brotherhood until he could take what he considered his rightful place as "Supreme Guide" of the movement, which he did in 1996. He was Banna's fourth successor.

I used to visit Mashur in his office in Star of Tawfikia. Then in his seventies, he favored dark suits and had a dour aspect. His smiles looked more like grimaces and lasted about a nanosecond. He was always polite, accessible, and consistent in his views, which included a belief that he was implementing God's will. As we talked, my eyes used to drift to the large, childlike drawing over his head on the wall. It showed a map of the world locked in the smothering grasp of a multi-tentacled octopus labeled "USA."

"The Muslim Brotherhood wants to return the people to true Islam because after the English invaded, there were things which spread which are not Islamic, like alcohol and interest and corruption in the media, films, television, and cinema," Mashur explained during one of my visits. Colonialism "also resulted in the government's separation from *shari'a*. An Islamic government should be run by *shari'a*. The Muslim Brotherhood is trying to get people to return to *shari'a*. . . . Our actions are no more than God's orders."

Unlike socialism and capitalism, Mashur continued, "Islam is from God and not from human beings. . . . God made this system. He asked us to implement *shari'a*. . . . Every Muslim is required to call for the law of God. We don't work for worldly gains or positions but only to please God and to win a happy future—at the end of the day, to go to heaven."

Shari'a, Mashur insisted, had "to be implemented as a whole, and not selectively." This would benefit Egypt because "if we apply the punishment for theft and cut hands three or four times, we would see no theft anymore."[28]

It was after one such meeting with Mashur that I met Erian for the first time. He was waiting outside the Supreme Guide's office, obviously hoping to chat with a reporter. He smiled a lot and his vocabulary was less religious and less stern than Mashur's. Often trained as doctors, engineers, or computer scientists, Erian and others of his generation were politically astute, media-savvy, and comfortable with new technologies and ideas. They were also less secretive, authoritarian, and insular than their elders.

"They were motivated by religion, Islamic principles, and Islamic shar-i'a, but they were not building big walls between themselves and society. They were interacting," Kandil said of the younger Brothers. "This is my point of view, although I'm not part of the group. I'm against . . . a big part of their practices, in particular concerning the rights of expression and concerning women. But I still can think and assess them on my experience [over] ten years. They accepted the rules of the game and they . . . were involved in it, in the heart of the political process. Essam was very intelligent in respecting these rules."

Erian's legislative career was cut short when parliament was dissolved in 1990 after a court ruled that the 1987 election law had been unconstitutional. The Brotherhood and other opposition parties boycotted the next election to protest government restrictions on campaigning. As a result, the 1990 legislature had no Muslim Brothers. Erian called his three years in parliament one of his "most important" experiences. "My horizons were broadened and I became better informed with . . . how a state is managed."

In 1992, Erian was elected deputy secretary-general of the medical association. He got his law degree from Cairo University, enrolled in a course in shari'a at Al Azhar University, and entered a doctorate program in clinical chemistry.

Around Cairo, he became one of the most visible Brothers, earning a reputation for grabbing almost any opportunity—an embassy dinner, an interview, a seminar—to engage in friendly political debate. When he gave interviews to female journalists, he did not insist they wear a kerchief. "He was the bright open face of the Muslim Brotherhood," said Saad Eddin Ibrahim. Another friend, describing Erian at an Islamist conference in Beirut, said that "he was going from person to person like a bee from flower to flower."

Erian was eventually appointed to the Brotherhood's Shura Council, the second-highest governing body after the Guidance Council. He represented the movement at conferences overseas, making three trips to the

United States between 1983 and 1993. While critical of U.S. policies, he did not share the visceral anti-Americanism of older Brothers. In fact, he seemed eager to be taken seriously by the global octopus. Because the concept of an Islamic state "is some sort of unknown for the United States," he told me, "real dialogue must be held between Islamists and the West, not just the Americans."[29]

On another occasion, Erian stressed the Brotherhood's conservative economic policies and added, "I don't understand why a capitalist country like the United States is so opposed to us. We're the best economic friends they could have out here."[30]

When I asked Fatma about her husband's attitude to the United States, she laughed, recalling how he'd tried to persuade her to join him on one of his U.S. trips because she was pregnant and "he wanted me to give birth there to get U.S. nationality" for the child.

Like her husband, Fatma is friendly, resourceful, and self-confident. She is a part-time teacher and used to speaking her mind. The day we met, her long, gray chiffon veil, pulled tight about her face, billowed onto her lap when she sat down. A loose-fitting, green skirt fell to her ankles.

The Erians and their four children live in a large, walk-up flat in Talbiyah, a sprawling shantytown on the way to the pyramids. The area's main thoroughfare, Osman Mutharam, looks like a street scene out of *Les Enfants du Paradis*. Donkeys, taxis, wagons, shoppers, children, and a camel or two form a throbbing, dusty stream on the unpaved road. There are no sidewalks so shoppers step directly out of the hubbub into tiny, fly-swarmed butcher shops and bread booths.

The Erian home hovers over this chaos like an insulated spacecraft, calm and clean. In the study, two brown sofas face each other across a tiled floor. Long, white curtains shift lazily in the breeze, muffling the din of the street below. On the bookshelves are medical texts in Arabic and English with exciting titles like *Blood and Hematology*.

Voluble as Erian was, however, it was difficult to draw out specific details of his Islamist political vision. I tried to do this one day in his first-floor office at the medical association. It was a brightly lit, high-ceilinged room with a large brown rug. There were no greedy octopi on the wall. "Is there any other model for a state than the Western model?" Erian asked from behind his desk. "That's the question. The communists tried and failed and now the Islamists are trying."

I pressed him to describe exactly what he meant by an Islamic state. "We have a majority of people who are Muslims. The land on which they live has an Islamic history. What is missing is that they follow and respect a legal system and constitution that sprout from Islamic concepts," he explained. An

Islamic state would have "freedom of opinion, free publications . . . and a change of power" through elections. Unlike the current Egyptian government, he added, it would "allow all its subjects the freedom of forming parties irrespective of the ideas they represent as long as they respect the constitution, the law, and the basic rules of society."

With some exasperation, I told Erian he seemed to be describing a Western democratic state. How would an Islamic state be different?

"It differs in the general spirit which motivates the people and the message carried out by the state," he replied. "What is the message of the Islamic state? It is the liberation of humanity from slavery to anything but Allah, even from desires and evil instincts. And to have the good dominating the evil, which is the mission of all heavenly religions and the hope of all man-made ideologies."

Unlike non-Muslims who "depend on their minds only," he added, "Muslims have a divine inspiration, the holy Qur'an, may Allah protect it, and a practical guidance which is the honored Prophet's Sunna. . . . Muslims use their minds to understand these texts and project their understanding on the changing human realities, which is a matter that takes a long time to explain."

Erian's gauzy vision left a lot of unanswered questions. But it clearly involved less talk about "implementing *shari'a*" and more about implementing democracy. In this, it illustrated a key feature about today's moderate Islamists. The core of their politics is an attempt to fuse two powerful desires, one for democratic government and the other for Islam to be their society's main reference point. This effort to create an "Islamic democracy" is a hallmark of moderate Political Islam.

CHANGING THE RULES

In the early 1990s, an anxious state saw its control slipping away, first in the professional associations and schools, then in the streets as the Islamist insurgents ratcheted up their violent campaign. Pious Islam was still on the move. Growing religious conservatism was evident among civil servants, journalists, judges, university professors, teachers, and sheikhs at Al Azhar. The government warily watched this personal religiosity for harbingers of religious-based dissent.

The Shura, parliament's upper house, released a ninety-three-page report warning that "Islamist extremists" were infiltrating government institutions and that some religious scholars usually viewed as "moderates" were indirectly supporting the cause of the violent rebels in the media. "Extremist" teachers, the report said, were using their own curriculum instead of the state's and teaching Islamist songs instead of the national anthem, which they regarded as a Western invention. At Cairo University, Islamists shut down theater, poetry, cinema, and music programs because they brought men and women together and distracted people from religious activities.[31]

Some senior government officials began to speak darkly of Islamists "penetrating" Egyptian institutions as if they were spies for a foreign power. In McCarthy-like tones, they portrayed a state bureaucracy honeycombed with closet Islamists waiting to turn Egypt into another Iran. "This penetration was genius," said one official as he sipped a scotch on the sunny verandah of a Nileside restaurant. In an intimate hush suggesting that a coup d'état had been nipped in the bud, he said the government had "discovered" how financial institutions, the judiciary, and university campuses had been "infiltrated." "Try to imagine Egypt without discovering all this penetration!" he said. "In a few years it would be some fundamentalist country!" But the government had dealt with the problem, he added, and "the country is totally safe."

Even Egyptians normally skeptical of official propaganda began speaking of a peril greater than bomb-throwing terrorists. "The danger is not terrorism. It's the systematic, unknown penetration of society," said Ali Hillal Dessouky, then chairman of Cairo University's political science department and now youth minister in Mubarak's cabinet. "Terrorism is easy to handle and if you want to be brutal you can put hundreds in prison. But how can you handle thousands of Islamic schools and teachers who have their own sympathies? You change the curriculum and they refuse to teach it! How do you handle it? To whom does every Egyptian have loyalty? An Islamic banking system, an Islamic educational system, Islamic social services. Already we have a problem. It's as if we already have two parallel societies. One administered by the state. One administered by someone else."

Education Minister Hussein Kamel Bahaeddin heightened public fears when he declared that the government was dealing only with "the tip of the iceberg" and that sympathy for Islamist ideas was deeper than most people realized. In an interview, the minister said that "extremist" teachers were forcing schoolgirls to cover their hair, separating Christian and Muslim students in class and giving fire-and-brimstone sermons about the horrors of hell.

Deciding to cover one's hair, the minister stressed, was a "personal" matter. "If some teacher is going to force girls to wear the veil, I would consider this a fundamentalist act. It's against human rights. It's against the constitution. It's against some international agreements we have signed."

In his view, it was also dissidence. Teachers who imposed the veil on students, Bahaeddin said, "want to show people they are in power and can force the government to do whatever they like. It's a political act."[32]

When the minister transferred about a thousand "extremist" schoolteachers from classrooms to administrative positions and ordered administrators to get parental consent before making schoolgirls wear scarves in class, some Islamists reacted just as the government feared they might: By portraying it as godless and un-Islamic.

"God help our children," bleated the Islamist newspaper *Al Nour*. "Anyone who calls them to repentance and to return to God is banished from his post and considered a criminal while the ministry leaves untouched secular and Marxist teachers. If the teacher had played a tape that invites students to dancing and debauchery, we would not have heard the minister objecting and maybe he would have promoted her!"[33]

The rising rebel violence and surge of religious conservatism alarmed Mubarak's government, which was already concerned about the mayhem going on in Algeria. There, Islamist rebels were locked in bloody confrontation with the state following the military's cancellation of the 1992 election that an Islamist party was all but certain to win.

In response, the Egyptian government moved to exert its control in places as diverse as villages, universities, and newsrooms. The state became a massive flyswatter, thwacking affronts to its authority and control, no matter how slight. The measures it introduced were primarily aimed at Islamists, both the radicals and the moderates. But the constriction of civil liberties affected everyone. Step by step, the government changed the rules of the game to favor itself. The result was a diminished democracy or, as one European diplomat put it, a "pharaocracy."

In professional associations, for example, the government was aware that the Islamists had been able to exploit low turnouts in association elections, making sure their supporters got to the polls. But instead of rallying his troops to compete directly with Islamist candidates, President Mubarak had parliament pass a new law on association elections. The 1993 measure stipulated that such elections would be valid only if at least 50 percent of an association's registered members voted. If that threshold was not reached, then a second round of voting would be conducted in which turnout had to be at least 33 percent. If that didn't happen, the government would take over running the association.

Here was an astonishing spectacle. A parliament that had been elected in 1990 with a voter turnout estimated at around 42 percent was now requiring lawyers, doctors, engineers, and other professionals to have a minimum of 50 percent turnout when choosing representatives in their own associations! "This is a strange law," Brotherhood leader Mashur said evenly through his straight, thin lips. "If they're saying that you can't have elections unless there are 50 percent of the voters present . . . then there wouldn't be a parliament."

Writing in a Cairo newspaper, Erian charged that the law was aimed at "hitting the Islamist trend which has gained popular support" and "poses a danger to the ruling clique." Using the law and a subsequent one allowing courts to approve candidates in association elections, the government reasserted its control over the medical and engineers associations as well as the bar association by mid-1995.

There were other antidemocratic moves. In December 1992, groups that did not have legal status as political parties were barred from making alliances with established parties. In other words, electoral coalitions like the one the Brotherhood had made with other parties for the 1984 and 1987 elections were no longer possible.

Minister of Religious Affairs Muhammed Ali Mahgoub announced that the government would henceforth appoint imams for all of Egypt's esti-mated seventy thousand mosques and send out "approved" sermons for Fri-day services. This was necessary, he said, "to secure the people ideologically." The measure was intended to deprive Islamic Group and other radical movements from using mosques to spread their ideas. But it also deprived others of what had long been considered a protected free speech forum.[34]

The decades-old practice of elections for the country's twenty thousand village mayors, some of whom were not enthusiastic supporters of the police's harsh counterinsurgency campaign, also ended. From now on, mayors would be appointed by the central government. Also in 1994, pro-fessors at Egypt's fourteen state-financed universities were informed that they could no longer elect their faculty deans. Instead, deans are appointed by university rectors—who are named by Mubarak. The government was clearly uneasy about the growing number of Islamist-oriented professors, many sympathetic to the Brotherhood, in senior faculty positions. Rectors also were instructed to be more diligent in weeding out students with Islamist sympathies by ejecting them from campus housing and vetoing their candidacies in student elections.

The press was next. On the evening of May 27, 1995, a parliamentary ses-sion opened with a legal quorum of 223 members present. But as the session dragged into the night, members dribbled out to go home. With a sleepy rump of only 45 legislators left in the 444-seat chamber, a bill with draconian restrictions on the press was introduced. It had not been on the official agenda or publicly debated. But within two hours, as most of Egypt was climbing into bed, it was passed into law.[35]

"The Assassination of the Press Law," as Egyptians dubbed it, allowed reporters to be detained while complaints of slander were investigated. It raised fines and imposed mandatory prison terms for libel and defamation convictions. It also imposed vague restrictions on what could be reported, making it a crime to publish "untruthful or biased" news that could create public panic or terror, harm the national interest, damage the national economy, or "ridicule state institutions or the officials governing those institutions."

The law also broadened the definition of reporting deemed "offensive" to Egypt's president. It now included "insults, the use of abusive language or defamation . . . assaulting the honor of an individual, the reputation of families, or violating the sanctity of private life."[36] Many Egyptians viewed this provision as an effort by Mubarak to stop press stories about official corruption, including ones hinting at financial wrongdoing by his own sons.

Even journalists at state-run publications were outraged by the law and the way it had been sprung on them—literally overnight. Taken aback by their vehement protests, Mubarak proposed a commission to study the law's implementation. But by February 1996, forty-three journalists, writers, and artists had been interrogated by police or criminally charged under the new law. The Islamist newspaper *Al Nour* was temporarily suspended because of the headline: "Suggestion . . . Mubarak, King of Egypt."

Mubarak finally backed away from some of the harsher penalties of the press law, including pretrial detention for reporters. But reporting deemed insulting to the president remains a criminal offense.

The government's tolerance of the Brotherhood, which had marked their relationship through the 1980s, began to wither as the Islamist rebellion escalated, leaving Egypt's crucial tourist industry in tatters and its policemen ambushed almost daily. Increasingly, the government was less willing to make a distinction between the violent extremists and the Brotherhood.

The Brothers did not help matters with their response to the terrorism. After Islamic Group gunned down writer Farag Foda in June 1992, Brotherhood spokesman Hodeiby infuriated the government and many secular-minded Egyptians when he charged that the government was partly responsible for Foda's murder because it "supports people who use their pens to stab Islam in the back."

The Brotherhood also declined to issue the blanket condemnation of the militants' violence demanded by the government. Instead, the organization always coupled its denunciations of the terrorism with criticism of torture and long-term detention. By this middle road, the movement sought to preserve its credibility with both sides. But the government accused it of being an ally of the insurgents and the rebels condemned it for abandoning *jihad* and "appeasing" the government.[37]

"We condemn these acts," Mashur said of Islamic Group's violent attacks during one of my visits. But, he added, "We cannnot condemn [the rebels] without saying that the government also has some responsibility. . . . We have to study this phenomenon and its reasons and provide a plan for curing it at its roots. It's not enough to have just a security solution . . . with laws that squeeze civil liberties." The better way to respond to the violence, he continued, is "through liberty and dialogue and freedom to speak opinions. Otherwise, these groups are forced underground and into using violence."

It was not a popular stance in government circles but it also was not unique. Egyptian human rights groups also urged the government to complement police actions with political reforms and dialogue. Still, the Brotherhood was increasingly seen as subversive and senior officials began publicly linking it to the extremists. After the death of Islamic Group lawyer Abdel Harith Madani, Interior Minister Alfi noted that some of the attorneys protesting his death in the streets belonged to the Brotherhood. This, he said, "confirms their links with terrorists and terrorism."

If Erian and other Brothers were concerned about Alfi acting on those accusations, they did not show it. They had grown used to government claims in the press of having uncovered Brotherhood plots, which later evaporated for lack of evidence. Ever the politician, Erian began strategizing for the next election, to be held in 1995. He was convinced that if it were genuinely free, it would produce a large Islamist bloc in parliament.

The Brotherhood, he told me, still wanted to amend the constitution so *shari'a* was formally enshrined as the highest law of the land. "But our opinion is that it must be done in a constitutional way, as the constitution says. This can only be done by the parliament," he added. "But which parliament is the question? It must be a real one. So, the first step is fully free elections. Our goal in the Muslim Brotherhood is gradual, constitutional, peaceful change. Abrupt change is dangerous for all. It looks like a coup d'état."

8

Guilty of Practicing Democracy

"O believers, be you securers of justice, witnesses for God. Let not detestation for a people move you not to be equitable; be equitable—that is nearer to godfearing."

—QUR'AN 5:11

"Civil society is a very vague concept. It is composed of a parliament, of a free press, a free system of education, a free trade union, an independent judicial system and so on. But in Egypt . . . all these elements are linked together in a key chain. And the key chain is in the pocket of the president."

—RIFA'AT AL SAID,
SECULAR OPPOSITION POLITICIAN[1]

Egypt was ripe for change in 1995. People were fed up with the rebels' violence. Many were just as disturbed with the government's harsh response. Corruption in high places was providing grist for many a coffeehouse conversation and the economy was faltering. There was a sour after-taste, too, from the referendum two years earlier when Mubarak, the sole candidate, had been given a third, six-year term in office by a previously unheard-of 96 percent of the voters. In the run-up to that vote, Cairo had suffered an identity crisis. It mistakenly thought it was Baghdad. As in the Iraqi capital, huge poster pictures of Al Rais, "The President," materialized on block after block of the cityscape. Banners urging "Yes and a Thousand Yeses to Freedom, Democracy and Mubarak!" flapped in the wind. Leaflets urging a "yes" vote fluttered down from airplanes. "We're verging on hysteria!" shrieked economics professor Essam Al Din Montassir. "Have you ever seen government ministers and officials going on such a propaganda spree? Talking about achievements which are not there? Making the president sound like a superman? It sounds like Romania!"[2]

Cairenes whispered that their president, catapulted into power by Sadat's 1981 assassination, had grown "hard of hearing" because he seemed to ignore his shrinking circle of advisers. The man who'd bravely flown a Soviet MiG fighter jet against Israeli forces in the 1973 Arab-Israeli War was now obsessed with being "First Pilot" of Egypt, the only one at the controls. He had morphed into a pharaoh.

Erian believed the nation's disgruntled mood would favor Islamist candidates in the upcoming parliamentary elections. Mubarak's ruling National Democratic Party was not offering an attractive alternative to the Islamists' emotional slogan "Islam Is the Solution." Another plus for the Brothers was that court-ordered changes in election regulations meant that candidates no longer had to run on a party slate but could offer themselves as independents.[3] For the first time, the Brotherhood would not have to enter parliament on the coattails of another party.

But months before campaigning began, Erian was sidelined from the race. He was arrested.

He'd come home from work around 11:30 P.M. on the night of January 21, 1995, and "was so tired he went right to sleep," his wife, Fatma, recalled. She stayed up, reading the newspaper. Around one A.M., there was a knock on the door. When she opened it, she saw several plainclothes security policemen standing on the landing. Others were racked on the staircase.

The policemen did not brandish firearms because they knew they would find no weapons here. Erian was no stranger, like "The Ghost." He was a former member of parliament and his propensity for talking with just about anyone had led him into numerous "chats" with security police over the years. Several policemen entered the flat and began collecting books and papers. Fatma recalled her husband being slightly "amused" by the visit. He'd anticipated some preelection harassment but nothing serious. "He was laughing. He expected it. I expected it," she said. Two hours after arriving, the nocturnal search party left with a stack of papers and Erian.

Escorted into the wintry night, Erian thought he'd soon be home. It was awhile before he realized that he was headed for a long separation from his family.

Erian and about thirty other Muslim Brothers arrested that night were detained indefinitely without charges while prosecutors investigated their activities. More arrests followed in July. The targets of the dragnet were the younger generation of activist Brothers. Most senior Brotherhood officials, like Mashur, were still free. The detainees included school officials, physicians, former members of parliament, a senior cleric at Al Azhar, a former deputy minister of industry, a banker, and a journalist.

Wearing their best poker faces, government officials denied the arrests had anything to do with the elections in November. Nobody believed them.

In August, Erian and forty-eight other detained Brothers were indicted under the antiterrorism law and ordered tried in a military court, the same tribunal that had been prosecuting radical, violent Islamists for almost three years. The indictment accused them of forming an illegal, secret group whose aim was to topple the government. "The defendants ran the Muslim Brotherhood Group with the aim of inciting people to render the Constitution and the laws of Egypt inoperable," it said. "They formed pockets of said group in various governorates and held secret meetings and seminars at which they set out the principles of resistance to the Constitution and laws of Egypt and brought together a new cadre of leadership. They also formed a so-called [Governing] Council for the organization. The above are deemed criminal acts" punishable by "hard labor."[4]

A second indictment against thirty-three other Brothers alleged that they had "operated the Muslim Brotherhood group, whose purpose is to disrupt constitutional decrees and laws, in that they participated with the rest of the leadership of the group in preparing and overseeing the election campaigns of the group throughout Egypt." Other accusations included distributing pamphlets alleging that the government was striking at Islamists in Egypt "with the help of foreign powers" and possessing publications that "sympathize with" extremist Islamists.

Finally, in an apparent attempt to tie the Brotherhood to the rebels, the second indictment charged that four of the defendants had provided "financial support for the families" of convicted extremists in order "to gain their sympathy and to have them join the group and the group's objectives."[5]

None of the eighty-two defendants was accused of using violence or being associated with extremist groups. Having failed to come up with evidence that they had broken their pledge not to engage in or support violence, the government was now criminally indicting the Brothers for things they had done openly since the mid-1970s. An American lawyer following the case said the charges sounded as if the Brothers "are guilty of practicing democracy."[6]

The indictments signaled that after more than twenty years of tolerating the Brotherhood's activities, the government was revoking its tacit recognition of the group. The precarious gray area in which it had operated and prospered was being shut down. Essentially, the government was no longer willing to differentiate between violent Islamist radicals and Islamist moderates like Erian working within the political system. It had telescoped the wide spectrum of Political Islam into the single rubric of Radical Islam.

"The most worrying factor," protested a group of Egyptian human rights lawyers, is that "civilians who politically oppose the government and whose views differ from those of the government" are being brought before military tribunals even though they are "carrying out their political . . . activities within the law, are respectful of the Constitution and refuse to have anything to do with violence or terrorism." The U.S. State Department noted that it was the first time in thirty years that the Egyptian government was trying civilians in a military court on political charges.[7]

Even opponents of the Brotherhood found the charges farcical. To demonstrate their outrage, over three hundred lawyers, including secularist leftists and liberals, and even two Christians, mobbed the military courtroom on the first day of the trial to enter their names as defense attorneys. About twenty of them formed the actual defense team.

The government pressed its case against the Brotherhood in the media. One anonymous official offered *Al Ahram* newspaper a list of reasons why the movement was "dangerous." Its publications claim that security forces violate human rights and practice torture, he said. And some of its members are lawyers who defend terrorists in court, using the trials to criticize the government and promote the ideas of "these criminal organizations." In addition, Brothers active in professional associations had given money to families of detainees and convicted extremists so the families could get apartments. In other cases, they gave the father of an extremist a job at an Islamist-run school and waived school fees for the children of another militant.

"This is like what drug lords do with members of their gangs when they are behind bars. They take care of the family," the exasperated official said.[8]

The two groups of Brothers pleaded not guilty before a panel led by Major General Ahmed Abdullah. They denied doing secret, illegal work, noting that the Brotherhood had even published its denunciations of the rebel violence in government newspapers. The defendants, who included a seventy-five-year-old Brother, were not tortured. But they were humiliated when they were herded into the same courtroom cages that had earlier held violent insurgents. Unlike the younger rebels, the Brothers did not disrupt the proceedings with angry tirades or insist that they be tried under *shari'a*.

But Erian was very angry. "How come," he asked reporters during a break, "we are being tried in the same chamber that witnessed the trials of those who attack tourists or wrestle with the government with bullets?" By treating him and the others this way, the authorities "are encouraging the armed Islamist opposition groups not to lay down arms."[9]

Military prosecutors drowned the defense team in more than two thousand pages of allegedly incriminating documents. But in the end their evidence was a joke. One government exhibit was a ruler seized from a defendant's home that was etched with "Islam Is the Solution." Similar rulers were available in the school supply section of many Cairo bookstores.

The highlight of the prosecutors' case was the "Vegetable Videotape," supposedly offered as proof of a secret, conspiratorial meeting held by the defendants. Shot by security police cinematographers, the thirty-minute video showed the sidewalk outside Star of Tawfikia. The action shots consisted mainly of transactions between vegetable vendors and their customers. "Some people are eating sandwiches or buying vegetables or apples. Others are walking by," said Mahfouz Azzam, an Islamist defense lawyer at the trials. The video opened with a close-up of the Brotherhood logo on the outside the building. "So it wasn't a secret meeting," Azzam said. "If it's to be a secret meeting, I would have gone to a different place."

The tape, which provoked barely concealed laughter among courtroom spectators, then captured five of the defendants ambling past carts stacked with tomatoes, lettuce, and eggplant as they headed into the building. The government's principal witness, security police officer Mohsen Abdul 'Aal, testified that one of the five was Hussein Shahata. But when asked to point out Shahata, Abdul 'Aal couldn't find him among the caged defendants. Shahata later presented documents to the court verifying that on the day the video was filmed, he was at a conference in the Persian Gulf with a former Egyptian prime minister.

Under cross-examination, Abdul 'Aal was asked why he had not arrested every known member of the Muslim Brotherhood since it was an illegal group. "I was asked to make a case only against these eighty-two," Abdul 'Aal replied. "I only bring [to court] those who my superiors asked me to bring because I'm not free to make a case."

In another memorable moment, Abdul 'Aal was cross-examined by defense lawyer Ahmed Al Khawaga, then chairman of the Egyptian Bar Association and senior figure in the secular, liberal Wafd Party.

Khawaga: "What was wrong with the objectives of the Brothers" who are on trial?

Abdul 'Aal: "They want to alter the constitution."

Khawaga: "So, is wanting to change the constitution a crime?"

Abdul 'Aal: "Yes."

Khawaga: "I am in the Wafd Party and I want to change the constitution. And Harid Abdel Karim, who is a lawyer, is in the Nasserist Party and he wants to change the constitution. So why did you not arrest us?"

Abdul 'Aal: "I don't know."

More giggles rippled through the gallery.[10]

The accusation that the Brothers had given "financial support for families" of insurgents also fizzled at trial. It turned out that four defendants had been arrested at a roadblock in the southern town of Minya after police got a tip that they were going to pay money to families of terrorists. The car's driver, Mohammed Omram, claimed that the cash was his and he was going to buy cows. The police officer called to testify about the incident could not disprove that claim or give details about any payment being made.[11]

Military prosecutors also entered as evidence the transcript of an audiotape allegedly recorded at a secret meeting of Brothers that purported to show their conspiracy to resist Egypt's constitution. Judge Abdullah would not allow the defense lawyers to hear the tape itself or cross-examine the person who transcribed it.

Chief defense lawyer Mohamed Salim El Awa said later that the transcript was of a strategy session for the upcoming elections attended by about eighty Brothers. They were taped "discussing whether to enter the elections and what they have to do to prepare for it," Awa said.

As he recalled it, the transcript went something like this: "Someone says 'Should we go to the elections?' And Essam El Erian says, 'Yes, I think we should go to the elections in all the constituencies.' And [Brotherhood spokesman Maamoun] Hodeiby says 'We cannot go in all the constituencies. We should choose only a few targeted ones.' And Essam says 'No, we have hundreds of people everywhere and we should go even if only to propagate our ideas.'"

"These people," Awa added, "were only accused of attempting to coordinate their efforts for reelection. This is the only accusation. . . . And that's the whole story. If this is a crime in any democratic system, okay, it should be a crime in Egypt."

Shortly before the verdicts were announced, Interior Minister Hassan Al Alfi gave an interview to a leading newspaper in which he called the Brotherhood "extremely dangerous" and accused it of trying "to seize power by any means." Some people "want to distinguish between those who bear arms and those who do not," he added, "but those who incite are more dangerous than those who bear arms. People have a right to know this." Alfi said the government had "evidence of full cooperation between these groups" and asserted there was "a distribution" of roles between the Brotherhood and the extremists. "They may differ among themselves over who should hold the leadership," he said, "but ultimately they are one."[12]

The minister's remarks flew in the face of the evidence presented at trial as well as the scorn heaped upon the Brotherhood by the rebel groups. Alfi left no doubt that the state's aim in criminally prosecuting the Brotherhood was to put it out of business. "This organization is unrecognized. It is dissolved. It does not exist," he said. "This is the main issue in the case."[13]

On November 23, 1995, less than a week before elections, hundreds of nervous relatives gathered outside the army base north of Cairo hoping to enter the courtroom for the reading of the verdict. Refused admittance at the front gate, they waited by the roadside under a dull, overcast sky.

General Abdullah's tribunal convicted fifty-four defendants of all the charges against them. Erian and four others were sentenced to five years at hard labor. Forty-nine others, including the seventy-five-year-old, were given three years in prison. The panel acquitted twenty-seven Brothers. As for the charge that four defendants were dispensing aid to families of terrorists—or possibly on their way to buy cows—the verdict was silent. It never addressed that charge.

The defendants, dressed in white galabias, listened to the verdict in silence. But as the military officers left the stage, the Brothers began to chant the motto of their movement: "The Qur'an is our constitution, the Prophet is our leader, holy war is our way, death for the sake of God is our most valued hope." Then they began waving tiny Egyptian flags that they had drawn on paper and broke into Egypt's national anthem, "Biladi, Biladi," "My Country, My Country." One defendant began to cry.[14]

Soldiers began shooing lawyers, reporters, and spectators from the crowded courtroom as Erian read a statement on behalf of the defendants. In the end, his words of sadness and anger fell on a mostly deserted gallery.

"We have worked very hard . . . in serious and sincere participation to solve the problems of Egypt and to alleviate the suffering and injustice suffered by its people," he said. "You people were behind us and that was clear in your support in all previous elections. We believe that a passion for Islam penetrates your being and that you are looking forward to the day when *shari'a* will prevail."

The trials, he added, showed that the government's case against the Brothers was political and not criminal. "Our method in reform and change is based on the principle of . . . using good words and good example through legal and constitutional means," he said. "We'd like to stress our absolute refusal for the logic and ways of violence, regardless of its source."

Addressing "our mothers, fathers, wives, sisters and brothers," Erian advised them that "this is the time for patience and taking the stand of Allah and bearing all this for him." He urged them to vote in the upcoming elections and to choose their representatives from among "honorable people of opinion from all political and nationalist forces.

"As for those who treated us unfairly or assisted in this [trial]," Erian added, "we say that you won't escape Allah's punishment and the calls of the victims will follow you always. Learn from those who preceded you. Where are the presidents now? Where are their influence and power? Where are their entourages? On Judgment Day you will have a painful, disgraceful and sorrowful end."[15]

The court also ordered the Brotherhood's office in Star of Tawfikia closed down. Within hours, police descended on the third-floor suite from which the movement had operated since 1977, evacuated the staff, and sealed the door with red wax.

The United States and most other Western governments maintained a studied silence about the military trials and verdicts, though they were widely condemned by Western human rights groups. Even some members of Mubarak's ruling party objected to the political nature of the prosecution.

"We thought that this was unfair," said Hamdi Sayed, chairman of the medical association and Erian's onetime colleague in parliament. "It's not the practice in this country that anybody who has allegedly committed an offense on political grounds should be prosecuted before a military court . . . we do not agree with that."[16]

If Erian and his fellow defendants hoped the "passion for Islam" they saw in their countrymen would provoke a public protest against their convictions, they were disappointed. Apathy still ruled the street. The government read this silence as approval of its actions. But many Egyptians squirreled the affair away in their collective memory as more proof of why justice seems as hard to hold in their hands as rain.

"We couldn't believe it," Erian's wife, Fatma, said of the verdict when I visited her several months afterward. "I felt that it was so unfair and unjust. There was no evidence against them. All that [the prosecutors] had was that they were meeting to prepare for the elections."

Fatma said her husband, who was serving his sentence at Tora Prison, a sprawling, high-walled complex a few miles south of Cairo, was not depressed. "Being detained for God is something they will have to endure," she said. "It's fate, but it's something like *jihad* for God [who] makes them patient and rewards them for their work for him and makes them happy. This is because they are doing work for him."

Erian's eldest daughter Sarah, seventeen, was listening to our conversation. Speaking softly, she said of her father, "He is an optimistic man."[17]

*   *   *

The 1995 election from which the Brotherhood was forcibly removed was one of the liveliest, most violent and most fraudulent in Egypt's history. An unprecedented number of candidates—nearly 4,000—competed for 444 parliamentary seats. Many were women and Christians running as independent candidates. Although the Brotherhood's best campaign organizers were behind bars, it fielded about 150 candidates.

The long-standing emergency laws meant that candidates could not meet with more than five people at a time or use loudspeakers without police permission. On top of that, opposition candidates faced constant harassment from security police. "As we handed out leaflets to passersby, the two policemen walking behind us confiscated the material from their hands," one Islamist candidate reported.

In Alexandria, two candidates were arrested when they entered a coffee shop and began shaking hands with patrons. One would-be parliamentarian woke up to find himself a prisoner in his own home: His front door had been chained and padlocked from the outside. Cafes where opposition candidates pressed the flesh suddenly lost electricity. Firms that rented chairs and electrical supplies for large gatherings were ordered by police not to service campaign events. One Brotherhood candidate was arrested in a town eighty miles north of Cairo with about 125 supporters and charged with "disturbing public order and causing a traffic jam." This, in a country of perpetual traffic jams.[18]

There were shenanigans in the assigning of ballot symbols. Since half of Egypt's twenty-one million voters cannot read, ballots bear a symbol beside each candidate's name. These are supposed to be assigned on a first-come, first-served basis as candidates register to run. But lo and behold, every single candidate of Mubarak's ruling party ended up with the camel, which stands for Egypt, or the crescent moon, a sign of Islam.

Meanwhile, "it just so happened in some funny way that . . . the vast majority of Islamist candidates got the sword or the revolver," observed Egyptian reporter Dina Ezzat. "It was a good tactical move because on buses and on streets there were big banners saying 'Vote for the camel and crescent for democracy, freedom and prosperity.' "[19]

Hundreds of Islamist candidates were briefly detained, apparently to disrupt their campaigning. On election day, many monitors from opposition parties were blocked from polling stations and there were numerous sightings of security forces stuffing or moving ballot boxes. As many as fifty-one people were killed and several hundred injured in election-related violence, according to citizen monitoring groups. Angry citizens also destroyed four police stations, a post office, a bank, a government-owned supermarket, twenty public buses, and a railway station.[20]

The final results were no surprise. Mubarak's ruling National Democratic Party took 317 seats outright and controlled about 100 more won by independent candidates closely allied to the NDP. It was the largest majority in the history of the country.[21] Although more than a dozen opposition parties put up candidates at a time of widespread discontent, they captured a paltry 13 seats. Every Islamist candidate but one was defeated.

Sociologist Saad Eddin Ibrahim, who chaired an independent election-monitoring group of prominent citizens, charged that the election saw "the biggest rigging ever in Egyptian history." The group's final report concluded that Egypt was "headed for troubled times" if elections were not reformed. "These irregularities falsify public opinion and cause citizens to lose faith in the whole electoral process and . . . will close the door on any change or turnover in political authority."[22]

The U.S. government, whose officials often reminded Islamist movements that they oppose "one-man, one-vote, one-time," averted its eyes. But the poll reinforced what many Egyptians knew all along about the ruling National Democratic Party: That the only appropriate part of its name is "National." Less a party than a huge patronage machine, the NDP greases the wheels of Egypt's bureaucracy and provides a facade of democracy to mask the country's real power structure, which is the army and security police agencies, with the president at the top.

As Zawya Al Hamra trucker Ahmed Sadek observed, the NDP "is the party which protects the government from other parties."[23]

The manipulated election, the military trials of Erian and others, and the expanded curbs on civil society eroded the integrity of Egypt's political institutions. Many Egyptians saw this as a regrettable but necessary price to be paid to avoid something worse. Having concluded that the Brotherhood was a Trojan Horse for the radical rebels, they supported the government's moves to repress the organization.

"Have you forgotten the millions and millions of people who died under communism in the last seventy years?" a retired general demanded in an interview. "Are we ready to give Islamic fundamentalism another seventy years until it proves it's not an accepted system of life? I don't think so. It's more dangerous than communism because the spread of ideas could be quicker than communism. You just say 'God tells you to do this.' "

Retired ambassador Hussein Amin, whose last posting was Algeria, noted that the Nazis "came to power as a result of general elections" nine years after Hitler published *Mein Kampf,* where "he told people plainly what his politics were going to be once he was in power." Similarly, Islamic writings and newspapers "foretell what it is going to be like under an Islamic regime," Amin added. "It's all there. They consider themselves as the 'Party of God.' They consider other parties the 'parties of the Devil.' . . . They do not intend to have democracy, to have pluralism. They only say that in order to gain ground until they come to power."[24]

But other Egyptians were dismayed at the road their country was taking.

"One question remains which we are not alone in asking," said an almost despairing editorial in the opposition Wafd Party's newspaper. "So long as the president appoints cabinet ministers, provincial governors, [rectors] of universities, deans of colleges and village headmen, then why does he not appoint the members of parliament, too?"[25]

Political scientist Kandil did not share Amin's certainty about how the Brotherhood would behave once in power. "If truth be told, in my point of view, some of these people are much better than the people in the government who pretend that they are very liberal," she said. She had found no evidence in her research on professional associations, she said, that those controlled by the government were more democratic than those dominated by Islamists.

"Democratic procedures and values were more respected in some—I'm not saying all—but in some" associations controlled by Islamists, Kandil said.[26]

Some Egyptians argued that as long as moderate Islamists rejected violence, they should be allowed to participate in the country's political life. In this way, their claims to have a superior political vision would be tested. If they didn't measure up with the public, they would suffer at the next election, a scenario that has occurred in some Middle East countries.

"Islamic fundamentalism is a fact of life," said Egyptian economist Said Naggar. "History tells us you cannot kill an idea by repression. Ideas have to be killed by ideas."

History also teaches that once civil liberties are diminished for one group, no group is secure. Egyptians of all political persuasions were shocked when Saad Eddin Ibrahim was arrested at his Cairo home on a summer night in 1999. Ibrahim was known throughout the Middle East for his academic work and pro-democracy activism, which had included the 1995 election monitoring. He also had been a political consultant to the Mubarak presidency for years. But his increasingly outspoken criticism of government policies had ignited rancor in the presidential palace.

Ibrahim, who is in his sixties, and twenty-seven employees of his Ibn Khaldoun Center for Development Studies were tried in a security court on what most observers consider trumped up charges. They included bribing officials to get publicity for his research center, disseminating false information designed to undermine Egypt abroad, defrauding the European Union and taking foreign funds without government permission, a reference to a $246,000 European Union grant for an educational project on electoral reform. Though the European Union issued a statement saying its audits had found no fraud, Ibrahim was convicted on all but the first charge and sentenced to seven years in prison in May 2001. His employees were also convicted and six were given prison terms ranging from two to five years, with the rest receiving suspended sentences. It would be nine months before an appeals court ordered a retrial and the defendants were released from prison.[27]

Ibrahim's twelve-year-old center, which did political and social research and published a magazine, was shut down as a result of the case. The center was an example of the expanding civic activity that has marked Egyptian life for two decades. By 1995, three thousand clubs and fourteen thousand voluntary organizations were officially registered with the government. Fed up with government incompetence and the hassles of everyday life, ordinary people have been banding together to promote their interests. They include feminists, environmentalists, businessmen, workers, athletes, neighbors, human rights activists, family planners, and people caring for the prison population. Both Islamist and secular, these groups have been giving their members practical experience in grassroots organizing and coalition-building. In doing so, they have challenged the state's authoritarian ethos.

Uneasy with this expansion of civil society, the government had parliament approve a law in May 1999 that imposed onerous new restrictions on all types of nongovernmental organizations, giving the state unprecedented control over their internal affairs and funding. Though declared unconstitutional a year later, the law demonstrated the extent to which the government seeks to restrict civil society and control the public space.[28]

Meanwhile, even as the government continued to squeeze the Brotherhood, bringing scores more of its members before military courts on charges of advancing the goals of the organization, the movement was unable to dispel widespread fears among secular-inclined Egyptians about its agenda.[29] Part of the problem stemmed from the group's lack of candor and its contradictions, which flow from its pinched version of *shari'a*. A woman's decision to wear a headscarf is voluntary but the Brotherhood believes the Qur'an requires head coverings. The movement believes in democracy but Muslims must abide by the "unchangeable principles of Islam" in *shari'a*. It believes in political pluralism, but in an "Islamic system" a "specialist committee" would determine if political parties met the right criteria to be legal. Ambiguous statements like these left the Brotherhood open to charges of incompetency for not thinking through its ideology, or worse, duplicity for harboring a hidden agenda. The essential problem was something else. Under its elderly leadership the Brotherhood failed what I call the "Abduh Test": It did not reinterpret its faith's holy scriptures to produce a coherent, Islamically informed ideology relevant to modern Egypt. It did not distill the essence of *shari'a* and apply it to the challenges facing contemporary Egypt.

It is one thing for the Brotherhood to declare, as it has on many occasions, that it is for social justice and democracy. It is quite another to harness *shari'a*'s power into a modern idiom that inspires a nation to reach those goals. Demands for "implementing *shari'a*" are just not enough.

How to explain this failure? One reason is the Brotherhood's long tradition, set by Banna, of obedience and practical action. As a result, Muslim Brothers always have been dynamic actors more than deep thinkers.[30] Another reason is the Brotherhood's secretive hierarchy, which is not known for democratic inclinations. This internal lack of democracy hindered intellectual innovation and allowed the Brotherhood's more dogmatic, rigid old guard to maintain its grip on the organization.

As a result, the chasm between the Brotherhood's elderly viziers and its younger activists widened. In 1995, some junior Brothers decided they had endured enough and broke away to launch a new Islamist political movement. They called it Al Wasat, which means middle, center, or moderate. The name instantly appeals to Muslims because of the famous Qur'anic injunction that they are called by God to be an "*umma wasat*," a "justly balanced community."[31]

Wasat's program, published in early 1996, was strikingly free of the usual Brotherhood jargon about doing God's work and "implementing *shari'a*." The table of contents did not even include the word *Islam*. *Shari'a*, the program said, should be interpreted and applied in a way that does not hinder progress. It stressed that while the party had an Islamist perspective, it wanted to work with all political trends and groups, including Christians. Indeed, two of Wasat's seventy-four founders were Christians. Confronting the generational conflict head-on, the program stated "it's about time that this middle generation carries the flag and does its duty for the nation."

Calling for democracy, the program said that "the people are the source of all authority." There should be "respect for the rotation of authority," it added, as well as the freedom to form political parties, to demonstrate and to strike in the workplace. There should be no barrier to women and Christians in top leadership positions. In sum, said one founder, Wasat was an attempt "to go beyond the slogan of 'Islam Is the Solution.' "

One of Wasat's prominent leaders was Abou Elela Mady, whose history of Islamist activism paralleled Erian's. As a university student in the 1970s in the southern town of Minya, Mady was in a campus Islamist group. He joined the Brotherhood in 1979, the same year as Erian, and was an organizer of its advance into the professional associations. He was elected deputy secretary-general of the engineers' association.

"We are not seeking to establish a religious party per se," Mady said of Wasat. "We are talking about a civil party with an Islamic frame of reference.

"We know that the hardest choice is moderation, and the easiest choice is extremism," he added. "We seek to form a part of Egypt's political landscape in the coming century. . . . We want to be viewed as an oppositional force and not a resistance movement."[32]

The government reacted predictably when Wasat announced itself in 1996. Mady and twelve other leaders were arrested and tried in a military court for allegedly forming a Brotherhood front organization. Five, including Mady, were acquitted but seven others were convicted and given three-year prison sentences. In later years, the movement twice applied to register as a legal political party but was rejected by the government both times. It finally got permission in early 2000 to operate as a sort of think tank under the name of Egypt Society for Culture and Dialogue.

The Brotherhood leadership was furious at Wasat's display of independence, which they regarded as a challenge to their presumed custodianship of the Islamist message. Mashur complained that Wasat did not project a "pure image of Islam." So great was the Brotherhood's distress that it went so far as to openly oppose Wasat's bid to gain legal status as a party during formal hearings on the matter.[33]

Wasat's organizers were taken aback by the fierceness of the Brotherhood's anger. "This small group of people waged a war against us that we didn't expect," Mady told an Arabic newspaper. "We expected them to say we disagree with you or we have nothing to do with this project. But waging a comprehensive war against us on all levels was a big shock that took us some time to absorb. . . . Their attack was even worse than what the government did with us."[34]

Wasat and two other Islamist parties founded by former Islamist rebels brought a new sense of pluralism and openness to the Islamist movement of Egypt. "We are very different from the Brotherhood," said Mady. "We do not claim to be the sole representative of Islam."[35]

Still, the Brotherhood is not a depleted force. Despite continuing arrests and harassment, it ran candidates in the 2000 parliamentary elections and emerged with 17 seats. While minuscule compared to the NDP's 388 seats, the Brotherhood again was the largest opposition bloc in parliament—the first time it held that position since 1987. Part of the reason for its success was that the 2000 poll was conducted under court-mandated judicial supervision, which made it a fairer election than the one held in 1995.

Missing from the Brotherhood bloc in parliament this time, however, was one of its most effective members. Essam El Erian was released from prison in January 2000, having served his five-year sentence. He immediately returned to his old job as assistant secretary-general of the Doctors' Association, where he received a steady stream of well-wishers, greeting them with smiles and mint candies. As before, Erian also worked evenings in a hospital set up as part of the Brotherhood's network of social services. Shortly after his release, he wrote an article for the Islamist newspaper *Al Shaab* thanking those who had supported him during his years in prison, especially his wife, Fatma. Typically, Erian did not dwell in interviews on how his prison experience had changed him, except to say he hoped "it won't be repeated," noting the hardship of being separated from his family.

Erian, who chose not to run in the 2000 elections, also deflected journalists' questions about his views on the tensions between the Brotherhood and Wasat. No doubt he was torn. The Brotherhood has been his political home for two decades and he feels an organizational loyalty to it. But Wasat's openness and more moderate orientation have been hallmarks of Erian's personal political style. In an essay on Hasan Banna that Erian published in early 2000, he noted that part of the Brotherhood founder's success was that "he presented Islam in a new and attractive light suitable for the time."[36]

By the end of the 1990s, it had become evident that Egypt's political system lacked the flexibility and imagination to compete on democratic turf with its main political opposition, the moderate Islamists. Instead, it fell back on coercion and authoritarianism. In doing so, it starkly revealed that Egypt's fundamental problem is not terrorism but lack of democracy and respect for lawful institutions. Like the generals who aborted Algeria's 1992 election to stop an Islamist movement from winning, the Egyptian government sent a message to its moderate Islamist opposition: The ballot box is a narrow gate through which you will not pass as long as we are in charge.[37]

This stance begs questions. If this is how secular, Western-modeled governments dispense justice and holds elections, then why shouldn't people give Islamists a whirl in power? Is it any wonder that many in Muslim countries view secularism and Western-style constitutions with reservations? Would the military trial of Erian and others have drawn different reactions from Western governments if the judges had worn turbans instead of chevroned uniforms and invoked *shari'a* instead of antiterrorism laws?

And were radical Islamists right when they said the only way to change an Egyptian government is by *jihad*?

Mubarak was given another six-year term in a 1999 referendum, though this time the "Yes" votes had dropped to 94 percent. The president defends his approach by saying that economic stability and reform are priorities, and once achieved, political liberalization can gradually follow. But as politicians from China to Central Europe have been learning since the end of the Cold War, enduringly vibrant and competitive economies require intellectual creativity, entrepreneurial courage, and a transparent commercial environment. All these are best fostered by democratic freedoms, including the freedom to peacefully change the government.

"The government of Egypt has opted for stability," said the late Tahseen Basheer, one of Egypt's most clear-eyed political observers. "But too much stability is the mummification of Egypt." Other Egyptians questioned what kind of stability had been achieved. "Vacuous tranquility occasionally punctured by gunfire and political violence," wrote Nabil Abdel Fattah, "is not the same thing as political stability."[38]

The choices facing Egypt's government and others in the Arab world are not easy. Have totally open elections and unrestricted political freedoms and you may have to share decision making with Islamists. But exclude them from legitimate political activity and you risk underground extremism that may explode down the road. Successfully moving from authoritarian rule to a free society is a messy process, requiring huge amounts of political goodwill and imagination. Nowadays in the Middle East, it also requires recognizing that moderate Islamists are likely to be part of that process.

Given the opportunity to compete legally in a free and fair election, Islamists in Egypt would likely do very well. They might even capture a slim majority of seats in parliament. But even then, they would have to contend with other centers of power in Egypt, notably the army and the secular business elite. Moreover, the appearance of Wasat and other groups shows that Islamists, far from monolithic, are not immune from the fractiousness of Egyptian politics.[39]

But for now, two realities are clear. Despite the Brotherhood's role as the strongest opposition party, it has failed to offer an Islamist ideology suitable to the needs of a modern, pluralist state. The government, meanwhile, has not lived up to the democratic values it espouses. This mutual failure is Egypt's dilemma at the start of the twenty-first century.

9

Middle Ground

"The image people have is one of the early caliphs. A strong, just state whose president would be able to sleep under a tree without guards because he is just."
— KHALED SALAH HASSANEIN,
EGYPTIAN JOURNALIST

"This is Islam. It has to have a vast meaning, not just a small, narrow meaning."
— MOSTAFA ROSTOM,
EGYPTIAN TRANSLATOR

You aren't long in Egypt, or any Arab country for that matter, before you run into someone like Mostafa Rostom. The young translator tools around in a gray, Egyptian-made Nasr 127 long past its vehicular prime. Bearing the scars of traffic battles, the tiny car has the heft of an empty tuna-fish tin. Its owner is talkative, friendly, and ambitious. In his mid-thirties, about four inches shy of six feet, Rostom has pasty white skin, a small mustache, and hollow-set, black eyes.

To maintain his middle-class lifestyle he juggles several interpreting jobs at once, passing out different versions of his business card to suit the needs of each new acquaintance. One card describes him as "head of the International Relations Affairs Department" at Egypt's state-run federation of trade unions. He and his wife live in an apartment complex on Cairo's eastern edge, where the city's asphalt tentacles slither farther onto the desert sands each day.

Rostom was blessed with a good start in life. Educated in private schools, he could speak both English and French by the time he was twelve. He has traveled to Russia, Europe, and the United States on business trips and is well aware of how the world beyond Egypt is changing. He desperately wants to be part of that world and partake of its prosperity and opportunities.

I encountered many Rostoms across the Arab world. They are engineers laying pipelines for Cairo's new sewers, urban planners designing new neighborhoods, doctors counseling patients with AIDS, and entrepreneurs listing new ventures on stock exchanges. These men and women want to be modern and Muslim and see no contradiction in that. They call themselves secular and they fear, as one calls it, the "turbanization" of their governments. Still, Islam is their moral code for personal behavior. It is also their guidepost for good government, for they know it demands justice, order, and freedom in society.

Arab governments and their Islamist opposition both grandiosely claim to speak on behalf of these young Muslims. But when the two plummet into open warfare, as they did in Algeria and Egypt, the Rostoms of the Arab world become the bloody turf on which they battle. Along the way, many of them are trampled to death.

Meanwhile, Rostom and his counterparts withhold their allegiance from both sides, for neither, in their view, lives up to Islam's commands. Their mental bumper sticker might read "A Pox on Both Your Houses." Leaderless, politically disengaged, and uncertain of their future, Rostom and those like him have one eye on their computer icons and the other on their minarets as they search—they hope not in vain—for the middle ground in the Middle East.

Rostom has thickened around the waist since we first met in 1989 when he was twenty-seven and single. I had gone to interview the head of the trade union federation. Seated beside the graying, self-important functionary, Rostom dutifully translated his pontifications about how happy and content Egyptian workers were. After the interview, when we were alone, Rostom scoffed at the rosy picture painted by the government-appointed official, describing how riot police had recently crushed a string of wildcat strikes at state-owned industries. He also told me he'd once been a member of the banned Communist Party.

Rostom grew up one of four children in Shoubra, a predominantly Christian, middle-class neighborhood of central Cairo. His father, Zaki, owned a factory that made automobile engines. Though Zaki and his wife, Nawal, are Muslim, they sent their children to St. Paul's College, a French-run school where most students were Christian.

He went on to Ain Shams University in Cairo, getting a degree in translation and interpretation in 1988. He was active in student politics on campus and participated in demonstrations protesting police interference in student affairs. This led to a brief detention in 1985, which he called "a very good experience." Some of the older political prisoners, including Muslim Brothers, "respected us students very much. I took the decision to join an illegal political group. I joined the Communist Party."

Despite this clandestine activity, which at the time would have sent him to prison if discovered, Rostom got hired as a translator by the trade union federation. He continued studying English and landed a second part-time job interpreting for visiting delegations of the International Labor Organization. In 1992, he left for Saudi Arabia to work for a private firm supplying technical support to the Saudi military. He was earning $2,000 a month—astronomical pay for an Egyptian. But he hated the job because he didn't have enough to do and didn't like the way he was treated. His Saudi boss was "illiterate," Rostom said, "but when I would read for him, he would correct me!"

Frustrated, he packed it in after seven months and came home. He got his old jobs back and opened his own translation business on the side. With his Saudi earnings, he was flush enough to marry his longtime fiancée, a cousin named Nahla. After the wedding, the couple moved into an airy, five-room apartment that they bought for a little over $10,000 with help from Rostom's father. They named their first child, a daughter, Reem.

A couple of years after their marriage, they invited me to lunch. Their new living room set of furniture was still covered in clear plastic to shield it from Cairo's omnipresent dust. Nearby, there was a large dining table and a tall china cabinet. On the wall, a faux needlepoint portrayed a seventeenth-century European country scene. A buffet table was appointed with peacock feathers standing in a vase. Off the living room, a small balcony offered distant views into the desert.

Rostom had just picked up a new Panasonic fax machine and we went into the study, where he hitched it up to his personal computer, an IBM-clone sporting Windows and a modem. He planned to link into the Internet as soon as he had enough money to pay the monthly connection fee.

Nahla is six years younger than her husband. At home, she is bareheaded but whenever she leaves home she wears a headscarf. She said she began wearing the veil at fifteen "when a sheikh at school . . . said 'Before you talk with me, you have to be better dressed.' The next day, I wore the veil. I wanted to wear it since primary school but no one in my family accepted it."

As she prepared lunch in the kitchen, Rostom recounted how communism had lost its attraction as he made the transition from student to businessman and he dropped out of the party. "I prefer just to be a good Muslim. It's enough," he said, sipping orange juice as we sat in the living room. "If I go through the Islamic tradition, it's better than the communist tradition. There isn't anything new in what they propose. . . . So why go to communism when I have God who has given us tradition and these rules written in a book which never changes?"

Rostom said he did not regularly attend Friday prayers at the mosque and occasionally had a beer. But Islam was indispensable to him as a moral compass, which became clear to me as he talked. "I'm not a good Muslim, I don't follow all the regulations of Islam, that I shouldn't drink, that I shouldn't go here and there. I don't follow the Islamic rules, practically," he said. "But I don't think I'm a bad Muslim. Because I don't attack people for nonsense. I always help weak people. I don't like to sell even my knowledge. In other words, if anybody needs help and can't pay, I help him as an interpreter.

"I find that people in the United States, in Japan, in all the modern countries, are better Muslims than our people because they follow all the Islamic traditions," he added. "In other words, they never come late to their appointments. They never say 'I forgot' because Islam asks you to remember all things and not say 'I'm sorry I'm late, the traffic is bad.' No, Islam says you have to be accurate in your time, you have to be clean, you have to be kind. In other words, all the things that lead you to a good character.

"And Islam asks you to be fair. If you go to Europe, if you go to the States, you never find anybody who cheats you. In the market, they say, 'This is Taiwanese,' or 'This is made in China.' But here in Egypt, if it's Egyptian-made, they never say it. In Islam, it is said that if you are a merchant, sell things at an acceptable profit, but in Egypt we never do."

Rostom recalled an incident during a trip to the States, which he said, "impressed me very much." It was late November. He and his friends were staying in a hotel close to Dupont Circle in Washington, D.C. "Every day we had to take the Metro to go somewhere. There was an old woman and she was begging. When I saw her face, I remembered my grandmother. So I gave her every day some small tip.

"On Thanksgiving Day, I woke up late. I went out for a walk and when I went to give her some money, she refused. She said, 'I need money to eat but now I have a lot of food,' " he recalled. The woman indeed had "a lot of hot rice and some chicken," he said. "And this is Islam, helping this woman to eat."

Rostom confided that he and Nahla had had difficulties early in their marriage and even discussed divorce. He was distraught but instead of seeking help from parents or friends he went instead to Dar Al Efta'a. "It's a special governmental office," he explained, "where you go if you have a question and you can get the answer." No appointment is needed and "sometimes you can do it by phone."

The government-employed sheikh whom Rostom consulted in his two visits to Dar Al Efta'a asked him about his temper, advised him not to talk with his wife about divorce and selected some quotations from the Qur'an and early Islamic writings to encourage him. Rostom said the conversations helped him through that difficult period. Most of the religious scholars at Dar Al Efta'a, he added, have studied Islam "deeply. When you go, you feel you are in good hands. Because you don't like to do anything against religion."

Rostom emphasized that he regards Islam as a thinking man's religion. While the Qur'an is God's Revelation and its words do not change, he explained, God expects Muslims to use their brains to interpret those words in a way that is appropriate for their times.

"Islam asks us to think," he said, his voice rising with conviction. "In Prophet Muhammad's day, I know they did not have cigarettes. But when they say, 'All that destroys your life is bad,' I can understand that cigarettes are bad. So this is Islam. If I go through the books, I can understand what is Islam." But one needs to read carefully, he said, adding that he uses a computer software program to search for words in the Qur'an.

It is natural, he said, to find different interpretations in the Qur'an "because Islam is not a monopoly." "Even Prophet Muhammad himself was corrected by a regular citizen. We have in the Qur'an a chapter called 'Abasa,' which tells how a blind man who wanted to learn about Islam was frowned at by the Prophet."

But then Prophet Muhammad was told in a revelation from God "that you are not allowed to choose to whom you present your mission because this person may be better than anybody else," Rostom added. "So Prophet Muhammad apologized to the blind man. This is Islam."[1]

Rostom's expansive appreciation of his faith gave him little in common with the Islamist extremists who brought grief to Egypt in the early 1990s, most of whom were younger than him by a decade. He was insulted by their intolerance. "I don't believe that any person has to come to explain to me what Islam means because I have the same mind, the same capability as they do to understand," he said.

"The problem with these people is that they like to brainwash you, to have you fall down blindly. They don't want people to think about what they are being told, but just to say it's the right thing," he added. "And even when they choose some verses from the Qur'an . . . they choose all the things that ask you to fight. But they forget that Prophet Muhammad and the Arab conquerors didn't attack others who didn't believe in Islam."

The extremists, he said, "can't accept a lot of modern equipment like television and radio. They say it's something from the devil. . . . But Islam accepts all modern things. . . . Islam is always asking people to be knowledgeable, to know more. . . . It has asked you to go and even learn languages. Because when you learn the language of other people it helps you to prevent enmity."

Rostom has even read the Bible. "I don't see anything strange in it, although I did not understand a lot of things," he said. "But I have to try because it's the only way to understand."

He also saw nothing Islamic in the violence of the Islamic Group rebels. "Islam doesn't mean to be rude or to be stupid or to be savage or to kill, like to attack the tourists here in Egypt in the name of Islam. Islam doesn't ask any person to kill anyone," he said. "I'm not pro-police . . . when we were at university, I attacked policemen physically and verbally. But we never thought to kill a person. . . . It's unfair, to kill anybody."

He does not find the message of moderate Islamists attractive either. He would not like a government led by Muslim Brothers because they "don't have any government experience. We don't need such a period. I don't have to start from the beginning. I think the best place for the Muslim Brotherhood Party is the mosque."

The slogan " 'Islam Is the Solution,' doesn't make any sense to me because Islam is a very vast word," Rostom continued. "When I talk about Islam I have to talk about many things so I don't think 'Islam Is the Solution' is a good concept. I believe in government, in institutions. I consider myself a secularist because this word means I apply religion in its right way, not a narrow-minded way but an open-minded way."

Like most secular-minded Egyptians, Rostom's first response when asked about the Brotherhood's call "to implement *shari'a*" was a frightful vision of amputated hands. "I can't accept that a thief, as an example, should have his hand cut," he said. "Because in accordance with Islam, before you cut his hands, you have to ask yourself . . . whether you provided him with a suitable way of living or not" so he would not become a thief.

But apart from these archaic criminal penalties, I asked Rostom, what else did *shari'a* mean to him?

"Nothing," he replied. "I believe in the law. It is enough. Egyptian law."

So does this mean that Rostom likes the government he lives under? Hardly. Like many young Egyptians he resents it for being inefficient, pompous, and repressive. Knowing that he can do nothing to change his rulers, Rostom opts for a strategy of silent retreat, flying below the government's radar as much as possible. He does not belong to a political party nor does he vote.

"People who enact the laws like to rob us, they like to take our money for nonsense," Rostom said. "I never received any good service. Never. This is the truth. I will give you an example." He proceeded to describe the experiences of his wife and sister in two different hospitals, one privately run and the other state-run. When his sister entered the government facility to give birth, he said, his family was not allowed in and the nursing staff mostly ignored his sister during labor, not even giving her painkillers. But when Nahla went to a private hospital, "they checked her immediately. Everything was prepared. The doctor came and asked me, 'Please go outside and wait and when we need you we will ask for you.' So you have this emotional relaxation," Rostom said. "I can't tell you the difference in procedures in the two different hospitals."[2]

Rostom digressed into this story as we were discussing what Islam meant to him. I asked what the tale had to do with his religion. "I will tell you," he answered, moving to the edge of his chair as he pulled up another story from Islam's past. This one was about Umar Ibn Al Khattab, the second successor to Prophet Muhammad as leader of the new Muslim community. It was a parable about the duties of a ruler.

Khattab "ruled all the Islamic nations," Rostom recounted. "And one day they found him a little bit worried. And they asked him, 'Why are you worried?' And he said, 'I'm afraid that there is a small lamb outside which is suffering and that God will ask me on Doomsday, 'Why didn't you protect her?'

"As a ruler, you have to put all these things into consideration," Rostom said. "This is Islam."

Rostom seemed to be saying that contemporary Muslim rulers have strayed from the ideal of Umar Ibn Al Khattab, whose sense of duty reached even to caring for a little lamb.

Part of the reason for the wave of Islamist violence in Egypt, Rostom said, was poverty and a lack of jobs. "It's economic," he said. "The solution is not to arrest people, but to find employment. But the government doesn't care about these very dangerous things."

When our conversation turned to the way Egyptian police treat ordinary people, Rostom became very agitated. "We know, all the people know, about these things since Nasser's time. But no one has told people . . . how to say to an officer, 'No you don't have to arrest me.' Who dares? A regular citizen? To tell an officer 'Don't arrest me because you are not allowed to?'

"You know, we are not in the United States or in Britain where nobody can arrest you except after reading you your rights as we see in the films.

. . . But really, I don't imagine I will see this in Egypt. An Egyptian officer in a police station gets astonished when you enter and sit down because all the people are supposed to wait until they ask for permission to sit. This is the mentality. Even a student in the police academy calls himself 'pasha,' which means a high rank. But all the police officers are 'pashas' right now."

This behavior is contrary to Islam, Rostom said, because it teaches equality. "They say that people are like a comb. If you look at a comb one way, it's all level. But look at it in another way, you can see all the differentiations" in the teeth of the comb, Rostom said. "And that's what Islam says. That people, with all these differences, are all the same. For all the religions, it is the same. People are all the same and must be treated the same.

"Here, we want to oppose the system because we feel there is something wrong," he concluded with a flash of anger. "The political leaders are the cause of all this downfall of our destiny."

An obvious question, then, is why secular opposition parties have not been able to tap into the frustrations of people like Rostom. Don't these parties represent a middle way between undemocratic regimes and Islamist forces?

In fact, the secular opposition is usually the last place young people in Arab countries look for inspiration and leadership because almost everywhere they are miserable failures. Nowhere more so than in Egypt. Of all Arab nations, Cairo has the most crowded stable of legal opposition parties, more than a dozen. While this makes the country appear politically vibrant, the reality is that decades of authoritarianism have created a wasteland of political thought.[3] Peddling Western-based ideologies or riding the limp hobbyhorse of Arab nationalism, Egypt's secular opposition parties draw about as much attention as a muted television in one of the capital's chatter-filled coffeehouses. Not one could fill Cairo's central Tahrir Square with supporters. To be sure, opposition groups labor under absurd legal restrictions. By law, all parties must be licensed by a Political Parties Committee—most of whose government-appointed members are from the ruling National Democratic Party. In its first two decades, the committee denied more than thirty requests to form new political parties. It approved none.[4]

The government's near-total control of radio and television means little news about the opposition reaches the public. Every legal party has its own newspaper, but the government licenses these and can shut them down at will. Even when a party manages to jump through all the hoops and achieve legal status, it faces restrictions on rallies and large gatherings imposed by the emergency laws and, at election-time, harassment by security police.

There are other reasons for Egypt's anemic secular opposition. Most parties are led by a coterie of upper-class, armchair politicians who pay little attention to the working poor's frustrations over inadequate housing, poor health care, unemployment, and illiteracy. Several of these graybeard leaders trace their political careers back to the era of King Farouk, the monarch overthrown by Nasser in 1952. These men are often consumed by petty rivalries and are notorious for lording it over subordinates in their own parties.[5]

"You need people who understand what it means to reform," sighed Ahmed Mostafa, a young journalist. "These people are still working with ways of the 1960s when subordinates always said 'Everything's wonderful, boss!' These people are not fit to reform anything. They are used to old-fashioned management, which is always related to totalitarian regimes. It's a strict, structural mentality. It's the fault of the political atmosphere in which they have been brought up."[6]

In addition, Egypt's secular opposition leaders cannot begin to match their ideologically motivated Islamist rivals when it comes to doggedness, courage, and risk-taking. Loud protests to government policies by secular opposition politicians usually turn into tepid retractions or "clarifications" after a call from the presidential office. As for organizational skills, Islamists leave secular parties in the dust.

"The Islamists are full of this idea of the necessity of organization," said retired diplomat Hussein Amin. "I have seen demonstrations in Algeria, both of secularists and Islamists. And one cannot help but be very impressed with the organization of the Islamists as compared to the unorganized secularists."[7]

Rostom recalled how, during his youthful fling with the Communist Party, the Islamist student activists were "better at organizing" on campus, selling cheap photocopies of textbooks to attract students to their movement. Secular activists never considered providing such services "because they don't think," he said. "Really, they are just thinking about how to make a demonstration or cause problems. But they don't think how to serve the people. . . . The communists and all these people like to talk only. You see them sitting in cafes. The same old people."

I once asked an Egyptian whose small think tank had been shut down by security police why he didn't fight back in court like Islamist activists who regularly used the courts to air their grievances and score political points.

"They do it because they are outside the system," he replied, showing surprise at the naïveté of my question. "I'm a liberal. I'm in the system, I'm not a revolutionary. Besides, the Islamists have the stamina to do it. Liberals just don't have the stamina. When and if the revolution comes, and they take power, it will be because they have the stamina."[8]

Egypt's secular opposition is also hobbled by the fact that their ideologies, whether socialism, Nasserism, or Western-style liberalism, have all failed to deliver the peace, prosperity, and freedom they once promised. Moreover, at a time when Islam is the most popular medium of political opposition, it is hard to raise the banner of secular ideas.

Even the word *secular*, a label proudly worn thirty years ago, is shunned. In the Islamist lexicon, it is a pejorative code word for "Western" or "American" that is used to besmirch their foes. People like Rostom will call themselves secular in private conversations but politicians don't boast of being secular. "In Egypt, it's as taboo to talk about 'secularism' as it was to talk about 'atheism' five years ago," said Egyptian journalist Mohammed Sid Ahmed. "There is only one frame of reference now: religion."[9]

In this environment, Egypt's secular opposition finds it hard to articulate an ideology. "There are secular forces," said the late Tahseen Basheer, "but no secular ideology."

Finally, there is the overall political culture of the country that affects both Islamists and secularists. "The problem," said Rostom during our talk in his apartment, "is that we don't have this modern system of give-and-take." Politics in Egypt is seen as a zero-sum game. Ideas are not judged by their intrinsic value but by who espouses them. And for all the rhetoric about democracy, a hypersensitivity to the prerogatives of authority leads to inertia, apathy, and stunted thinking in Egyptian political life.

"We have all the resources in our country to become a model for development and progress, but we don't open our heart to differences of opinion," wrote Egyptian playwright Alfred Farag. "Sure, we have a multi-party system, but voices are kept low and discussion is virtually mute. Our behavior at work has inherited the military line-of-command attitude passed down to us. To hear is to obey. There can be no discussion and the subordinate never has the right to say to his superior, 'Let's take the matter up with a higher authority.'

"The boss still takes it for granted that he has the sole concession on opinion and that anyone who differs with him must be a sworn enemy," Farag continued. "As a result, qualified people with the courage of independent thought have been sorted out and left behind in the process of rising to the top, leaving the way open to those who subscribe to the precept, 'Don't bite the hand that feeds you,' regardless of the great harm this causes to us all."[10]

Such political habits are to be expected, perhaps, when election results are predicted in advance and change at the top comes only with a state funeral. Which is why one of my Kuwaiti friends tells this joke:

"Why are Arabs fatalists?"

"Because progress depends on the fatality of our leaders."

*   *   *

At the end of our long conversation in Rostom's living room, chock-full of the young couple's new furniture and their dreams of the future, I asked him what his ideal leader would be like.

"I must go back to history, to Muhammad Ali," he said, referring to the Egyptian leader who launched Egypt's modern development in the early 1800s. "He liked this country very much. So he sent people abroad to learn and he brought the best industrially trained people to Egypt during this time," Rostom explained. "He built the first Egyptian army, the first Egyptian artillery, the first Egyptian print shops.

"So this is what we need: a person who likes the country, not himself. Who will sacrifice. A person who can perceive the future, who is able to give what we have missed. Because we have good potentialities and resources. Any Egyptian who goes abroad becomes a success. But he has to be put in the right atmosphere. . . . So we need only to make a kind of preparation, to prepare the right person in the right place. This is what we miss and what we really need."

And what, I wondered would be this ruler's understanding of Islam? "He has to understand Islam in its right meaning, in what Islam really asks. If a leader is a fair person he won't suffer," Rostom replied. "Again, I have to refer to Umar Ibn Al Khattab," he added. "When the commander of the Roman troops came to surrender to Umar's troops, he asked for Umar. He found him wearing humble clothes and sleeping under a tree. He was astonished to find him sleeping under a tree without any guards. He thought he would meet the head of state in a palace! So he told him, 'Umar you are good person, a fair person. You are secure because you have ruled people in a very proper way. So you are not afraid now of anybody coming to kill you.' This is the right interpretation of Islam."

Five days after the September 2001 terrorist attacks, I received an e-mail whose subject line read, "Our sincere condolences on the occasion of the deaths after bombarding [of] Pentagon." It was a message from Rostom, who called the attacks "extremely barbarian and cowardly acts against civilization." As for whoever was responsible, he added, "How he can sleep or breathe, I don't know."

In our subsequent conversations, Rostom told me that in the last few years he'd gone through a spiritually difficult time and as a result had become more devout. He joined a religious movement that stresses the importance of prayer and Qur'anic study, attends mosque services every Friday and no longer has an occasional beer. But his attitude toward the Egyptian political scene had not changed. He hadn't bothered to vote in the 2000 parliamentary elections. "I don't believe in it," he said. "I see it as something stupid."

At the turn of the century, Political Islam had Egypt boxed inside a square of failure. An Islamist insurgency had blistered the gentle land like a raging sandstorm, inspiring the disillusioned and destitute but alienating many more with its illiberal, violent version of Islam. Moderate, nonviolent Islamists had made impressive political gains in trade unions but were still striving to show that their religion-based politics could accommodate democracy when they were dispatched to kangaroo courts and prison. A feckless secular opposition flitted about the political stage like fleas on a camel. And a repressive, uninspiring, and unaccountable government ruled on.

All in all, a portrait of impasse.

Viewed through a wide historical lens, this impasse reveals Egypt's real predicament: that it is still struggling to define itself as a modern Muslim state. All the people we have met so far—Muhammad Abduh, Hasan Al Banna, Sayyid Qutb, Abdel Harith Madani, Talaat Yassin Hammam, Bestawi Abdel Meguid, Essam El Erian, and Mostafa Rostom—have been fellow travelers on Egypt's long journey toward a new national consensus on Islam's place in its society. Some blazed luminous paths. Others smashed into dead-ends. But all are proof that Egypt's pilgrimage is not yet over.

Many Egyptians, both secular and Islamist, call themselves reformers but are really partisans of "trickle down" reform. They speak of "orderly" change and a need for "national projects" to "galvanize the masses." They refer to the burden of "leading the masses" because they are "easily deceived." Deep down, these people are pseudoreformers who presume that they alone are destined to captain the Arab ship of state. None is a believer in true democracy.

Only new thinking in Islam can crack the authoritarian political culture from which these faux-reformers spring, usher in what Rostom called the "modern system of give-and-take" and inspire new norms of political behavior. With these aims in mind, more Muslims than ever before are exploring how to harness their faith as a vehicle for introducing more representative governments in their societies. They believe that power is not the privilege of "pashas" living in large, walled homes and driving Mercedes but rather the privilege of the *umma*, the "community of the faithful," the people. They are laying the foundations for Islamic democracy.

But these men and women have not yet coalesced into a critical mass that can bring revolutionary change to the Middle East. They are marginalized by the police forces and controlled media of authoritarian states. They contend with religious establishments steeped in orthodoxy. No Arab government, including Egypt, allows unfettered public debate over Islam's place in its society and its role in political life. Most insist that they are best equipped to interpret the holy texts and that their brand of "official Islam" is the right one.[11]

As a result, nonviolent Islamist activists lack the domestic platforms to spread their ideas, mobilize politically, and engage in dialogue with their secular counterparts, which is essential to complete the unfinished business of melding Islam and democracy. These Islamists are far more important actors within Political Islam than those who speak with bombs. But they are drowned out by a louder chorus of Muslims who meet the challenge of modernity by rejecting it and who use violence to get their way. We have examined Islam's contemporary revival through Pious Islam, the grassroots return to personal religious values. We also have seen how this revival is manifest in public life, or Political Islam. But the quest for a modern Islam also travels through the lands of culture and theology. We turn now to these frontiers of Islam's revival.

CULTURAL ISLAM

10

A Culture of Our Own, or Madonna and Belly-Dancing Have to Go

"We don't want the films or plays with sex, AIDS and Mafia, which are well known in American and European countries. We want to be a pure Muslim society. . . .It's a matter of the life of the American people now, which we don't agree with."
—YUSSEF ATHEM,
ISLAMIST AND FORMER MEMBER OF JORDAN'S PARLIAMENT[1]

"[T]here is nothing that protects the Arabness of Egyptians any longer today except Islam."
—TARIQ AL BISHRI,
EGYPTIAN JUDGE[2]

"We Muslims once had a great civilisation, and played an active role in human history. Today, we lack the position and role we once enjoyed. . . . The world we live in today is the world of the West, not only in a geographical sense, but also intellectually, morally and technologically."
—IRANIAN PRESIDENT MOHAMMAD KHATAMI[3]

Knock-off designer shades. Fashionably cropped hair. Blue denim jacket. Khaled Salah Hassanein is no slacker when it comes to style. Sitting in the upscale coffee shop of Cairo's Nile Hilton, the tall, slim journalist looks like a poster boy for the cafe crowd. Around us, on the outdoor piazza, Egyptians argue in spirited Arabic while sipping sugary tea and warm whiskey.

Some puff on the long, snaky tubes of water pipes. Gray-haired tourists in Bermuda shorts and baseball caps order beer and swap stories in American drawls that are more than a match for the background din of clacking plates. At other tables, young backpackers scribble memories into dog-eared journals. Like everyone else, Khaled hails friends who come over to barter dollops of gossip. When a lithe, micro-skirted beauty prances past our table, his green eyes feast. "Nice legs!" he quips, flashing a smile across the table.

Had you been there, you would not have suspected that this relaxed, attractive twenty-seven-year-old once loathed scenes like this. You would not have guessed that once there'd been another Khaled who shunned such places as sinfully un-Islamic because of their free-flowing alcohol, mingling of sexes, and tableaus of bare female limbs. You also would not have known that even now the two Khaleds tug his soul in opposite directions and sometimes leave him wondering, at some level, who in fact he really is.

To know all this you have to flash back to the late 1980s when Khaled was in high school. His parents, both civil servants, provided their four children with a comfortable life despite the poverty around them in Imbaba, one of Cairo's poorest districts. Khaled recalled late afternoons watching television with his father while his mother prepared dinner. Afterward, he'd meet up with friends. His crowd liked to party and their A-list included music by American pop idols like Michael Jackson. Khaled's favorite was Diana Ross.

But the teenager wanted something more. Encouraged by an uncle, Khaled began hanging out at a mosque near his home. It was run by angry young men who accused the government of "suppressing" Islam. Many of them were members of the underground Islamic Jihad, the radical Islamist movement. After awhile, Khaled caught their fire and joined the group. Its ideas "were strongly linked to religion and through that religion you could be active and moving," he explained during our chat in the coffee shop. "Islam is a style of life, a way of life which pushes one to participate in running his country. Besides that, it guarantees you a better life after Dooms-day. It's very idealistic."

Having committed himself to the movement, Khaled's lifestyle under-went what he called "a radical change." He prayed five times a day, grew a beard, donned a white galabia and adopted a different name. To his new friends, he was "Nasser Salah," a name he said was inspired by the twelfth-century Egyptian ruler and Muslim warrior Salah Al Din, who routed the Christian Crusaders from Jerusalem.

Khaled also stopped listening to Michael and Diana because, according to Islamic Jihad, Western music was *haraam*, meaning religiously forbidden. To his family's great annoyance, he'd switch off the television because the programs showed women "in ways not acceptable to Islam." Instead, he'd tune the radio to broadcasts of Qur'anic recitations. "The Qur'an," he said, "was the only voice you could hear in our house, either from the radio and from tapes." He also stopped shaking hands with women when introduced, berated his sixteen-year-old sister for not wearing an Islamic headscarf, and badgered his father to stop smoking because cigarettes are *haraam*. "My father wasn't really convinced of what I said," he noted with a wry smile. "He's a moderate Muslim."[4]

Khaled's youthful trajectory into an extremist Islamist movement, followed by his subsequent disillusionment and departure from the group, illustrates how many young Egyptians live between two compelling and competing worlds. One easily accepts Western culture. The other scorns it. The tension between these two worlds is another reason for Islam's new potency in the Middle East. Pious Islam offers Muslims personal spiritual solace. Political Islam arises from their demands for new types of governance and a voice in how they are ruled. Cultural Islam reflects their search for an identity that is truly their own.

At a time when traditional ways of life are yielding to new ones that all seem to bear the label "Made in the West," many Muslims are unnerved by what they see as a threat to their Islamic identity and culture. Convinced that their societies have become too enamored of the West, they feel a need to break free from what they see as a humiliating imitation and psychological dependence on a foreign culture. The way to do this, they believe, is by restoring Islam as the dominant cultural standard, or as one scholar has described it, by "reconnecting with the 'pre-colonial' symbolic universe" of their society, which is Islam.[5]

Cultural Islam manifests itself in many different ways. It includes violent attacks by extremists on cinemas because they show American films, as well as students wearing headscarves as a badge of Islamic identity.[6] It is also seen in the shunning of Western pop culture, like Khaled's rejection of Diana Ross. At a more sophisticated level, it is evident in assertions of cultural independence by Muslim intellectuals as they seek to replace Western concepts with ones grounded in Islamic traditions.

Islamists have long chided fellow Egyptians for adopting Western lifestyles and ideas. In the 1930s, Muslim Brotherhood leader Hasan Al Banna called it undignified, unpatriotic, and insulting to their Islamic heritage. "Formal political independence," he warned, was worthless without "intellectual, social and cultural independence . . .We want to think independently, depending on . . .Islam and not upon imitation which ties us to the theories and attitudes of the West in everything. We want to be distinguished by our own values."[7]

Nowadays, Western, and especially American, culture has a much greater reach than in Banna's time and so is perceived as a greater menace. Faced with a "cultural invasion" that they fear is endangering their Islamic identity—perhaps even Islam itself—many Muslims are taking refuge in their faith and its traditions. Islam is their vaccination against becoming a cultural clone of the West.

The cultural dimension of Islam's resurgence in Egypt and other Arab countries is intimately intertwined with Political Islam. The same question that is at the heart of Political Islam occupies the center of Cultural Islam: "What kind of society are we going to be?"

But Cultural Islam is a distinct force on its own. It extends beyond politics and casts a wider net. Islamist activists may be the most vocal about calling for an "authentic" Islamic culture and identity. But that call resonates outside their normal constituencies, appealing also to many secular Egyptians. Although they want nothing to do with an orthodox Islamic state, they, too, are anxious about the perils to their Arab customs and culture from an increasingly ubiquitous Western culture.

Western governments often overlook or minimize the cultural aspect of Islam's contemporary revival. Concerned about the stability of Arab governments, they tend to be preoccupied with Political Islam's armed rebels and well-organized activists. But culture and politics are Siamese twins, and what happens in one arena affects the other, sometimes with major consequences. In the 1970s, Iran's Shah Reza Pahlavi accelerated the Westernization of his country in the belief that imitating the West was the ticket to modernity and power. "Iranians thought that if we make our country look like the West, if we make our parliament look like a Western one, it will solve our problems," observed Iranian political scientist Farhang Rajaee. "People thought to be successful we had to look like the West."[8]

The Iranian elites who bought into this idea flaunted a dangerous disdain for traditional culture. Tehran's upper crust, which got rich on lucrative military contracts and business deals with Western partners, staged lavish parties featuring Paris couture and fountains of champagne. On university campuses, officials who wanted their country to look "modern" discouraged female students from wearing the long, black chador. Women who showed up in hotel lobbies wearing this traditional garb were discreetly hustled out because they jarred with the Western image that Iran's capital city sought to project. Islamic sensibilities were further abraded by posters promoting foreign movies that often featured women in low-cut or tight clothes.

Many Iranians were upset by the implication that Iran's traditional

Islamic lifestyle was inferior or "backward." Their resentment helped fuel the antishah storm that climaxed in the 1979 revolution. Firebrands of Iran's new order popularized a word for an inordinate love of things Western: "Westoxification."[9]

Egypt has not turned its back on local tradition nor discouraged Islamic dress to the extent Iran did. Female news anchors cannot wear Islamic head scarves on state television and the full-face veil, or *niquab*, is banned from university campuses. But the government would never dream of banning headscarves from parliament, government offices, or universities, as Turkey's ferociously secular government has done.[10] Still, the extent to which Egypt's political and business elites favor Western lifestyles and tolerate expressions of American pop culture is noticed by those who are alienated from the system. To them, an un-Islamic taste for Diana Ross and heavy metal music goes hand in hand with the pro-Western orientation of their rulers who are seen as conduits for the foreign "cultural invasion."[11]

The preoccupation with identity that is at the core of Cultural Islam is also important to understand because of its influence on religious reform. I often wondered why the most orthodox and conservative interpretations of Islamic law and scripture had shown such staying power over the last century even as Egyptians made ever-increasing contacts with the West. Why had these contacts not led to more innovation in religious doctrine and greater intellectual openness among Islamic scholars? In fact, just the opposite occurred. The more Egypt interacted with the West, the more its scholars and society held fast to traditional, conservative renditions of Islamic scripture.

Part of the explanation seems to be that whenever a society feels threatened by outside forces, whether military or cultural, self-reflection and internal reform are dampened. Arab Muslim societies are no exception. Expanding contacts with a militarily and technologically superior West made societies like Egypt insecure and fearful about the survival of their Islamic cultural identity. This gave religious conservatism the upper hand.

"When Islam shows its dogmatism, it is often from the dread of becoming rootless. It is an attitude of self-defense," Egyptian judge Tariq Al Bishri once observed. "One does not advance when one is on the defensive. . . . Western thought presents itself as a model and an example. Islamic thought goes on the defensive and ignores from then on what can prove profitable to it. A good number of Muslim thinkers are reformists until they feel the existence of a danger threatening the foundations of their thought. They then swing toward conservatism."[12]

A recurring lament in the opinion pages of Egyptian newspapers is that a backward Europe once turned to Islamic civilization for enlightenment, but now it is Arabs who are ever the students. "Our relation to the West has always been lopsided," wrote Hassan Hanafi, an Islamist philosophy professor at Cairo University. "They create and produce, we imitate and consume. They are the perpetual teachers; we, the perpetual students. Generation after generation, this asymmetry has generated an inferiority complex, forever exacerbated by the fact that their innovations progress at a faster pace than we can absorb."

Hanafi's remedy is a greater identification with Islam, which he called "the best tool to reverse the inferiority complex to a superiority complex. Islam would give the whole culture a sense of dignity."[13]

But spend a day walking around Cairo and you might wonder what cultural "inferiority" or "humiliation" I am talking about. The city appears enthralled with American consumer culture. Hungry? Have a hamburger at Roy's Country Kitchen. Or a large pepperoni-and-onion at Pizza Hut. Or a hero at Subway, followed by a scoop of fudge ripple at Baskin Robbins. Western pop tunes show up on morning radio's "Top-20." American movies fly out of video rental shops. Kellogg's Corn Flakes are stacked on supermarket shelves. Kids hang out in video arcades. And next to the Nile in the heart of Cairo is a shopping mall with sixty-four boutiques. Its name? The World Trade Center.

Consumerism oozes from state-run television like toothpaste from a tube. The ads are in Arabic but the antics are pure Madison Avenue: dirt-defying genies leaping from detergent boxes and teenagers in blue jeans dancing around a park. TV trailers for the 1994 film *Back in Action* featured frenzied shots of car chases, gun battles, fistfights, karate kicks, blazing fires and defenestrated bodies, which all climaxed in a frozen vision of men pointing guns, one in each fist, at viewers in Egyptian living rooms.

Every night during Ramadan, families gather around their television sets to watch extravaganzas of dancing and entertainment. "The Bold and the Beautiful" was so beloved in Egypt that fans grew incensed when it was moved from its prime-time slot and replaced with "Oshin," a Japanese soap opera about a girl who endures poverty, disease, and earthquakes. "Who needs misery?" cried a popular Cairo magazine. "There are thousands of 'Oshins' in Egypt already!"

A popular hangout that opened while I was in Cairo was House of Donuts. Located in the glitzy commercial quarter of Mohandseen, it had a modernistic decor of shiny chrome and pastel-hued walls and served a luscious variety of doughnuts and muffins all made with imported American flour. Its sales pitch was "Have a Sweet Day." When it started up, the doughnut place advertised staff openings in local newspapers for young women who spoke English and had *"slimmy"* figures. Behind the counter, the women wore American-style uniforms with caps. Their Islamic head-scarves, which they wore traveling to and from work, were stored in the changing room.[14]

So pervasive are American cultural symbols in Cairo they hardly seem foreign to some. One afternoon, eight young women poured into a newly opened Kentucky Fried Chicken that was decorated with pictures of James Dean, Marilyn Monroe, and Elvis Presley. The menu was in English and the piped music was American pop hits. The women, all in headscarves, were pre-med students from Cairo University across the street. When I asked if they considered the eatery a cultural intrusion, one of them looked nonplussed.

"Is there a KFC in America?" she asked.

Another one, tucking into her fried chicken and French fries, replied, "Food isn't culture. My mother makes this at home."

And surely, you might argue, the long lines of Egyptian visa-seekers that form daily at the U.S. embassy can't despise American culture. Nine out of ten Egyptians, it seems, would hop on the next New York–bound plane if they could get a visa. "There *is* Muslim fanaticism in this country," joked one longtime American resident of Cairo. "It's a fanaticism to go to England, France, and the United States."

As your tour would indicate, many Egyptians are clearly not bothered by America's "cultural invasion." Some are even wildly enthusiastic about it.

But alongside this acceptance runs an undercurrent of unease and resentment about America's cultural presence, whether in trivial matters like doughnuts or the more insidious idea that they should be served by "slimmy" women. The recurring reminders of American culture in Cairo's streets are semaphores to some Egyptians of their own culture's attenuated influence on the global scene and its domination by a foreign one.

Fears of American cultural influences are heightened by the widespread view among Egyptians, from secularists to the most radical of Islamists, that America has gone too far in its sexual freedoms. Egypt is a very conservative society and its people generally disapprove of America's open acceptance of gays and lesbians, the uninhibited sexuality of its entertainment and media industries, and the extent to which it practices gender equality. For most Egyptians, the role of women in society is still primarily seen within the context of the family. Only a minority of the most liberal and Westernized Egyptians would accept the same freedoms for women enjoyed by American females.

Western-style gender equality is therefore widely seen as a bad cultural influence. Conservative Islamists in particular see this issue as a cultural Rubicon. To cross it by allowing Egyptian women the same political and social freedoms enjoyed by Western women represents the ultimate in Western cultural penetration. They believe it would put their society on the slippery slope to the moral decadence and social ills they see endemic in the West, such as high rates of divorce and abortion, broken families, illegitimacy, AIDS, prostitution, and pornography.

Indeed, such ills are just the beginning for some Islamists who see America as morally irredeemable because it has left religion behind. They conveniently ignore the fact that the United States has one of the most religiously active populations in the developed Western world. To hear some Islamists describe American society is to hear echoes of Cold War Soviet propagandists. In these scenarios, which are driven as much by willful distortion as ignorance, the United States consists solely of money-grubbing, drug-addicted, sex-crazed citizens who crave nudity and violence, spend all their earnings on consumer goods and live in broken families.

"What does the West have to offer other than Coca-Cola, hamburgers, blue jeans, Madonna, Michael Jackson, and the whole gamut of ephemeral pleasures?" asked Islamist author and community activist Mustafa Mahmoud. By contrast, he noted, "Islam offers mankind heaven and immortality . . . [and] the eternal spirit that God breathes into all of us."[15]

These conservative Islamists, much like Christian right-wingers in the United States, have special disdain for America's acceptance of homosexuality. At the close of one long interview with Mustafa Mashur, the "Supreme Guide" of the Muslim Brotherhood, he pulled himself up in his chair and announced that he wanted to tell me something. Pen poised, I listened.

"The West nowadays in sexual freedom and homosexuality makes people not bother to get married," Mashur said. "As a result, there is a reduction in population and this represents a danger for these countries." Family ties are so weak in the West, he continued, that "maybe an old man would die in his home alone without his daughter or son caring about him." The West's moral failures, he concluded, "are threatening destruction of these countries. The curve is going down in the West. If you cannot take care, you will fall."

Such warped notions of American life, which come mainly from movies and television, have convinced many Egyptians, not just Islamist activists, that American culture is best kept at a very long arm's length. As journalist Khaled explained, "People look at the West as a society that is morally loose and they imagine taking anything from the West would introduce a loose society. This fear . . . persuades them to hold more to our heritage."[16]

It is not only Islamists, however, who worry about their culture's future.

Faced with "a new world order led exclusively by the U.S.," the Arabs once again confront "foreign political, economic and cultural hegemony in all its aspects, from the marketing of consumer goods to the direction of political decisions, passing through the plundering of resources, the conditioning of minds, the taming of wills and the coloring of thoughts." Arabs therefore must begin "fortifying the Arab cultural identity against the foreign cultural invasion."[17]

The author of these words is not an Islamist zealot. He is Salah Eldin Hafiz, deputy editor in chief of Egypt's *Al Ahram* newspaper and a self-described secularist. He has been to the United States many times and is on the U.S. embassy's permanent roster of invitees to its receptions in Cairo.

Hafiz believes his culture is under siege. The ideology that has shaped his life, and probably still does, is Arab nationalism. But he shares the Islamist discontent over the West's cultural insinuation into Egypt and to a certain extent, his secularist ears are not deaf to their assertions that Islam "protects" Egyptian culture. For where does Islam leave off and Egyptian culture begin?

Hafiz is in his sixties and has a corona of gray hair circling his otherwise bare head. He emanates a dignified, patrician air. The day we met in his *Al Ahram* office, he wore tinted glasses, a pinstriped suit, and a silk tie of blue and gray. The aroma of his cigar mingled with the scent of jasmine floating through an open window five floors above Cairo's boisterous streets.

American culture has a "heavy impact" on Egypt mainly through "the films, the television programs, 'Dallas' and so forth," Hafiz said. It affects "not only the behavior of the people but also the way of thinking . . . in a way that contradicts Arab values.

"We have to explain to our people that our culture is different," he continued. "We have very clear values and Western societies have other clear values. Western values are not applicable for other societies. [The West] is not the only model in the world. Maybe it's a good model for Westerners but it is not very good for us."

When I asked for an example of these differences, Hafiz said that "in the Arab or Muslim families . . . there is a kind of good and strong relationship between father and wife and his daughter or his son. This kind of relationship is a continuing one, for a long time." But in the West, "the family accepts that a daughter is going out after sixteen years of age . . . to do anything, to live individually, to exercise her freedom for instance. This is not acceptable in Arab culture. It is not a matter of Islam only, it's a matter of Arab values of family life."

Hafiz is not, of course, in favor of burning video shops or shooting up movie houses that show American films. But he would like to see more respect for his culture from outsiders. "We don't accept cultural hegemony. We are ready to accept a kind of balance in cooperation. You have to study our civilization and our culture and you have to understand it, as we are trying to understand Western culture."

The secular editor agreed that he shares the concern of Islamists on the issue of America's cultural influence in Egypt, though they part ways at a certain point. "The point of agreement is that both of us are defending our culture," he said. "I accept some of the Western values" he added, but many Islamists "cannot accept Western culture. That's the difference."

During their insurgency, Islamic Group extremists firebombed video stores because they rented "immoral" American movies. They also opened fire on a theater at the 1993 Cairo International Film Festival, declaring in a fax that it really should have been called the Cairo International *Nudity* Festival. Such acts arose out of the rebels' belief that they were battling to keep Egypt from losing its Islamic identity. Their violent campaign, one analyst wrote, was in part "a cultural struggle between Western consumerism and a traditional culture trying to assert its . . . values in the face of inexorable Westernisation, which is . . . strongly felt to involve a loss of identity and to threaten the national culture as it is replaced by the [Western] Other."[18]

The desire to avoid Western imitation is apparent when one considers how Islamic Group rebels differed from their guerrilla counterparts of the Cold War era. In those days, national liberation movements in Africa, Asia, and Latin America spouted ideologies that were rooted in the West's intellectual tradition: socialism, communism, capitalism. Some rebel leaders welcomed journalists in cluttered offices hung with pictures of John F. Kennedy, Martin Luther King, Fidel Castro, or Che Guevara. In forest enclaves, military commanders proudly showed off armed, camouflaged "female cadres" to demonstrate that they had modern ideas about gender equality. And late-night confabs often included whiskey, cigarettes, and song. Behind it all was an implicit message for visitors, whether they arrived by Pan Am or Aeroflot: "We want to be like you."

By contrast, Egypt's Islamic Group insurgents wanted to restore the Islamic caliphate, a type of government most Westerners know only from history books. Their ideology regarded secularism as heresy and democracy as alien. Instead of pumping up crowds with cries of "Power to the People," they held prayer meetings and chanted "Power for God." Their communiqués were sprinkled with sayings like "Hearts set on the creed have no fear, nor can they grasp the meaning of loss" and "God will have what he orders but most people don't realize this." These militants would never tack a snapshot of King or Castro to their wall, for neither is Muslim nor a source of inspiration. And compared to their Cold War predecessors, the Egyptians were prudes. They abstained from alcohol and cigarettes, interrupted interviews to pray and kept their women hidden.

Their implicit message to visitors was very different: "We don't want to be like you."

Islamic Group members were also sending a message to their own people, particularly the older generation. With their aggressively Islamic lifestyle, one Egyptian observer noted, they were claiming to be "the elite, the clean ones who have left society which is impure and infidel and corrupt."[19] When they wore Islamic garb, prayed diligently five times a day, and tuned their radios to Qur'anic readings, these militants were telling fellow Egyptians, "We are different from you Western-fawning, pseudo-Muslims."

For some Islamic Group militants, Western influences were not the only danger to their Islamic culture. They also denounced belly dancing as un-Islamic. And in a foretaste of the Taliban's dreadful destruction of Afghanistan's world-famous Buddhist rock statues, Islamic Group announced that the pyramids and other pharaonic temples had to go. These national treasures, they said, were relics of the country's "pagan" era before Islam.

The battle to protect Egypt's Islamic identity from Western "contamination" was also joined by conservative Islamists. But instead of picking up guns, these self-appointed guardians of public virtue went to court, filing lawsuits against those they regarded as co-conspirators in the foreign assault on Egyptian culture. In scores of cases, actresses, writers, and journalists were sued for allegedly "defaming Muslims" or "offending" Islamic moral norms. The plaintiffs included preachers, lawyers, and Al Azhar University faculty members, intent on making Islam the cultural benchmark for all works of art, whether films, books, or paintings. But the Islam that these Islamist activists were promoting was a narrow, orthodox, sexually puritanical version of the faith, making for a dangerous, intolerant return to roots.

Youssra was among their prime targets. The longhaired brunette is one of Egypt's most popular film stars. But her sexy screen image and acting roles, including one as a prostitute, offended conservative Islamists. When she appeared on the cover of an Egyptian film magazine dressed only in a flimsy nightgown, she was hit with a lawsuit accusing her of violating Islamic moral standards.

"I was shocked," she said indignantly. "Look, there is something wrong going on. . . . It's about fundamentalism. . . . It's the whole climate. It's a different one . . . if you see the old films you will see our previous actresses they used to wear the bikinis, used to wear chiffon, transparent things, baby doll, whatever it was.

"I'm a symbol. They would like to go for the head and cut it off," she added, laughing nervously. "This is ridiculous. I can't find that this is right. Nobody can come and tell me, 'You are against God or you're not a Muslim or you're not a good person.' . . . My relationship with God is totally personal."[20]

In another case, Islamists tried to block distribution of *The Emigrant,* a film by Egypt's best-known director Yousef Chahine. They claimed the movie's portrayal of the biblical figure Joseph violated an Islamic ban on visual portrayals of holy prophets.

Portrayals of human sexuality were another big complaint. An Islamist member of parliament went after the minister of culture for allowing a play with homosexual characters to be staged and for putting a "nude pornographic" picture on the cover of an arts magazine. The picture was Gustav Klimt's *Adam and Eve.*

Books that had a secular outlook or questioned belief in God were also challenged. In May 2000, Al Azhar University students clashed with police during two days of protests against the government's decision to release a new edition of *A Banquet for Seaweed,* a 1993 novel in which one character is a religious skeptic who calls God "a failed artist" and commits suicide. The students shouted "Back, back to Islam! Back, back to the Qur'an!" during their demonstrations. Even though the book was written in Arabic by a Syrian, Islamists associated its antireligious theme with the West. The book's release, a prominent Islamist said, showed how Egypt was subject to "a wave of Westernization that targets its religious beliefs and its Arab, Egyptian and Islamic identity."[21]

To secular Egyptians, these Islamist activists were "cultural terrorists" who stifled intellectual creativity and aimed to turn Egypt into another Saudi Arabia, a country with no art museums, movie theaters, or statues depicting human forms. "This is a very dangerous form of fascism," an enraged Chahine said at the height of his two-year court battle with the Islamists.[22]

Many lawsuits were eventually dismissed, but they cost the defendants time and money. Some were patently absurd. An Islamist lawyer sued a newspaper editor because a cartoon in his paper allegedly ridiculed God. The cartoon actually ridiculed Islamists for seeing mortal danger to their souls in almost everything. It showed a couple riding Cairo's Metro and looking annoyed at a bearded sheikh, flies buzzing around his head, seated next to them. "Oh, worshipers of God," the sheikh was lamenting, "Metro

Goldwyn Mayer leads us astray. . . . The Underground Metro leads us astray!"[23]

The Islamists' rejection of Western pop culture is quite understandable to many Americans, who have their own quarrel with its celebration of sex, violence, and drugs, be it gangsta rap, Madonna's provocative gyrations, or Jennifer Lopez's sartorial minimalism. Even assertions that America is all about money and materialism get a sympathetic hearing from plenty of homegrown critics who decry a consumer culture that seems built on the Cartesian shopping principle: "I buy, therefore I am."

But Cultural Islam becomes far more unsettling for Americans when they hear Islamists reject as un-Islamic values believed to hold universal appeal, such as individualism, pluralism, secularism, feminism, and even democracy. "It's unpleasant because Islamists are saying 'We no longer want to use your categories, your system of expressing yourself. We want to use our own references,' " said François Burgat, an expert on Egyptian Islamist groups. "They want their symbolic system to be the symbolic system of Egypt."[24]

This intellectual return to roots involves neither guns nor frivolous lawsuits. Its proponents reject the idea that in order to be "modern" they have to look, act, and think in a Western way. Or that history is inevitably moving to a time when everyone will adopt Western lifestyles, dress, and cultural values. Instead, they are harvesting their own heritage for Islamic alternatives to handle modern social issues and seeking to ground values long associated with the West in an Islamic cultural context. Thus, businessmen establish "Islamic banks," scholars write about "Islamic finances," and political activists speak of "Islamic democracy."

"Can we learn from the West? . . . Yes, we can. But we should also learn from the bitter lessons of modernity in the West," wrote Heba Raouf Ezzat, a young Islamist political scientist in Cairo. "We need to be open to new ideas, but we do not have to repeat the same mistakes. . . . We have a golden opportunity to construct our own modernity, and to carefully see where things went wrong."[25]

One place that Ezzat believes Western modernity went wrong is feminism. Which might seem strange coming from this peppy, cheerful woman who delivers strong opinions in rapid-fire sentences. In her mid-thirties, Ezzat is married to a psychiatrist and has three children. She teaches at Cairo University, is a writer for an Islamic Web site, and is completing her doctoral dissertation on the concept of citizenship in Western liberal thought. She has worn an Islamic headscarf since she was thirteen.

"I don't call myself a feminist because I think feminism revolves around individualistic, secular conceptions," Ezzat said. "I would rather work to foster women's rights within a more communitarian conception of society that respects the different circumstances of women in the public and private spheres."

In Ezzat's view, Western feminism is inappropriate for Muslim societies because it comes out of a secular worldview that "marginalizes God." In the end, she believes, "it just ruins society because it breaks down the family, it deconstructs the family itself."[26]

Islamists who think along the lines of Ezzat make an argument strikingly similar to the one made by secular editor Hafiz: It's not that Western values are intrinsically bad. It's just that some are not right for Egypt. "Imitation cross-culturally is something very difficult," said Rafik Habib, one of the founders of the moderate Islamist political movement Wasat. "We have to look at our circumstances and at our history and shape our ideas. We can benefit from any other country, take what is suitable for us and leave what is not suitable for us. Then we can make the model which belongs to us and at the same time is suitable and effective for us."

Habib is a social worker and an author whose books examine the intersection of politics and culture, specifically Arabic Islamic culture. He is in his forties and holds graduate degrees in psychology and philosophy. He is also somewhat of a maverick because, unlike most other founders of Wasat, he is Christian. He helped start the movement, he said, because it stressed Egypt's Islamic and Arab culture, with which he also identifies.

I found Habib on the fourth floor of a building set amid the twisting alleys around Cairo's Metropole Cinema. His office windows were shuttered and we sat amid tall piles of cardboard boxes stuffed with files. He wore large-framed glasses and his roughly textured, jet-black hair was accessorized with a black mustache. "All our ideas depend on our culture and our cultural experience and from this identity we try to initiate new ideas," Habib said. "We are not aiming to make the Arab Islamic culture internationally spread out. We know that this culture belongs to us. It is not suitable for Western people."

The drive for cultural independence is stronger in his generation than his parents', Habib noted, remarking on how his father "thinks about modernization in Western meanings and I think about renewal in Arabic culture meanings. He doesn't think Westernization is something bad. He thinks what the Western countries are doing is something that can benefit any culture. I think the contrary. Western values are not international."[27]

The desire for indigenous cultural expressions is particularly evident in Islamist discussions about democracy, which they want anchored in an Islamic cultural framework, in their "symbolic universe" of Islam. "I think we can develop a universal system of governance from within our Islamic faith that can also be relevant to different societies, even if they do not convert to Islam, just as much as Western democracy has been claiming to be universal as a model of governance," said Ezzat, adding that she would like to see "new forms of direct democracy in an age of telecommunication."[28]

Transplanted Western political systems failed because the Islamic cultural context was disregarded, Habib said. That was the case, he added, with the modern bureaucratic state established in Egypt in the early nineteenth century. Egyptians took "this idea of a state from Western countries and tried to make something similar," he said. But now "we have a Western-style state [that] is not effective like the Western states and at the same time it is not suitable for us."

Hundreds of books have offered blueprints for an "Islamic democracy," using traditional Islamic terms like *shura*, meaning consultation, and describing the electorate as the *umma*, or community of believers. But Islamic democracies, Islamists say, also need to reflect cultural values. That means, for example, striking a different balance between individual and community rights than the balance struck in the West. "If we think about democracy as individualism, it's not for us because we [believe in] group values, not individual values," Habib explained. Westerners think first about individuals but "we think first about the *umma*, which carries a holistic identity . . . and the individual is not existing itself, the individual is a member of a group."[29]

Human rights is another arena where Islamists have balked at a Western framework. Extremist Islamists reject the very notion of human rights as a Western concept, saying that *shari'a* has all the rights a Muslim could ask for. Moderate Islamists do not reject human rights but protest that they are defined within the Western tradition of secular liberalism, which emphasizes an individual's liberties as opposed to his or her duties. In order for Muslim societies to fully embrace international human rights standards, Islamists say, they need to be adapted to and expressed in an Islamic context and vocabulary.

"We have to take this building, this structure of human rights standards, and put it on pillars," Ezzat has argued. "These pillars represent different cultures and religions. Human rights should rest on all of them, if they are to be truly universal. The human rights movements in each country or region or culture must find their own philosophical foundations. They all agree upon the basic rights and freedoms, but the issue is how to explain that according to each philosophical background. We have to accept diversity.

"The problem," Ezzat added, "is that . . . once religion jumps in, people start feeling uncomfortable. They insist that the discourse has to be purely secular, and everyone has to leave his culture . . . outside the door."[30]

Cultural Islam is perhaps most problematic for Westerners in its challenge to their cultural value par excellence: secularism. Islamists contend that secularism is alien to Islam because it violates *tawhid*, Islam's core belief in God's Oneness and the unity of all things in God. It is *tawhid* that gives Islam a mandate over all aspects of a Muslim's life and makes it difficult to separate religion from politics and culture. It also works against any tendency to compartmentalize religion from other aspects of one's life.

To call oneself "secular" implies that you have *demoted* Islam to just one part of life: the strictly private or personal sphere. In other words, it implies that you are thinking like a Westerner instead of a Muslim. In Islamists' eyes, to accept secularism as a cultural value means abandoning *tawhid*, which is key to Islamic identity. It means surrendering a fundamental difference between Muslims and Westerners. As one Al Azhar faculty member wrote, secularism is contrary "to the all-embracing Islam . . . [and] rejects the substance of Islam. Moreover, it is one of the instruments of the colonial and intellectual invasion."[31]

Islamists tend to be the most antisecular, but even Egyptians comfortable with Western culture say secularism as practiced in the West cannot thrive in Egypt. Islamic tradition "is still anchored in the hearts of the people," explained Hanafi, the philosopher. "If you say religion is only in the private sphere, between you and God, and has nothing to do with society, with the state, with politics . . . some intellectuals may understand you and the elite may join you, but not the masses. This is the crisis of secularism in the Middle East. It is the choice of the elite but not the choice of the masses."[32]

As Khaled, speaking above the bustle of the coffee shop, observed, "Islam is a style of life and the sayings of Prophet Muhammad organize the life of a Muslim from the time he wakes until the time he sleeps."

If Islamic identity means a society and culture reflecting *tawhid*, how is this accomplished? The answer for many Islamists is to restore Islamic law, or *shari'a*, to a primary place in society. Implementing *shari'a* would, in their view, attach Egypt more closely to Islam, strengthen its Islamic identity, and fortify it against creeping secularism. For them, *shari'a* is their culture's coat of mail, a protective armor against the cuts and thrusts of the West's globalizing, secularizing influence. So while implementing *shari'a* is a political slogan, it is also a cultural statement, an Islamic version of running Old Glory up the flagpole.[33]

For many years, Tariq Al Bishri has argued that applying *shari'a* would stave off the peril to Egypt's Islamic identity posed by the West's intellectual and cultural penetration. Now in his sixties, the retired judge, who has written extensively on Egypt's political system, is regarded as a moderate Islamist. His view of *shari'a* is more sophisticated and nuanced than the dogmatic version of those who rush to court to stop a movie, ban a book, or harass a journalist. But he shares with them a desire to more closely connect his culture with its precolonial "symbolic universe" of Islam. He has described Egypt's Islamist movement as one that calls "on society to return to values which had previously been dominant and to Islam as a source of legitimacy and of social order."[34]

As a young law student at Cairo University in the early 1950s, Bishri was a staunch secular leftist. But after Egypt's shattering military defeat by Israel in 1967, he began reassessing his worldview. Increasingly, he came to see religion as the essential glue of Egyptian society and key to its development. He abandoned his secular leftist ideology for an Islamist one.

"I found that . . . national belonging had something to do with Muslim religious thinking," Bishri told one interviewer. Religion, he concluded, was crucial for society's "internal cohesion" and that if "the future of the country demanded sacrifices, it was Islam which would make us capable of performing them. . . ."[35]

Before Bishri retired, I went to see him at his judicial office. It was on an upper floor of an elegant, colonial-era building shaded by towering palms next to the Nile. He is a tall man with stooped shoulders, ruddy cheeks, a long, thick nose, and a mustache. His brown hair is slightly frizzy. During our interview he spoke in quiet, judicious tones and fingered a circle of prayer beads made from mother-of-pearl. His desk was neat and newly dusted, a rare sight in government offices.

"To implement *shari'a* is part of the belief of Muslims. It's not just getting rid of a foreign influence. It's part of complementing your understanding of life and your relation to life and your relations to society [so] that both would have *one* source of reference," Bishri said. "Nowadays, the moral side is related to religion. [But] the aspect of day-to-day dealings is not related to religion and this makes some sort of schizophrenia."[36]

Bishri's desire for "*one* source of reference" grows out of *tawhid*. When a Muslim society like Egypt's strays from *tawhid* and attempts to straddle the two worlds of Islam and the secular West, it produces, as he put it, a "sort of schizophrenia." Not all Muslims, of course, are bothered by this cultural "schizophrenia." But it concerns Islamists like Bishri who want Egyptian culture to openly reflect *tawhid* and display a strong Islamic identity.

As Western culture encroaches even more into Muslim societies, these concerns are growing. When some seven hundred Muslim scholars from one hundred countries met in Cairo for their annual conference a few years ago, they complained that the "information revolution" had exposed Islamic states to a variety of cultures. As a result, they said, some young Muslims had drifted from their religion and developed a "split personality."[37]

This cultural cleavage vexes Muslims from Tehran to Cairo and has even drawn comment from Iranian president Mohammad Khatami. "Western culture is at least in harmony with their civilisation, and consequently [Westerners] do not suffer from conflicts in their personalities," he wrote. But for Muslims, "our private and social lives are strongly influenced by the West . . . [while] our culture . . . belongs to a civilisation of a bygone era." Khatami said this "contradiction" was "the source of the aggravated crisis in the lives of most of us non-Westerners."[38]

At one point in our coffee shop chat, Khaled said he thought that Egyptian society "is far from Islamic thinking" because "society is divided in two. Half is taking exactly from the [Islamic] heritage and the other half is imitating the West. Each is doing it literally and both are imitating. And the authority in society is in the hands of those who imitate the West. So society is neither Islamic, nor Western, neither secular nor religious. There is some sort of disruption."

Khaled was articulating the sense, which I heard often from Egyptians, that something is out of whack in their country, that there is a disturbing lack, as Bishri would put it, of "national belonging." Cultural Islam, the desire for a more Islamically oriented national identity, is a response to this sentiment.

But as Khaled's experience suggests, the pull of two competing worlds remains strong. His clandestine stint as a radical Islamist was intense but short-lived. One day in 1989, only two years after joining Islamic Jihad, he received news that one of its jailed leaders had been beaten by prison guards. Khaled and some of his militant friends decided to take revenge by staging a bomb hoax and he was tasked to place the calls. He rang up the British embassy and the airport, claimed to represent a group named "Islamic Revenge" and announced that there was a bomb onboard the British Airways flight set to depart Cairo for London in half an hour. Although there was no bomb, the threat forced an evacuation and search of the plane, delaying its departure four hours.[39]

A few months later, Khaled was arrested at the gates of Cairo University, where he was then studying. He promptly confessed to his part in the hoax, which he now calls "a mistake" and something he did "just for propaganda." He was detained four months and released without charges. This was long enough for him to grow disillusioned with his Islamist compatriots, who came from several different militant factions. Khaled watched as they bickered endlessly over minor theological points, refused to pray or eat together, and called each other *kafir*, or infidel.

"This destroyed the idealistic image I had," recalled Khaled, who also began to doubt his radical beliefs. "I asked myself, 'Could someone follow an idea all his life and at the end find out he was not correct?' " This possibility, he added, "terrified me."

His release from prison, he said, precipitated "a psychological crisis. I was not able to live without believing in something. Meanwhile, I was not able to get rid of this status of doubt within me. I found myself outside everything, even religion. I stopped praying totally. I started smoking. I started listening to music but away from my family because I was afraid to face them with these new ideas I had."

Eventually, he graduated from university, married a fellow journalism student and started a family. He also landed a job with *Al Arabi*, the newspaper of the Nasserite Party, which carries the torch for the late Nasser's socialist ideas. Khaled said he doesn't believe in the party's ideology. In fact, no ideology really appeals to him.

"I'm disoriented because I've just got out of a trend which was very comfortable . . . guaranteeing happiness here and in the afterlife. I don't have an alternative ideology which is as attractive. . . . I don't have any more a holistic vision," he said. "It's a good thing to believe in something. Now I feel sorry because I have nothing to believe in."

Then this hip young Egyptian, who'd derived his rebel moniker of "Nasser Salah" from a legendary Muslim fighter, called to mind another warrior. But this one was a Westerner and he had entered Khaled's life the way so many heroes do nowadays—through the celluloid images of Hollywood.

"Have you seen the movie *Braveheart?*" Khaled asked, leaning forward in his chair. "William Wallace was a true believer. This belief moved him to face Britain and made him different from the nobles, who had nothing to believe in. Belief in itself creates a real hero. It's a beautiful feeling to be a hero."

We left the hotel and took a taxi to the Nasserite Party headquarters near Lazoghly Square. We walked past Nasser's large colored portrait in the entryway and went upstairs to Khaled's workstation, where I took his picture sitting at his computer. Then I left, heading for the square to hail a cab. Standing at the door, Khaled waved good-bye and then, with an impish grin, he shouted, "Remember me to Demi Moore!"

FAITH AND MODERNITY

11

New Thinking in Islam

"We need people who will practice ijtihad and can tell us, if Prophet Muhammad were living in a time like ours, what he would do."

— Khaled Salah Hassanein,
twenty-seven-year-old reporter in Egypt

"Our countries need to be modernized. There is a technological revolution. We need to be part of that. I don't think we have succeeded yet in combining our modernization with the indispensable part of our life, which is Islam."

— Dirgham,
twenty-seven-year-old teacher in Jordan

Cairo is no longer rocked by the bombs of Islamic Group insurgents. But it does reverberate with explosions of a different kind, ones that come from the mind. The perpetrators of these blasts are still on the loose. Middle-aged and law-abiding, they are far more interested in footnotes than fuses as they pose fundamental questions about their faith.

Take for instance portly, merry-eyed Hassan Hanafi.

"What is the *first* duty of a Muslim?" the Islamist philosopher asked a visitor to his air-conditioned Cairo study. "What's the *first* statement? What's the *first act* for a Muslim to be a Muslim?"

Startled by the pop quiz, I fumbled for an answer. "The first duty," I replied, summoning up Islam's basic tenet of faith, "is to say 'There is no God but Allah and Prophet Muhammad is His messenger.' "

"*You* are a fundamentalist!" Hanafi shot back, gleeful at snaring another student in his professorial trap. "This is the fundamentalist's answer. Now let me give you the philosopher's answer! The first duty of a Muslim, to be a Muslim, is thinking. . . . In Arabic, *awwali wajibat.*"

Hanafi, to borrow his phrase, is an "enlightened Islamist." He has spent decades thinking and writing about how to "restructure" Islam's intellectual and theological heritage so that it speaks to what he calls the "human predicament" of modern Muslims. Rationalism and reason, he insists, are essential to that restructuring.

"Why is thinking the first duty of a Muslim?" Hanafi continued. "Because to say 'There is no God but Allah,' you have to think. You have to know what that means. It's an act of consciousness. It's thinking. This is our Cartesianism. I think therefore I am."

Perplexed by such complicated thoughts, some sheikhs at Al Azhar University demanded that Hanafi be put on trial for undermining Islam. One called him a "raving atheist."

Then there's Nasr Hamid Abu Zaid. This detonator of intellectual explosives is short, chubby, and bushy-browed. As a Cairo University student, his curious, analytical intellect lapped up Hanafi's philosophical theories. But Abu Zaid's first love is language. For decades, he has applied modern techniques of literary criticism to writings about the Qur'an.

"The Qur'an was revealed, of course, by God," said Abu Zaid, sporting a wrinkled lavender T-shirt the day I visited his office at Cairo University. "But from the moment it was revealed from eternity in the Arabic language, it was a cultural and social phenomenon." In order then, to faithfully and completely comprehend Islam's universal message, one must understand the seventh-century cultural and linguistic environment of Prophet Muhammad, the Arabic-speaking human being to whom God revealed the Qur'an, Abu Zaid explained.

Underlying his scholarly work is the premise that people "need to differentiate between religion itself and human understanding of religion," he said. "The Qur'an," he added, "is divine as revelation and human as interpretation."

Abu Zaid also takes issue with those who restrict freedom in the name of Islam. "You are free to choose Islam and then you lose your freedom? I don't think God intended it this way," he said. "I don't think God is illogical and would say you're free until you choose Islam. Freedom is guaranteed by the simple fact that God created us free."

In 1995, an Egyptian court ruled that Abu Zaid's ideas about the Qur'an made him an apostate from Islam and therefore unfit to be married to a Muslim. It ordered him to divorce his wife. The couple was forced to flee their homeland so they could continue living together.

And what about erudite, courtly Mohamed Salim El Awa, the law pro-

fessor, attorney, and moderate Islamist with a penchant for smartly tailored suits and reasoned argument? He, too, has been pitching bomblets.

Awa has defended scores of Muslim Brothers before military tribunals,
among them Essam El Erian. His columns in *Al Shaab*, an Islamist newspaper, are widely read by Islamists and secularists alike. And his 1980 book
On the Political System of the Islamic State has been reprinted several times in
both Arabic and English. In it, Awa argues that Islam mandates "a government which takes its basic law from the Islamic *Shari'ah*, and which subjects the rest of its institutions and authorities to that law."[1]

Awa is grappling with the core dilemma for Egyptian Islamists: how to
construct an Islamic state based on *shari'a* that is also genuinely democratic. He has not yet perfected a workable model. But he is trying. During an
interview in his book-lined law office, he was dismissive of Islamists who say
there is "nothing new" in Islam. "If there is nothing new in Islam, then Islam
has no relation to our life," said Awa, peering over the top of tinted eyeglasses. "We should exert [ourselves] to get the answers, the new answers,
to new instances from the original Islamic sources. . . . And this is what I
mean by a new reading of the Qur'an."

The secular Egyptian government regards Awa with suspicion, as someone who challenges its official brand of Islam. Until recently, he was not
allowed to appear on state-run television. Even now, his ideas on an Islamic
state remain off-limits for the camera. Instead, he is allowed to talk about
"Islamic culture."[2]

Hanafi, "enlightened" Islamist philosopher.

Abu Zaid, secular Muslim linguist.

Awa, moderate Islamist attorney.

All three are part of an unprecedented intellectual and theological ferment that is roiling Islam not just in Egypt but around the world. As the
twenty-first century gets under way, more Muslims than ever before are
reexamining their faith in light of the political, economic, and intellectual
challenges of contemporary life. They are reshaping Islam for the next
millennium.[3]

This global undertaking is the fourth layer of Islam's ongoing revival.
It is a far more important enterprise for Islam's future than the headline-
grabbing events of Political Islam. For it holds out the promise of a new
Islamic theology as it plumbs the toughest questions: How should the
Qur'an be read? What is the proper relationship of religion and the state in
Muslim countries? What role, if any, should religious scholars have in
political governance? Who holds authority in Islam? What is the nature of
religious knowledge and how does it differ from religion itself? Should the

rules of Islamic jurisprudence be modified? Should *shari'a* be overhauled and can it be applied in a modern state? Is there such a thing as "Islamic secularism"? If intellectual freedom is a right, how far can a modern Muslim go in expressing doubts about his faith? Does critical analysis of long-held assumptions constitute apostasy? Who is to judge that?

Similar questions, of course, have riveted Muslim minds since Islam began in the seventh century. But in recent decades, the search for new answers has quickened. Today it is unfolding on a scale never before seen in Islamic history.

It is a quest propelled by a deep yearning among many Muslims for new thinking in Islam, which they deem essential for political reform, cultural vitality, and even the survival of their faith. "The most urgent problem facing us, the Muslims, is neither political nor economical, but a crisis of our thinking and learning process in relation to ourselves, Islam, Muslims and humanity at large," wrote Laith Kubba, an Iraqi-born Islamist thinker. "Without an objective, relative and rational Islamic discourse, our relationship to Islam will remain as that of a sentiment to the past or a mere slogan at present but it will not become an alternative towards a better future."[4]

The craving for new thinking has led to an explosion of *ijtihad*, the Islamic practice of "exerting one's utmost to understand." Bubbling up in universities, newsrooms, and Qur'anic study groups, *ijtihad* is recharging Islam as never before.

Ijtihad springs from the root word *jhd*, meaning to struggle, strive, or exert. Its provenance makes *ijtihad* a cousin to *jihad*, a word of many meanings, but known in the West mainly as "holy war" or "holy struggle." *Ijtihad* is the *intellectual* counterpart of *jihad*—the struggle to resolve a problem or reach a new understanding of some issue through serious reflection on Islamic teachings and scripture.[5]

Traditionally, *ijtihad* was a competence reserved to Islam's *ulama*, the religious scholars who for centuries have been looked to by Muslims to interpret their sacred scriptures. The *ulama* typically spent years committing the Qur'an and Sunna to memory and mastering Arabic grammar and *shari'a* rulings. But nowadays, Muslims with no classical theological training are claiming the right to do *ijtihad*. So great is the impulse for *ijtihad* that the word has taken on new meaning, often denoting any individual's effort to apply the moral message of Islam to contemporary problems guided by his or her own conscience, experience and knowledge. It is *ijtihad* in this more expansive meaning—a sort of grassroots, mass effort beyond the traditional *ulama* ranks—that is proliferating.

As they exercise *ijtihad*, these Muslims still consult the writings of influential *ulama* and *shari'a* experts from the past. But they do not regard the opinions of their intellectual forebears as sacrosanct or definitive, rejecting what one young Muslim called "hero-worship of past scholars." In addition, many Muslims are insisting that secular disciplines such as linguistics, history, science, and sociology are legitimate tools in their struggle to understand the divine message of their holy scriptures for modern times. This is what makes the contemporary wave of *ijtihad* so exciting: It is taking modernity into account.[6]

At its core, the exuberance for *ijtihad* is an ardent embrace of the plea to reject *taqlid*, or blind imitation of the past, that was made to Egypt's *ulama* by the nineteenth-century reformist thinker, Muhammad Abduh. If the revered masŧer were around today, he undoubtedly would be pleased to see reason and science being harnessed to revitalize Islam's ancient message. But he might be a tad alarmed to see how an expanding corps of *ijtihadistas* is poaching on the turf of his elite profession.

Indeed, some Islamic scholars complain that too many ordinary folk are offering the outcome of their own personal *ijtihad* as the one their community should adopt. This "phenomenon didn't lead to *ijtihad*," said Awa. "It led to factions . . . led by young people." Simply being able to read and write does not make one competent to do *ijtihad*, he explained. It is a task requiring "a deep knowledge of the Qur'an, the Sunna and past interpretations of those texts," Awa said, as well an understanding of the "needs and necessities" of one's community.

Awa has a legitimate point. In its formal, historical sense, *ijtihad* demands a recognized level of religious scholarship and personal integrity in its practitioners. Also, their conclusions require widespread community acceptance in order to become authoritative.[7] But in addition to what we might call this formal official "major" *ijtihad*, recent years have seen a groundswell of "minor" *ijtihad* by thousands of Muslims working in all fields, from lawyers to teachers to politicians to scientists. While they are not qualified to issue a formal religious opinion, or *fatwa*, their efforts to better comprehend their faith are influencing the Muslim communities in which they live.

Muslims describe what is happening today by saying that the "gates of *ijtihad* are opening."

But when did they close, and why?

From its start, Islam was a religion that encouraged believers to acquire knowledge. As one famous Islamic proverb states, Muslims were to "seek knowledge even unto China." This religious sanction for learning made Islam's earliest centuries intellectually vibrant. While Europeans were groping around in the Dark Ages, Muslims were making advances in medicine, mathematics, and astronomy. *Ilm*, or knowledge, was "the basic driving force of Islamic culture."[8]

Early Muslims valued empirical observation of the natural world as a path to knowledge. They saw no conflict between scientific learning and belief in God. They produced great science in part because all kinds of knowledge were held in esteem. As American Muslim author Imad-ad-Dean Ahmad noted, this early period of Islam was "an era of tolerance, of freedom, and of a deep love for the pursuit of knowledge. It was an era in which it was understood that *all* knowledge is religious knowledge. There is no sacred and no profane."[9]

It was, in other words, a golden age for *ijtihad.*

But early Islam's intellectual brilliance dimmed over the centuries. Political, economic, and social factors played roles in this decline. So did Islam's scholarly class of *ulama* and other intellectuals, who had gained prestige and power by aligning with political leaders. As the faith spread to far-flung lands, these Islamic authorities were troubled by the variety of popular devotions and local customs retained by ordinary people after converting to Islam. They also were suspicious of Muslim philosophers trying to understand God through metaphysical inquiries and rational thought, a pursuit they perceived as a threat to the divine message revealed in the Qur'an.

In response, the *ulama* sought to make Islam more uniform in thought and practice. At the same time, their approach to knowledge evolved. They became seized with the notion that religious knowledge was superior to natural science and philosophy. Gradually, the pursuit of learning was truncated into the pursuit of *religious* knowledge. In turn, religious knowledge increasingly became identified with expertise in one specific area, namely, Islamic law, or *shari'a*. As a result, *ijtihad*'s once expansive scope was narrowed and the *ulama* became its most legitimate practitioners, as opposed to the Muslim community as a whole.

Religious scholarship degenerated into rigid, legalistic elaborations on what had already been written. The spirit of the Qur'anic message became smothered in the letter of *shari'a* law. By the fifteenth century, the written corpus of legal rulings and Qur'anic interpretations already produced by the *ulama* came to be viewed as a complete system that required no updating. Everything essential that needed saying had been said. This gradual historical development culminated in an ever-widening consensus among leading *ulama* that "the gates of *ijtihad* had been closed."

With the collapse of early Islam's spirit of robust *ijtihad*, the long reign of *taqlid* set in. Advances in academic pursuits dwindled as *ijtihad* became confined to an elite of legal experts unsympathetic to innovation. "Muslim thought ossified," observed one writer. "Muslim culture lost its dynamism and degenerated, while the Muslim community was transformed from an open to a closed society."[10]

Muslims of course did not commit intellectual suicide when the "gates of *ijtihad*" were ostensibly padlocked. Individuals continued to pursue all types of knowledge in matters scientific and religious. Some modern scholars even contend that historians exaggerate the effect of "closing the gates of *ijtihad*." Still, most agree that Muslim lands of the Middle East after the fifteenth century were more discouraging than encouraging of independent, creative thinking. The pursuit of all kinds of knowledge through the *umma's* collective *ijtihad* was no longer the driving force of Muslim advancement. Many contemporary Muslims associate their scientific and technological backwardness with this historical shunning of *ijtihad*. "Political backwardness and scientific backwardness come from the same root," said author Ahmad. "It was falling away from *ijtihad*."[11]

Only with nineteenth-century reformist thinkers like Egypt's Abduh did the "closed gate" of *ijtihad* begin to crack open. Widening by fits and starts at first, today it is swinging open.

The reexamination of Islam is significant first of all because of its sweep, drawing in all social ranks and professions. Among its most avid enthusiasts are women, ones like Heba Raouf Ezzat, the Islamist writer and political scientist in Cairo. Ezzat has a special interest in promoting women's participation in politics but has had to fight what she considers outmoded thinking on women by other Islamists.

"God in the Qur'an never put restrictions on a woman in a ruling position," she wrote. "Contrary to what the traditional Muslim scholars . . . teach, a woman in a leading political position is not against God's system or against the Qur'an. It might be against the chauvinistic views of some men."

Ezzat believes that Islamists have not always dealt adequately with women's issues, sometimes leaving the impression that women are inferior to men. So she did her own *ijtihad*, finding Islamic texts on women not usually mentioned in current Islamic discourse. Assisted by these, she said, "I have been trying to develop an Islamic approach to women's issues."

Her arguments have a ring of legitimacy with other Islamists because they are bolstered by Islamic texts interpreted by the same rules that male scholars have long used. "I'm doing my *ijtihad* according to the same lines of the classic methodological rules of interpretation," Ezzat said wryly, "but, amazingly, reaching different conclusions."[12]

The tools now available to Muslims facilitate the contemporary interest in *ijtihad*. Just as Gutenberg's printing press helped spread the ideas of the Protestant Reformation, the Internet, e-mail, and jet travel are now giving

Muslims unprecedented access to knowledge of their religion and the world. A mere generation ago, *ulama* had to tap their memories or delve into thick, yellowed volumes to find relevant Qur'anic citations when asked for advice. Today, the Qur'an and commentaries on it are instantly accessed on CD-ROMs at the click of a mouse. Muslims can debate different interpretations of Qur'anic verses in digital chatrooms, exchange ideas with Muslims around the world, or even become authorities themselves, giving online advice to other Muslims. The Internet has allowed a thousand *ijtihads* to bloom.

The contemporary zest for *ijtihad* is also exceptional because it involves millions of Muslims living permanently in the West, a relatively new development in modern history. Turkish guest workers in Germany, second-generation Pakistanis in Britain, longtime Algerian immigrants in Paris, and recent Afghan and Iraqi refugees in the United States are all part of Islam's expanding presence in the West. Most of them regard Europe and North America as home and are raising children and grandchildren who will do likewise. All live in secular societies where religion and politics occupy separate compartments and their faith has no place of privilege, as it often does in their homelands. These experiences cannot but affect the conclusions they reach in their *ijtihad*.[13]

Muslims in the West also have greater freedom to debate the future of their faith. "Islam in America now is safer than in its lands of origin . . . where the impulse of the power structure is to control Islam and manipulate it for political use," said Muslim scholar Sulayman Nyang. "Here, Islam is free to be Islam." It is no surprise, then, that some of the most innovative thinking in Islam is coming from those who live in the West. While they have only a limited impact in their native lands for now, their ideas are affecting the future of Islam.[14]

Still, the expectation is not that this period of questioning and introspection will result in a uniform new understanding of Islam around the globe. Islam has always been a pluralistic, versatile faith with a diversity of views on how divine revelation should be understood and applied. *Shari'a*, for example, developed five different schools of thought. Moreover, those who sincerely exercise *ijtihad* can differ in their conclusions, as the stories of Awa, Hanafi, and Abu Zaid illustrate. The fruit of *ijtihad* depends on one's life experiences, knowledge of Islamic teachings, and sense of how Islamic values should be manifested in social and political life. Moreover, Muslims of all stripes—Islamists and secularists, liberals and conservatives—are all engaging in *ijtihad*. So there will be disagreements.

What is significant, however, is that all of them are stirring the pot of intellectual and theological inquiry that is now simmering on the stove.

"The sheer abundance of people actively seeking answers to religious questions," observed Richard Bulliet, an expert in the history of Islam, "affords a better augury of the future of the Islamic world than the specific teachings or political policies of particular religious leaders." And while "a new Islamic synthesis will be achieved" out of all this questioning, Bulliet adds, "the final shape of 'modern' Islam is still too distant to discern."[15]

ONE ISLAM, MANY VOICES

As *ijtihad* proliferates, the issue of *authority* in Islam becomes more insistent. Who speaks for Islam in any given community? How is religious authority recognized? Whose *ijtihad* should prevail? When the faith was new, Muslims accepted the Companions of Prophet Muhammad as authorities because of their close personal relationships with him. Later, when literacy was still the prerogative of an elite, the *ulama* were accepted as religious authorities, esteemed for their lifelong scholarship of the Qur'an and Sunna and ability to memorize large parts of these scriptures. They guided the faithful by issuing *fatawa* on questions of faith, morals, politics, commerce, and family matters. Each opinion, or *fatwa*, was based on the scholar's personal *ijtihad*. Although these rulings were taken seriously, they were never regarded as infallible or binding on all Muslims.

Traditionally, an individual scholar gained authority informally and gradually as the community came to accept his *fatawa* as reasonable and legitimate. "It is the general acceptance of people that gives authority to the scholar," Awa explained. If his *ijtihad* "meets the needs of people and their general acceptance, he gradually becomes an authority. When he mistakes their needs and necessities time after time, he loses authority."

Over the past century, this pattern of religious authority has badly frayed for a number of reasons. The refusal of establishment *ulama* to modernize their interpretations of Islam is one factor. The rise of secular-oriented nation-states also weakened the authority of *ulama* because those who sided with the state often lost credibility with the people. In addition, better-educated Muslims increasingly gained direct access to Islamic scriptures. Their broadened access to Islam's primary texts broke the *ulama*'s monopoly on interpretation. As a result, wrote Muslim technology expert and writer Ziauddin Sardar, *ulama* "are being confronted by nonprofessional theologians who can cite chapter and verse from the fundamental sources, undermining not just their arguments but also the very basis of their authority." This has eroded "the role of the *ulama* as human memory banks, and the power they command by virtue of that role."[16]

The *ulama* are still revered by Muslims, particularly those with little formal education in societies like Egypt that put a premium on tradition. But the *ulama* no longer enjoy the uncontested religious authority they once did. The upshot of all these changes is that at the beginning of the twenty-first century, Islamic authority has badly fragmented and competing *fatawa* are flying thick and fast.

Recognizing that consensus is essential for the cohesion of any society, moderate Islamists, joined by some secular-oriented Muslims, are demanding greater freedom to openly debate *everyone's ijtihad,* be it that of the *ulama,* students, political officials, orthodox Islamists, liberal Islamists, secular Muslims, or opposition figures. This public debate, they argue, would facilitate agreement on whose *ijtihad* is most acceptable within a particular community and who, therefore, speaks most authoritatively for Islam in that community.

The fracturing of Islamic authority has thus fostered a greater appreciation of the need for pluralism in religious matters. And because of the spider web connection between religion and politics, demands for more open debate on religious matters have reinforced calls for more democratic societies. If multiple interpretations of Islam's holy texts can be aired among Muslims, the argument goes, then so can multiple views of the national budget or the qualifications of individuals who want to be president.

"Anybody can make *ijtihad,*" said London-based Islamist writer Abdelwahab El Affendi. "The question is how to get this *ijtihad* accepted by other people; this is the problem. So to get it accepted, you need dialogue to make this *ijtihad* into a consensus, not a point of view of a certain individual. I think the way negotiations and dialogue should start is through the initiatives of democrats in each country."[17]

A Long Journey Just Begun

Some have compared this period of intellectual ferment in Islam to the Protestant Reformation in Christianity. The comparison is inexact. Europe's sixteenth-century Christendom was dominated by the Roman Catholic Church, a hierarchical, centralized institution exercising both spiritual and political power. Islam has no such institution. There are, however, similarities in the two periods.

Just as ecclesiastical abuses and corruption impelled Martin Luther to nail his 95 Theses to Wittenberg's cathedral door, disillusionment with government and religious authorities in the Middle East is helping fuel a reexamination of Islam there. Egyptians are still vexed by questions like those that once plagued Abduh: If we possess the "final, perfect revelation" in Islam, why do we depend on Western foreign aid? Why did we need

American military forces to push Iraq out of Kuwait? Why don't our universities produce cutting-edge scientific research? Why am I poor? Why am I tortured in prison?

Questions like these have driven many Muslims into Political Islam. But they also are kindling wood for *ijtihad* and the impetus for new thinking in Islam.[18]

The theological questioning that is percolating through Islam today is also likely to have long-term consequences for the Muslim world, just as the Protestant Reformation did for the West. As Muslims parse their Islamic heritage for its essential, universal truths in order to understand the meaning of God's revelation for modern times, they are resurrecting something they lost when the gates of *ijtihad* closed down. They are reviving what one Muslim author described as "the continuous interpretative relationship" with their sacred scripture.[19]

Restoring that "interpretive relationship" is a key to many doors. Individuals who revitalize their faith through *ijtihad* unlock their own spiritual powers and take responsibility for their lives. When this occurs on a large scale, new political and cultural attitudes emerge and intellectual creativity blossoms. These long-term effects are why the current devotion to *ijtihad* is likely to be the most important and enduring aspect of Islam's contemporary revival.

But Muslims are only at the beginning of their latest communal journey. Decades of *ijtihad* lie ahead before "modern-friendly" *ijtihad* achieves critical mass. Along the way, there is likely to be messiness, experimentation, and discombobulations. Some Muslims will distort the process of *ijtihad*, producing warped versions of their faith for personal and political ends. Osama Bin Laden comes to mind. And in many Muslim countries, including Egypt, the winds of orthodoxy still blow strong. Resistance to new thinking in Islam comes from several quarters. Authoritarian governments restrict public debate and tradition-bound religious establishments, allied to the state, reject new interpretations of Islamic scriptures. Political opportunists who prefer religious slogans to genuine reform are another barrier. As are orthodox Islamists who read the Qur'an in a literal way and maintain that theirs is the "correct" version of Islam and all others heretical. Finally, extremists threaten new thinkers in Islam with violence.

These conservative forces are likely to remain powerful for some time to come. And in a world shaken by terrorism in the name of Islam, it is often difficult to notice, never mind heed, those working to modernize their faith with ideas instead of debasing it with bombs. Like a giant forest fire, terrorists easily draw the most attention. Closer scrutiny is required to see the stubbly mushrooms of new thinking sprouting all over the forest floor.

Even then, these sprouts are imperiled by those who ignore Hanafi's admonition that a Muslim's first duty is to think.

No one better illustrates this predicament than Abu Zaid.

I*JTIHAD* OR APOSTASY?

"Abu Zaid is demolishing the temple."
—Iraqi journalist SALAH NASRAWI

"No, no! I don't agree. I'm cleaning the temple!"
—NASR HAMID ABU ZAID

In the spring of 1993, Abu Zaid was just shy of fifty and living with his wife, Ebtehal Younes, in Sixth of October City, a state-planned community south of the Egyptian capital. The two had met at Cairo University and were attracted by a mutual love of scholarship. He taught Arabic and Younes, the daughter of an Egyptian diplomat, lectured on French civilization and Spanish art history. He was roly-poly. She was razor-thin. Younes, then in her mid-thirties, also had a steely will and a dagger-sharp tongue. It was she who discovered, quite by accident, the happily married couple's impending divorce.

"I was in the office of a friend of mine and there was a magazine," she told me. "I opened it and I read it."

"It" was an article saying that a group of Islamists had asked a local court to order Abu Zaid to divorce his wife. Their reason? That his scholarly writings denied the divine status of the Qur'an. According to the Islamists, this made him an apostate from Islam and as such, he could not be married to a Muslim woman because *shari'a* forbids such alliances.

Younes was infuriated. "They say they are defending God's right. I don't know if they have permission from God for this," she snapped. "They said an apostate is like a dead man and I can't be married to a dead man." Furthermore, they piled insult on injury by treating her "like a minor," she added tartly. "They want to decide for me. Thank you very much but no, I am not sixteen years old."[20]

Abu Zaid was astonished that strangers could challenge his marriage in court. But he had no doubt about the origins of the lawsuit. It had everything to do with his ideas on interpreting the Qur'an.

Abu Zaid was born in Kahafa, a village near the Nile delta town of Tanta about sixty miles north of Cairo. As a boy, he studied the Qur'an at the local mosque school. But he "learned to love the Prophet as a human being," he recalled, "from the stories my father told me." When he was four-

teen, his father, who ran a small grocery shop, died. In order to help his wid-
owed mother support her seven children, Abu Zaid switched to a vocational
school to learn a trade and worked as a wireless technician for more than a
decade. He never lost his ambition to go to college.

When he finally was admitted to Cairo University at the age of twenty-
five, "I walked onto the campus with tears in my eyes," he said. "The university for me was . . . a dream." Tapping the wireless by night and hitting
the books by day, he graduated in 1972 and got a job teaching Arabic at his
alma mater. In the late 1970s, he spent two years on a fellowship at the University of Pennsylvania. Returning to Cairo University, he got his doctorate in 1981, and six years later became associate professor of Arabic.

As he waded through early Islamic writings during his postgraduate
studies, Abu Zaid became fascinated with the pivotal role of the Qur'an in
Arab-Muslim intellectual history. "I became preoccupied with the idea
that interpretation of Qur'anic texts was, within Arab culture, the base
upon which any idea had to be founded," he said. Put another way, "any
intellectual concept had to find its legitimacy by virtue of not contradicting
the Qur'an," he explained. As a result, interpretation of the Qur'an became
"an integral part of the cognitive framework" of Middle Eastern Muslims.[21]

Abu Zaid also noticed how Qur'anic interpretations had been used as
tools of persuasion in early Islam's intellectual and political struggles and
how those varying interpretations had been influenced by the authors' cultural and linguistic environment as well as their social and political views.

All this did not mean that the Qur'an is not divine. "There is no question about the divinity of the Qur'an, that it comes from God," Abu Zaid
said. "But God spoke to man in human language and it has a history before
God spoke to man." Thus, Abu Zaid believes, both the divine and human
aspects of the Qur'an must be recognized.

He argues that one must approach the Qur'an like a detective, looking
within its text for signs of the linguistic, cultural, social, and political realities of the time in which it was written. Only by deciphering these contextual clues, he insists, can one comprehend how the first Muslims
understood the words of the Qur'an. And with this knowledge, one can then
better discern the profound spiritual meaning of the Qur'an that makes it
vital for every age.

"I say we must understand the words as Muslims in early times understood them, and only then can one begin interpreting," Abu Zaid said. "In
the end, the aim is to find the 'direction' of the Qur'an. Then, taking that
'direction' as guidance, one can do *ijtihad* for modern circumstances and
times."

If a document is read without its historical context, "it is very simple to put one's own opinion into it, to let the text say what one wants," he said. "Instead of studying the meaning from the inside, an opinion is forced upon it from the outside. This happens on a large scale and it is the reason why Islam always has been politically manipulated."

For example, on the matter of inheritance. Why does the Qur'an give a man twice as large a portion as a woman? Abu Zaid said the answer lies in "the Arab bedouin way of life before Islam" when women had no rights and a man could marry as many wives as he wanted. The Qur'an commanded that a man could not marry more than four women and that women should get a share of inheritance. Both teachings, he observed, were big improvements for women.

"The conclusion we should draw, if we want to be good Muslims at the present day," Abu Zaid said, "is to give women an equal portion [of inheritance with] men. We should not follow the literal meaning in the Qur'an, but the spirit of God's Word. . . . The same may be said about polygamy. If we now say that a man may only marry one wife then that remains in the spirit of the Qur'an."[22]

After years of examining ancient commentaries on the Qur'an, Abu Zaid switched to contemporary Islamist writing. In his 1992 book *A Critique of Religious Discourse*, he argued that just as early Islamic writers had sometimes interpreted the Qur'an to suit their political, social, or philosophical interests, so do certain Islamists today. He faulted them for holding on to outdated interpretations that ignore the Qur'an's linguistic and cultural context and that render the holy book archaic and irrelevant to modern times. He also contended that some Islamists manipulated Qur'anic interpretations to advance their own financial interests.[23]

His book appeared at a volatile time. The Islamist rebels and security police were lurching toward their national duel of violence. In addition, orthodox Islamists had acquired new prominence in public institutions, including the ruling National Democratic Party and university faculties. Many of these religious conservatives were sympathizers of the Muslim Brotherhood and some were members. They viewed Abu Zaid's emphasis on understanding the human context of the Qur'an as heresy and objected to his contention that political aims had shaped Qur'anic interpretations. This heretic, they decided, had to be stopped.

An opportunity to do this arrived in May 1992 when Abu Zaid requested promotion to full professor. He submitted *Critique* and several other writings to a faculty committee for review. Three peers were asked to evaluate his work.

Two reports came back favorable, including one from Mahmoud Mekki, Abu Zaid's former doctorate adviser. He called Abu Zaid's work a good example of *ijtihad*, writing that it demonstrated "progressive and enlightened thought based on an informed, comprehensive reading of the Islamic heritage."

Abu Zaid, Mekki continued, recognizes that religion "is fundamental to any project of revival, but only if religion is correctly understood and scientifically interpreted in such a way as to free it from superstition and preserve its inherent rationalism." He also praised his former student's forthrightness about the fact that "contemporary religious discourse is responsible to a large extent for the state of backwardness from which the Islamic world has suffered since an end was put to *ijtihad* and adherence to tradition became widespread."[24]

But the third peer review lambasted Abu Zaid's work as inept and irreligious. It was written by Abdel Sabour Shahine, a professor of linguistics at Cairo's Dar Al Ulum College. Shahine was active in Mubarak's ruling party as chairman of its religious committee. He was also a preacher during Friday services at Cairo's oldest mosque and a host of television and radio programs about Islam.

Insiders also knew that Shahine had been a consultant in the late 1980s to the Rayyan Investment Company. Rayyan had touted itself as an Islamic financial outfit, appealing to pious Muslims who believed that Islam forbids them to receive interest. It promised to pay them instead with Islamically sanctioned "dividends." Badly run, the firm went bankrupt, depriving thousands of Egyptians of their life savings. In his book, Abu Zaid cited Rayyan as an example of how some Islamists used religious discourse for ulterior motives and material gain. Shahine had not been pleased with the criticism.[25]

In his review of Abu Zaid's writings, which he described as "similar to atheism," Shahine was clearly more interested in religious orthodoxy than academic soundness. He wrote that he had found "doctrinal flaws" and "abominable disdain for the tenets of religion" in Abu Zaid's work. He also faulted Abu Zaid for rejecting "the categorisation of those of different faiths as infidels." In Shahine's view, Abu Zaid's textual analysis of the Qur'an had impugned Islam itself.[26]

Shahine's report had its intended effect. The faculty committee, by a 7–6 vote, denied Abu Zaid's promotion. Its deliberations were not public, but its members apparently wanted to duck an open clash with ultraconservatives like Shahine at a time of growing Islamist dissent and violence. Secularist professors vehemently protested the committee's vote but to no avail. It was endorsed by the Cairo University Council in March 1993. Most amazingly, the government-appointed rector of the university, a bastion of secular thought for decades, ratified the decision to deny Abu Zaid's promotion.[27]

Shahine was still not satisfied. From his pulpit at Amr Ibn Al 'Aas Mosque, he denounced Abu Zaid as an apostate in a Friday sermon. He and like-minded Islamists wanted to make an example of Abu Zaid in their battle against what they regarded as dangerous, secularist thinking. Only a formal judgment of apostasy would do. This was their goal when they filed the divorce petition in April 1993.

Their suit invoked an old Islamic legal concept known as *hisba*, which derives from the obligation of all Muslims to promote good and forbid evil. At one time, Islamic governments had an official, the *muhtasib*, who filed *hisba* cases against Muslims who were committing wrongs and thus disturbing the public order. But that state function gradually lapsed, and as most Muslim countries replaced *shari'a* with secular-based law codes, *hisba* cases became rare. By resurrecting the concept to justify their lawsuit against Abu Zaid, the Islamists were challenging the court to recognize the supremacy of *shari'a* over Egypt's Western-based legal code. *Hisba* was a convenient legal tool for them because it did not require that a plaintiff be directly affected by a defendant's alleged wrongdoing, as Western legal tradition requires. It was enough that the plaintiff be Muslim.

Islamist attorney Mohammed Samida Abdel Samad, one of the plaintiffs, explained that the petitioners had "no desire to separate Abu Zaid from his wife." But the suit was "the only legal avenue for us to prove that he is an atheist and to stop him from teaching apostasy to youth." Egypt's constitution, Abdel Samad noted, "protects the rights of members of all three religions: Christianity, Islam and Judaism. But it does not protect those who choose to leave their religion."[28]

As news of Shahine's sermon and the divorce action spread, Abu Zaid's reputation was blackened. "It took one week for my name to be cursed all over Egypt," he recalled. "Even in my village they were saying I was teaching heresies to the students. You can imagine the people in my village. My family was terrified. They came to me and said what is going on?"

Religious conservatives wasted no time demanding Abu Zaid's head. The *Islamic Banner*, a newspaper published by Mubarak's ruling political party, urged that the "heretic" be fired from his job and added that "execution" was a fitting penalty if he did not repent.[29]

Threats arrived in Abu Zaid's mail. "What idiot can think these thoughts of demolition!" read one anonymous note. "There is no discussion with you. The important thing is that within three days you emigrate from Egypt to any spot in the world far away from the Arab/Islamic world. Or else you will not live in a country you wanted to demolish. No matter how much the police tries to protect you, you will not get away."

A police guard was posted outside the besieged couple's apartment. Abu

Zaid considered resigning but Younes would not hear of it. "We first met in the university," she said, calling it "an integral part of our relationship."[30]

Hearings in the case plunged the tiny courtroom into pandemonium. At one session, the judges struggled to be heard as Abu Zaid's detractors and supporters screamed epithets and shook fists at one another, sometimes climbing up on tables and chairs. Policemen leaned against the door to keep out a throng of men in the corridor chanting anti-Islamist slogans. "This is a terrorism case," shouted one of Abu Zaid's lawyers. "We have nothing like the killing of apostates. . . . These people have their own version of the Qur'an."

Down the hallway, a publicity-hungry preacher and critic of Abu Zaid named Yousef Al Badri informed us journalists that Abu Zaid "should be charged with high treason" since his writings "resembled atheism" and sentenced to death unless he repented.

"He must say 'Everything I wrote is incorrect,' " Badri said. "Islam is not against ideas. But they must be respectable."

And who, I asked Badri, decides what is "respectable"?

"The judges," he replied.

But when the judges spoke in January 1994, they dismissed the suit, saying the plaintiffs had no legal standing to interfere with Abu Zaid's marriage. In effect, they rejected *hisba* as a legal principle in Egyptian courts.

Undeterred, the Islamists appealed.

Eighteen months later, a legal thunderclap stunned Egypt's secular-oriented elite.

On June 14, 1995, a panel of Cairo's Court of Appeals reversed the lower court, found Abu Zaid to be an apostate and ordered him to end his marriage to Younes. For the first time in modern Egypt, a couple was told to divorce because of the religious views held by one of the spouses.[31]

The panel was headed by Judge Farouk Abdel Alim, a graduate of Al Azhar who had worked for several years in Saudi Arabia, where he had imbibed its ultraorthodox version of Islam called Wahhabism. Abdel Alim and his fellow judges never questioned Abu Zaid, basing their judgment solely on his writings. Their ruling is a remarkable window into the mindset of orthodox Islamists.

It begins by excerpting a passage from Abu Zaid's 1992 book where he distinguishes between divine revelation and its human expression and argues that interpretations of the Qur'an should keep pace with human intellectual development.

The text [of the Qur'an], from the moment it descended over the Prophet, has been transformed from being a divine text to a human understanding because it has changed from revelation to utterance. . . . Since language develops with the development of society and culture, providing new ideas and developing its terminology to express more developed relations, then it is necessary and only natural to reinterpret texts in their original historical and social context, replacing them with more contemporary interpretations that are more humanistic and developed. . . . .Clinging to the literal meanings which culture has long transcended is considered a denial of development and insists on an image which history has long transcended.

In this context, Abu Zaid wrote that magic, jinns, and devils, as well as the image of God on a throne surrounded by angels were concepts "related to a particular time and age . . . in the development of human consciousness."

These excerpts, the judges said, showed that "the defendant denies the divinity of the Qur'an and emphasizes that it is a human text." He also "denies that God is King although this fact exists in many Qur'anic verses" and "denies the throne, the seat and the soldiers of God who are the angels." The defendant additionally "denies the existence of devils and makes their presence a merely psychological matter in the minds of the first Islamic believers and [he contends] that the Qur'an merely acquiesced in their understandings and culture."

Abu Zaid concluded, the judges wrote, "that the Qur'anic text represents a period in the minds of the Prophet and his people, and that there have been developments in minds and history, and the psychological imagery has now changed and has to be now understood according to people's current culture. As such, the defendant has denied God's affirmation that the Qur'an is the Truth and that what it contains is the truth."

The judges also attacked Abu Zaid's contention that some *shari'a* rulings are outdated because they arose from "the social reality during a specific historical period." He had cited rulings on inheritance, owning slave women and *jizya*, the poll tax non-Muslims once paid to Islamic governments. "It is not acceptable," Abu Zaid had written, "that *ijtihad* . . . should stop at the point where the divine revelation stopped, or else the idea of its applicability to all time and place will have been destroyed. . . ."

The judges belittled Abu Zaid's reasoning on these issues, and with obvious sarcasm noted that he "refuses stopping *ijtihad* at the divine revelation and . . . finds he must further develop it." The panel declared that owning slave women is allowed under certain conditions by "clear" Qur'anic verses "that we must follow" and that the verse authorizing the *jizya* tax "is not subject to discussion."

Summing up, the court found that Abu Zaid had "made fun of God's

Book" by denying angels and devils; called some Qur'anic verses myths; denied that the Qur'an is God's Word by "claiming that it is a human text and not a divine text"; refused to accept *shari'a* by calling for "contemporary meanings that are more humane and progressive . . . than the literal meanings," and denied that there were unchangeable Qur'anic verses, especially on "inheritance, women [and] slaves."

The judges also rejected the argument of Abu Zaid's lawyers that his writings were legitimate academic research. "Any researcher," they stated, "knows that [Islamic jurisprudence] has a basis and conditions for research, and if the researcher did not abide by . . . such principles, then his writing is no longer research." This is especially true when the research deals with "matters of belief and the Qur'anic fields of knowledge."

Moving to their conclusion, the judges wrote that most *shari'a* scholars agree that "anyone who trivializes the Qur'an" or calls anything in it "a lie" is guilty of apostasy. Abu Zaid's writings speak for themselves and since "there is no need to prove intentions," they wrote, "the defendant is an apostate." If he repents, they added, "then he has to remarry the wife should they so wish." But for now, the panel "announces the separation" of the couple.

Judge Abdel Alim and his fellow jurists did not stop there. They also declared Abu Zaid a threat to national security, saying that by attacking Islam, he had attacked "the state on which it is founded."[32]

The ruling was significant because it set a precedent for applying *shari'a* in Egyptian courtrooms. Abu Zaid's lawyers had argued that his case did not belong in a courtroom because the country's Western-modeled legal code has no provisions for determining apostasy. Such determinations can only be made, they contended, if a person makes his apostasy "clear beyond a shadow of a doubt" by "direct confession" or openly converting to another faith. As for what someone writes in books, "people's understanding and interpretations may differ, and the Holy Qur'an accepts such differences."

But their arguments fell on deaf ears. The appeals panel ignored Egypt's secular legal code and based its verdict on *shari'a*, where they wrote, "apostasy is a material action and a crime that is proven legally just like other crimes." Orthodox Islamists saw the verdict advancing their long struggle to have *shari'a* replace Egypt's secular code.[33]

For secular Egyptians the verdict was a threat to intellectual freedom and they mounted a full-throated protest against what one called "dark medieval nonsense." Rallying to Abu Zaid's defense, they lambasted the Islamists for "intellectual terrorism." Magazine editor Ghali Shukri protested that Egypt was "withdrawing to the back of the back."

"What will our country gain?" asked philosophy professor Fouad Zakariya. "Nothing—except that we shall become the laughingstock of the world." Why, he demanded, did Judge Abdel Alim not busy himself with more important national problems such as "the briberies that are prevalent in all corners of this state . . . instead of exercising his militancy in a field whose final impact does not exceed a single bedroom?"[34]

In his moment of triumph, an elated Shahine advised Abu Zaid to request a court hearing to announce "his repentance" because "if he is a true Muslim, he has to prove it. The only way . . . is to disassociate himself from the erroneous beliefs contained in his books." By claiming that "the Holy Qur'an is not in keeping with the spirit of the age," Abu Zaid had written "sheer lies," Shahine added. Obviously feeling vindicated, Shahine advocated a wider investigation of his ideological foes. "Any just court looking into [the works of] secularist intellectuals," he wrote, "will declare them all apostates."

At Al Azhar University, one official called the ruling "a shining landmark in the history of the Egyptian judiciary. Any other ruling would have been a violation of *shari'a*." Abu Zaid was wrong, Mohammad Abdelmoneim El Berri added, "to say that Islamic rulings should not be applied exactly as they were mentioned in the Qur'an [and] that we should bear in mind the current changes that occur on a daily basis. . . . His only aim was to attack Islam and claim that it has some weak points. If *shari'a* were applied, this man would have been killed."[35]

The Muslim Brotherhood took its usual straddle-the-fence stance and said little, reinforcing perceptions that the organization was quietly backing, perhaps even funding, the legal assault on Abu Zaid. Many old-guard Brothers certainly shared the conservative, literalist version of Islam promoted by Shahine & Co.

Finally, the extremist Islamic Jihad movement weighed in, declaring that Abu Zaid must die. "Based on our faith in God's law rather than man-made law, we affirm that the apostate ruling stems from Islamic law and whoever denies it or objects to it under false pretexts, such as freedom of expression or opinion, is an infidel and an apostate from Islam," the group asserted. "Based on this, it is legitimate to shed Nasr Abu Zaid's blood, whether anyone likes it or not."[36]

Abu Zaid and Younes, who flatly refused to divorce, now feared for their lives. Given the 1992 slaying of secular writer Farag Foda and 1994 stabbing of novelist Naguib Mahfouz, it was not an unreasonable fear. A few weeks after the court ruling, they fled their homeland for an indefinite sabbatical in the Netherlands, where Abu Zaid became professor of Islamic studies at Leiden University. Though his books were not officially banned in Egypt, they were pulled from the library shelves of his alma mater.

Still, the beleaguered scholar left Egypt with one victory in his pocket. Two weeks before the judges issued their decision, he was promoted to full professor. In an about-face, the university's Council declared that his "prodigious academic efforts demonstrate that he is a researcher well-rooted in his academic field, well-read in our Islamic intellectual traditions. He has not rested on the laurels of his in-depth knowledge of this field, but has taken a forthright, critical position . . . and has mastered the issues before him, investigating them by way of both traditional and modern methodologies. In sum, he is a free thinker aspiring only to the truth.

"If there is something urgent about his style," the Council added, "it stems from the urgency of the crisis which the contemporary Arab-Islamic World is witnessing and the necessity to honestly identify the ills of this world in order that an effective cure be found. Academic research should not be isolated from social problems."[37]

The Council had found its backbone. Unfortunately, it was a bit too late.

From the beginning, the government strived to ignore the Abu Zaid controversy. When publications of the ruling party labeled him a heretic, it said nothing. And its state-run media only briefly reported the 1995 appeals court ruling, "as if it were on some other planet of the universe," a frustrated Abu Zaid observed. "This is very dangerous. I know people are misled [and] confused about the whole matter. No one is explaining."[38]

The government appeared to fear that if it openly condemned Abu Zaid's persecution, it ran the risk of seeming to be anti-Islam. When it finally acted, it did so quietly and after the fact. First, it had parliament enact legislation to restrict the use of *hisba*. Henceforth, anyone who wants to sue someone for allegedly harming Islam must first get approval from the public prosecutor. In addition, plaintiffs have to be directly affected by the alleged offense. The government also deprived Shahine of his public soapboxes. He was barred from preaching at the mosque, removed as head of the ruling party's religious affairs committee, and ousted from his radio and television programs.[39]

What lingered most with Abu Zaid's supporters, however, was the dismal fact that no government official publicly rose to his defense. No official championed his right to do *ijtihad* without being labeled an apostate just because his conclusions challenged prevailing orthodoxy. As a result, those Egyptians seeking a more modern understanding of Islam through *ijtihad* were forced once again to watch their words. "The state is outbidding the religious groups and the religious groups are outbidding the State," wrote philosopher Hanafi. "And we, in the middle, are the sole losers."[40]

So, were Judge Abdel Alim and his fellow jurists on solid ground when they found Abu Zaid an apostate under *shari'a*?

Yes and no.

The Qur'an upholds freedom of conscience, declaring that there is "no compulsion" in religion and that apostasy is something punished in the afterlife. It does not state anywhere that apostates should be killed or divorced from their Muslim spouses.

However, some passages of the Sunna, the huge compendium of Islamic writings that includes the sayings of Prophet Muhammad, do prescribe death for unrepentant apostates. These texts have been cited for centuries by *ulama* to justify *shari'a* rulings for determining apostasy and its penalty. Needless to say, these *shari'a* provisions are not aggressively implemented in most Islamic countries. But their existence inhibits public debate on sensitive issues in Islam and creates an atmosphere of fear and danger for those who think critically. Not surprisingly, some contemporary Muslim scholars are urging that these texts on apostasy be subjected to *ijtihad* and reinterpreted in light of the modern world's recognition that freedom of religious conscience is a basic human right.[41]

Abu Zaid's experiences heightened secular Egyptians' suspicions of collusion between the violent rebels and the conservative Islamists who held senior positions in some of Egypt's public institutions. The court ruling, one secular group declared, was part of "a broader conspiracy" to spread "fear and terror amongst scholars, intellectuals and artists, aimed at coercing" the government into accepting demands for an Islamic state. The Islamists' "mouths have fairly watered," they added, "ever since they succeeded in infiltrating the different institutions of the State."[42]

It is certainly true that faxes of the Islamic Group rebels, the public sermons of Shahine and the religious decrees of Al Azhar University all drew from the same well of Islamic orthodoxy. And just as the climate of instability provoked by the Islamist insurgency emboldened Abu Zaid's adversaries to pounce on him, their spiteful rhetoric and incendiary apostasy accusation encouraged the rebels. Witness Islamic Jihad's quick announcement after the apostasy ruling that Abu Zaid should be executed.

But it is important to note that not all Islamists viewed Abu Zaid as an apostate and that some openly deplored the bushwhacking of his marriage. "If this is the first case in the history of the Egyptian judiciary separating a couple because of the defendant's thoughts, we look forward to it being the last time a man of opinion is taken to court before a wide public discussion on his ideas," wrote Islamist attorney Awa. Egyptians should hope, he added, that "the judiciary keeps [to] its original mission."

Awa was even more blunt in an interview, calling the ruling "one of the most stupid . . . in the modern history of Egypt." Although he disagreed "with hundreds" of Abu Zaid's statements, Awa said, he did not regard him as an apostate. "He has his own interpretation of the relation between divine revelation and human life and this interpretation doesn't [contain] apostasy ingredients," the attorney explained. "I see views which I don't accept and I'm ready to debate with him. . . . Islam is wide enough to accept different views."

Mohammed Emara, another Islamist intellectual, warned those who took Abu Zaid to court that "it is the Islamists who are going to lose if constraints are put on the freedom of expression. It is in the interest of Islamists and the Islamist movement that all should be allowed freedom of expression; in this way they will win over millions of people and only a few will go astray.

"I am asking," he added, "what will Islam gain from separating a married couple?"[43]

An Essential Theological Issue

Abu Zaid's work is part of an embryonic and controversial movement in Islam that extends beyond Egypt and has potentially revolutionary implications. To fully understand this movement and the hysterical response to Abu Zaid's ideas, it is necessary to look more closely at the Qur'an.

Sometimes called the "charter" of the Islamic community, the Qur'an is Muslims' most cherished book. They believe God revealed its contents to Prophet Muhammad over two decades beginning around 610 C.E. and continuing until his death in 632 C.E. When he related these revelations to family and friends, some memorized them. Others wrote them down. According to Islamic tradition, the written texts were assembled by the middle of the seventh century into one book of 114 chapters whose title, Qur'an, means "recitation" or "reading."[44]

For Muslims, the Qur'an is not Prophet Muhammad's recollection or interpretation of what God told him. Rather, it *is* the Word of God and, like God, divine and perfect. This is why Muslims often call the Qur'an a "miracle." They consider it divine in the same way that Christians consider Christ divine.

Some early Muslims approached the Qur'an differently. While they believed that it is God's Word, they did not regard it as divine and they adopted a more metaphorical reading of its text. This "rationalist" school of thought, known as Mu'tazilite, dominated Islamic theology for a time. But it was always controversial among Muslims, and eventually lost influence. Thereafter, for most of Islam's history, the dominant Muslim view has been that the Qur'an is God's literal Word and, like God, perfect.[45]

By contrast, most Christians and Jews accept that the narratives making up the Bible were authored by individual human beings with the help of divine inspiration. This explains why Christians and Jews widely accept biblical criticism, which involves applying literary, historical, cultural, linguistic, and archaeological knowledge to biblical texts in order to better comprehend their origins, biases, and contexts. In other words, secular disciplines are used as guides to understanding scripture.

Of course, some Christians and Jews reject biblical criticism because they regard the Bible in the same way that Muslims regard the Qur'an: as the infallible, literal Word of God. Despite their objections, however, biblical criticism has gone forward over the past three hundred years and significantly altered how both faiths view their scriptures. For the most part, it has not shaken their reverence for the Bible's message of salvation. Despite dissection by humans equipped with the scalpels of secular knowledge, the Bible retains its spiritual authority as divine revelation.

The Qur'an has not undergone similar scrutiny by Muslims. Because they believe it is authored by God, not humans, most Muslims have deemed it improper, even sacrilegious, to probe its historical and literary origins. Past attempts to do so were always fiercely beaten back.[46]

That has begun to change.

Notwithstanding Abu Zaid's unhappy saga, an increasing number of Muslims are raising what he once called the "devil question" of the nature of the Qur'an. They are taking up the distinction between the Qur'an as divine revelation and the Qur'an as human interpretation. These Muslims are saying that it is possible to believe the Qur'an is God's revealed Word and also slide its text under an academic microscope. More than ever, they are accepting that the Qur'an's linguistic history and cultural context can be studied without challenging what one Muslim called the "cognitive certainty" that God spoke to Prophet Muhammad.

Muslim scholars also are showing new appreciation for how faulty human memories may have affected the Qur'an's early oral transmission and how cultural and literary norms may have influenced those who wrote down what Prophet Muhammad told them. The new openness to studying the literary origins of the Qur'an got a boost when scholars began examining a cache of Qur'anic manuscripts discovered in a mosque in Yemen in 1972. They noticed that some of the Arabic parchments, which included fragments from some of the oldest ever Qur'ans, had small variations from the standard text of the Qur'an. These discrepancies challenge the dominant Muslim belief that their holy book first appeared exactly as it reads today. They suggest that the Qur'an's text evolved over time, that it has a linguistic history.

Qur'anic criticism is still in its infancy, embraced so far by only a minority of Muslim scholars. But it is one of the most exciting and important frontiers in Muslims' contemporary *ijtihad*. Its implications for Islamic theology are enormous because, as Abu Zaid said, how the Qur'anic text is understood is "an essential theological issue." Critical exegesis of the Qur'an is likely to lead to new interpretations of its message more in tune with contemporary times. When sacred writings—be they Christian, Jewish, or Islamic—are interpreted literally and without change, they become increasingly meaningless to new generations of faithful. But when writings are scrutinized through the lenses of culture, linguistics, and scientific knowledge, interpretations will vary to meet the spiritual, moral, and psychological needs of contemporary believers.[47]

Efforts at Qur'anic criticism could also transform how Muslims approach secular knowledge. Some scholars argue that a literal reading of the Qur'an has hindered Muslims from fully incorporating modernity's technoscientific mind-set. If the Qur'an is read literally, the scholars ask, how can Muslims reconcile contradictions between what it says and the knowledge derived from human reason and scientific observation? One only has to read Abu Zaid's apostasy verdict to see how a literalist reading of the Qur'an clashes with a modern outlook.[48]

One of the clearest signs that Muslims are interested in exploring a new approach to their Qur'an was the reception they gave to an eight-hundred-page tome called *The Book and the Qur'an: A Contemporary Interpretation*. Despite being banned in some Arab countries, the book by Muhammad Shahrur of Syria has been a best-seller in the Middle East since its 1990 publication.

Shahrur, a civil engineer by training who taught at the University of Damascus until his recent retirement, argued in his book that human understanding of the Qur'an is relative and changing and requires the continuous exercise of human reason. Muslims have a responsibility, he added, to interpret their holy book in light of modern secular knowledge. Shahrur has also criticized contemporary Islamic thought for not having an "objective scientific approach." The "fault of Muslims," he once said, "is that they have no modern theory of knowledge."[49]

Beyond its implications for Islamic intellectual life, the new interest in Qur'anic criticism harbors a long-term potential for revolutionary social and political change because it is fostering a new relationship between Muslims and their holy book. As they begin to read it with critical intelligence, they see through the myths, cultural prejudices, and literary devices imposed by humans on interpretations of the text. This allows them to better grasp the Qur'an's profound spiritual meaning. Rather than passive receivers of revelation, they become active interpreters of God's Word. Millions of such personal transformations among individual Muslims in the decades ahead will affect how they act collectively on that sacred message within their communities.[50]

Releasing the *Umma*

"The history of the Islamic state is this, that everyone was free to put his . . . own *ijtihad* and present it to the people. And the people followed whatever they wanted and left whatever they didn't like."

—Mohamed Salim El Awa

Mohamed Salim El Awa's law office is a quiet refuge from Cairo's noisy streets. Its shelves are filled with neat rows of bound legal volumes. A prayer rug with a Qur'anic verse hangs on the wall. A globe lamp dangles over Awa's glass-topped desk, softening the fluorescent glare from overhead lights. The place is spanking clean. Awa, who is in his sixties, keeps his curly gray hair short and is clean-shaven. He was wearing a pink, pinstriped shirt and paisley-patterned tie the day of my visit.

Back in the 1960s, Awa was fired from his job as a deputy public prosecutor because of his sympathies for the Muslim Brotherhood. He went overseas and enrolled at the University of London, where he got a doctorate in Islamic and Comparative Law. He taught Islamic law in Nigeria, Sudan, and Saudi Arabia and was a legal adviser to Islamic banks and represented top-flight Arab and Western corporations in international arbitration proceedings. In 1984, he returned home for good.

Awa said he counts himself among those who "devote their lives to study Islam and work for it." Like many Islamists, his education, professional experience, and travels have given him a familiarity with the West and its institutions. "We are still all committed to Islam and we are trying to put our efforts toward its revival," he said. "This is why we are seeing every day *ijtihad* all over the world."

He reads the Qur'an daily and "every time, I read it anew," he said. "I see how, in the light of modern life, in the light of what's happening today, how it can be applied."

Awa admits there are problems trying to reconcile Islamic precepts with the demands of a modern state. "He knows there is a problem squaring the circle," said Egyptian journalist Mohammed Sid Ahmed. This, along with his dignified, calm demeanor, explains why many secular Egyptians give Awa a hearing even though they reject his ideas for an Islamic state.

Awa is still sympathetic to the goals of the Muslim Brotherhood and has defended many of its members in court. But his *ijtihad* leads him to more moderate positions than those held by old-line Muslim Brothers and people like Shahine. As would be expected, however, Awa is more religiously conservative than Abu Zaid. A good illustration is inheritance. Whereas the secular linguistics professor emphasizes the Qur'an's "direction" on this matter, Awa more strictly interprets the Qur'anic injunctions that give sons a larger inheritance than daughters. "This is a Qur'anic rule" said Awa. "It's not going to be changed and we don't accept this to be changed."

However, in the best tradition of his profession, Awa the lawyer contended that "the so-called famous rule whereby a woman should take half of a man is not applicable in all cases." A sole surviving female child, for example, gets half her father's estate with the rest going to other relatives whatever their gender. "So there is no such thing as a golden rule for inheritance in Islam that a man takes double of the woman. Nothing like that."

Awa was still a young law professor at Saudi Arabia's King Saud University in Riyadh in the mid-1970s when he wrote *On the Political System of the Islamic State*. In it, he contended that the raison d'être of an Islamic state is to attain "Islamicity," which he defined as "obedience to the teachings of Islam in all its various aspects." An Islamic state's "fundamental goal" is "the establishment of faith. . . . Indeed, it is the justification for its existence and the intangible quality which distinguishes it from other states." While an Islamic state must also secure "the interests of the ruled," that is a secondary function.[51]

Islamic states can differ from one another in form depending on local situations, but they all must rest on the Islamic political values or "constitutional principles" contained in *shari'a* that are binding on all Muslims, Awa wrote. These principles include justice, liberty, equality, obedience, and *shura*, meaning consultation between ruler and ruled. *Shura* includes the right of the people, or the *umma*, to choose and question their rulers. In addition, Awa stressed, the *umma* is "required to remove a ruler who relinquishes *shura*."[52]

For Awa, the *umma* is not just Muslims but everyone living within the territorial boundaries of an Islamic state. In our conversation, he called the *umma* "the repository of sovereignty," and described it as "everyone and every faith living on the land." As for determining the *umma*'s wishes, Awa was clear. "I said it many times. I can see no way but voting. . . . The majority [of the *umma*] is not only made from believers but from the majority of voters. . . . Whether they be Christians, Jews, atheists, as long as they are [living] on the land, they form part of the *umma*."

Non-Muslims within the *umma* have political rights equal to Muslims with one exception: They cannot become head of state. Why? "Because the duty on the state to propagate [Islam] would be a burden on a non-Muslim," Awa explained. "It would put him in personal conflict between his own beliefs and the duty imposed on him as a head of state . . . so we just relieve him from this burden and keep it for Muslims."

An Islamic state should propagate Islam "by preaching, by education, by publishing books, by allowing for preachers," Awa explained. While "in modern times the duty of the state is only limited to the national boundaries," he added, individual Muslims still have a personal duty to spread Islam everywhere.

I asked Awa how a state whose main purpose is spreading Islam would not become intolerant of other faiths.

"The duty of the state to propagate the faith is not a duty of eliminating or eradicating other faiths," he replied. "It is a duty of protecting faith preachers, scholars, workers for Islam from being forbidden or barred from reaching the people. What is happening in modern states like Egypt," he continued, "is that groups like the Muslim Brotherhood, which are trying to propagate the ideas of applying *shari'a* and an Islamic state, are barred by all means from reaching the people. If this was an Islamic state, no one who claims to be calling for Islam or preaching Islam would be forbidden."

Awa cited the example of religious tolerance in Western countries. "In any European state, no faith is forbidden from reaching the people. It is completely left to the people," he said. "You have Jehovah's Witnesses, Mormons, Catholics, Protestants . . . each church has different little points from the other and they're all allowed to reach the people. Now this duty on the democratic state is the same duty on the Islamic state. . . . It is only left to the people to accept and follow the ideas of Muslim preachers whom they think are more in accordance with their original faith as expressed in the Qur'an and Sunna."

This was how it was in early Islam, Awa said, when "everyone was free to put his . . . own *ijtihad* and present it to the people. And the people followed whatever they wanted and left whatever they didn't like."

Awa clearly was talking about freedom to propagate Islam, not other faiths. I pressed him on the issue of tolerance for other faiths. He contended that a modern Islamic state would have "two guarantees" to keep it tolerant. "We have the popular guarantee, the people's guarantee, the majority would stand against [intolerance]," he said. "And we have the judiciary. . . . In an Islamic state, we should have an independent judiciary and free expression of ideas and views and freedom of speech, freedom of movement and so on and so forth."

But in his book, Awa wrote that freedom of opinion must be "restricted by one provision, that is, adherence to the boundaries of Islamic law." In exercising this freedom, "the view presented by Muslims should, therefore, not be a refutation of the religion or cause dissension in it, for this is against public order in the Islamic state. A holder of such opinion should be detained and may, under certain circumstances, be punished for it."[53]

So I asked Awa what an atheist's chances would be in an Islamic state. "He's not a Muslim if his *ijtihad* leads him to be an atheist," he responded. But he would still be "protected, provided that he does not preach atheism to people," he added. "Under an Islamic state, under Islamic theology, if someone becomes an atheist and keeps his belief to himself, nobody can touch him. But if he goes out and preaches atheism to people in an attempt to lead them out of their faith to his own idea of atheism, then he's forbidden to do that," Awa continued. "If he does not accept the orders to remain silent and keep his atheism to himself, then the government will take action against him as it is happening everywhere if someone is preaching anticonstitutional ideas," he said. A book by an atheist "should not be allowed . . . if it contains apostasy," he added. "No one is allowed to try and lead people outside of Islam to atheism or to any other religion."

Besides these limitations on freedom of opinion and speech, Awa's model of an Islamic state lacks clarity on the composition of the *umma*. Awa insisted in our conversation that it includes all residents, regardless of their religion. Anything else would be absurd in Egypt, which has millions of Christian citizens.

But in his book, Awa stated that the Muslim community, or *jama'ah*, "in its political association constitutes the state," which seemingly makes it, and not the *umma*, the essential body politic in an Islamic state. This begs questions: What is the relationship between the diverse, multifaith *umma* Awa spoke of in our conversation and the Muslim *jama'ah* described in his book? Which has priority in matters of governance?[54]

Another problem lies in his contention that an Islamic state's duty is to propagate Islam. But whose version of Islam would be officially propagated? Awa's? The Ghost's? Mubarak's? The Muslim Brotherhood's? Shahine's? Abu Zaid's? Al Azhar's? Like many Islamists, Awa appears to assume there would be little or no disagreement among Muslims once an Islamic state is established. But unlike some right-wing Islamists, he recognizes a need for pluralism. "There is no reason why political diversification or pluralism cannot be recognized and tolerated," in an Islamic state, which "incurs no reproach today by licensing political parties and permitting political pluralism," he wrote. The only caveat, he added, is that "these parties must abide by the values of Islam."

Awa's political theory is lean on details about the process and mechanisms of governing, especially for power-sharing and protecting minority rights. His book gives short shrift to the rights of the individual. *Shura* requires the ruler to consult with the *umma* or its representatives, but what happens when they disagree? And how exactly would the *umma* remove a ruler who, as Awa states, "relinquishes *shura*"?[55]

A younger generation of Islamists in Egypt has not been shy about facing such questions and refining the theory of an Islamic state. One example was the political program offered by Al Wasat, the group founded by breakaway Muslim Brothers in 1996. Like Awa, who acted as a mentor for the group, Wasat contended that the *umma* includes non-Muslims and is "the source of authority." Wasat founder Rafik Habib compared the *umma* to civil society in the West, describing it as a collection of "religious groups, professional groups, family groups or any groups" that share "the same culture, and values and aims."

Wasat believes that the *umma*, rather than the state, will be Egypt's "catalyst of progress," Habib said. In order for this to happen, the state's wide-ranging powers should be curtailed to allow the *umma* to organize professional associations, political parties, and civic groups that are not "under the power of the state by any means," he added. "We are talking about the release of the *umma*."[56]

At least in theory, Wasat was saying that civil society should take precedence over the state when it comes to political authority and responsibility. This is a different view from the one held by the Egyptian government, which rather than "releasing" the *umma*, of course, has been steadily tightening its grip over civic society.

Ezzat, the political scientist, also said she is revising her ideas on an Islamic state. "For the last hundred years we've been trying to Islamicize the nation-state," she said. "But I'm thinking now this was wrong because it led us to overemphasize law . . . as a tool of change. I think Islam is about a small state and large Islamic community. . . . What was wrong since the 1950s about the Islamic state paradigm was not the Islamic bit but the state bit.

"I don't say no to an Islamic state absolutely, I say no to the Islamic state in which most of the focus has been on law . . . through the application of a strict definition of *shari'a* as only a penal code," Ezzat added. "I want a small, powerful state more directed to security . . . while the real power is in the domain of the *umma*. It is what we could call governance of the civil society." Ezzat said she was even "reconsidering calling myself an Islamist" if that term means someone "using law as the main tool of authority and change and advocating a strong state apparatus. . . . I would be reluctant to identify myself with this view."[57]

The ideas of Wasat and Ezzat, with their echo of John Locke's concept of limited government, characterize contemporary political thinking among moderate Islamists. They also illustrate how moderate Islamists, through *ijti-*

had, are working toward an accommodation of Islam and the imperatives of modern democracy. They still have a long way to go and plenty of issues to resolve. It may be that a workable synthesis will only emerge from tooth-and-claw street politics rather than polite back-and-forth discussions at academic seminars. But the more that moderate Islamists refine their concepts of an Islamic state so it is truly democratic, the more they will threaten existing authoritarian states because they will have a hard-to-beat combination: Islam plus democracy.[58]

A reminder of that authoritarianism greeted me when I left Awa's office and got into my car. As I fastened my seat belt, my driver and good friend Mohamed Abdel Salam discreetly pointed out a young, bearded man leaning on a motorcycle. Like most Egyptians, Mohamed can smell an undercover security cop like a cat smells dead fish. Sure enough, as soon as we sped off, the man hopped his bike and began tailing us.

"But are you sure?" I asked Mohamed, pointing out that our pursuer had a beard. This was a time when young Egyptian men were diligently shaving every day so police wouldn't suspect them of being Islamist rebels.

Mohamed laughed. "Now, the police are all wearing beards," he explained, "so people won't suspect them of being policemen!"

Looking in the rearview mirror, Mohamed declared, "Okay, now I'll drive like in an American movie."

He pressed the pedal hard, leaving our hirsute escort in the dust.

RESHAPING THE PYRAMID

"Ijtihad means the new is coming out of the old . . . inventing the new from the old as the baby from the womb of its mother . . . changing through continuity."

—HASSAN HANAFI

Hassan Hanafi devotes his *ijtihad* to an endeavor beyond language and politics. The philosophy professor believes that Islam's spiritual message is destined for all humankind. But Muslims can effectively spread that message, he contends, only if they first reinterpret their Islamic heritage so that it facilitates, instead of impedes, human progress and freedom. With that aim in mind, Hanafi has undertaken a sweeping reinterpretation of Islamic philosophy and theology. Begun two decades ago, this work-in-progress is entitled "Heritage and Renewal." Through it, Hanafi hopes to liberate the Arab-Muslim intellectual heritage from the cloister to which it has been confined by Muslims who view their heritage as immutable and untouchable.

Hanafi's work poses a more fundamental question than the one most often asked by Westerners: "Are Islam and democracy compatible?"

The Egyptian philosopher instead raises the question: "Are Islam and liberalism compatible?"

Hanafi, a liberal Islamist, believes they are.[59]

"I would like to liberate minds before liberating the sociopolitical structure," he told me one warm spring evening in his Cairo home. "I want to make a movement of enlightenment. And then through the democratic process, Islam can come into power."

Now in his sixties, Hanafi has curly, graying hair and ample jowls. His eyes, shielded by thick glasses, have a permanent crinkle and his mouth a slight smile, as if he's always hearing an amusing story. Born in Cairo in 1935, he was one of six children in an artistically inclined family. His musician father played the trombone and Hanafi, in his youth, studied violin, which he still plays now and then. He was seventeen when Nasser and his fellow officers overthrew Egypt's monarchy and launched a revolutionary era of Arab nationalism and socialism. Like most of his teenage peers, Hanafi became an ardent Nasserite.

But he was also drawn to the Muslim Brotherhood's emphasis on Islam's cultural heritage and traditions and was an active member of the organization while attending Cairo University, even soliciting donations for families of imprisoned Brothers.

Still, Hanafi and the Brotherhood sometimes differed on what was properly Islamic. He recalled how he used to visit the organization's offices after lessons at Cairo's music conservatory, his violin under his arm.

"Once, one Brother said to me, 'Brother, don't you know this music is the voice of Satan?' " Hanafi related, a smile crossing his face.

"I said, 'No-o-o.' "

"'Don't you know this activity may distract you from praying?' "

"I said, 'No-o-o.' "

The differences between Hanafi and the Brotherhood went beyond music. When Iran nationalized British holdings in Iran's oil industry in 1951, teenager Hanafi was exhilarated by this display of Third World independence, particularly since Britain also had once been Egypt's colonial master. But his fellow Brothers, who were ardent anticommunists, were far less enthusiastic. They looked askance at the nationalization and referred to Iran's bold prime minister as "a bad Marxist."[60]

By the time he graduated from university, Hanafi had drifted away from the Brotherhood, but not from Islam. Setting off for Paris for postgraduate studies in 1956, he dutifully packed his prayer rug. For some years after, he recalled, he'd interrupt his studies at Islam's prescribed times for daily worship, lay out the small mat in the stacks of the Bibliotheque Nationale, and say his prayers. Ten years later, with a doctorate in Islamic jurisprudence and comparative religion from the Sorbonne, Hanafi returned home to teach medieval Christian thought and Islamic philosophy at his alma mater. He served as chairman of the philosophy department from 1989 to 1995 and helped found the Egyptian Philosophical Association. Temporary teaching assignments took him to Japan, Morocco, Germany, and the United States, where he spent four years at Philadelphia's Temple University in the 1970s. In 1999, the Iranian government honored him as its Muslim Thinker of the Year.

Like all good teachers, Hanafi reaches into the past to explain the present. In the last hundred or so years, he said, Egypt saw "three big philosophical trends." The first held that "nothing will change in reality without beginning by building a modern state." Its proponents took Europe's nineteenth-century liberal nationalist state as a model and stressed the importance of politics, a constitution, industrialization, and educational reform.

The second trend, Hanafi continued, held that "science and technology is the point of departure" and "that nothing will change in reality without beginning with natural science." Its enthusiasts insisted on adopting the West's scientific, secular worldview and complained that Egypt fell behind Europe "because we are still intermingling religion with politics, religion with the state."

The third trend, Hanafi said, "begins by one simple statement: Nothing will change in reality without change in our view of religion. Religion is the point of departure. A new understanding of religion is the prerequisite of any social change.

"I, as someone who is making *ijtihad,* which one should I choose? Religion as a point of departure? State and politics as the point of departure? Or science, technology, and secularism as the point of departure?" asked Hanafi.

"I chose the first one," he said.

The choice made Hanafi an Islamist.

For him, the premises of the two other trends are valid but insufficient by themselves to achieve lasting reform in Egypt. The most effective vessel for that, he believes, is a renewed Islam because for most Muslims, their faith remains the ultimate authority.[61]

"People are religious, the tradition is still lived, people are still moved by religion," he said. "If you hear a Muslim speaking anywhere what is his argumentation? If he would like to prove something to you what is his art of demonstration? He will say, 'God said, the Prophet said, the tradition said.' The tradition for him is a legitimizing device. Here I am not being an idealist or a traditionalist, I'm being very realistic.

"So I take from the mouths of the people their argument of authority. . . . I tell him that I'm with him on the premise that religion, tradition, is a value which has been inherited. But in what sense? Religion in the hand of the despot? Religion in the hand of the capitalist? Religion in the hand of the upper class? Or religion as the cry of the oppressed, as a liberating function, as a social function?"[62]

At the same time, Hanafi insists that rationalism and reason are essential. Islamic civilization atrophied, he believes, because Muslims did not embrace "the rational method which constitutes the frame[work] for a scientific view of the world. The unscientific character of our life is the result of the prevailing irrationalism."[63]

Hanafi wants to rectify that through his reinterpretation of Islam's intellectual heritage. The seeds of this project were planted during Hanafi's student years in Paris when, for the first time, he eyeballed the European civilization that had both burdened and besotted his people since Napoleon Bonaparte took Egypt in 1798. The experience forced him to reexamine his fundamental assumptions.

"When I was in France I had the idea of how can I be liberated, a free man, a free citizen, a free individual," he recalled. "What are my big impediments? What are the big walls of my prison?"

"I found myself cornered between three sides of a triangle," he said. "The first side was my [Islamic] heritage," which began to seem "archaic, obsolete, irrelevant. So I began asking how can I renew my tradition in order that I can feel that my soul is modern . . . because I felt my soul is living in the old days and my body is living in the twentieth century. And there was a huge discrepancy in time between body and soul.[64]

"The second wall of my cell was fascination with the West," he explained. "I did not want to get rid of one master to fall into the hands of another. How can I continue my liberation from the fossilized [Islamic] tradition without being fascinated by that attractive terminology of freedom, progress, reason, science, social contract . . . all the big themes of Western philosophy." In other words, if he rejected his own "fossilized" heritage, he did not want to end up captive to another as a completely Westernized, secular Muslim.

The third wall of Hanafi's cell was reality. "How can I understand it? How can I make a diagnostic of my time?"

Here then was Hanafi's three-sided "prison": an archaic Islamic past, a seductive Western future, and the problematic present. As he explored these questions in Paris, he realized that Islam was "much deeper" than he'd previously thought. "I hung my prayer rug on my wall as a decoration," he said. "I began to shy from ritualistic Islam to one that is modern, open."

Years later, he is still attempting to "reconstruct" the various components of Islam's intellectual legacy—its theology, philosophy, jurisprudence, and culture—in light of "my actual predicament, which is decolonization, liberation, unification, social justice, development, identity, mass mobilization. These are the big questions of my time."

Like many Egyptians who came of age under Nasser, Hanafi has never abandoned the populist, socialist ideals of his youth. He still uses "socialist-speak," referring, for example, to ordinary folks as "the masses." His vestigial socialism informs his political philosophy, which he calls the "Islamic Left." It is "a revolutionary Islamic ideology," he said, that combines "Islam and the Nasserist national project." Hanafi sees the religious values of his "Islamic Left" as scaffolding on which to build a movement of political liberalism, something he regards as "practically a myth" in contemporary Arab society.[65]

Something else Hanafi hopes to change is what he calls the "pyramidal" worldview of his fellow Arabs, which sees authority entrenched at the top, far from the reach of "the masses" at the bottom. "I'm Egyptian," he quipped. "I like pyramids very much." But the pyramid represents the "metaphysical structure of authoritarianism," he said. His hope is that his reinterpretation of Islam's heritage will shape "a more populist, a more egalitarian" Arab worldview.

Unlike the young radicals of Islamic Group or the orthodox Islamists who menaced Abu Zaid, Hanafi does not view Islam as a means to control others or attain short-term political goals. "I don't want to control, I'm not interested in power," he said. "I'm working on the long-range. They are working on the short-range. They would like to be the successors of Mubarak. For me, it's not in my thinking.

"I've passed the age of somebody telling me how to pray or that having a beard . . . is one of the Islamic symbols. These are battles which we have already won. I do not want to repeat them," Hanafi said. "For me, the essence of Islam is . . . solving the problems of social justice, of freedom, of development and dependency, of alienation and identity and . . . entering into the big challenges of the time. . . . The battles which everyone is afraid to enter."

Hanafi also approaches *ijtihad* differently from conservative Islamists. Those wedded to an unaltered Islamic tradition, he said, go looking for a Qur'anic verse to answer a problem. But he first looks at the world in which he lives, he explained, because *ijtihad* requires that you consider "your own time, your own life, your own people, your own society.

"For instance, in Cairo we are fourteen million people. We have a big problem of mass transportation. To solve this problem should I go to the

Qur'an? Or do I go directly to my own assessment, counting how many millions of cars there are and how many highways are needed? If you have five million cars, you cannot have two kilometers of highways. Science says this. Then I follow science, technology.

"If I go to the texts, picking a verse on mass transportation—provided I can find one—another man, let's say the Sultan of Brunei or King Fahd or Khomeini, will say, 'Mr. Hanafi, you are such a respectable professor of philosophy, but you picked the *wrong* verse. *Here* is a *better* verse.' They will begin fighting over verses!" Hanafi said. "And we will lose the poor fourteen million people waiting until scholars solve the problem of which verse will solve the problem of whether we should have underground or overground transportation!

"This is the big distinction," he added. "They begin by the text. I begin by reality."

Hanafi is the first to admit that his ideas reach a limited audience. His lengthy, dense books are not best-sellers and his "Islamic Left" is more theory than grassroots movement. It is also difficult for progressive Islamists like himself to defeat the biases of fellow Muslims. "The Islamists think we are disguised secularists and the secularists think we are disguised Islamists and the state thinks that we are communist Muslim Brothers," he said. "This is our deadlock."[66]

But Hanafi believes his ideas and those of other enlightened Islamists eventually will bear fruit. "History," he once wrote, "tells that ideas are the beginning of movement." And so the professor continues his work on "Heritage and Renewal," a project whose completion is still years away.

"A life's work?" his visitor asked.

"Maybe posthumous also," he chuckled.

A year after our conversation in Cairo, Hanafi was invited to lecture at Al Azhar University. Alarmed that this Islamist liberal might taint their citadel of orthodoxy, some conservative Azhar figures launched a scathing verbal attack on Hanafi, accusing him of undermining Islamic teachings. One critic alleged that he'd raised doubts about Prophet Muhammad's mystical Night Journey, when Muslims believe he briefly ascended into heaven from Jerusalem. In doing so, wrote critic Yahya Ismail, Hanafi had denied "the indisputable divine nature of the Qur'an in his writings," which previously "resulted in the emergence of an apostate like Nasr Hamid Abu Zaid." Hanafi is a "raving atheist," Ismail added, who had no right to lecture at "the bastion of Islam."

Ismail and his conservative colleagues demanded that Hanafi be put on trial for apostasy and his books removed from Cairo University. "He has a destructive plan against which the entire [Muslim] nation should be mobilized," Ismail wrote. "Every zealous Muslim must expose his intellectual project, reveal its hidden contents and remove it from the university."[67]

After the Abu Zaid controversy, there was no appetite for another apostasy trial in Egypt. But a couple of months after Ismail's screed was published, three men armed with swords and daggers were caught approaching Hanafi's house. According to Hanafi, the trio allegedly intended to execute him "in the name of God."

After that, a round-the-clock police guard was posted outside his home.

DIMMED BRILLIANCE

The verbal brickbats hurled at Hanafi came from an institution with a glorious past and a troubled present, which is a major problem for new thinking in Islam.

Al Azhar University, whose name means "The Brilliant," was once the Harvard of Egypt. For centuries after its founding in 970 C.E., its scholarship was renowned, rulers dared not ignore its decrees, and ordinary people revered it as their protector and teacher.

Those days are long gone. Egypt's government does not ask Al Azhar's counsel in its decision making. Islamists accuse the university of selling its soul to the secular state. Secularists see it as hopelessly reactionary. And what passes for theology at Al Azhar is far from cutting-edge. Behind its crumbling walls in central Cairo, *ijtihad* is suffocated in *taqlid* and a very traditional interpretation of Islam holds sway.

This predicament is largely of Al Azhar's own making. Fearful of losing their status as exclusive guardians of Egypt's Islamic heritage, the university's *ulama* resisted change as Egypt began developing into a modern national state two hundred years ago. Leader after Egyptian leader goaded Al Azhar's sheikhs to update their curriculum and modernize their interpretations of Islam's holy texts. But their calls went unheeded because, as one writer observed, "it has not been admitted that a divinely ordained system can be in need of reform."[68]

As a result, Al Azhar became increasingly isolated from Egypt's modernizing elite, whose secular political agenda undermined the religious institution. In the 1960s, Nasser delivered the coup de grace to Al Azhar's independence by turning the ancient citadel of Islamic learning into a government department. By doing so, he transformed its *ulama* into what one scholar called "marginalized state functionaries."[69]

Most of Azhar's senior officials would prefer Egypt to be an Islamic state ruled by *shari'a*. As a second-best option, they support the government's brand of "Official Islam," sometimes sarcastically called "Radio Islam" because of its high profile on the state-run media. "Official Islam" is tolerant, theologically traditional, and has little appetite for fighting social injustice. As state appointees, Al Azhar's senior officials can usually be counted on to bless government decisions, even controversial ones such as Egypt's 1979 peace treaty with Israel and its dispatch of troops to the U.S.-led war against Iraq in 1990–1991.

Even before Nasser made Al Azhar an appendage of the state, its authority had ebbed. For decades, educated laymen had challenged Al Azhar's jealously guarded monopoly over Islam's theological patrimony by offering their own interpretations of the Qur'an and Sunna. In recent years, the institution has faced competition from such players as Islamic Group, the Muslim Brotherhood, Wasat, secular Muslims, and independent Islamist intellectuals.

Resentful of the rivalry, Al Azhar is forever insisting that its version of Islam is the "correct" one and objects when others presume to present their own.[70] Yet even within Al Azhar itself, the "correct" version of Islam is disputed. In recent decades, growing numbers of professors, students, and preachers at the university have spurned "Official Islam" in favor of a more militant version of their faith, reflecting the rise of religious conservatism. These dissidents regard state control of Al Azhar as a dishonor to Islam and share the Islamist opposition's disdain for the government. Some are sympathetic to the Muslim Brotherhood. Others use the radical religious vocabulary of extremist organizations like Islamic Group.

The influence of these ultraconservatives has been evident in the university's intensified rhetoric against secularism and aggressive attempts to censor all books and films. It also has been visible in numerous *fatawa*, or religious rulings, contradicting official government policies. Among these edicts—not always approved by the school's top officials—were ones declaring that the genital mutilation of girls is an Islamic "duty," that Muslim women must cover their hair in public, that cosmetic surgery and tinted contact lens are immodest, that organ transplants and artificial birth control are immoral, that the government is duty-bound to execute unrepentant apostates, and that interest on loans is forbidden. Al Azhar also waged a high profile campaign against a 1994 international population conference in Cairo, charging that it condoned extramarital sex, homosexuality, and abortion.[71]

One of the most vocal dissident groups within the university was the Al Azhar Scholars Front, an association of ultraconservative faculty and alumni. Although not an official body, the Front often claimed to speak for Al Azhar. More than once, it publicly criticized positions taken by the university leader, Grand Sheikh Mohamed Sayed Tantawi, who was appointed by the government in 1996 because of his support for "Official Islam." Fed up with the Front's recalcitrance, Tantawi dissolved the organization in 1998. Nevertheless, the antigovernment sentiments of the Front are still found within Egypt's premier religious institution, indicating that the state has not totally succeeded in making Al Azhar its handmaiden.[72]

The Islamist rebellion in the 1990s put Al Azhar in a difficult situation. To some extent, it gave the university increased leverage with the government because, more than ever, the state needed Al Azhar's imprimatur to maintain its Islamic legitimacy with the people. Al Azhar, meanwhile, was mindful of rebel accusations that it was the lapdog of a secular government and sought to demonstrate its independence.

Al Azhar officials vigorously denounced the rebels' violence. Tantawi's predecessor once accused them of being false Muslims who "should be killed, or crucified, or have their hands and feet cut off."[73] However, Al Azhar's criticism could only go so far since its theological orientation was similar to the rebels. Both wanted Egypt to be an Islamic state under *shari'a*. In addition, the interpretation of *shari'a* that Al Azhar upheld decreed that women inherit less than their brothers, that alcohol is forbidden, that Christians should pay the *jizya* tax, that interest on loans is forbidden, and that unrepentant apostates should be killed. How, then, could Al Azhar challenge Islamic Group militants when they demanded enforcement of these rulings?

Many secular Egyptians complained that what they regarded as Al Azhar's inflexible orthodoxy provided intellectual cover for Islamist violence. For example, when two Islamic Group members stabbed Egyptian Nobel Laureate Naguib Mahfouz in the neck in 1994, they justified the attack by citing his 1959 novel *Children of the Alley*. Al Azhar regards the novel as blasphemous, which is why it is not sold openly in Egypt even though the rest of the world regards it as a masterpiece of Arab literature.

It was Farag Foda's murder, however, that vividly illustrated why many Egyptians felt Al Azhar was less an ally and more a tacit accomplice of the extremists. In June 1992, an informal group of conservative *ulama* petitioned the government to block Foda's plans to form a new political party because of its secular platform. The group included a dozen lecturers at Al Azhar's faculty of Islamic preaching and was led by one of them, Sheikh Abd Al Ghaffar Aziz.

Four days after Foda was murdered, Aziz published a two-hundred-page tract condemning his killing and saying the perpetrators should be punished. However, he went on to say that Foda's secular ideas clearly made him an apostate and therefore liable to the death penalty, though this punishment should only occur after he had a trial and an opportunity to recant. Aziz based his theological arguments on the same Islamic writers and *shari'a* rulings often cited by the radical Islamists, demonstrating that his version of Islam was not all that different from theirs.[74]

In the late 1990s, Al Azhar's Grand Sheikh Tantawi introduced curriculum changes that eliminated some religion courses and added others to give students wider knowledge and more proficiency with critical thinking. However, the university still follows a classical approach to *ijtihad.* This was clear in a visit I had with Tantawi. Seated in his large, semicircular office, bathed in fluorescent lights because its windows were shuttered, Al Azhar's most senior figure wore a long, brown robe and a red fez, its black tassel neatly tucked into a circular band of white cloth. The sheikh, who is in his sixties, had a pale, impassive face with eyelids that slowly fluttered up and down as he spoke. Cordial but not warm, he reminded me of a long-tenured professor who had concluded there was not much new to learn.

"We are with the side of the good *ijtihad* or the correct one and this cannot happen except in the hands of the specific scholars and *ulama* who are well-educated in all fields or branches of religion," he said. *Ijtihad* must comply with "the stable rules of *shari'a,*" he added, and it should not be applied to "whatever is known basically in the *shari'a*" but rather to "new things [faced by] the Islamic community, to give the opinion of Islam to the common people."[75]

In other words, the university's prevailing approach to *ijtihad* is one in which it is done by an elite of experts following traditional rules of Islamic jurisprudence. This approach limits the revision of *shari'a,* because it gives primacy to its sacred quality over changing social and political conditions.

Al Azhar's reluctance to adapt Islam's theological heritage helps explain why it is a bastion of rigid, deeply antisecular instruction rather than a vibrant center of modernizing Islamic theology. Its resistance to new thinking in Islam is troubling for Egypt's long-term future because it hampers the nation's intellectual creativity. It also makes Al Azhar incapable of providing inspiring religious leadership for thousands of frustrated young people, creating a spiritual void that is sometimes filled by radical Islamists.

Al Ahzar continues to be revered as a center of Islamic learning by many Muslims, who come from Asia and Africa to study there. But at home, its indifference to social justice, its unwillingness to criticize the government, and its refusal to shed an ossified, legalistic interpretation of Islamic teachings have made Al Azhar's prestige more historical than real. It is a crippled player in the struggle for Egypt's soul. One can only imagine the powerful contestant it would be if it became an engine of theological renewal in Islam. But given its historical resistance to change, that it is unlikely to happen. Such a renaissance is far more likely to come from people and forces far beyond Al Azhar's ancient walls.[76]

VOICES IN THE WEST

"The Muslim *Umma*'s chances of a better future are linked to the success of the modernisation movement in Islamic thinking. This requires a thorough review of Islamic heritage, and a re-establishment of this heritage in the spirit of the age."
—LAITH KUBBA, Washington, D.C.[77]

New thinking in Islam is taking shape among Muslims living in the West. Take for instance Abdelwahab El Affendi, a former Sudanese diplomat and journalist who heads a London-based project on democracy in the Muslim world. In his 1991 book *Who Needs an Islamic State?*, Affendi challenged prevailing assumptions about such a state, arguing that Muslims had erred by "camouflaging the key political questions as theological arguments." Traditional Islamist conceptions of a ruler as "a replacement of the Prophet . . . created confusion and unrealistic demands," he wrote, because such rulers were perceived as above criticism.

In Affendi's view, another error was believing that a state based on Islamic principles "is one which forces people to live according to Islam." This created a "totalitarian" vision of "a mighty state dragging an unwilling community along the path of virtue and obedience to the law," he wrote. For too many Islamists, he added, the citizen "is essentially someone who is deprived of the freedom to sin, even if there is not the freedom to be virtuous either. This was certainly not God's purpose when He created man and woman and endowed each with free will."[78]

The quest for a truly Islamic state, Affendi contended, "must start with the search for freedom for Muslims" and democracy. He suggested Islamists shift their focus from an Islamic state to "a state for the Muslims, or an Islamic political community" that is "a decentralized pluralistic association based primarily on choice rather than on coercion."[79]

As an Islamist, Affendi believes that *shari'a* must be the basis for Islamic governance because if a community rejects *shari'a*, "it is by definition not Islamic." But Affendi criticizes those who demand that *shari'a* be forcibly applied. "*Shari'a* can rule truly only when the community observing it perceives this as a liberating act, as the true fulfillment of the self and moral worth of the community and each individual within it," he wrote. "When only coercion underpins *shari'a*, it becomes hypocrisy."[80]

But even if implementing *shari'a* were by the people's choice, it still poses a quandary since many of its rulings conflict with democratic principles and widely accepted international norms in the areas like women's rights, equality between Muslim and non-Muslim citizens, and freedom of conscience.

Historically, Muslims have handled this dilemma in a variety of ways. Egypt, prodded by its British colonial masters, replaced *shari'a* with a Western-modeled legal code, shuffling the Islamic legal system into family courts that handle matters like divorce and inheritance disputes. Other countries, notably Sudan, Iran, and Afghanistan, enforced *shari'a* regardless of its adverse consequences on women and non-Muslims. A third option has been to gloss over, ignore, or explain away—in sometimes convoluted language—clashes between *shari'a* and international conventions.

In another example of Islam's theological renewal, some Muslim thinkers are proposing a way out of this dilemma. They are suggesting an overhaul of *shari'a* itself and of the rules governing how Islamic jurisprudence is practiced. One advocate of this approach is another native of Sudan, Abdullahi A. An-Na'im, a law professor at Emory University in Atlanta, Georgia. Na'im believes in the divine nature of the Qur'an as "the literal and final word of God," and recognizes that *shari'a* plays an important role in shaping individual Muslim behavior as well as government policies.

But in his book *Toward an Islamic Reformation*, Na'im contended that *shari'a* lacks an adequate legal framework for democracy because it "does not afford non-Muslim subjects of an Islamic state constitutional and legal equality with its Muslim citizens."[81]

To make *shari'a* workable in today's world, Na'im recommends reformulating its problematic rulings to reflect advances in human rights and constitutional norms. In order to accomplish this, he writes, Muslims must revise some long-held notions. They need to stop regarding *shari'a* as divine, which obscures the fact that it is "the product of *human interpretation* of" the Qur'an and Sunna. If Muslims recognize that "the public law of *Shari'a* is not really divine in the sense of being the direct and invariable will of God," Na'im wrote, they will not feel that it is heresy to revise it to fit the current historical context.[82]

Na'im also challenged the traditional way that most *ulama*, including those at Al Azhar, develop *shari'a* rulings. Calling for a "paradigm shift" in the practice of Islamic jurisprudence, he has urged *shari'a* scholars to abandon ancient conventions that restrict the scope of formal *ijtihad*. Under these conventions, for example, *ijtihad* is not used in matters considered long settled in Islamic jurisprudence or to interpret passages of the Qur'an and Sunna deemed to be unambiguously explicit.

"It is true that the modern proponents of *Shari'a* often speak of *ijtihad* as the answer to all the problems facing the modern application of *Shari'a*," he wrote. But doing *ijtihad* under conventional rules of Islamic jurisprudence is "inadequate," he feels, because many problematic *shari'a* rulings are based on explicit passages of the holy texts. Na'im believes Muslims should exercise *ijtihad* in all areas, "as long as the outcome of such *ijtihad* is consistent with the essential message of Islam."[83]

Na'im's proposals for reforming *shari'a*, which are considered controversial and, to orthodox Islamists, even heretical, are endorsed by only a small minority of Islamic scholars. But he believes they offer a better alternative to the two options now available to Muslim societies: either reject *shari'a* and proceed down a completely secular path, or implement it in its present form and defy international norms. Na'im's approach to *shari'a*, he wrote, allows "the development of alternative *Islamic* principles of public law for modern application."[84]

The contributions to new thinking in Islam being made by Muslims in the West are significant. But they certainly will not be adequate to resolve the tensions within the faith that exist in the Middle East. In Egypt, two hundred years after Napoleon Bonaparte brought Europe to the Nile, Islam and secularism co-exist in an edgy, de facto truce. Each side has its extremists. Militant secularists want a society that looks and acts like the West. Militant Islamists say secularism is equivalent to atheism and apostasy. The chasm is reflected in the language of those competing to control Egypt's future. "We are facing now a dilemma with two types of discourses," observed Hanafi. "The first one is the fundamentalist discourse. . . . It is a discourse which knows exactly how to speak to the people, using the language of religion, the tradition, piety, belief. . . . But it is a discourse which does not know what to speak about. What is the content of this discourse? Telling me to pray five times a day? I know this from my early kindergarten. Telling me the five pillars of Islam? I learned this from my kindergarten.

"The second discourse is the secular discourse," Hanafi added. "It's a discourse which knows very well what to speak about: freedom, social justice, progress, science, technology, planning, modernism. But it refers to liberalism, Marxism, socialism, nationalism, and all these 'isms.' And people don't know who is John Stuart Mills or who is Marx. And they wonder, 'Are these new Companions of the Prophet?' "

The unresolved standoff between Islam and secularism, which is also evident in other Arab countries, exacts a heavy toll. Intellectually, it hinders the pursuit of knowledge acquired solely through human reason and scientific observation. As a result, intellectual curiosity and a willingness to question assumptions take a backseat to conspiracy theories.[85] Politically, the standoff reinforces undemocratic political systems because secular-inclined political elites and tradition-minded ordinary people are tugging in different directions. Shortly after the 1991 Persian Gulf War, Cairo's *Al Ahram* newspaper published the results of a poll of nearly five thousand Arabs. Among Egyptians polled, 54.9 percent called for "real democracy" while 53 percent wanted immediate application of *shari'a*. These results not only show the deep division between secularists and Islamists but also underscore the urgency of reinterpreting *shari'a* so it is a complement to democracy, not its polar opposite.[86]

Neither hard-line Islamists nor hard-line secularists on their own will bring meaningful change to Egypt. Resolving the impasse will require a new discourse developed during a long period of *cooperative ijtihad* by both sides. This endeavor will surely involve new insights into *tawhid*, the theological concept that for centuries has led Muslims to see life holistically, as a continuum, with all of it subject only to God. How is *tawhid* to be understood in a twenty-first century world of diverse faiths, transnational economies, horizon-breaking advances in science and technology, grassroots demands for democratic institutions, and a widening gulf between rich and poor? *Ijtihad* on these questions no doubt will lead some Muslims to a new theological articulation of *tawhid*, which is the necessary prelude to a felicitous convergence of Islam and secularism.[87]

New thinking in Islam has begun to emerge in the Middle East but it will take time to mature and spread. In the meantime, there is need for Muslims who are unafraid of critical thinking.

"We are very few," said Hanafi, "and we must plant some time bombs in people's minds."[88]

PEOPLE OF
THE BOOK

12

We Were Here First

"Those who believe [in the Qur'an]. And those who follow the Jewish [scriptures], and the Christians . . . Any who believe in Allah and the Last Day and work righteousness, shall have their reward with their Lord on them shall be no fear, nor shall they grieve."

—QUR'AN 2:62

"This country is a palimpsest, in which the Bible is written over Herodotus, and the Koran over that."
—LUCIE DUFF GORDON, 1865[1]

"We pride ourselves on having unity between Christians and Muslims. All the Christians can do their rituals. They even broadcast their prayers in the open—with microphones! And this is rare in Egypt."
—ABDU ABDEL RAHMAN, MAYOR OF MUSHA,
A VILLAGE IN SOUTHERN EGYPT[2]

I met the ironer when he still was an emotional wreck. He was a tall, slender man who reckoned his age at "about forty." Until a few months earlier, he'd supported his wife and two children by pressing wrinkles from other people's clothes in a small rented room. Now, his wife and son were dead and his right arm ended in a stump three inches above where his wrist had been. It is the same wrist where millions of Egyptians like the ironer have tattooed a small, blue cross. The ironer had suffered these catastrophes because he is Christian.

He is from Tima, a town about 250 miles south of Cairo, and he asked not to be named. Sitting in a large, stuffed chair in the home of friend and wearing a galabia, he described what happened. His impassive face and flat voice registered his depression. A mob of young Muslims intent on avenging the murder of a local Muslim by a Christian went on a rampage in Tima. They set alight Christian-owned stores, pharmacies, and a church. Amid the mayhem, four men armed with butcher knives broke down the locked door of the ironer's second-floor apartment. They slashed his wife and eighteen-year-old son and as he held up his hands to protect himself, they severed his right arm. His daughter saved herself, the ironer said, by jumping from their balcony to another apartment. He spent two months in the hospital.

He didn't know the assailants personally but he called them "ordinary" Muslims as opposed to the Islamist rebels then terrorizing southern Egypt. "The problem is the ordinary Muslims," he said. "It happens all over the republic."

Why, I asked, had they picked on him?

"Only God knows," he answered. "But what did we do to deserve it?"[3]

About two hour's north of Tima by car in the hamlet of Manshiet Nasser, farmer Abdullah Massoud wondered the same thing. A hardy man in his fifties with a brown, weather-lined face and mustache, he wears his white turban tightly wound. Massoud invited me into his living room, which was as spartan as a monastery. There were wooden benches around three sides of the small cement-floored room. On the wall were four pictures of Jesus, a painting of St. George and an icon of the Blessed Virgin Mary.

"My kid was killed because of me," Massoud said, "because I refused to pay."

What Massoud declined to pay was a "tax" of about $166 to the local leader of Islamic Group. Running what was essentially an extortion racket, he was demanding a "tax" every time land changed hands in the hamlet. He'd also stopped Christians from holding wedding celebrations and ordered them to stay away from their fields. For a while, Christians in Manshiet Nasser shortened their Sunday Mass from two hours to twenty minutes because they feared being together in one place for very long.[4]

After Massoud refused to pay the tax, his son Badr Abdullah Massoud, an employee of the state forensic medicine department, was gunned down in the town of Assiut. The murderers then hacked his body with knives. One morning a few weeks later, the extremists who had been intimidating Manshiet Nasser's Christians for weeks, methodically shot thirteen of them to death. Victims of the May 1992 massacre included ten farmers and a child tending their fields, a doctor leaving his home for work, and an elementary school teacher giving a class.

"It's the first time ever something like this happened in Manshiet Nasser," said Massoud. "I'm asking God to calm down the times. We pray."

Massoud's prayer has been a common one among Egypt's Christians as they cope with Islam's revival—and particularly the rise of radical Islamist movements—in an overwhelmingly Muslim country. The violence that took place in Tima and Manshiet Nasser are not everyday occurrences for Christians in Egypt and most Muslims were revolted by the attacks, which they widely condemned. But the incidents spotlight the broad range of difficulties faced by Christians in recent years. To begin with, Islamist insurgents in the 1990s targeted Christians because of their faith, killing more than 120.[5] In addition, a more self-consciously Islamic society has brought increased anti-Christian bigotry that sometimes fuels Christian-Muslim street clashes. Growing religious conservatism has also fostered a widespread sentiment, nurtured by some Islamist activists, that Christianity is an inferior faith that must be kept in check. As a result, the government finds it difficult to reverse decades of discrimination that has severely limited the building of new churches and shrunk the Christian presence in many Egyptian institutions, including the army, police, and universities.

Across the Middle East, but especially in Egypt, Christians are anxiously pondering what Islam's new assertiveness means for them. In the region where their faith was born, are they destined to become an increasingly harassed minority enjoying, at best, second-class citizenship? What, they are asking, is their long-term future in societies where an ardor for Islam sometimes means diminished tolerance for their Christian faith?

Perhaps no other Arab country is as pivotal for the future of Middle Eastern Christians as Egypt. Its Christian population, most of whom belong to the indigenous Coptic Orthodox Church, is the largest in the Arab world. While the exact number is disputed, they are believed to make up from 6 to 10 percent of Egypt's nearly seventy million people.[6]

Egypt's role in early Christianity also gives the country special meaning to Christians around the world. Each year, thousands of tourists flock to Egyptian churches built on sites where tradition holds the Holy Family rested while in flight from Herod. Egypt is also where some of Christianity's earliest theological disputes were fought and its desert countryside gave birth to the West's Christian monastic tradition.

Egypt is also an important barometer of regional Muslim-Christian relations because here, more than in any other Arab country, members of the two faiths have lived in intimate proximity for centuries, sharing a common culture and racial background. Though many rural villages tend to be predominantly Muslim or Christian, there are no Christian ghettos in Egypt and the two groups live side by side in urban areas. Uncountable are the streets where two spindly spires rise within yards of each other—one the minaret of a mosque, the other a church steeple.

Foreigners have a hard time telling if an Egyptian is Christian or Muslim until they hear an unmistakably Christian name or spot the tiny cross tattooed on a wrist. Both groups believe in angels, use the same word— "Allah"—for God, and express with equal conviction that before the will of the Almighty, they are powerless. They both know that Prophet Muhammad had a child by a Coptic woman and both revere Mary as the mother of Jesus. Indeed, women of both faiths earnestly claimed in 1968 that they saw Mary appear in a Cairo church.[7]

Muslims and Christians eat the same foods and observe the same social customs, including the ancient Egyptian tradition of *mulids*, the popular street festivals honoring saints and other holy people. Despite the common assumption in the West that female genital mutilation is an Islamic practice, Muslim and Christian families alike observed the custom, which is now banned by the government. As for love of homeland and soccer, the two communities are indistinguishable. Unlike Christians in Lebanon, those in Egypt have never sought a share of political power based on their religious identity. Instead, they have always viewed themselves as an integrated part of the broader national polity, even rejecting the label "minority."

This shared cultural, racial, and political identity between the two communities is the wellspring of the Egyptian dogma of "national unity," an ideal fervently professed by government and religious leaders whenever Christian-Muslim violence shakes the peace. This dogma affirms that every citizen is Egyptian first, Muslim or Christian second. It is what once moved an Egyptian politician to declare that "Islam is my country, Christianity is my religion!"[8]

It is precisely this cultural kinship, religious coexistence, and national togetherness that has been strained by Islam's resurgence in recent decades. The increased emphasis on religion as a source of culture and identity and the challenge to Egypt's secular orientation, which are both integral parts of the Islamist trend, are threatening to undermine the shared national identity of Muslims and Christians in Egypt. "This is the biggest change now," lamented the prominent Coptic intellectual Milad Hanna. "Religious affiliation comes before nationalism."

ANCIENT ROOTS

It is Easter Sunday and St. Mark's Cathedral in the Abbasiyya district of Cairo is buzzing with excitement. The liturgy in the capital city's largest Coptic Orthodox church is over and crowds are straining to glimpse their bearded patriarch, Pope Shenouda III. Others are waiting in line to enter the basement crypt holding a relic of St. Mark. Out of respect, they take off their shoes before going inside. On the broad concrete plaza surrounding the church, which also serves as the patriarchal seat of the denomination, families sit in the sunshine and teenagers clown around, setting off firecrackers. A block away the capacious dome and soaring minarets of El Nour Mosque bask in the sunshine. President Mubarak sometimes prays here. He has not yet visited St. Mark's.

The Coptic Orthodox Church is the largest Christian denomination not only in Egypt but also in the Middle East. Its name is derived from the Arabic *qubt*, which in turn arose from the Greek *aiguptios*, meaning Egyptian. The church traces its origins to the missionary activity of the Apostle and gospel writer St. Mark. According to Coptic tradition, St. Mark came to Alexandria around 60 C.E. and converted the indigenous people, who then spread Christianity throughout the country and as far up the Nile as Ethiopia. In the middle of the fifth century, many of Egypt's Christians broke with their brethren in Rome and Constantinople in a theological dispute over how to understand Christ's human and divine natures.[9] The schism brought the Copts into conflict with the Byzantine imperial authorities then ruling Egypt. As a result, Copts were receptive to anyone who would rid them of Byzantine persecution.

In 641 C.E., barely a decade after Prophet Muhammad's death, an Arab warrior named Amr Ibn Al-'As rode out of Arabia, crossed the Sinai Desert, and entered Egypt with four thousand horsemen. With his conquest of the Nile Valley, Egypt slipped from Byzantine control into the rapidly expanding Muslim domain that would soon stretch from southern Spain to northern India. Slowly at first, but then steadily, Egyptian Copts converted and somewhere between the ninth and twelfth century Islam became the dominant faith of Egypt.[10] Arabic also replaced Coptic as the national language. Rooted in the ancient Egyptian language, Coptic is still used in the church's liturgy.

In the twelfth century, when Egyptian ruler Salah Al Din husbanded Muslim forces to retake Jerusalem from the Crusaders, Copts joined his campaign. Eight hundred years later, Copts were active in Egypt's independence movement, just as eager as Muslims to end British colonial rule in their country. The pro-independence movement, which became the Wafd Party, took as its symbol an Islamic crescent encircling a Christian cross. It also became the emblem of the dogma of "national unity," a central ingredient in the emerging political ideology of secular nationalism that prevailed in the 1920s and 1930s. In 1928, for example, a Copt was elected to the high-profile post of parliamentary speaker with no objections from Muslims.[11]

Today, it is hard to imagine any Egyptian political party choosing the crescent-and-cross icon or a Christian, no matter how talented, being elevated to such a position.

PEOPLE OF THE BOOK

Muslims believe that Islam was revealed by God to perfect the monotheistic expressions of Judaism and Christianity, whose followers had failed to fully adhere to God's revealed Word. Revering Abraham as the spiritual father of Jews, Christians, and Muslims, they see biblical figures such as Moses and Jesus as holy prophets who received divine revelations prior to God's final revelation to His last prophet, Muhammad. Though Muslims do not believe Jesus is God or the Son of God, they hold him in special esteem and the Qur'an recounts how he was born of a virgin and performed miracles. Mary, too, is accorded high status in Islam; the Qur'an's nineteenth chapter is named for her.

Islam's special relationship to Judaism and Christianity is laid out in the Qur'an, which calls adherents of these two religions "People of the Book" and commands Muslims to respect their beliefs. Thus, Christians and Jews were not pressured to convert, and when Islam spread outside of Arabia, they were given a special status as protected minorities, or *dhimmis*. They were allowed religious freedom provided they submitted to Muslim rule, observed some social restrictions, and paid a poll tax called *jizya*. For much of Islam's history, this arrangement made Jews and Christians second-class citizens in Muslim lands. But it afforded them personal security and religious freedom unheard of in medieval Christian Europe. Instances of forced conversions and persecution were rare.[12] The *jizya*, which was rarely rigorously applied in medieval Islamic societies, generally lapsed throughout the Islamic world during the nineteenth century.

Today, Islam's affinity with Judaism and Christianity, as embodied in the "People of the Book," is a powerful incentive to religious harmony and ecumenical dialogue. But this teaching and its corollary that Jews and Christians are "protected minorities" are not adequate foundations for contemporary political arrangements, given expectations of legal equality for all citizens in modern democratic states.

Yet some Islamists still use these concepts in their political discourse. In Egypt, the Muslim Brotherhood has been at pains to win over Copts and other Christians to the idea that an Islamic state under *shari'a* would not mean second-class citizenship for them. "Christians are our partners in the country and were brothers in the long struggle to liberate the nation," the Brotherhood said in a 1995 policy statement. "They enjoy all rights of citizenship, whether financial, psychological, civil or political. To care for and cooperate with them in every good cause is an Islamic obligation."[13]

However, the Brotherhood has not explained how Christians would enjoy equality in an Islamic state when *shari'a* ordains that they are a protected minority subject to legal restrictions. Likewise, Muslim Brothers and other Islamists have not come up with a realistic, practical explanation of how Christians would fit into the *umma*, which usually means the community of believers in Islam.

As a result, most Christians see the Brotherhood's program as one in which they would be subordinate to Muslims. Comments by the organization's Supreme Guide Mustafa Mashur have not helped matters. In 1997, Mashur told an Egyptian paper that he thought Copts should pay the long-abandoned poll tax. He went on to say that while "we do not mind having Christian members in the People's Assembly . . . the top officials, especially in the army, should be Muslims since we are a Muslim country." This is necessary, Mashur explained, because "when a Christian country attacks the Muslim country and the army has Christian elements, they can facilitate our defeat by the enemy."[14]

More troubling for Christians, however, is the rise in recent years of an extremist, intolerant version of Islam that displaces the "People of the Book" tradition altogether and preaches that Christians are infidels whose faith is a danger to Islam. Rather than spiritual companions of Muslims in the Abrahamic tradition, Christians in this interpretation of Islam are seen as foot soldiers of a hostile West. They provoke sectarian strife so Western powers can intervene in Egypt on the pretext of protecting fellow Christians. And like Jews and "pagan" Muslims who reject applying *shari'a*, they are an obstacle to establishing an Islamic state in Egypt. As such, the growth of Christianity must be stopped. It is in this context that the building of new churches and the repair of old ones are seen by some Muslims as provocative and subversive.

Radical Islamists who preach this anti-Christian outlook typically use "Crusader" to refer to the West, playing on the deep and widely felt resentment about the "holy wars" waged by European Christians against Muslims in the eleventh and twelfth centuries. Thus, Osama Bin Laden named his international network the "World Islamic Front for Jihad Against Jews and

Crusaders." And Bin Laden's senior aide, Ayman Zawahiri, an Egyptian, wrote in his autobiography that he wanted the "Islamic nation" to know "how the new crusaders hate Muslims."[15]

This radical Islamist ideology, which turns the "People of the Book" tradition on its head, is rejected by the majority of Muslims. But a minority in Egypt adopted these anti-Christian ideas with destructive results during the insurgency of the 1990s. Islamic Group leader Sheikh Omar Abdel Rahman called Christians "cunning and deceitful" and told his followers that it was acceptable to rob Christian jewelers because they financially supported their church, which is "inimical to Islam."[16]

During its violent campaign, Islamic Group used anti-Christian propaganda to provoke attacks by Muslims on Christians, such as the ones that wracked Minya province for two days in early 1990. By the time I arrived in Minya, an ancient center of the Coptic faith about 150 miles south of Cairo, five churches, two charity organizations, and thirty-eight mostly Christian-owned businesses had been torched. Witnesses said the destruction was carried out by gangs of young Muslims wielding iron bars and Molotov cocktails and shouting "God is Great!" A Catholic nun said that during the melee, she was spat at by one youth and called a prostitute by another.

In the village of Abu Qurqas, a shaken Khalil Abadere Abdel Malek showed me around the scorched chapel where he was the custodian. The floors were littered with broken glass and altar vessels. "I've never seen anything like this," he said.

Residents recounted how a local imam had been heaping abuse on Christians in his Friday sermons for some time. Days before the rioting, a handwritten pamphlet signed by Islamic Group was slipped under the doors of Muslim homes. It objected to a health-care center for poor women recently opened by two private charities, one Christian, the other Muslim.

"Are we living in a Muslim society," the pamphlet asked, "or are we living in a Christian empire, whose leaders are the sons of Crusaders?" It accused Minya's Muslim governor of abetting a Christian conspiracy to control Muslims.

This orchestrated mob action was an early indicator of the even greater anti-Christian violence to come as Islamic Group's insurgency went into high gear. Over the next few years, the rebels deliberately targeted Christians, including priests and church guards. The 1992 massacre at Manshiet Nasser was one of the worst incidents. Five years later, three masked terrorists entered St. George Church in Abu Qurqas and shot dead eight Copts at a weekly youth group meeting. As the attackers fled, they gunned down a Christian farmer watering his fields.

The rebels' anti-Christian violence was most intense in the southern governorates of Assiut, Minya, and Qena, where Copts comprise between 30 to 40 percent of the population, a much larger Christian presence than elsewhere in the country. These provinces also were Islamic Group's power base, home to most of its militants.

While the attacks grew out of the movement's ideology, which demonized Christians, they had a political rationale, too. Like attacks on foreign tourists, anti-Christian violence was meant to show that the government was weak and ineffectual. The attacks "are a means to disturb the security of the towns," said Amin Fahim, then head of a private Catholic educational organization in Minya.[17]

Unlike tourists, however, Copts had no way to escape the violence, and many of them came to see the extremists' attacks as a campaign of deliberate intimidation. It is meant, said Fahim, "to encourage Christians to become Muslim or to emigrate. If I feel myself a stranger in my own country, I cannot stand that for long. And if I stay, I am demoralized."

Some Copts were embittered by feelings of being unwanted in what they consider their ancestral homeland. I remember asking a Christian cabdriver in Minya how he felt living among Muslims. "We were here first," he replied angrily. "They came in historically to protect the Christians but they made it an Islamic state. We have become the strangers."

The government always forcefully condemned the insurgents' anti-Christian violence as an affront to Egypt's "national unity." But Copts often complained that the government had been slow to take the insurgents' attacks on them seriously, and only confronted Islamic Group head-on after it began attacking foreigners. Before the massacre in Manshiet Nasser, for example, extremists had been harassing Christians there for years, according to a Cairo-based human rights group.[18]

Occasionally, the insurgents' hostility toward Christians led to unusual situations. Naim Labib, a Christian human rights attorney in the southern Egyptian town of Aswan once told me how years before the insurgency started, he had joined a team of Muslim lawyers to defend Islamic Group's spiritual leader Sheikh Abdel Rahman after one of his many arrests. "He met me and was happy that there was a Christian on his defense team," Labib recalled. "He asked me if Pope Shenouda had permitted me to defend him. I told him . . . that as a Christian I must ask for the freedom of everybody.

"But after this, he ordered his people to burn some churches and kill Christian gold store owners," Labib sighed. "They don't recognize the right of the Copts to live peacefully in Egypt."[19]

Say "Hello" Instead of "Peace"

As frightening and disturbing as the rebels' anti-Christian violence was, it was the work of a minority. Many Christians are more concerned about what they see as a broader trend of less tolerance for Christians in society as a whole. In interviews, they described, sometimes painfully, how their Muslim neighbors seemed to view them less kindly than in the past.

Sitting in the cool shadows of his rectory's drawing room, a young Catholic priest born in Minya, asking not to be named, related the changes in personal terms. "When I was a kid, relations were very good," he said. "I remember my mother was very good friends with many Muslim women. . . . There was a big sense of togetherness. Trade, agriculture, everything was done together."

But in the 1970s, he added, "relations took on a new tone" and "there was a self-consciousness about being Christian. Christians felt things had changed. The problem is, it's instilled in children in schools and in mosques. The children now, when they see a priest, they insult him. Many times, it happens to me. A child says, 'You're an infidel, and I'm going to pray for you to become a Muslim.' "[20]

Sometimes it was small things that made Christians realize that Muslims were looking at them in a new, discomforting way. Shadi George, a Christian physician in Assiut, recalled his shock when a Muslim surgeon, suiting up to operate on a Christian woman lying before him, began berating her faith, asking, "Why don't you fast? Why do you eat pork?"[21]

"The root of the hatred is . . . in the hearts of people. It needs treatment," added George, sitting in his clinic beneath a picture of Christ kneeling in the Garden of Gethsemane. "They found in *shari'a* something against Christianity. And I think many of the youth groups have the feeling and belief that Christians are against Islam."

Christians say the change in relations began in the 1970s under President Anwar Sadat, who liked to stress his personal piety and Islamic credentials. Sadat also curried favor with the Muslim Brotherhood and student Islamist groups in order to counter his secular, leftist critics. In addition, the Egyptian leader developed a rocky relationship with Pope Shenouda, who became the Coptic Patriarch in 1971. There were numerous points of dispute. Sadat was angered when Pope Shenouda organized a large contingent of Coptic priests to protest the burning of a Cairo church. The two men disagreed over how many new churches the government would allow to be built each year. The pope publicly protested the constitutional amendment making *shari'a* the principal source of Egyptian legislation. He also refused to lift his ban on Copts visiting Jerusalem despite entreaties from Sadat, who wanted to normalize relations with Israel after the 1979 Israeli-Egyptian peace treaty. The president's pique with the pope sharpened after Sadat was confronted with Coptic demonstrators during a visit to Washington in April 1980.

Soon after returning to Egypt, Sadat gave a speech to parliament in which he claimed that the Coptic leader was planning to set up a separatist Coptic state in southern Egypt. "The Pope must understand," Sadat declared, "that I am the Muslim President of a Muslim country."[22]

Copts were shocked not only by the accusation leveled against Pope Shenouda and the open hostility between the two leaders, but also by Sadat's description of himself. They were left wondering about their place in Egypt.

More than a year later, Muslim-Christian fighting erupted in the Cairo neighborhood of Zawya Al Hamra, leaving eighteen dead and worsening tensions between the two men. When Sadat ordered the arrest of 1,536 journalists, opposition activists, and religious figures in September 1981, the detainees included, for the first time in modern Egyptian history, eight Coptic bishops and twenty-four priests. Shenouda was confined to a desert monastery.

Many Christians believe that the feuding between Sadat and Pope Shenouda, who remained under virtual house arrest until Mubarak released him four years later, hardened anti-Christian feelings among ordinary Muslims. Those feelings, meanwhile, were being reinforced by some teachers in the public education system. Many of these teachers had spent time in Saudi Arabia or graduated from an expanded network of Al Azhar University satellite campuses, whose construction had been financed by Saudi money.

In some classrooms, teachers separated Muslim and Christian students as a way of underscoring their differences. History lessons no longer mentioned Egypt's pre-Islamic Coptic heritage, leading some Christians to fear that younger generations of Muslims were growing up with the mistaken impression that Copts had migrated to Egypt from someplace else or converted to Christianity during nineteenth-century foreign missionary work in Egypt.[23]

Anti-Christian commentary also began appearing in the mainstream popular media. The late television personality Sheikh Mitwali Al Sharawi, for example, sometimes mocked Christian beliefs in his popular weekly program. He made fun of the Trinity and joked that Jesus couldn't be the Son of God because God wouldn't get married. Christians saw such comments breaking a long-standing Egyptian taboo against insulting other religions. "Years ago, it was shameful in Egypt to mock or attack another religion, especially a revealed religion or a religion of the book," said Fahim, the Catholic educator.

Other Muslim religious leaders encouraged the notion that Christians were inferior and untrustworthy. One sheikh, for example, advised Muslims not to greet Christians with "Salaam," meaning "Peace," but instead to just say "Hello." A professor from Al Azhar wrote in a government-run newspaper that "Islam does not prevent dealings with non-Muslims, but prevents affectionate feelings and alliances, because a Muslim can only have true affection with a brother Muslim."[24]

"These are tiny things, but they hurt," said Milad Hanna.

Nearing eighty, Hanna is an author, professor of engineering, and former member of parliament. A prominent figure in the Coptic community, he was among the fifteen hundred people detained by Sadat in 1981. Hanna lives on a cozy residential street in Cairo's Mohandseen district, where his phone rings constantly with calls from both Muslims and Christians. A courtly, white-haired man, he is fond of signing off on these calls by saying *"Rabina yikhallik,"* or "May God preserve you."

"Society is getting Islamicized. This is something beyond the government's control," Hanna said the day I visited him. "What I'm angry about . . . is that Egypt is a treasure. Egypt is a wonderful country because the people are tolerant. We have Egyptian Islam. . . . But Egypt has been gradually shifting from tolerant Egyptian Islam to a bedouin, Saudi, fundamentalist Islam."[25]

Hanna was referring to Saudi Arabia's ultraconservative brand of Islam, Wahhabism, which is less tolerant of other faiths than Egypt's version. Saudi Arabia is the only Arab country with no churches because public worship of any religion other than Islam is forbidden. Although Christians are officially allowed to hold worship services in private, they do so fearfully because Saudi religious police sometimes harass, and even arrest, those who attend. After its oil wealth accumulated in the 1970s, Saudi Arabia began funding schools, mosques, charities, and Islamist movements around the Arab world, including Egypt, to spread its ascetic, rigid form of Islam. Eventually, the Wahhabi influence began affecting Egyptian social attitudes in general.[26]

The Egyptian government's response to this shift, in Hanna's view, was misguided. "Its policy fighting this is not by secularism and advocating democracy but by selling more Islam," he explained. "And hence, the whole society becomes Islamicized in the Saudi way, where there is only one religion, Islam, and not the Egyptian way of coexistence and pluralism."

The spread of anti-Christian bigotry that came with society's growing Islamicization since the 1970s has contributed to outbreaks of sectarian violence in recent years. These clashes have been rare, but violent. Unlike the

1990 rioting in Minya, they were not directly instigated by radical Islamists but instead usually erupted after minor altercations between individuals. Other times, they were a matter of Muslims taking the law into their own hands, such as the rampage in Tima.

Some incidents occurred in parts of Egypt that had no rebel Islamist activity, such as Kafr El Demien. This village in northern Egypt is half Muslim and half Christian. In early 1996, more than forty Coptic homes were burned by thousands of Muslims, some of them shouting, "Convert, Convert, Admit there's no God but God." The spark for the violence was an argument between a church guard and a policeman after the officer halted construction of a shrine saying the church lacked a building permit.

The most serious clash came in January 2000 in Al Kosheh, a predominantly Christian town in southern Egypt. Kosheh was already on tenterhooks for a couple of reasons. During a heavy-handed 1998 murder investigation, police detained thousands of Christians and used torture on more than a score to extract information. This abuse was not necessarily because they were Christian. Police treat Muslims the same way. Still, it left Christians angry. In addition, the town's Christian shop-owners had long been feuding with Muslim street vendors over sidewalk space.

So when a Muslim customer and a Christian shoe-store owner fell into an impromptu argument, it quickly escalated into three days of Muslim-Christian street fighting. When it was over, twenty Christians, including four children, and one Muslim were dead. The town also suffered widespread property damage.

These explosions of communal fighting almost always occur in rural areas and are the result of many factors, including the frustrations that come with poverty and an expanding population. In addition, both Muslims and Christians in rural Egypt are accustomed to a culture in which family and blood feuds have long been settled by violence. Nevertheless, many Egyptians say that anti-Christian attitudes have also played a part in provoking the violence and sometimes prolonging it. Christians often complain that local police and firefighters, who are predominantly Muslim, are slow to arrive on the scene when clashes break out and sometimes even join the melee. "The situation, in fact, is that there is some sort of growing popular anti-Coptic feeling," said Mohammed Abdel Moneim, a human rights activist who investigated the Kafr Al Demien episode.[27]

Rafik Habib, the Protestant social worker and writer who helped found the Islamist Wasat movement, blames the rising tension on a loss of a shared identity between Muslims and Christians and a growing feeling among Christians that they are "the other." "The sense of belonging is very weak now," Habib said in an interview. "They say 'we,' and it means Christians. 'They' means Muslims. When you belong to your own small group, you already think that anyone outside this group is different. Then there is something negative about him because what is right is . . . inside the group. Everyone in Egypt thinks like this now."[28]

Instances of sectarian violence, Habib added, "shows the whole circumstance is very dangerous . . . that there is a kind of prejudice, that Muslims and Christians are not in good relations these days because anything small can make a very big fire. . . . There is some tension between Christians and Muslims from the 1970s."

Sometimes this sense of separateness comes out in conversations with ordinary Muslims. When I visited Ahmed Sadek, the trucker in Zawya Al Hamra, he was clearly well disposed toward Christians—up to a point. "Islam says don't destroy a church and don't build a church. Leave it as it is," he said. "But it also says to treat Christians kindly. . . . In normal transactions, no preference is given to Muslim or Christian. . . . But there still is a reservation in the heart. A Muslim is Muslim in his heart and a Christian is Christian in his heart."

PROTECTED BY GOD

Violent attacks by extremists and sectarian fighting are not everyday occurrences for Egypt's Christians. Discrimination is.

The government insists that all citizens are equal. But its actions send a different message to Christians. Of thirty-two cabinet ministers, only two are Christian. None of Egypt's twenty-six provincial governors, who are appointed by the central government, are Christian. No university presidents or deans are Christian. And among senior military and police officers, they are rare.

In the 1995 parliamentary elections, the ruling National Democratic Party did not put up one Christian candidate for 444 seats. And though 57 Christians ran as independents or on opposition tickets, not one was elected. Christians fared a little better in the 2000 elections, when three Copts—two nominated by the ruling party and one by an opposition party—were elected. Copts were also named to four of the ten presidentially filled parliamentary seats. But this is a meager Christian presence in the national legislature compared to earlier times in Egypt's modern history.

Coptic leaders have complained that the government also underreports the size of the Christian population in its census figures, ignores qualified Christians for faculty appointments at public universities, and gives little coverage to Christian subjects in state-run television and radio. Many Christians also feel that the courts are overly lenient with Muslims accused of killing Christians. After the Kosheh fighting, thirty-eight Muslim defendants were charged with murder in connection with the deaths of twenty Copts. But the court acquitted all thirty-eight on murder charges, convicting four on lesser charges, including manslaughter. The longest sentence imposed was ten years. Pope Shenouda angrily rejected the verdict. In this instance, the government agreed. It appealed and asked for a new trial, which was granted.

Perhaps the most grating discrimination for Christians is the government's continued application of an 1856 Ottoman decree requiring presidential permission to build a new church or repair existing ones. The permits were so time-consuming and difficult to obtain that for decades few new churches were built and many churches became decrepit for lack of maintenance. When I visited Assiut's First Evangelical Church in 1993, for example, its interior had not been repainted since its construction in 1896.

In recent years, the government has moved to address some of these discriminatory practices. Mubarak has facilitated church repairs by delegating authority to approve repair permits to provincial governors. He has also increased the number of annual permits for new churches.[29] Egyptian radio and television now air the Coptic Mass on Easter and Christmas and are giving more attention to Christian affairs. They also are more sensitive about not broadcasting commentaries that denigrate Christian beliefs. Lessons on Egypt's Coptic history have been added to the public school curriculum.[30]

Still, the government moves gingerly and quietly in tackling this institutional discrimination, lest it appear to be catering to or favoring Christians. It does not want to jeopardize its Islamic identity at a time when Muslims, including many in the government itself, have become more assertive about their own religious identity. Yet these discriminatory practices, which affect Christians of all social, economic, and educational levels and which also mar the private employment sector, are a far greater source of frustration and anger to the Christian population than the episodic anti-Christian violence.

Copts have responded to their difficulties in a variety of ways. Some have emigrated, joining an estimated 400,000 Copts now living in the United States and Canada. It is difficult to know, however, how many have left primarily to escape religious discrimination and how many have gone for the same reasons that Muslims leave Egypt: to pursue educational and economic opportunities.[31] At home, Christians increasingly have tended to take refuge in their church life and communities. And if provoked, they try not to make waves. As Labib, the civil rights attorney in Aswan, told me, "we do advise Copts to let it pass. In peace."

Pope Shenouda also takes every opportunity to show solidarity with Muslims on important national issues. To the consternation of many Copts, he still discourages them from going on pilgrimage to Jerusalem until there is peace between Israelis and Palestinians. As an elderly Coptic priest in Minya, who gave his name only as "Father John," told me, "Shenouda forbade Copts to go because he doesn't want them to go without Egyptian Muslim compatriots. He wants us to go together. He doesn't want us to be seen as going without them."

The pope, who passionately promotes the dogma of "national unity," also insists that the word *minority* not be applied to his flock. He fears that its use could drive a permanent wedge between Copts and the larger Muslim community. Besides, to him it implies that Copts are not indigenous to Egypt. "We are not a minority in Egypt," he once declared, "We are Egyptians and a part of the Egyptian people." The terms *minority* and *majority*, he added, "indicate segregation and discrimination. This does not befit the sons of a single homeland, especially if this homeland is beloved Egypt."[32]

Another way that Copts are coping with their disadvantages is by converting to Islam, often because they believe it will help them land a job. "Mainly young people . . . are told, 'All you have to do is call yourself Mohammed and there is a job waiting for you.' I have endless examples of this," said a source who asked not to be named. There have also been cases of young women converting in order to facilitate marrying or eloping with a Muslim boyfriend. There are no reliable numbers on how many Christians convert to Islam but it is a big enough trend to worry some Coptic and other Christian leaders.[33]

While it is not illegal under Egyptian civil law for Muslims to convert to Christianity, *shari'a* regards it as apostasy. As a result, such conversions are rare and usually provoke severe social repercussions from family, friends, and employers. In addition, such conversions are not legally recognized because authorities do not permit those who convert to Christianity to change their religious affiliation on their national identity cards. There also have been occasional instances of security police arresting and physically abusing Muslim converts to Christianity.

Christian proselytizing, while not technically illegal under Egyptian law, draws immediate police attention. Some Christians who spoke enthusiastically about their faith to Muslims have been detained briefly for questioning. Police sometimes threaten to charge them under a section of the criminal code that forbids "disparaging or belittling any divinely revealed religion . . . or disrupting national unity and harmony."[34]

The Egyptian government is extremely sensitive to external criticism of its treatment of Christians, which has increased in recent years as Coptic emigrants, particularly in the United States, have become more vocal about anti-Christian discrimination in their native land. One U.S.-based lobbying group has a Web site that speaks of "Persecuted Copts in Egypt" and features photographs of those killed in sectarian violence under the heading "Coptic martyrs."[35] The plight of Christians in Egypt also has been a focus of increased criticism from Western human rights organizations and governments, especially the United States, which all have increased their monitoring of religious freedom around the world.[36]

Copts in Egypt are of two minds about this external attention. It is reassuring, they say, that someone is concerned about their situation and pressing the government on their behalf. But some fear that such pressure could backfire and fuel the contention of extremist Islamists that Christians are an extension of "Crusader" forces that want to harm Islam and interfere in Egyptian affairs.

To say that Copts and other Christians are persecuted or endangered in Egypt seems an exaggeration. For the most part, they openly practice their faith without fear, Coptic services are well attended, and in recent years the Copts have erected two magnificent new churches. On the edge of Cairo the Church of St. Simeon, which holds twenty thousand worshipers, was carved out of limestone cliffs. And at the other end of the country, a huge Coptic cathedral was recently completed in Aswan. Personal relations with neighbors and coworkers are generally without problems, most Christians say, and they note that moderate Muslim religious leaders have been quick to condemn anti-Christian rhetoric and violence. In almost every incident of sectarian violence, there were Muslims who stood against the bigotry to rescue or assist their Christian neighbors. When extremists murdered nine Christians in Abu Qurqas in 1997, a local doctor recalled, "mosques called on people to hurry to the hospital to donate their blood" and the victims' funerals "included people from the two religions."[37]

Still, the difficulties of Christians in Egypt are real and Muslim-Christian relations are not always as rosy as government officials and the official media suggest. Islam's new power in the Middle East is testing Egypt's long history of relative religious harmony. Christians are nervously watching Islam's inner turmoil from the sidelines, praying that after this stormy passage, Islam's traditional tolerance will prevail.

When they feel besieged, as they sometimes do, Christians draw on two enduring assets of the Coptic heritage: forbearance and faith.

"Copts are living with a real strong feeling inside them that they are protected by God," said Milad Hanna. "Without that feeling," he added, "the rich would emigrate and the poor would convert to Islam."

13

One Dream Fulfilled, Another Denied

"Shalom"
—"Peace" in Hebrew

"Salaam"
—"Peace" in Arabic

"slm"
—Semitic root shared by both words

On a warm, sunny day in May 1948, 250 men and women bearing coveted invitations gathered in a large hall in the Tel Aviv Museum. Two white flags with a blue Star of David hung from one wall. Between them was a picture of the bearded Zionist visionary Theodor Herzl. Below his visage, the men about to make his dream come true sat at a long table facing the assembled crowd. At precisely four P.M., David Ben-Gurion stood up and began reading a declaration establishing an independent Jewish state called Israel. It was, the document stated, "the natural right of the Jewish people, like any other people, to control their own destiny in their sovereign state." Their new nation, it added, would "be loyal to the principles of the United Nations Charter." The straightforward ceremony lasted a mere half hour and concluded with the singing of the new state's unofficial anthem "Hatikvah," meaning "The Hope." Outside, crowds on Rothschild Boulevard danced with joy.[1]

The birth of Israel was a triumph for the Jewish people. After centuries of persecution and pogroms, after the horrors of the Holocaust, Jews would have a safe refuge and a national home to call their own.

But for Arabs living in what was then Palestine, Israel's appearance was a disaster. To this day, they call it Al Nakba, "The Catastrophe."[2]

Palestine, which historically stretched from the Mediterranean Sea to beyond the Jordan River, is a land of ancient religious memory. For Jews, it is the home of biblical patriarch Abraham and Kings David and Solomon. It is where the Jew later known to the world as Christ lived and died. It is also the land where Muslims built a revered mosque in the seventh century and then ruled for the better part of the next twelve hundred years, pledging allegiance for the last several hundred of those years to the Ottoman Empire.

When that empire was broken up after World War I, Palestine became a British mandate. But at the end of World War II, Britain set up the Kingdom of Jordan east of the Jordan River and prepared to withdraw from the rest of its mandate. Zionists, pointing to their faith's ancient roots there and to the presence of a growing Jewish community, wanted a Jewish state in the Holy Land. Western powers, which were beginning to absorb the full horror of the Holocaust, were sympathetic. In 1947, the United Nations announced a partition plan for Palestine, carving it into a Jewish state and a larger Arab state. The plan called for Jerusalem to be a separate, internationally run city. But the Arab majority in Palestine did not think it fair of Western states to take part of their country for a new nation dedicated to a single ethnic group. They rejected the U.N. partition plan. Amid this political uncertainty and months of guerrilla fighting between the Jewish and Arab communities, Britain's troops departed. Within hours, Israel declared its independence and the first full-blown Israeli-Arab war broke out. When it was over, about 700,000 Palestinians had fled the fighting or been expelled from their homes by Israeli forces. They were not allowed to return home by Israeli authorities.[3] As for territory, whatever parts of historic western Palestine were not seized by Israeli forces in the fighting, were taken by the neighboring states of Egypt and Jordan.

Thus were the seeds planted for the Palestinians' long struggle for a sovereign national state of their own so that they, too, like the Zionists of 1948, could "control their own destiny."

That struggle is not over and it is a major reason for today's troubled landscape in the Middle East. Indeed, the impact of the long-running Israeli-Palestinian conflict has been so profound and diffuse that it bears retelling. It has deeply compromised the entire region's psychic, political, economic, and cultural health. It has prompted Israel and the Arab states to spend billions on military armaments, and it has kept the area on a warlike footing for decades. It has led to four more Israeli-Arab wars—in 1956, 1967, 1973, and 1982—and to the most vicious Israeli-Palestinian combat ever beginning in late 2000. It has given authoritarian Arab governments cover to defer internal political reforms and justify restraints on civil liberties. It has led

Israel into the role of brutal occupier, subjugating Palestinians by force. And it has deferred prosperity for millions by impeding the normal regional connections that promote economic development. Tourism, trade, business ties, cultural exchanges, educational dialogue, even the sharing of electrical grids and water sources, have all been stunted for half a century.

As the Israeli-Palestinian conflict dragged on, it also fueled Jewish and Muslim religious extremism, complicating efforts to reach a settlement. In 1981, Egyptian president Anwar Sadat was slain by extremist Islamists angered by his 1979 peace treaty with Israel. Secular nationalists led by Yasser Arafat, who were without serious competition for decades, now see their leadership challenged by tenacious Islamist nationalists who want to replace the Jewish state of Israel with an Islamic one.

On the Israeli side, an extremist Jew gunned down Israeli prime minister Yitzhak Rabin in 1995 for signing a peace agreement with Palestinians. And militant messianic Jewish settlers, who vow never to leave Israeli-occupied land on which Palestinians hope to build their national state, comprise a pressure group no Israeli government can easily ignore.

Neither Israel's creation nor the extended conflict that it spawned caused Islam's contemporary resurgence. But at this time of religious revival within Islam, the conflict has given radical Islamists a galvanizing cause. Osama Bin Laden justified his terrorist attacks on the United States in part by invoking the Palestinian cause. It did not matter that he was a latecomer to their national struggle, or even that his concern for Palestinians was questionable. What is significant is that simply by including their cause on his long list of grievances, he got the ear of millions in the Middle East.

Finally, the prolonged Israeli-Palestinian conflict has fueled anti-Americanism among Arabs who contend, not without foundation, that the United States has been overly deferential to Israel for decades and thus, they believe, helped to perpetuate the conflict. Perceptions of American favoritism toward Israel have warped America's relationship with the Arab world, creating in some quarters a hatred for the United States. Evidence of these sentiments surfaced in the ambivalent Arab response to the 2001 terrorist attacks on New York and Washington. To be sure, there was sympathy. But there was also the suggestion that U.S. policies were partly to blame, particularly America's unbending support for Israel.

It was a reaction heard in Egypt.

First to Make Peace

Egypt was among the Arab states that attacked Israel within hours of its founding. But it was the first to break from the Arab fold and make peace with Israel. Secretly assured by Israel that it was ready to return Egypt's Sinai desert seized in the 1967 Israeli-Arab war, President Anwar Sadat visited Jerusalem in 1977 in a gesture of acceptance of the Jewish state. Two years later, Egypt and Israel signed a peace treaty. For this, Egypt was booted out of the Arab League and ostracized by its Arab brethren for a decade. Its hope of being a bridge between Israel and the Arab world was further dashed by its peace partner. Less than a year after their 1979 treaty, Israel formally annexed Jerusalem, declaring the entire city its "complete and united" capital. In 1981, it annexed the Golan Heights, seized from Syria in the 1967 Arab-Israeli War, and a year later, Israel invaded Lebanon, setting off a war that left thousands of Lebanese and over a thousand Israeli soldiers dead.

Egyptians felt betrayed. Today, they live in a stew of emotions over the Israeli-Palestinian conflict. They resent the United States for its bias toward Israel but feel utterly dependent on Washington to resolve the conflict, seeing it as the only power capable of influencing Israel. They deeply want peace but fear and distrust Israel. They spew vile anti-Jewish propaganda in public but privately admire Israelis for their military and business acumen. They condemn Israeli shootings of rock-throwing Palestinian teens but are mute on suicide bombings by radical Islamists that kill and maim Israeli civilians. They are not totally in love with Palestinians or their leader Arafat, who have sometimes meddled in Arab countries with disastrous results, but they remain passionately attached to the Palestinian cause.

In one recent poll, 79 percent of Egyptians said the Palestinian issue was "the single most important issue" to them personally. In four other Arab states polled, an average of 60 percent said the same thing.[4] What explains this attachment to the Palestinian question, which is evident among Egyptians of all social strata, economic classes, and political persuasions?

For Egyptians, as for other Arabs, it is a matter of Arab honor and dignity. Arab pride was dealt a devastating blow in the 1967 Arab-Israel War. Besides taking the Sinai and Gaza Strip from Egypt, and the Golan Heights from Syria, Israel also captured East Jerusalem and the West Bank from Jordan. Though Egypt has regained the Sinai, it remains frustrated by its inability to reverse all the other Arab territorial losses of 1967. For decades, Egyptian leaders have told their people that Arab destiny is intimately linked to the fate of the Palestinians and that Arab honor can only be restored by a regional peace settlement that includes Israel's return of all Arab lands and a viable Palestinian national state.

Egyptians are also attached to the Palestinian cause because they see an injustice that requires redress. The 700,000 Palestinians deprived of their homeland and property at Israel's creation now are a refugee diaspora of about 3.7 million, including more than 820,000 living in utmost poverty in the Gaza Strip.[5] The harsh treatment of Palestinians by Israeli occupation forces, which Egyptians see nightly on television news, adds to their sense of outrage. Egyptians may be more vocal about the Palestinian cause than other Arabs because they regard themselves as leaders of the Arab world. They also would like to see their pioneering peace treaty with Israel, which was initially so controversial, vindicated with a region-wide peace settlement.

Finally, concern about the future of Jerusalem drives Egyptian devotion to the Palestinian cause. They have not forgotten that it was an Egyptian ruler, Salah Al Din, who recovered Jerusalem from the Christian Crusaders in the twelfth century. The city's mythic importance in the Egyptian mind, however, derives mainly from its religious significance. Al Quds, the Arabic name for Jerusalem, is where Muslims believe Prophet Muhammad made his miraculous Night Journey, ascending into heaven with Angel Gabriel to meet Allah. The rock from which tradition holds he began his journey is now enclosed by Islam's oldest large sanctuary, the Dome of the Rock. Built about sixty years after the Prophet's death, the shrine sits on an elevated esplanade that also includes Al Aqsa Mosque and is known to Muslims as Haram Al Sharif or the Noble Sanctuary.

Sparkling in the sun, the golden-roofed Dome of the Rock dominates Jerusalem's skyline and on a clear day can be seen from miles away. Pictures of it adorn classroom walls and student notebooks around the Middle East. In southern Egypt, I saw its photograph on the wall of a mosque. Beneath was the exhortation: "Men of Islam, we are calling on you to return to al Quds."

The esplanade holding the Dome of the Rock is also sacred to Jews, who call it the Temple Mount. Here stood Solomon's Temple and later, the Second Temple of Herod's time, which was destroyed by the Romans in 70 C.E. Judaism's holiest site, the Western Wall, is actually part of the foundation of the elevated esplanade. For centuries, Jews around the world have expressed their attachment to these holy places with the liturgical proclamation, uttered every Yom Kippur and Passover, "Next year in Jerusalem!"

Among Egyptians, it is not only Muslims who are enamored of Jerusalem. Christians are also spiritually transfixed by the city. Almost every conversation I had with Copts in southern Egypt ended with a curious question, "Have you been to Jerusalem?"

"The most important thing is Jerusalem," said Bardilla Mossad Atta, a tailor in Cairo. "As a Christian man, I am concerned about Jerusalem."

The United Nations recognized Jerusalem's importance to these three faiths in its 1947 partition plan, when it said the city should become an internationally run enclave. That never happened. When the first Arab-Israeli War of 1948–1949 ended, Israel controlled the city's western half and Jordan had the eastern half. During the next conflict, in 1967, Israel pushed Jordan out of the eastern half, which holds the Dome of the Rock and the Western Wall, and has held the entire city ever since.

Despite their peace treaty, Egypt, for the most part, has treated Israel like an angry spouse, keeping it at a distance to signal its disapproval of Israeli policies. Apart from correct diplomatic ties, the government has done little to facilitate or encourage tourist, cultural, and educational exchanges between the two countries. In two decades as Egypt's leader, President Mubarak has visited Israel only once and that was to attend Rabin's 1995 funeral.

The government also does little to restrain venomous anti-Jewish propaganda in its semicontrolled press. The slanders are often accompanied by racist cartoons. If the Egyptian media is to be believed, Israelis have sent Egypt tainted seeds that produced rotten tomato crops, infected Egyptians with AIDS and HIV, and distributed chewing gum that makes young people sex crazy. During the Islamist insurgency of the 1990s, some Egyptians suggested Israel was hiring Egyptians to kill tourists in Egypt. More recently, some commentators suggested that Israel was responsible for the 2001 terrorist attacks on the United States.

The government tolerates this demonizing of Israel and Jews partly to allow public opinion to blow off steam. It also diverts attention from economic and political frustrations closer to home. Like other Arab governments, Egypt also does nothing to counter the widespread refusal among Arabs to acknowledge what happened to Jews in the Holocaust. Many Arabs deny the Holocaust happened, and even if it did, they show no interest in it. Egyptians can rent *Schindler's List* from video stores, but it is banned from cinemas.

Taking their cue from the government, Egyptian professional associations of lawyers, musicians, doctors, writers, actors, and journalists still bar members from having contacts with Israelis. The Egyptian Writers' Union recently expelled playwright Ali Salem because he openly advocates normal ties with Israel and has made frequent visits there, which he described in a 1994 book, *A Trip to Israel*.[6] Despite criticism from his professional colleagues, Salem's book sold well, underscoring Egyptians' curiosity about their Jewish neighbors.

I remember talking one day with my Egyptian driver Mohamed Abdel Salam about an Israeli commando operation some years ago that had killed senior Palestinian leaders then living in Tunisia. "Yes, that was really good," he said. Seeing my puzzlement, Mohamed hastened to explain.

"No, I mean it's bad, the killing, but it was a good operation, the way it was done, the timing. I don't like Israel but the Israelis are smart people."

That their passions on the Palestinian issue have clouded Egyptians' judgment is evident in their attitude toward Palestinian suicide bombers. Islam bans suicide and the Qur'an prohibits deliberately killing innocent civilians during military operations. But many Egyptians take the questionable position that the target of a suicide bombing determines its moral legitimacy. So while they condemn Al Qaeda's terrorist attacks in New York and Washington, they justify Palestinian suicide bombings against Israeli civilians as acts of "national resistance" to Israeli occupation.

Al Azhar's Grand Sheikh Mohamed Sayed Tantawi, Egypt's most senior religious figure, has rejected targeting Israeli civilians as "abhorrent to Islam." But he, too, slips around Islam's ban on suicide, saying that those who blow themselves up "on a battlefield"—presumably targeting Israeli soldiers—are "martyrs."[7]

Oslo Spring

In the fall of 1993, Israeli prime minister Yitzhak Rabin and Palestinian Liberation Organization leader Yasser Arafat signed the landmark 1993 Oslo Accords in the White House. The agreement, reached over months of secret negotiations between Israel and the Palestinians, marked the first time that the Palestinians formally recognized the state of Israel and that Israel formally recognized the Palestinians' right to self-rule.

The Accords also held out the promise of a lasting peace settlement. The Declaration of Principles on Palestinian Self-Rule in Gaza and Jericho, as the agreement was formally titled, did not mention a Palestinian state. But it called for discussions on "permanent status issues," including Jerusalem, borders, Jewish settlements in the Israeli-occupied territories, and the Palestinian refugee problem. It also set out a timetable of five years to complete the negotiations that would lead to the "permanent status." These provisions raised expectations among Egyptians that the Israeli-Palestinian conflict might finally be on its way to a resolution.

This implicit vision of peace led many in the region to begin imagining how this would change the Middle East at large. During this "Oslo Spring," the edifice of anger, humiliation, and resentment that had supported Egyptian attitudes toward Israel for decades began to crack. Like Czechs during their brief fling with freedom in early 1968, Egyptians and Israelis lived through several tantalizing months. There was a collective grab for normality in a region that had not known the feeling for forty-five years. Egyptian businessmen flew to Israel on scouting trips. Israeli and Egyptian officials took dusty plans for joint industrial ventures out of the drawer. Egyptian Copts took off on a pilgrimage to Christian holy sites in Jerusalem, the first organized tour of its kind in four decades. Intellectuals discussed political and economic realignments in the region with Israel as a partner. Why not a Middle East League, some asked, instead of the Arab League? Egyptian soccer fans, meanwhile, boasted that their beloved Al Ahly team would trounce any Israeli contenders.[8]

"The main thing is that there is no hostility in the hearts of Egyptians now against Israel," journalist Abd Al Satar Al Tawila told me at the time. "Nobody thinks of war."

Mahzer Abdel Ghani thought he saw a real difference in the air. "It seems things have changed from the past," said Ghani, twenty-two, as he browsed through the offerings at the 1994 Cairo Book Fair. "The feelings in Israel are somewhat sympathetic for the Arabs. I hope to go to Israel, so I can know how they think. I don't know if I will go. Will I really find animosity, like we have animosity or will it be different? It's a matter of time and good intentions. The Arab people in nature are people who make up and we have a history which says so."

Elhamy Al Zayat, chairman of Emeco Travel, was hopeful, too, but pragmatic. "People are more realistic and they are exhausted. They want to live," said Zayat in his tiny Cairo office near Tahrir Square. "We've always been told to tighten our belts because we are at war. . . . There are some fundamentalists on both sides, yes. But these are difficulties that will be overcome. The whole thing is to sell peace to the people. People don't want to lose face. You have to help them."

But even when it looked like walls might be tumbling, there was resistance and skepticism. Looking out from their bunker, many Egyptians seemed to be seized with an inferiority complex, fearful that they would not be able to compete economically with the Israelis. The press was filled with commentaries questioning Israel's motives and suggesting that it would pursue its "expansionist" aims by new means. Instead of its vaunted military, some writers suggested, Israel would use economic clout to "colonize" Arab economies and create Israeli commercial "hegemony" in the region.

"It's dangerous to open everything to the Israelis," said an Egyptian lawyer. "All the banks in Egypt will be affected by the financial power of the Israelis because the Jews are running most of the banks in the world." He hastened to add that he was "not anti-Semitic, I have Israeli friends. But I don't believe they really want peace. They want to utilize this area for their benefit, for their interests. They still think they are the chosen people of God. I have nothing against them, even as a state, but I want them to prove they want real peace."

As another prominent businessman explained, "We live in the past. We are still taken by our prejudices, our suspicions. . . . You cannot think that the devil overnight has become an angel. And it's a total mentality of conspiracy. Even if they do something nice, what do they want in return?"

Other Egyptians sensed, even hoped, that as the Arab-Israeli wall began falling, Arabs would increasingly question why their countries did not have the same level of prosperity, press freedom, and political rights as Israel. "The Israelis are very serious about what they want, and they have . . . a clear-cut democracy so they can do what they think they should," said Cairo businessman Mustafa Nahas. "As for us . . . the Arab world now has to go through a very, very serious reshuffling of its internal affairs."

But the Oslo Spring did not last. Its glimpse into a new and different Middle East slowly faded as Israeli-Palestinian negotiations foundered. The 1995 assassination of Rabin, who had made the Oslo process possible, brought to power Israeli prime minister Benjamin Netanyahu, a hardliner with no intention of executing the Accords. Islamist suicide bombers did not help matters. Slowly, even before it had fully bloomed, the Oslo Spring withered.

Egyptians generally fall into two categories when it comes to Israel. One stream of thought begrudgingly recognizes the reality of Israel's existence and accepts a two-state solution, in which Israel coexists beside a Palestinian state in the West Bank and Gaza, with Jerusalem as a shared capital. This is the mainstream view and it gained ground after Oslo. But it is based on pragmatism rather than preference. "The real and genuine attitude of Arabs is that they would prefer that Israel does not exist," Salah Eldin Hafiz, deputy editor in chief of Egypt's *Al Ahram* newspaper, said in a 1996 interview. "But Israel now is status quo. Israel is now a state in the Middle East . . . and we have to accept it."

A second stream of thought, which is found predominantly but not exclusively among Islamists, is rejectionist. Its adherents vow never to accept Israel, which they steadfastly refer to as "the Zionist entity." They are not against Jews or Judaism, they say, but against Zionism and its legacy, a Jewish state on Arab Muslim lands. In place of Israel, some say they want an Islamic state in all of Palestine; others speak of an Islamic democracy in which, they claim, people of all faiths, including Jews, would live as equals. Still others want a binational state that allows for "group identity" as the basis for political organization. The rejectionist camp also includes some secularists who envision a secular democracy in all of Palestine.[9]

"Our position comes from Islam," said Mustafa Mashur, Supreme Guide of Egypt's Muslim Brotherhood, whose views on Israel are typical of those among Islamists in most Arab countries. "Palestine is not for Palestinians only but for all Muslims. We do not allow the enemy to take one foot of the land of Palestine." Israelis "are saying that Palestine is owned by them from a long time ago," he added. "But it's well known that Muslims were in Palestine for fourteen hundred years. . . . We want Jews and Christians and Muslims to live together in Palestine as they used to live there before the Jewish gangs came."[10]

MUSLIM ZEAL FOR THE HOLY LAND

In January 1965, a small force of less than thirty Palestinians began launching attacks on isolated Israeli water and agricultural installations in rural areas. The guerrillas belonged to Fatah, a Palestinian nationalist group formed in 1958 and led by an engineer named Yasser Arafat. Fatah's immediate objective was to get the Palestinian cause on the radar screen of Israeli and Arab leaders alike. Its long-term goal was to destroy Israel and replace it with a Palestinian state. The head of Israeli military intelligence at the time would later call Fatah's initial operations "a nuisance, not a strategic threat—not politically, nor militarily." Indeed, the first Fatah fighter captured was carrying a rusty gun that wouldn't fire. Over the next two and a half years, until the outbreak of the 1967 Arab-Israeli War, Fatah raids killed eleven Israelis.[11]

Thirty six years later on a warm August day in the heart of Jerusalem, fifteen Israelis, including six children, were murdered in a blinding instant when a twenty-three-year-old Palestinian walked into a Sbarro Italian restaurant and blew himself up. Izzedin Masri, who detonated an explosive device packed with nails, turned the crowded pizzeria filled with chattering families into a grotesque scene of bloody carnage. Unlike his Fatah precursors in 1965, Masri had no intention of surviving his deadly attack. He'd been trained by the Islamic Resistance Movement, usually known by its Arabic acronym, Hamas, a word meaning zeal. Masri, who was not yet born when Fatah launched its first attacks, believed he was headed for paradise as a martyr who had sacrificed himself for his Palestinian nation.[12]

The contrast between the Palestinian attacks of 1965 and 2001 offered a sobering insight into the price that both Palestinians and Israelis were paying because of their protracted conflict. Over thirty-five years, amateurish assaults on rural water installations had evolved into sophisticated, deadly attacks in crowded urban spaces. Masri's suicide bombing also illustrated the role that religious militancy now plays in the Palestinian nationalist struggle.

Hamas has its roots in a network of schools, mosques, libraries, and clinics run by Islamist social activists affiliated to the Muslim Brotherhood. Like Sadat, who had turned to Egypt's Muslim Brotherhood to help counter his leftist critics, the Israeli military authorities had funded some activities of these Palestinian Islamists because they saw them as a counterweight to the more radical, secular Palestinian nationalists.[13]

But that all changed with the outbreak of the first Palestinian *intifada*, the spontaneous revolt against Israeli military occupation that erupted in the Gaza Strip in late 1987. Hoping to harness the sustained fury of that uprising, the Islamists formed Hamas under the leadership of Sheikh Ahmad Yasin. The organization seeks to eradicate Israel and replace it with an Islamic state. According to its Covenant, Hamas "strives to raise the banner of Allah over every inch of Palestine," which has been "consecrated for future Muslim generations until Judgment Day." The only way to solve the Palestinian question, the document adds, is through *jihad*, which is an "individual duty" of every Muslim. Negotiated peace deals with Israel such as Egypt's "treacherous Camp David agreement" are rejected.

Hamas issued its Covenant in 1988. Ironically, that was the same year that Yasser Arafat's Palestine Liberation Organization, the nationalist umbrella movement that includes Fatah, announced that it accepted Israel as part of a two-state solution and renounced terrorism. In other words, 1988 was the year that the two main organizations of Palestinian nationalism took historic turns and passed each other like two ships in the night.

Hamas's strength comes from several potent forces: religious zeal, hatred of Zionism, Palestinian nationalism, and despair. It has escalated the deadliness of Palestinian terrorism with suicide bombers, who are nearly impossible to detect. Fighting the Jewish enemy for Hamas is not merely a nationalist duty but a religious one. As one of its supporters explained, it is "an act of worship for which God rewards a struggler in the form of victory in this life and eternity in the Gardens of Eden in the life after death."[14]

This religious context helps explain why Hamas rejects the term *suicide bombings* and instead says that it conducts "martyrdom operations," which it regards as legitimate retaliation for Israeli "terrorism" against Palestinian civilians. A senior Hamas official once explained, "We want the enemy to withdraw from the occupied territories so that Palestinians can live freely, like other people. Negotiations didn't work, the international community didn't help, so the only way we had was to let the occupying force pay the price of the occupation."[15]

Hamas's social welfare activities, which are delivered in a less corrupt and more efficient manner than those of Arafat's organization, have brought it solid support among Palestinians. But their enthusiasm for Hamas's military operations fluctuates with their frustration level. When they are optimistic about an end to Israeli occupation, as they were in the post-Oslo months of 1994, support for Hamas's suicide bombings drops. When they despair of release from the occupation and feel that no one is listening to their national aspirations, support for Hamas's operations soars. At times like that, it is not unusual to meet a Palestinian mother who says she hopes her sons will become "martyrs" for their nation.[16]

In Egypt, Islamists openly support Hamas. It has presented "a good model," said Abou Elela Mady, a founder of Wasat, the moderate Islamist movement. "We consider it an Islamic nationalist movement that deserves our admiration and appreciation.

"We should not ignore that Israel is a religious state and it was founded on that," he added. "Israel is a country which uses religion in its confrontations and in its discourse. Putting aside this religious aspect then can weaken our confrontation with Israel because you can only fight iron with iron. . . . That's why Palestinians are confronting the Jewish faith with their Islamic martyrdom faith."[17]

Jewish Zeal for the Holy Land

Palestinians have not been alone in buttressing their nationalist struggle with religion. When Israel captured East Jerusalem and vast reaches of Arab territory in the Arab-Israeli War of 1967, some Jews saw this as the handiwork of God. Embracing a messianic strain of Judaism, these Jews believed that Jewish control of these lands was essential to God's redemptive plan and that to relinquish any part of them would be a sin. The West Bank in particular, they contended, could not be returned to Arabs because it is the core of Jews' biblical patrimony from God. They call the West Bank by its ancient biblical names of Judea and Samaria.

This apocalyptic, mystical interpretation of Zionism, which was promoted by the influential Rabbi Tzvi Yehuda Kook, also held that the world is eternally hostile to Jews and Israel; the struggle with Arabs is a cosmic one against evil and a negotiated peace with Palestinians is impossible because there is no possibility of giving up the Promised Land. "The State of Israel was created and established by the council of nations by order of the Sovereign Lord of the Universe," Kook said, "so that the clear commandment in the Torah 'that they shall inherit and settle the Land' would be fulfilled."[18]

These ideas eventually crystallized in Gush Emunim, "Bloc of the Faithful," a movement of militant religious Jewish settlers who began colonizing the West Bank and Gaza Strip in the late 1970s with the aim of solidifying Jewish control there. The long-term goal of Gush Emunim is to see Israel, a secular democracy, ruled by Jewish religious law and its borders expanded to the Jordan River. Its slogan is "The Land of Israel, for the People of Israel, According to the Torah of Israel."

Though a minority, this radical Jewish movement had an impact beyond its size because for much of the time between 1977 and 1992 Israel was led by secular politicians of the right-wing Likud Party who shared Gush Emunim's goals of holding on to Arab lands seized in 1967. They were only too happy to facilitate the group's colonizing activity.[19]

Menachem Begin was a secular expansionist who believed that it was Jewish "destiny" to incorporate the West Bank in order to create "Greater Israel." Elected prime minister in 1977, he embraced Gush Emunim's missionary zeal toward his goal of populating the West Bank with so many Jews that it would be impossible ever to give up. As Begin's first agriculture minister, Ariel Sharon launched a vigorous program to increase the 5,023 Jewish settlers then living in the West Bank and Gaza Strip. Yitzhak Shamir, who was Israel's prime minister from 1986 to 1992, had similar views to Begin and Sharon and once called settlement building "holy work."[20] The fruits of their colonizing drive, which continued even when the more centrist Labor Party was in power, are evident. By early 2002, there were 213,672 Jewish settlers in the West Bank and Gaza.[21]

The fusion of Gush Emunim's religious radicalism with the expansionist policies of the secular Likud Party meant that for years Israel rejected the essential compromise required for resolving its conflict with the Palestinians. That compromise involves giving up the West Bank and Gaza, as well as part of Jerusalem. In diplomatic jargon, it is called "trading land for peace." This principle was enshrined in U.N. Security Council Resolution 242 of 1967 at the end of that year's Arab-Israeli War. But it did not become the governing principle of Israeli-Palestinian negotiations until the 1993 Oslo Accords.

Israel's political life has been affected by increased religious conservatism in other ways. Political parties that espouse ultraorthodox Judaism have won seats in Israel's parliament, the Knesset, where they have pressed their religious concerns into legislation. Though small, these religious parties have often been crucial to create governing coalitions and used that bargaining power to get cabinet seats. Also, an estimated 25 and 40 percent of all officers in the Israeli military, which had been a predominantly secular Jewish institution for decades, are now religiously oriented Zionists.[22] Many in this group have attended special seminaries that combine religious education with military service. Some of these seminaries share Gush Emunim's more extreme messianic Zionism.

It was a graduate of one of the militant religious seminaries who sidled up to Rabin after a peace rally in Tel Aviv in 1995 and pumped three bullets from a nine-millimeter Beretta pistol into the prime minister. Yigal Amir later said he believed that Rabin had to be killed because he was preparing to give up land that God had given to Jews. The twenty-five-year-old assassin justified the murder by citing the "doctrine of the pursuer," or *din rodef* in Hebrew. Under this concept from medieval Judaism, one can kill a pursuer to stop him from murdering his intended victim. "According to Jewish law, the minute a Jew gives over his land and people to the enemy, he must be killed," Amir told a judge. "My whole life has been studying the Talmud and I have all the data."

Amir is serving a life sentence—Israel does not have capital punishment. Unlike with Palestinian terrorists, Israeli authorities did not demolish his family's home as punishment.[23]

It is hard to quantify how much Jewish and Muslim extremists have fed the flames of each other's hot zealotry. But it is clear that the persistence of the Israeli-Palestinian conflict has contributed to the rise of both Islamic and Jewish religious militancy. On the Jewish side, this militancy has blurred the distinction between Judaism and Zionism. On the Muslim side, it has led to perceptions that Islam is an aggressive, militant faith.

THE AMERICAN ROLE

Among Americans, the Palestinian struggle for self-determination has never evoked the same level of emotional and political support as the struggle of black South Africans against apartheid. Yet here are a people with equally legitimate grievances: unlawfully dispossessed in 1948 and since 1967 subjected to violations of their basic human rights by a foreign military occupation. In the West Bank and Gaza, Palestinians have been jailed and tortured. They have had their homes demolished, their water rationed, their olive groves uprooted and their land confiscated. They have been forced to live under curfews, stand in line for hours at checkpoints and get Israeli permission to build a home and travel abroad. They have watched their teenagers fired on with guns for throwing stones.

"The Palestinians are not the only members of God's children with no rights to self-determination, but their attitudes and interests are not understood in the U.S," wrote the former Democratic senator from Illinois Adlai E. Stevenson III. "It is as if we did not want to understand." Stevenson wrote that in 1980.[24]

Part of the explanation for the disparity, perhaps, is that Americans saw in the battle against apartheid a familiar replay of our own civil rights struggle. A second reason surely lies in the violent tactics, including terrorist attacks on civilians, adopted by the Palestinians. True, South Africa's

African National Congress used violence and was once regarded as a terrorist organization by the U.S. government. But compared to the Palestine Liberation Organization and Hamas, the ANC seems like a lamb. How much closer to their national aspirations, it is fair to ask, would Palestinians be today if from the start they'd adopted the nonviolent tactics of Mohandas Gandhi or Martin Luther King Jr.?

Then there is the matter of leadership. Arafat has made his mark on history by igniting the flame of Palestinian nationalism and sustaining his people's aspirations through their darkest hours. But he was never able to charm the world or sear its conscience as Nelson Mandela and Desmond Tutu did.

Another explanation for the different American reaction, however, is that there is virtually no serious, sustained public debate in the United States about its approach to the Israeli-Palestinian conflict or the assumptions that underlie U.S. ties with Israel. America's exceptionally close relationship with the Jewish state has become so embedded in the national political consciousness that it is not regarded as a subject that requires examination or discussion. It is as if Israel is on a par with Hawaii—far away, its status taken for granted. By extension, therefore, debate on U.S policy toward the Israeli-Palestinian conflict is curtailed.[25]

But there are legitimate issues to be examined. In Israel, the United States has a close ally that is in continual conflict with its neighbors because the Israeli-Palestinian conflict has not been resolved. As a result, public opinion in more than twenty Arab countries is embittered against the United States, which does not serve the U.S. national interest.

The United States was the first government to recognize the new Jewish state in 1948, partly out of a sense of justice because of what Jews had suffered in the Holocaust.[26] Later, Israel was seen as a staunch ally during the Cold War and in need of U.S. protection against hostile Arab states allied to Moscow, in particular Syria and, up to the early 1970s, Egypt. Israel's close relationship with the United States is also due to Jewish Americans' effective, energetic lobbying on Israel's behalf with U.S. politicians. The American Israel Public Affairs Committee is one of Washington's most powerful interest groups.[27]

Since the end of World War II, Israel has received more U.S. foreign assistance than any other state in the world, a total of $87 billion by the end of 2002. The largest annual recipient of U.S. aid since 1976, Israel has received $3 billion every year since 1985, although its GDP per capita is $18,900, the highest in the Middle East. The U.S. assistance comes with unique features favorable to Israel not offered to other countries, such as receiving its aid in an upfront lump sum instead of by installments, allowing it to earn interest on the payment. Also, in both money and access to U.S. weapons research and development, U.S. military aid to Israel is unparalleled compared to any other Middle East state.[28]

However, despite this generous U.S. assistance, Israel's status as a close U.S. ally, the legitimate aspirations of the Palestinians, and a resolution of their conflict being in the U.S. national interest, the United States for more than three decades has not been able to achieve a settlement.

The track record suggests that part of the problem is that the United States has been overly tolerant of Israeli behavior. For example, one of the major obstacles to resolving the Israeli-Palestinian conflict has been the steady growth of Jewish settlements. Ever since 1967, official U.S. policy has been that East Jerusalem, the West Bank, and Gaza are occupied territories subject to the Fourth Geneva Convention of 1949, to which Israel is a party. That convention prohibits an occupying power from transferring its citizens into occupied territory and from making permanent changes not for the benefit of the occupied population.

Israel has violated this Convention by establishing Jewish settlements in the West Bank and Gaza and by dramatically altering the demographic balance of East Jerusalem. When captured by Israel in 1967, East Jerusalem had no Jewish residents. By early 2002, there were about 175,000, roughly the same as its Arab residents. Israel accomplished this by building Jewish settlements, mostly apartment buildings, in East Jerusalem while severely restricting Arab construction.[29] Although people speak of "Arab East Jerusalem," there are in fact only pockets of Arab neighborhoods surrounded by Jewish neighborhoods or by vacant land on which the Israeli government forbids development.

In August 1994, less than a year after the Oslo Accords were signed, I visited Fawzi Kiswani in the Zewahre area of southeast Jerusalem. Israeli authorities had just bulldozed his home, where two of his nine children were born, because he built it without a permit—something notoriously difficult for Palestinians to acquire in Jerusalem. Across the valley in clear view of his ruined home, however, was the site of a new Jewish development recently approved by city officials. It was projected to include a multistory hotel and three hundred apartments.

"I'm desperate, I'm collapsed, I'm confused," said Kiswani, forty-five, a hotel kitchen steward as he stood on the rubble of his home. "Peace didn't do anything for me."

On another day, I joined other reporters on a tour of Jewish neighborhoods organized by Jerusalem's mayor Ehud Olmert. We were shown the construction site of a new 2,100-unit apartment complex for Orthodox Jews in the East Jerusalem neighborhood of Reches Shoafat. The new settlement, going up at a hectic pace, was privately financed but the government provided the land, sewage, roads, and schools. "The construction pace is unbelievable," the project manager told us. "We originally planned that [the site] would be ready for housing in November 1995 but now we have pushed up the date by six months."

The United States has issued statements critical of Israeli settlement building. But it has never penalized Israel in any concrete way, such as withholding U.S. financial aid, for violating the Fourth Geneva Convention and ignoring U.S. entreaties to cease settlement construction. The United States has told Israel that U.S. assistance cannot be used for building settlements, but it has not set up transparent, strict monitoring of this restriction. "Because U.S. economic aid is given to Israel as direct government-to-government budgetary support without any specific project accounting, and money is fungible, there is no way to tell how Israel uses U.S. aid," a congressional report stated.

Only one U.S. president—George Herbert Walker Bush—bluntly and publicly demanded that Israel stop its settlement activities and then attempted to use American financial leverage to gain its compliance.[30] In 1990, Bush said his administration did "not believe there should be new settlements in the West Bank or in East Jerusalem. And I will conduct that policy as if it's firm, which it is. . . . And that's our strongly held view." Bush's secretary of state James A. Baker told American supporters of Israel in a speech that "now is the time to lay aside once and for all the unrealistic vision of a Greater Israel. Israeli interests in the West Bank and Gaza, security and otherwise, can be accommodated on a settlement based on [U.N.] Resolution 242. Foreswear annexation. Stop settlement activity."[31]

In 1992, the Bush administration informed Israel that it would not approve its request for a special $10 billion loan guarantee—a separate item not included in the annual U.S. aid package—unless Israel froze all settlement construction. This stance led to an open confrontation between the Bush administration and Israel, which was backed by its supporters in Congress. The ensuing tension contributed to Prime Minister Yitzhak Shamir's 1992 defeat at the polls. But a few months later, with the U.S. presidential election in the offing, Bush worked out an arrangement with Shamir's successor, Yitzhak Rabin, under which Israel received the loan guarantee with only minor restrictions. Israel suffered no decrease in its normal level of U.S. aid, and in the years that followed, the number of settlers mounted, almost doubling in the West Bank and Gaza after the 1993 Oslo Accords.[32]

The United States has frequently denounced Israel's actions in the occupied territories such as home demolitions, extended curfews, and excessive use of lethal force against civilians. But those reprimands were not backed up by U.S. actions to show its disapproval. The United States has frequently stood alone in support of Israel at the United Nations and other international forums when Israeli behavior was condemned. The United States went to war to reverse Iraq's 1990 occupation of Kuwait. But when Israel invaded Lebanon in 1982, and several hundred Palestinians were subsequently slaughtered in Beirut refugee camps by Lebanese allies of the Israeli forces, the United States limited itself to verbal demands for an Israeli withdrawal.[33]

From this history comes the Arab perception that the United States is biased toward Israel and, by extension, against Arabs. It is why they see the United States as complicit in the longevity of the Israeli-Palestinian conflict. Arabs do not understand how the United States, despite its economic generosity to Israel, cannot convince it to end its thirty-five-year-long military occupation of the West Bank and Gaza Strip. They do not know why the United States tolerated the erection of Jewish settlements on the land where Palestinians hope to have their own state. They cannot understand why the United States permits Israel to use U.S.-made rifles, tanks, helicopters, and jet fighters to attack Palestinians. As one Palestinian-American professor put it, when Arabs look at America's relationship with Israel they see "a vast reservoir of permissiveness stretching from Capitol Hill to Pennsylvania Avenue."[34]

U.S. officials who have spent hours nudging Israelis and Palestinians to the negotiating table over the years may protest that this is an unfair picture. They maintain that they cannot force peace, which can only come through negotiations between two willing partners. But while they cajole behind the scenes, perceptions of U.S. bias rule the public airwaves. Since these perceptions are a reality, they matter in dealings between the United States and Arab countries.

The Palestinians have done their part, too, to prolong their conflict with Israel. Arafat took far too long to renounce terrorism in 1988. He sided with Iraqi leader Saddam Hussein during the 1991 Gulf War. He was also partly, though not solely, responsible for the failure of the Israeli-Palestinian talks mediated by President Bill Clinton at Camp David in the summer of 2000.

In fact, the disastrous outcome of that summit was a collective failure of all the parties—Clinton, Arafat, and then–Israeli prime minister Ehud Barak. This was the first time that the two sides convened to discuss a final agreement on the hardest problems, the ones left as "permanent status" issues by the Oslo Accords. But there was no clear agenda, no formal working papers, and the atmosphere was all wrong. Clinton, with his eye on his presidential legacy and only a few months left in office, injected an air of urgency into the talks, reinforcing Palestinian fears that they were being coerced into a bad deal.

Barak did offer greater concessions than had any previous Israeli leader. He accepted Palestinian sovereignty over Arab areas in East Jerusalem and a Palestinian state in 90-plus percent of the West Bank. But Barak's offers were oral, not written. He refused to negotiate directly with Arafat, communicating instead through Clinton. He rebuffed Palestinian demands to implement earlier Israeli commitments to partial withdrawals from the West Bank before the talks started. Finally, Barak's terms fell short of what Arafat could accept. On Palestinian refugees, he offered only a "satisfactory solution." Instead of Palestinian sovereignty over Islam's holy site in Jerusalem, he mentioned "permanent custodianship." In addition, aiming to avoid the dismantling of as many Jewish settlements as possible, Barak's proposals for a final settlement on West Bank territory did not give Palestinians enough contiguous land to make a viable independent state and would have left them instead with large, semiconnected blocs.

The Palestinian delegation contributed to the failure of the Camp David parley by refusing to make concrete counterproposals. But contrary to widespread perceptions, the two sides continued to negotiate after Camp David, holding more than fifty secret negotiating sessions over the next few months. They then met openly at the Egyptian beach resort town of Taba, where they had fruitful talks employing the usual tools of tough bargaining: written proposals and counterproposals. As a result, they came the closest ever to what is likely to be the final framework of a peace settlement. The key points included the turnover to Palestinians of at least 94 percent of the West Bank to allow for a state with a mostly contiguous land mass; a swap of territory inside Israel for West Bank territory that Palestinians would give up so major Jewish settlements can remain under Israeli sovereignty; a shared Jerusalem as the capital of both states and Palestinian sovereignty over Arab neighborhoods in the eastern half of the city. As for Palestinian refugees, compensation would be paid, Israel would recognize their theoretical right of return but only allow a token number back to Israel proper in order not to compromise its Jewish majority. Though many details were left unresolved, including how to share sovereignty over Jerusalem's disputed esplanade that is holy to both Muslims and Jews, huge progress was made at Taba.[35]

Unfortunately, these achievements were not followed up because Clinton left office and Barak was about to lose elections to an adamant opponent of peace with Palestinians, Ariel Sharon. Of all Israeli politicians, Sharon is most anathema to the Palestinians. A prime architect of Jewish settlements in the occupied territories, Sharon spearheaded Israel's 1982 invasion of Lebanon. Later charged by an official Israeli inquiry with indirect personal responsibility for the massacre of several hundreds of Palestinian refugees in Beirut during that invasion, he was forced to resign as defense minister. He has opposed every single peace treaty Israel ever signed with Arabs and in the eyes of some fellow Israelis, has been unremittingly brutal to Arabs.[36] Shortly after the collapse of Camp David, Sharon made an in-your-face visit to the Dome of the Rock in Jerusalem to assert Israeli sovereignty over the disputed esplanade. He was accompanied by hundreds of police in riot gear, helicopters overhead, and TV cameras on the ground. This provocative act in late September 2000 triggered the second Palestinian uprising. Arafat's mistake was allowing the Palestinian violence, although it was a desperate cry of despair, to escalate to unprecedented levels. This contributed to Barak's defeat by Sharon in the February 2001 elections. The violence also allowed Sharon, now prime minister, to unleash an unprecedented level of Israeli military reprisals.

FROM DESPAIR TO HOPE

More than ever since September 11, 2001, the United States needs to consider what kind of Middle East it is helping to shape over the next few decades. This is a region of rising populations, political discontent, lagging economies, and robust Islamist political activism. It is well armed on all sides, in large part because of weapons sales by the United States. The continuing Israeli-Palestinian conflict adds yet another volatile element to this precarious environment, offering a ready-made rationale for those willing to walk the path of religious militancy. The Israeli-Palestinian conflict did not cause the terrorist attacks on America. Osama Bin Laden had his eyes on far more distant horizons when he made war on the United States. But his audience in the Arab world made an instant connection between his terrorist attacks and U.S. policies in the Middle East. It is noteworthy that there were no Palestinians among the perpetrators of the deadly attacks in New York and Washington on September 11, 2001. Their struggle is focused on something much closer to home. But that may not be the case forever if the Israeli-Palestinian conflict continues.

The United States must continue to guarantee that Israel, now home to one-third of the world's Jews, remains strong and secure. The Middle East needs Israel—not only for its economic contributions but also for its example as a strong democracy. No other nation in the region allows the same freedom for its press. No other Middle Eastern government would publicly investigate its own culpability in atrocities, as Israel did after the

1982 massacre of Palestinian refugees in Beirut. And none of Israel's neighbors would follow its example of allowing hundreds of military reservists to remain outside prison walls after refusing orders that they considered wrong.[37]

But any democracy, Israel included, whose security depends on guns, tanks, and missiles is not really secure. Genuine security comes through normal, friendly relations with neighbors who feel they are being treated fairly and with dignity. There is no getting around the reality that until a durable resolution is found to the Israeli-Palestinian conflict—one that is just to both sides—the Middle East will continue to be adversely affected. "We say the Palestinians behave like 'madmen,'" said Ami Ayalon, a former senior Israeli security official. "It is not madness but a bottomless despair. . . . As long as the Palestinian question is not resolved, the region will not know stability. Only a Palestinian state will preserve the Jewish and democratic character of Israel."[38]

The outlines for resolution to the Israeli-Palestinian conflict are no secret. They were put on the table at Taba in January 2001. What is required is *determination* to make a settlement happen. A resolution of the Israeli-Palestinian conflict will not mean a future of honey and roses for the Middle East. But it will improve the image of the United States in Arab eyes. It will begin to loosen the straitjacket of hatred, fear, and mistrust that fetters the region. And it will marginalize the hard-liners on both sides, lifting the voices of millions of Israelis and Arabs who sincerely and desperately want to live in peace with each other.

That was the lesson of the Oslo Spring.

THE PATH AHEAD

14

The Promise and the Passion

"He gives the Wisdom to whomsoever He will, and whoso is given the Wisdom, has been given much good; yet none remembers but men possessed of minds."
—QUR'AN 2:269

"Yet the people bore the outrages steadfastly, taking refuge in patience. They held fast to hope, and whenever they were persecuted, they said, 'Injustice must have an end, as day must follow night. We will see the death of tyranny, and the dawn of light and miracles.'"
—NAGUIB MAHFOUZ, *Children of the Alley*

I cannot claim to fully understand the minds of Osama Bin Laden and his fellow outlaws. Their megalomania and callous contempt for human life are breathtaking. Even more so when one considers that before the attacks in New York and Washington on September 11, 2001, Al Qaeda's men killed hundreds of innocent Africans in Kenya and Tanzania just to press their grudge match with the United States. The "collateral damage" of the 1998 U.S. embassy bombings in East Africa was 224 human beings.

I do not understand Bin Laden's ilk any more than I understand Hitler, the product of an advanced Christian civilization who perpetrated mass atrocities beyond belief. But just as historians have sought for decades to understand what led to Hitler's rise, it is necessary to understand the historical forces that contributed to the formation of Muslim radicals intent on killing thousands in the name of Islam.

This understanding is essential for two reasons. First of all because military and police measures, while necessary, can never alone vanquish terrorism. Whenever possible, the causes of the rage and resentment that moti-vate terrorists must also be addressed. It is also prudent to understand the environment that produced such terrorists because the men who plotted and executed the attacks of September 2001 came predominantly from Egypt and Saudi Arabia, two close allies of the United States in the Arab world of the Middle East.

In the aftermath of those attacks, millions of horrified Muslims around the world expressed outrage. They were angry and ashamed that Muslims had sullied their faith by such acts. But some Muslims expressed satisfaction. The United States, they claimed, had brought the attacks on itself through arrogant, selfish behavior.

This split reaction, which bewildered many Americans, indicated two things. It pointed to the existence of deep grievances among some Muslims toward the United States. Second, it was evidence of the divisions that mark Islam today as it passes through one of its most crucial periods since Prophet Muhammad received God's revealed word in the hills of southwest Arabia nearly fourteen hundred years ago.

As we have seen in this book, Muslims are in the throes of a historical resurgence of their faith. Islam has become a template for the culturally confused, a language of protest for the politically frustrated, and a vision for nations adrift in a competitive world. It has also become a subject of inten-sified scrutiny by Muslims seeking to make their faith more relevant to the challenges of modern times.

This revival of Islam is playing out on four overlapping levels: personal, political, cultural and theological. At its core, it involves an internal strug-gle among Muslims who hold very different views of Islam's place in their societies. It is this *internal* battle for the hearts and souls of fellow Muslims, rather than Bin Laden's call for *jihad* against the West, that is most crucial for the future of Islam's contemporary resurgence.

This revival has a global reach and is affecting to varying degrees mostly all of the world's 1.3 billion Muslims. But in the Middle East it has acquired a particularly intense and sometimes violent cast. There are several reasons for this volatile climate. Although Arabs make up only 20 percent of the world's Muslims, they have a special sense of ownership over their faith. Prophet Muhammad was an Arab. The Qur'an is written in Arabic. Arabs were the first Muslims and their faith's first missionaries. As a result, Arabs sometimes feel entitled to define Islam for the rest of the world.

In addition, like any other religion, Islam's expression is influenced by political and social factors. In the Middle East, authoritarian governments have deprived people of political, civil, and intellectual freedoms for decades. Young people, particularly Islamists who want their faith more closely identified with their politics, have found normal channels of political participation closed off. As a result, they have gravitated to underground extremist movements. In many countries, poverty, cronyism, and official corruption have heightened popular frustration.

The long-running Israeli-Palestinian conflict has also contributed to the precarious background in which Islam's revival is occurring in the Middle East. The conflict has aggravated Arab feelings of powerlessness and humiliation before the policies of a seemingly all-powerful United States, which they regard as Israel's main benefactor and protector. Their resentment has only been heightened by the decade-long U.S. insistence on United Nations economic sanctions against Iraq. Though aimed at weakening Iraqi leader Saddam Hussein, the sanctions have contributed to the deaths of thousands of ordinary Iraqis and crippled their country's intellectual and economic life. These U.S. policies, perceived by Arabs as unfair, are at the root of the anti-American sentiment in the region.

A final reason for the turbulence of Islam's resurgence in the Middle East is a crisis of theology, which has resulted in a literalist, ultraorthodox version of Islam gaining the upper hand. As we have seen, a vital aspect of Islam's global revival is the effort of many Muslims to bring new thinking to their faith through *ijtihad*. But in the Middle East, this theological renewal has been stymied. Decades of intellectual repression by authoritarian governments and the failure of Islam's traditional religious scholars, the *ulama*, to modernize interpretations of Islamic scripture contributed to this theological void.

In addition, Saudi Arabia has used its oil wealth to vigorously promote Wahhabism, its ultraconservative understanding of Islam. Wahhabism is not a terrorist ideology and there are many peace-loving, tolerant Saudis. But Wahhabism is based on a literalist reading of Islamic scripture and Islamic law, rejecting historical or contextual analysis. Its religious schools eschew disciplines like philosophy, rhetoric, logic, and sociology as aids in understanding Islamic scripture. Many proponents of Wahhabism are anti-Western, puritanical, and xenophobic. They are often intolerant of other faiths and of Muslims who do not follow their way of Islam. Some urge *jihad* against "enemies" of Islam. This version of Islam has won an increasing number of adherents in recent years and has strongly influenced religious attitudes throughout the region.

All these political, religious, and social factors have created an angry, unstable environment in the Middle East, of which Al Qaeda's terrorists were the most extreme manifestation.

If terrorism is to be defeated for good, this environment needs to be turned around. It is a long-term undertaking. But the sooner started, the better, especially with the United States increasing its military involvement in the region. As we learned in Vietnam, policies germinated in flawed appreciations of what matters to people in distant lands can lead to tragedies.

The first task of the United States should be to reach a final resolution of the Israeli-Palestinian conflict. This is an opportunity for the United States to show its commitment to justice for *both* sides. It should also be more overt in its criticism of human rights violations, no matter who is perpetrating them, and in its support for political liberalizing by Arab governments.

As this book shows, there is a wide spectrum of views among Islamist political activists. It is important to see the distinctions among them and support their right to participate in political affairs if they operate within the law and reject violence. The Islamists working to make their countries more democratic should not be dismissed simply because their models of governance are not yet perfect or differ from those in the West. At least for the foreseeable future, the secular state of the West is not going to be replicated in the Middle East, where people increasingly prefer Islam as the touchstone for their political life.

On another level, it is important to foster the conditions that nourish theological inquiry and debate, and that means a regional peace settlement and greater political freedoms. Muslims are eager for new thinking in Islam that is compatible with democracy and modernity and that gives them a sense of restored dignity. They know deep down that a closed, cramped version of their faith will not make them full partners in today's globalized world, and that new thinking will allow Islam to maintain its vibrancy as a spiritual force. But when societies feel defensive, humiliated, and beleaguered—like those in the Middle East do now—they are not at their most creative. Instead, more hard-line, conservative ideologies usually prevail in such circumstances.

There is only so much that outsiders can do, however. Muslims of the Middle East have to do the heavy lifting. And that means first of all dropping their debilitating dependency on conspiracy theories in which they are eternally the victims. This bad habit allows Arabs to avoid taking responsibility for their own future. More open, democratic societies are not going to be delivered on a silver platter. They have to be fought for.

Islamic countries of the Middle East want a bigger voice than they now have on the world stage, where they feel sidelined and pushed around by bigger countries, including the United States. The way to achieve that power is by building strong societies based on economic prosperity, political liberties, and intellectual creativity.

In the years ahead, the land along the Nile may offer this new paradigm of a modern Islamic society. Of all Arab countries navigating the shoals of Islam's resurgence, it is among those with the potential to achieve this. But getting there is not a certainty and faces roadblocks.

Egyptians, including Islamists, need greater freedom to debate their future, speak their minds, and engage in politics. The tug of war between Egyptians who want a more orthodox Islamic state and culture and those who prefer a Western-style, secular-oriented society is not over. A new generation of radical militants could cause mischief down the road. Egypt is not a revolutionary nation, but it has experienced periodic spikes of violence, most recently in the early 1990s.

Essential, too, will be the freedom to do *ijtihad* so that Islam's message can be articulated anew for modern Muslims. One hundred years ago, Muhammad Abduh perceived that far-reaching social and political reforms in Egypt would require a new understanding of Islam. That is still true today. For the vast majority of Egyptians, Islam remains the most legitimate source of authority. It is Islam, then, that can provide the road map for Egypt to become a successful modern state.

The task of reinterpreting Islam for modern times is the essence of Islam's contemporary revival in Egypt and around the globe. If this "interpretive imperative,"[1] as some Muslims call it, is fully embraced, Islam's revival will become Islam's renaissance, ushering in a new era of intellectual creativity for Muslims.

This reinterpretive endeavor will take *shari'a* beyond archaic criminal penalties and canonical minutiae, presenting it instead as a living, adaptable body of laws that embody Islam's mandate to make the world reflect God's justice. And it will give prominence to Islam's insistence on freedom, compassion, and fairness, thereby closing the gate to modern Muslim dictators in the twenty-first century.

This is the promise of Islam, and the source of passion for Islam.

NOTES

1. First Verses

1. Between 1992 and 1998, 1,357 persons, including terrorists, policemen, civilians, and tourists, were killed either by insurgents or police, according to the independent Egyptian Organization for Human Rights (EOHR), cited in *Human Rights Watch Special Report on Egypt, October 2001*. In May 1996, the now defunct Ibn Khaldoun Center in Cairo reported that from 1992 to 1995, 1,562 people were wounded in the insurgency—the most ever in political conflict in modern Egypt.

   My independent count showed ninety-six foreigners killed by the end of November 1997. A congressional report stated that ninety foreigners had been killed. Clyde R. Mark, *Egypt–United States Relations*, Congressional Research Service, Library of Congress, Washington, D.C., updated January 17, 2002, p. 5.

   By the end of 2001, eighty-eight death sentences handed down by military courts had been carried out, according to EOHR, as cited in *Human Rights Watch Special Report on Egypt, October 2001*.

2. Mark, *Egypt–United States Relations*, p. 12, for cumulative U.S. aid to Egypt since 1948. See also John Lancaster, "U.S. Aid Has Yet to Lift Most Egyptians," *Washington Post*, April 5, 1996. Requesting more than $2 billion in aid for Egypt in 1999, the Clinton administration described Egypt as "the most prominent player in the Arab world and a key U.S. ally in the Middle East" and noted that "[a] strong relationship with Egypt affords us political and security benefits that no single other Arab state can provide." *Human Rights Watch World Report, 1999*, New York, p. 351. For fiscal year 2002, the Bush administration requested $1.3 billion in foreign military aid; $655 million in economic support fund assistance and $1 million for Egyptian military officer training, according to Mark, *Egypt–United States Relations*, p. 12. Beginning in 1999, U.S. aid to Egypt is decreasing every year until it reaches about $400 million annually by 2008. This is in line with current reductions in U.S. economic aid to Israel. Egypt, however, is not receiving increased U.S. military assistance every year, as Israel is. Mark, *Egypt–United States Relations*, preface and p. 9.

   The 358,000 figure for Egypt's military comes from *Jane's World Armies*, at www.janes.com.

3. Atta information is from Neil MacFarquhar, "Hijack Suspect Called 'Shy and Tender,'" *New York Times*, September 19, 2001. Atef was apparently killed in the U.S. bombing of Afghanistan, according to news reports. Zawahiri's whereabouts in early 2002 were unknown.

2. Withered Dreams and "Zucchini" by the Bushel

1. Sadat's "Open Door" policy was presented as a turnaround from the external trade barriers erected by Nasser's socialist state. By 1996, the public sector still accounted for two-thirds of the country's industrial output, according to the World Bank, cited by John Lancaster, in "Egypt's Economy Fights to Junk Socialist Legacy," *Washington Post*, May 8, 1996. In 2002, the World Bank estimated that 17 percent of Egypt's GDP was still in state hands, according to a telephone interview with author.

2. A Mercedes Benz company spokesman said in an interview that Egypt in 1994 was number thirty-one in the world for importing its passenger cars. "So we can say that Egypt is very important for Mercedes Benz," he added. John Lancaster, "Desert Turns to Greens as Egypt's Affluent Revive Colonial Links," *Washington Post*, February 22, 1997; Youssef M. Ibrahim, "The Tower of Power: Something to Babble About," *New York Times*, August 15, 1995.

3. The CIA's *World Factbook* reports 22.9 percent of Egyptians live below the poverty line. In a population of 70 million, that would be 16 million. (In the United States, which has a GDP per capita of $36,200, 12.9 percent of the population lives below the poverty line, according to the *Factbook*.) The World Bank reported that in 1996, 56 percent of Egyptians living below the poverty line were in rural areas. The *Factbook*, using a benchmark that it calls "purchasing power parity," puts Egypt's GDP per capita at $3,600, higher than the $1,420 figure of the U.S. State Department in its Country Report on Egypt.

   The percentage of Egyptians who can read is 51.4; 63.6 percent of men and 38.8 percent of women are literate, according to the *Factbook*. Official figures place the unemployment rate at 9.4 percent, but some economists estimate it as high as 15 percent, according to Mark, *Egypt–United States Relations*, p. 7.

   The estimated annual population growth rate is from the *Factbook* and the projected 2015 population is from U.N. Development Program's *Human Development Report, 2001*, New York, p. 156. The figure for population under fifteen years old is from the *Factbook*.

   Although Egypt is a large country, only 3 percent of its territory, a little less than Maryland, is suitable for agriculture and the country must import food. Mark, *Egypt–United States Relations*, p. 7.

4. Mark, *Egypt–United States Relations*, p. 7, cites Egyptian officials estimating that one million Egyptians work in Europe and another million in the Persian Gulf states.

5. Salama Ahmed Salama, a senior editor at the government's main newspaper, *Al Ahram*, knows firsthand the frustrations of reporting on corruption in Egypt. Even when a paper ferrets out a scandal and prints it, Salama said in an interview, "nothing happens. You don't get an answer to what is raised. I tell you you are a thief and you don't answer. You just leave it. You don't even sue me for defamation."

   After a 1992 earthquake killed 560 people in Cairo, the press was full of stories about corrupt building inspectors. The owner of one apartment building, which became a grave for 72 persons, reportedly erected eight illegal floors on top of the six allowed by her building license. *Rose Al Yussef* magazine noted that even without earthquakes, three houses collapse every day in Cairo because of shoddy or illegal construction overlooked by bribed inspectors. The situation, wrote Salama, showed how "bribery makes the impossible, possible and reduces the laws of the land to no more than ink on paper."

6. Interview with Farghali, Cairo, 1993. The industrious Ragab also petitioned the minister of religious affairs to rename a mosque in Cairo after his mother, which was promptly done by ministerial fiat. This proved too much for one of the mosque members, who shot off a withering letter to the minister pointing out that the woman so honored "has done nothing for the mosque except that she is the mother of a well-known journalist."

7. Neil MacFarquhar, "Hijack Suspect Called 'Shy and Tender,' " *New York Times*, September 19, 2001. The alienation of Egyptians and other Arabs from their governments

is evident in language. While it is common in the West to hear references to "our government," Egyptians usually say "the government" or "the authority," noted Middle East scholar Augustus Richard Norton of Boston University.
8. *'Abd al-Rahman al-Jabarti's History of Egypt*, ed. Thomas Philipp and Moshe Perlmann (Stuttgart: Franz Steiner Verlag, 1994), p. 12.

3. PERSONAL AWAKENINGS

1. John Lancaster, "Cairo's Populace Enforces Ramadan's Fasting Rules; Eating and Smoking Become Hidden Vices," *Washington Post*, January 25, 1996.
2. The 1996 documentary film by Egyptian director Yousry Nasrallah *Boys, Girls and the Veil* is a good examination of why young girls decide to wear the veil.
3. The description of "Science and Faith" is in Yahya Sadowski, "Egypt's Islamist Movement: A New Political and Economic Force," *Middle East Insight*, 5, no. 4 (1987): 43.
4. Former presidential spokesman, the late Tahseen Basheer, explained that Egyptians used "setback" because it expressed their hope that the military defeat could be reversed. Other Arabs, he said, used "catastrophe," the same word they had applied to the 1948 establishment of the State of Israel.
5. The Egyptian journalist is Mohammed Sid Ahmed, whom I interviewed in New York in March 1996. I want to acknowledge here my debt to Ahmed. He was the first person I heard using the phrase "Pious Islam" to describe the grassroots revival of personal piety. The Lebanese scholar Ghassan Salame has also elucidated the distinction between Pious and Political Islam. See his analysis, "Islam and the West," *Foreign Policy*, Spring 1993: 22–37, where he states, "Whatever the outcome of Islamist attempts to dominate governments, the re-Islamization of societies is proceeding" (p. 26).
6. Fatemah Al Farag, "Neighborhood Takes Responsibility for Orphans," *Middle East Times*, March 31, 1996. Mustafa Mahmoud's hospital is an ambitious example of community service generated by Islam's admonition to help those in need. Its 1989 construction was underwritten by mostly private donations from Egyptians and Saudis. The staff of over three hundred serves both Muslims and Christians; its tidy rooms have air-conditioning, televisions, and telephones, and its overall efficiency and cleanliness make it a stark contrast to shabby, underfunded government hospitals.

"Though many Islamic associations are apolitical, these organizations and activities carry an implicit political critique of the Egyptian government's failure to meet the needs of society," wrote John L. Esposito in *The Islamic Threat, Myth or Reality?* (New York: Oxford University Press, 1992), p. 132.

"In highly secularized Middle Eastern societies, Islam becomes more and more a quest for meaning without being linked to political purposes. In these milieus, a new kind of Islamic community emerges, one that is based on personal piety rather than on commitment to political institutions. . . ." This "reconstruction of Islam" has encouraged "a more fully self-disciplined and self-directed autonomous personality," wrote Ira M. Lapidus in "The Golden Age: The Political Concepts of Islam," in *Annals of the American Academy of Political and Social Science* 524 (November 1992): 25.

See also Andrea B. Rugh, "Reshaping Personal Relations in Egypt," in *Fundamentalisms and Society*, eds. Martin E. Marty and R. Scott Appleby (Chicago: University of Chicago Press, 1993), p. 165.
7. The interviews cited in this chapter were all done in Cairo except Yousry Nasrallah's, whose remarks come from a 1996 New York workshop on Egyptian film. I interviewed Hussein Amin in February 1992 and April 1996, Ibrahim Mohammed Al Ataban in 1994, Mustafa Mahmoud in 1990, Mohammed Yusuf Al Qa'id in 1996, Gasser Shadi in 1992, Soha Abdel Kader in 1993, Nabil Al Din in 1993, Omayma Abdel Latif in 1996, and the Arab journalist, who preferred to remain anonymous, in 1996.

4. What Kind of Country Are We Going to Be?

1. Qur'an, 11:101
2. The Egyptian Organization for Human Rights, cited in *Human Rights Watch Special Report on Egypt, October 2001*, reported thirty-two trials from 1992 to 1998 and eighty-eight death sentences carried out. The military courts procedures were "grossly unfair," according to "Egypt Indefinite Detention and Systematic Torture: The Forgotten Victims," Amnesty International, London, July 1996. See also 1996 U.S. State Department Report on "Human Rights Practices in Egypt" (Sec. 1e).
3. Albert Hourani, *A History of the Arab Peoples* (Cambridge: Belknap Press of Harvard University Press, 1991), p. 282.
4. *Flaubert in Egypt: A Sensibility on Tour*, ed. and trans. Francis Steegmuller (Chicago: Academy Chicago Limited, 1979).
5. Nadav Safran, *Egypt in Search of Political Community* (Cambridge: Harvard University Press, 1961), p. 63.
6. Charles C. Adams, *Islam and Modernism in Egypt* (London: Oxford University Press, 1933), pp. 22, 93–144. I am indebted to Adams's excellent study of Abduh for the details of his life presented here.
7. Safran, *Egypt in Search of Political Community*, p. 63. Abduh's impatience with those who mistook slavish attention to ritual for spiritual maturity was vividly, if inadvertently, illustrated in an incident a few months before his death. Returning from a trip to Sudan, Abduh was met by a welcoming committee that included a sheikh who excitedly announced that he was instructing a prominent Christian who had converted to Islam in the details of the ritual washing Muslims perform before praying. When Abduh asked which details, the sheikh replied, "For instance, I explain the parameters of his face between the two ears widthwise and from the forehead to the chin lengthwise." Abduh, so the story goes, frowned and snapped at the fawning cleric: "O sheikh, every human being knows his face without the need of a surveyor." See Yvonne Y. Haddad, "Muhammad Abduh: Pioneer of Islamic Reform" in *Pioneers of Islamic Revival*, ed. Ali Rahnema (London: Zed Books Ltd., 1994), p. 62.
8. Abduh's professors who had tried to block his diploma got their revenge by giving him only a passing grade in his final exams. Adams, *Islam and Modernism in Egypt*, p. 43. Apart from his youthful support for the military officers' nationalist movement, Abduh generally steered clear of politics and his writings dealt mainly with social, moral, and theological issues. But he argued that an Islamic ruler does not get his authority from God, as many traditional *ulama* then taught, but rather from the community of Muslim believers, the *umma*. This view of the source of temporal authority is why Abduh argued that a representative form of government is compatible with Islam. He considered veiling "not of the essence of Islam since there is no" Qur'anic text for it. Abduh also taught that monogamy was preferable to polygamy since no man could be equally just to several wives, as the Qur'an requires. Haddad, "Muhammad Abduh," pp. 53 and 58; Adams, *Islam and Modernism in Egypt*, pp. 51 and 63.
9. At his trial, Abduh was found guilty of having given a religious opinion in favor of deposing Tawfiq Ali Pasha prior to the uprising of military officers, known as the Urabi revolt, according to some contemporary accounts. One of Abduh's earliest biographers, however, claimed he had not issued any such decree. Adams, *Islam and Modernism in Egypt*, pp. 54 and 56, note 4.
10. Ibid., pp. 58–61 and 89.
11. Abduh once wrote that his trips to Europe were part "of renewing his soul" because there he found hope that Muslim societies could be improved. He sent the Russian writer a letter after his excommunication from the Orthodox Church. Ibid., pp. 67, 95, and 92
12. Ibid., 129–130.
13. Ibid., 130–131. Abduh's attack on *taqlid* is in his primary theological work, *Risalat Al Tawhid*, or "Treatise on the Unity of God": "The hearts of the mass of the people have been infected by the *ulama* with the disease of *taklid*. For the *ulama* believe a certain

thing and then seek proofs for it; and they are not willing to have the proof be other than agreeable to what they believe."

Abduh was not the first or only Islamic reformer to call for a renewal of *ijtihad*, but he was the most forceful and influential of those who did. Safran wrote that Abduh's "most revolutionary enterprise" was "his reinterpretive initiative." He "rejected vehemently the orthodox view that the doctrine and law of Islam had been formulated once and for all by the medieval doctors, and insisted on the right of every generation to go back to the sources and understand them according to its own lights." Safran observed that in Abduh's time, with Britain occupying Egypt, "[T]raditional Muslim doctrine, having annihilated historical causality and natural justice in the inscrutable omnipotence of Allah, could offer neither hope of redemption from, nor a satisfactory explanation for, the possibility of subjugation by alien, less virtuous powers." Safran, *Egypt in Search of Political Community*, pp. 64 and 41.

14. Haddad, "Muhammad Abduh," p. 46. Adams wrote of Abduh: "Devotion to Islam was the controlling motive of his life. It was his deep conviction that only by a thoroughgoing reform of the whole system that amounted, indeed, to the evolution of a new Islam, although to him it meant but a return to the original form, could this religion prove its inherent adaptability to present-day conditions." Adams, *Islam and Modernism in Egypt*, p. 96.

Abduh was apparently discouraged at being unable to stir his people from their political apathy. "There is another thing that I called for while all the people were blind to it, whereas it is the foundation of their life in society and the cause of all their weakness and humiliation; and that is the distinction between the government's right to the people's obedience and the people's right that the government be just. . . . Yes, I was among those who appealed to the Egyptian nation to be conscious of its rights with regard to the ruler when this had not occurred to it for more than twenty centuries. . . ." Safran, *Egypt in Search of Political Community*, pp. 70–71.

For more on Abduh's thought, see P. J. Vatikiotis, *The History of Modern Egypt* (Baltimore: Johns Hopkins University Press, 1991), pp. 195–196.

15. Haddad, "Muhammad Abduh," p. 42 and Albert Hourani, as quoted in Nemat Guenena, *The "Jihad," An "Islamic Alternative" in Egypt* (Cairo: American University in Cairo Press, Summer 1986), Cairo Papers in Social Science, vol. 9, monograph 2, p. 30.

16. The Ottoman Empire, wrote the late Middle East historian Albert Hourani, was "the last great expression of the universality of the world of Islam." Of its end, Hourani added: "The political structure within which most Arabs had lived for four centuries had disintegrated . . . the dynasty which . . . had been regarded as the guardian of what was left of the power and independence of Sunni Islam had vanished into history. These changes had a deep effect on the way in which politically conscious Arabs thought of themselves and tried to define their political identity. . . ." Hourani, *A History of the Arab People*, pp. 207 and 316.

The modern Islamist Abdelwahab El Affendi wrote, "The period that followed the abolition of the khilafa [caliphate] in Turkey in 1924 was one of deep anguish and disorientation for Muslims. For the first time since the advent of Islam the believers were left without a central authority claiming to be the protector of the faith. . . . For the first time since the Prophet assumed supreme political office in Medina in 622, Islam became a stateless religion, an ideology in search of a home." Affendi, *Who Needs an Islamic State?* (London: Grey Seal Books, 1991), pp. 47–48.

17. By 1914, wrote P. J. Vatikiotis, a gap had opened between Abduh and his first disciples, who "were now under the spell of European thought . . . willing to adopt not only European ideas, but the very institutions that grew in Europe." Vatikiotis, *History of Modern Egypt*, p. 245. The "Great Arab Revolt" against the Turkish Sultan in Istanbul during World War I, fueled by the British agent T. E. Lawrence, indicated the new spirit of Arab nationalism. After that war, the country that swung farthest to the new secular nationalism was the modern state of Turkey, which arose from the ashes of the Ottoman Empire. In 1924, Turkish leader Mustafa Kemal Ataturk officially abolished the caliphate.

18. Richard P. Mitchell, *The Society of Muslim Brothers* (London: Oxford University Press,

1969), p. 230. My rendition of the Brotherhood's history and ideas, as well as many details of Banna's life, are principally from Mitchell's book, widely regarded as the most authoritative and detailed examination of Banna and the Brotherhood.

19. Ibid., pp. 40, 235, and 246. Mitchell called the Brotherhood "the first mass-supported and organized, essentially urban-oriented effort to cope with the plight of Islam in the modern world" (p. 321).

20. Ibid., p. 30. This passage comes from a 1943 "Farewell Address" that Banna wrote at a time he believed he was about to be sent into exile. Banna's idea of transforming a nation by transforming individuals (p. 234) was echoed in recent years by another religious reformer, this one an American evangelical Christian. Bill McCartney, founder of the Promise Keepers, said in an interview that "the way you change a nation is the way you change a man's heart. They think that government changes things. Government depends on men's hearts to be right." Transcript of "Larry King Live," CNN, November 21, 1997

21. The more rigid, moralistic approach was embodied in the work of Abduh's most prominent disciple, Rashid Rida. He stressed the need to go back to Islam's original sources for guidance in developing a social morality. This return to a "pure Islam" involved reinterpreting the Qur'an but stressing a return to orthodoxy as exemplified in the early days of Islam. See Hourani, *History of the Arab People*, pp. 307–308 and 347; "Modernism," in *Oxford Encyclopedia of the Modern Islamic World*, ed. John L. Esposito (New York: Oxford University Press, 1995); Vatikiotis, *History of Modern Egypt*, p. 197; Mitchell, *Society of Muslim Brothers*, pp. 325–327.

"Brotherhood leaders," wrote John O. Voll, "recognized that traditional teachers might be helpful, but they were not final authorities. One was freed from any obligation to accept the word of the medieval scholars, for the 'greatest fear of the Muslim Brotherhood is that Eastern Islamic peoples may let themselves be swept along by the current of blind traditionalism.' In practical terms, this meant that a basic 'principle of action' was the exercise of informed independent judgment, *ijtihad*, in order to guide 'the endeavor of present-day Muslims to meet the needs of the community.' " Voll, "Fundamentalism in the Sunni Arab World: Egypt and the Sudan," in *Fundamentalisms Observed*, eds. Martin E. Marty and R. Scott Appleby (Chicago: University of Chicago Press, 1991), p. 364.

22. Mitchell, *Society of Muslim Brothers*, p. 297.

23. Ibid., pp. 300 and 297. Mitchell, who used the phrase *moral rearmament* to describe the Brotherhood's mission, was eloquent on this aspect of the organization: "Profoundly genuine though it was, the call to return to Islam and its code of behavior was nevertheless vitiated by a sterility born of obedience to inherited forms and a self-righteousness born of sanctimonious claims to omniscience" (p. 325).

24. David Commins,"Hasan Al Banna" in Rahnema, *Pioneers of Islamic Revival*, pp. 142–143.

25. David Gardner, "A Cautious Man," *Financial Times*, May 11, 1995. Mubarak added that he was soon disenchanted: "There was a big Sheikh in our village, giving good speeches, good advice, good principles . . . then we realised it was not just about speeches but power." As an army officer, Egyptian president Anwar Sadat also had ties to the Brotherhood. "I myself believed that great things would come of our combined efforts," he said, discussing the alliance between the army and Brotherhood during the 1952 coup. Sadat, *Revolt on the Nile* (New York: John Day Co., 1957), p. 92.

26. Mitchell, *Society of Muslim Brothers*, pp. 243, 245–250. Despite the Brothers' demand for an Islamic state, they "perceived only intuitively" how that would actually work. Safran, *Egypt in Search of Political Community*, p. 232. Obviously, the Brotherhood regarded as un-Islamic the Egyptian monarchy's claim to royal authority by heredity. Banna always insisted that his movement was not a political one, arguing that political parties were not part of the "Islamic system." But the Brotherhood talked, walked, and acted like a political party. When it suited Banna's purposes, he directed members to participate in elections and was not above making secret alliances with secular parties or officials in the royal court. In a 1939 national conference, the Brotherhood defined itself as a "political organization." Mitchell, *Society of Muslim Brothers*, p. 16.

27. Mitchell, *Society of Muslim Brothers*, pp. 230 and 236.
28. Ibid., p. 233. This well-known statement from Banna underscores the difference between his idea of "nation" and Europe's. While Europeans regard ethnicity as the basis for "nation" and "nationality," Banna saw Islam as the defining ingredient of these concepts. Mitchell linked the Brotherhood's mission to the question of Egypt's destiny. "[T]he immediate concern of the Muslim brothers was not the organization of a 'Muslim state' (although, as we shall see, this was considered), but rather the more profound issue of the nature and destiny of Muslim society in the twentieth century—'the Islamic order,' the most important elements of which were: (1) the *shari'a* and its validity for modern times; and (2) the related question of 'the separation of church and state'" (p. 236).

   For background on the dispute over whether Egypt's national identity should be based on secular or religious values, see P. J. Vatikiotis, "The National Question in Egypt," in his *Arab and Regional Politics in the Middle East* (New York: St. Martin's Press, 1984).
29. Mitchell, *Society of Muslim Brothers*, pp. 206–208.
30. Ibid., pp. 30–32. Other underground groups included the "Green Shirts" of the right-wing Young Egypt movement and the "Blue Shirts" of the secular, liberal Wafd Party. Mitchell concluded that several factors contributed to the creation of the Brotherhood's secret unit. They included Banna's militant rhetoric, his proclivity for secrecy and the Brotherhood's frustration with obstacles imposed by the state when it tried to participate in elections. He stated that along with the Brotherhood's "pacifist" current dedicated to education and gradual reform, there coexisted another current that believed in action, sometimes violent, revolution. There was a definite perception both inside and outside the Brotherhood, Mitchell wrote, that it was a revolutionary party and "that the forcible overthrow of the political order was in fact its goal" (pp. 306–320 and 312).
31. Induction ceremony details and estimates of "Apparatus" membership are in Ibid., p. 206, and Sadat, *Revolt on the Nile*, p. 93.
32. Mitchell, *Society of Muslim Brothers*, pp. 62 and 68.
33. Ibid., p. 71. Most scholars agree with Mitchell that the government was responsible for Banna's killing.
34. Anwar Sadat met secretly with Banna. Ibid., pp. 24–25, 40–41, 96–97.
35. This summary of Nasser's concept of Islam's role comes from Abd Al Moneim Said Aly and Manfred W. Wenner, "Modern Islamic Reform Movements: The Muslim Brotherhood in Contemporary Egypt," *Middle East Journal*, 36, no. 3 (1982): 342–343; Hourani, *History of the Arab People*, pp. 405–407; and a 1996 interview in Washington with former Nasser spokesman, the late Tahseen Basheer. The changes in Al Azhar's status took place in 1961.
36. Many Egyptians "believed Israelis won the war because they are so much attached to their religion. That Israel is not really a secular state as it says," observed former Egyptian ambassador Hussein Amin. The Israelis, he noted, "are very attached to their religion." Amin interview, Cairo, April 1996. Also Aly and Wenner, "Modern Islamic Reform Movements," p. 345. Mitchell described how prominent Brotherhood scholar Muhammad Al Ghazali expressed "admiration for Zionists for returning to their past, unashamed of their religion, to call themselves Israel." He quotes Ghazali as writing: "'What evil must we not expect to befall Islam at the hands of such adversaries.'" Mitchell, *Society of Muslim Brothers*, p. 242, note 38.
37. Gilles Kepel gives an excellent elucidation of the link between Nasser's spread of social control and the radicalization of Islamist thought. Kepel, *The Prophet and Pharaoh*, trans. Jon Rothschild (London: Al Saqi Books, 1985), pp. 37, 46, and 55–56.
38. Qutb, quoted in Charles Tripp, "Sayyid Qutb: The Political Vision" in Rahnema, *Pioneers of Islamic Revival*, p. 171.
39. Qutb's personal history and political beliefs are taken mainly from Kepel, *Prophet and Pharaoh*; Tripp, "Sayyid Qutb"; Shahrough Akhavi's "Sayyid Qutb," in *Oxford Encyclopedia*, and Yvonne Y. Haddad's "Sayyid Qutb: Ideologue of Islamic Revival" in *Voices of Resurgent Islam*, ed. John L. Esposito (New York: Oxford University Press, 1983).
40. Kepel, *Prophet and Pharaoh*, pp. 28, 41, and 55.

41. Quoted in Yvonne Haddad, "The Traditional Response," in Yvonne Haddad, *Contemporary Islam and the Challenge of History* (Albany: State University of New York Press, 1982), pp. 92–93.

42. Kepel, *Prophet and Pharaoh*, pp. 51 and 53–55, and Haddad, "Sayyid Qutb." Haddad quoted Qutb as writing: "Anyone who grasps the nature of this religion . . . understands the imperative for the dynamic movement of Islam by *jihad* with the sword—side by side with the *jihad* through admonition—and would understand that it is not a defensive movement" (p. 83). Qutb drew on the ideas of the late Sayyid Abu Al A'la Mawdudi, the radical Islamist thinker who led Pakistan's Jama'at-I Islami party and who died in 1979.

43. Kepel, *Prophet and Pharaoh*, p. 46.

44. Voll, "Fundamentalism in the Sunni Arab World," p. 366. Three years after Qutb's execution, the head of the Muslim Brotherhood, Hasan Al Hodeiby, published his own book from prison criticizing Qutb's ideas. *Preachers, not Judges* never mentioned Qutb's name but rejected his characterization of Egyptian society as "pagan." It reiterated the Brotherhood's traditional outlook that just because a Muslim has sinned does not mean he is beyond the pale of Islam or "a pagan." Finally, in 1982, the editor of the Brotherhood's main publication, *Al Dawa*, or "The Call," disowned Qutb by name. Umar Talmasani wrote that Qutb had "represented himself alone and not the Muslim Brethren." Kepel, *Prophet and Pharaoh*, pp. 61–63.

45. Kepel gives a detailed description of the rise of Islamic Associations on campus and their capture of the national student union. Kepel, *Prophet and Pharaoh*, pp. 139, 140, 144, and 150.

46. *Facts on File*, 1981, p. 648. The description of Jihad's membership, structure, and conspiracy to kill Sadat is drawn principally from Kepel and Guenena. The man who later emerged as Osama Bin Laden's senior adviser, Ayman Zawahiri, was not a major player in the conspiracy to kill Sadat and only became a significant leader of Jihad in later years.

47. Kepel, *Prophet and Pharaoh*, p. 192. In April 1982, Islambouli, Faraj, and three other Jihad members were executed for their roles in Sadat's assassination, an attack in which seven others were killed. In a separate trial, 302 defendants were tried for a wider conspiracy to overthrow the government and lead a rebellion in Assiut. In September 1984, 174 were acquitted and 107 were sentenced to prison sentences ranging from two to twenty-five years. The other 21 were at-large or died during the trial. David Ottaway, "107 Extremists Are Sentenced," *Washington Post*, October 1, 1984.

When Islambouli was asked by Egyptian police why he had killed Sadat, he said, "I did what I did because the *shari'a* was not applied, because of the peace treaty with the Jews and because of the arrest of Muslim *ulama* without justification." Guenena, *"Jihad," an "Islamic Alternative" in Egypt*, p. 44. Islambouli was also very upset by Sadat's arrest of his brother (Kepel, *Prophet and Pharaoh*, p. 205). So while Sadat's peace overture to Israel was a reason for his murder, it was not the only one.

5. THE GHOST

1. Yusuf Idris, "The Stranger," in *Rings of Burnished Brass* trans. Catherine Cobbam (Cairo: American University in Cairo Press, 1990), pp. 4–5.

2. *Egyptian Gazette*, May 11, 1993, p. 7. One of Hammam's ancestors, it seems, had also been rebellious. According to Mamoun Fandy, who grew up in southern Egypt, Sheikh Al Araba Hammam from the town of Girga defied the government in 1776 by establishing his own independent fiefdom, which he called the "Republic of Girga."

3. Details of Hammam's early life came from Egyptian lawyer Montassir Al Zayat, interviewed in Cairo, April 1996, and Egyptian journalist Hamdi Rizk, who said his information came from Egyptian security sources. The Egyptian Interior Ministry said Hammam was expelled from Assiut because he failed many courses.

According to Hisham Mubarak, 115 policemen were killed in the Assiut uprising. At the time, the government said that only half that number—54—had been killed and over

100 wounded. Three years later, *The Washington Post* reported that 87 persons, most of them policemen, were killed and 156 others injured. David Ottaway, "107 Extremists Are Sentenced," *Washington Post*, October 1, 1984. Hisham Mubarak, who sought to understand the root causes of terrorism in Egypt, was one of Egypt's most dedicated human rights activists. Sadly, he died of a heart attack at age thirty-five in January 1998. I am indebted to him for sharing his insights with me during several interviews between 1992 and 1996.

4. Shinawy interview, Cairo, July 1993. A kindly, white-haired surgeon in his sixties, Shinawy had studied and written about Islamists for years when I met him.

5. Peter Waldman, "Holy Terror: How Sheik Omar Rose to Lead Islamic War While Eluding the Law," *Wall Street Journal*, September 1, 1993.

6. Maha Azzam, "Islamic Oriented Protest Groups in Egypt, 1971–1981: Politics and Dogma," Ph.D. thesis, Faculty of Social Studies, University of Oxford, 1989, p. 287.

7. The Qur'anic passage is 8:39. Abdel Rahman's courtroom statement is in Nemat Guenena, *The "Jihad." an "Islamic Alternative" in Egypt* (Cairo: American University in Cairo Press, Summer 1986. Cairo Papers in Social Science 9, monograph 2, pp. 57–58.

8. Zumur apparently later defected to Islamic Group and Ayman Zawahiri eventually emerged as leader of Islamic Jihad.

9. Most Muslims in the Middle East are Sunni Muslims, so-called because of the importance they ascribe to the Sunna. The other main branch of Islam, dominant in Iran, is Shi'a or Shiite Islam. The two branches arose from a dispute among early Muslims over who was the lawful successor to Prophet Muhammad.

10. Saad Eddin Ibrahim, "The Changing Face of Egypt's Islamic Activism," Ibn Khaldoun Center for Development Studies, Cairo, April 1994, p. 16. Cassandra [pseudonym], "The Impending Crisis in Egypt," *Middle East Journal* 49, no. 1 (Winter 1995): 17. The last article noted the longevity of the cabinet of Prime Minister Atef Sedky, who was appointed in 1987. Some cabinet ministers had been in their seats so long that they appeared not to know how fast time flies. I remember going to interview the minister of irrigation Osama Raddi in 1990, who'd then been in his job for many years. I asked if the government had a water management plan for the Nile. Of course, he replied. He buzzed his aide who handed me a report called "The Water Policy of Egypt." It was dated 1975!

11. Nabil Abdel Fattah, *Veiled Violence* (Cairo: Khattab Press, 1994), pp. 85–86. For a perceptive analysis of why Islamic Group appealed to the younger generation of southern Egypt, see Mamoun Fandy, "Egypt's Islamic Group: Regional Revenge?," *Middle East Journal* 48, no. 4, (Autumn 1994): 602–625; and Mamoun Fandy, "The Tensions Behind the Violence in Egypt," *Middle East Policy* 2, no. 1 (1993): 25–34.

12. Mubarak interview, Cairo, April 1996. Hisham Mubarak, *The Terrorists Are Coming!* (Cairo: Al Maharussa Center for Publication and Press Services, 1995), p. 268.

13. Milton Bearden is a retired CIA employee who was stationed in Pakistan to support the Afghan Islamist guerrillas in their *jihad* against the Soviets. He was interviewed at his Vermont home by telephone in February 1996. Bearden estimated that 3,000 to 5,000 Arabs went to fight in Afghanistan before the 1989 Soviet withdrawal. Estimates vary on how many Egyptians joined the *jihad*. They range from 375 (*Al Hayat* newspaper, October 21, 1993) to 600 (*Mussawar* magazine August 20, 1993) to 1,142 in the year 1987 (*Al Ahali* newspaper May 2, 1993). *Al Ahali* said the Egyptians made up the largest group among the Arab volunteers.

14. Sayyaf information is from Bearden; Barnett R. Rubin, *The Fragmentation of Afghanistan*, (New Haven: Yale University Press, 1995), and Mary Anne Weaver, "Blowback," *Atlantic Monthly*, May 1996, pp. 24–36. One reason Sayyaf set up a special camp for the Egyptians was because they refused to join a bigger training camp run by the Muslim Brotherhood. Egyptians affiliated with Islamic Group and Islamic Jihad despised the Brotherhood's more moderate policies and its willingness to cooperate with un-Islamic Arab governments. See Mubarak, *Terrorists Are Coming!*, p. 274

Mubarak provided the information on the Khilafa camp. The Egyptians, he added, later renamed the camp after Adli Yussef, the first Islamic Group member to join the

Afghan *jihad*. A former Assiut University student, Yussef arrived in 1985 and was killed in a clash with Soviet troops four years later. To honor him, his colleagues renamed their training center Camp Martyr Abu Suheib.

15. An often overlooked consequence of the Afghan war was the "internationalization" of the concept of *jihad*, according to the late writer and activist Eqbal Ahmad. He pointed out that for most of the twentieth century, *jihad* had a secular nationalist connotation. But with Afghanistan, the word reacquired its more classical, theological meaning, which emphasized its pan-Islamic character. "Not since the great crusades in the Middle Ages had *jihad* crossed cultural, ethnic and territorial boundaries. . . . Pan-Islamism grew on a significant scale as a financial, cultural, political and military phenomenon with a world-wide network of exchange and collaboration." Eqbal Ahmad, "Guns, Gold and Godspeak," *Al Ahram Weekly*, December 14, 1995.

16. A senior Islamic Group militant, Talaat Fouad Kassim, told Hisham Mubarak in a 1993 interview in Copenhagen that the movement's policymaking group, or *shura*, was formed in 1987 and, besides himself, included: Karim Zuhdi, Isam Derbalah, Najih Ibrahim, Salah Hashim, Usama Hafez, Asim Abd Al Majid, Sabri Al Banna, Ali Al Sharif, Hamdi Abd Al Rahman, and Rifai Taha.

   Kassim's list of *shura* members excludes many senior Islamic Group leaders and is probably not exhaustive. Hammam, for example, is not on Kassim's list, although he and Kassim were close friends. Mubarak said that based on other sources, he believed Hammam was a *shura* member along with others also not mentioned by Kassim: Mohammed Islambouli, Safwat Abdel Ghani, Ala'a Mohieddin, and Usama Rushdie. Mubarak also said Hammam's release from prison came in 1986.

17. Hamdi Rizk, "The Decline of Terrorism and Islamic Group After the Fall of Hammam, the Inside Emir," *Al Mussawar*, April 29, 1994.

18. Mamoun Fandy observed that the logo's spare lines and the sword's resemblance to an obelisk are strikingly reminiscent of the visual imagery of Egypt's pre-Islamic pharaonic art. This detail underscores Islamic Group's roots in southern Egypt's ancient culture. Fandy noted that, unlike other Islamist groups, Islamic Group "abandoned the crescent as an Islamic symbol in favor of the sun. Unless one reads the Qur'anic verse in the background, it is easy to mistake the symbol for a pharaonic emblem, specifically from the Ikhnaton era. In addition, the open book . . . look[s] very much like the wings of Isis in pharaonic tomb paintings." Fandy, "Egypt's Islamic Group," pp. 609–610.

19. Up to 1990, thirty-two leaders of Islamic Group were killed in clashes with police, according to Hisham Mubarak. In its 1996 and 1995 "Human Rights Practices in Egypt" reports, the U.S. State Department noted that the Egyptian security forces allegedly committed "extrajudicial killings" (Sec. 1a).

   Tension between police and Islamic Group increased in 1987 after another small group of radicals tried to kill two former government officials and a journalist in three separate incidents. The group, called Salvation from Hell, had no connection to Islamic Group. But the police often made no distinctions among Islamists and grew increasingly harsh with all of them.

   Hammam's second arrest in 1986 followed a clash between Cairo police and Islamic Group demonstrators celebrating the end of Ramadan. He was charged with attempting to reorganize an illegal group but was freed when the charges were dropped. Information on Hammam's two arrests in this period came from Hamdi Rizk, "Decline of Terrorism," and attorney Montassir Al Zayat.

20. Talaat Fouad Kassim claimed in his 1993 interview with Hisham Mubarak that Islamic Group's military wing and *shura* were both formed in 1987. But Mubarak said the movement's own literature and his independent research placed the military wing's creation in 1989.

21. Gamil Hussein Metwalli, a former member of Islamic Group, described its military operatives as "brainwashed" and illiterate in a 1993 interview prominently displayed in Cairo's *Al Ahram Weekly* at a time when the government was seeking to turn public opinion against the movement. His interview was headlined "An Emir Abdicates."

22. In a courtroom interview in April 1993, senior Islamic Group leader Safwat Abdel Ghani told me the violence of the movement was "not a method but a reaction and legitimate way to defend itself." Hisham Mubarak heard the same argument, which he reported in an article entitled "The Politics of Burned Land: New Escalation of Violence," *Al Yasar,* no. 38 (April 1993). Abdel Ghani's argument reflected Sheikh Abdel Rahman's belief that *jihad* was, in part, a defensive measure. He once told an interviewer that there "must be *jihad* that creates terror in the hearts of the rulers and makes them think a hundred times over before they think of attacking the Islamic movement." Azzam, "Islamic Oriented Protest Groups in Egypt," p. 284.

23. Caryle Murphy, "Egypt's Mubarak Fires Hard-Line Security Chief," *Washington Post,* January 13, 1990; Caryle Murphy, "Egyptian Minister Escapes Alleged Assassination," *Washington Post,* December 17, 1989; and Max Rodenbeck, "Egyptian Minister Survives Attack," *Financial Times,* December 18, 1989.

24. Reuters, January 19, 1990.

25. The description of how Abdel Rahman left Egypt was provided by one of his lawyers, Youssef Ahmed Saqr, who said he accompanied him to the airport. They were escorted by about twenty police cars "with motorcycles and loudspeakers" as if "they were afraid of both of us, even though he is blind and I have only half my sight," Saqr said. Interview, Cairo, July 1993.

26. Hisham Mubarak said police sent an ultimatum to Mohieddin through an intermediary warning him and another movement leader "to leave Cairo, return to [southern Egypt] and if they stay in Cairo we will kill them." Mohieddin ignored the warning and was murdered two months later. This account was corroborated by another source also in close contact with Islamic Group leaders. Mubarak elaborated on the government ultimatum in his "A Tragedy of Errors," *Cairo Times,* January 22, 1998. He wrote that the government said it would begin adopting a "shoot to kill" policy if the militants didn't leave the Cairo area. The same year Mohieddin was shot, so were twenty-seven other Islamic Group members.

27. Egyptian officials said the militants' plan had called for Interior Minister Mohammed Abdel Halim Moussa, who had replaced Zaki Badr, to be attacked as he arrived at Cairo's Nile-side Semiramis Intercontinental Hotel. Writer Hisham Mubarak and lawyer Montassir Al Zayat stressed that Mohieddin's killing drove Islamic Group's military wing into greater defiance and militancy. Zayat said that at the time of its bungled 1989 attempt to assassinate Badr, the military wing had been "a deterrent force against [police] excesses against Islamic Group. But as a fighting battalion which became independent and . . . had its own military mission, this was only after the killing of Ala'a [Mohieddin]." Mubarak noted that an Islamic Group booklet described Mohieddin's murder as "a serious stage in the escalation campaign of the government" against the movement. As a result, it stated, "we need to send new messages to [the government]. Clearer messages. Let's write our messages in blood and draw our future policies with bullets." Mubarak, *Terrorists Are Coming!,* p. 400.

28. The 1992 military coup sparked Algeria's long and horrifying civil war that led to the deaths of some 100,000 persons over the next decade.

29. *Al Hayat* newspaper quoted Egyptian security sources saying that Haridi had gotten military training in Afghanistan.

30. Transcript of Mubarak's 1993 interview with Kassim provided by Hisham Mubarak.

31. Meguid's story is from local press reports and interviews I had with his family on a trip to Hujairat.

32. The figure on jobs related to tourism was given by then-tourism minister Fouad Sultan, interviewed in Cairo, November 1992. Reuters reported that tourist revenue fell by $900 million in 1933. Western diplomats estimated Egypt lost $1.5 billion in tourism revenue in 1992–1993. Caryle Murphy, "Egypt: An Uneasy Portent of Change," *Current History* 93 (February 1994), p. 79. See also Caryle Murphy, "Poverty Breeds Despair in Egypt," *Washington Post,* July 15, 1994.

33. Survey and statistics in Ibrahim, "Changing Face of Egypt's Islamic Activism," pp. 8–9. Islamic Group communiqués routinely asserted that violent attacks on policemen

and other officials were "reprisals" for the slayings of militants or the torture of detained suspects. "The policy of an eye for an eye," declared one of its 1993 faxes, "will be the future policy awaiting the oppressive regime in Egypt in response to its declared policy of wholesale liquidation centered around fabricated military trials and the killing of helpless people without trials inside their mosques or in detention." Revenge also appeared to be a factor in the police choice of targets and tactics. The assassinations of Islamic Group leaders like Mohieddin and, later, the unexplained deaths of suspects in custody pointed to this.

34. Samia Nakhoul, "Egyptian Militants Are Dedicated, Well-Organized," Reuters, March 19, 1993.
35. Ibrahim, "Changing Face of Egypt's Islamic Activism," pp. 11–12.
36. "We have 7,000 years of civilization. We are the country of moderation," President Mubarak told Reuters, October 28, 1993, while on a visit to Paris. Egypt was first united into a single geographical and political unit by Menes around 3,400 B.C., which gives the country about 5,400 years of history as a geographically unified state. According to recent archaeological finds, however, Egypt has been settled since the Stone Age.
37. Reuters, February 5, 1994.
38. Qur'an, 5:32
39. The antiterrorism statute, tightened in 1992, is described in the U.S. State Department human rights reports on Egypt in 1993 and 1996 (Sec. 1d). The amendments also prescribed the death penalty or life imprisonment for membership in a terrorist group.

According to Hisham Mubarak, Al Khilafa held about two thousand Egyptians in the early 1990s, even though the *jihad* was over. In 1992, it was closed following pressure from the U.S., Egyptian, and Saudi governments, which were all alarmed by the Islamist insurgency in Egypt.
40. The Egyptians were not shy about accusing Iran. After an attempt on his life in 1995, Mubarak declared that Iran had trained his would-be assassins. Another Egyptian official alleged Iran had trained several Islamic Group members and helped them sneak back into Egypt. John Lancaster, "Iran Has Strong Links to Anti-West Terror," *Washington Post*, November 1, 1996.

Although Tehran wished to export its Islamic revolution, long-standing mutual suspicion between Iran's Shiite Muslims and Egypt's Sunni Muslims worked against a close relationship. The Iranians did appear to have some ties with Egypt's Islamic Jihad, though it is unclear why or how deep those ties were.

As for Islamic Group, far more important to it than Iran was the logistical, moral, and financial support it got from Saudi Arabia, which is mainly Sunni Muslim. The Saudi link started when Egyptian volunteers, on their way to *jihad* in Afghanistan, passed through Saudi Arabia. There they met conservative, wealthy Saudis who shared their desire to see a more orthodox Islamic state in Egypt. Later, Saudis helped Islamic Group by facilitating meetings of its leaders in Saudi Arabia, a destination convenient for both those living in Egypt and in exile. For example, senior Islamic Group officials convened in Saudi Arabia to discuss retaliation for the 1993 murder of their movement's spokesman, Hisham Mubarak told me in 1993. See also Mubarak's "Politics of Burned Land."

In a 1993 interview, Interior Minister Hassan Alfi said his government did "not know the exact amount" of money coming from Saudi Arabia and other Gulf countries to Islamic Group. "These operations took place secretly. It has to be large sums of money. The arms, and the items [the militants] use in their operations are expensive. And their continuous travel abroad is also expensive," he said. "So there must be large sums of money."

Asked if more money was coming from Saudi Arabia and the Gulf than from Iran, Alfi replied: "Maybe."

I once asked attorney Abdel Harith Madani, an Islamic Group member, about the movement's funding. He said it came from "Saudi individuals" and from "people in the street" in Egypt who believed they were contributing to "the defense of Islam in general." He said he did not know whether more money came from abroad or from inside Egypt. Madani interview, Cairo, July 1993.

In the early 1990s, Osama Bin Laden did not appear to have any ties, financial or otherwise, with Islamic Group. Rather, he worked with Islamic Jihad's Ayman Zawahiri. One reason the Saudi government stripped Bin Laden of his citizenship in 1994 was his support for the Egyptian militants.

41. Reuters, October 28, 1993.
42. Transcript of Mubarak 1993 interview with Kassim, provided by Hisham Mubarak. While Kassim was saying attacks on tourists would continue, a prominent Islamic Group leader in prison in Egypt, Safwat Abdel Ghani, was saying they would stop, according to Mubarak. In September 1995, Kassim was arrested in Zagreb and then vanished. It is believed that he was handed over to Egyptian authorities and taken back to Cairo, where he faced a death sentence imposed by the same military court that had condemned Hammam to death in 1992. Egypt never acknowledged capturing Kassim and did not comment on widespread press reports in 1995 that it had been tipped off to Kassim's location by U.S. intelligence officials.
43. Metwalli, "An Emir Abdicates."
44. Interview with Soghaiars, Hujairat, June 1993. They and other villagers said seven homes had been rammed by police bulldozers and about a hundred villagers arrested. A 1996 U.S. State Department report on human rights practices in Egypt (Sec. 1f) noted reports by press and human rights groups that, in January 1995, Egyptian security forces in the southern province of Minya demolished the homes of seventeen individuals suspected of membership in terrorist groups. The government confirmed the demolitions took place, but said they were "not authorized," the U.S. report stated. The State Department report of 1995 cited human rights groups' findings that Egyptian "security forces have subjected entire villages to collective punishments, such as curfews and mass arrests" (Sec. 1d).
45. Al Hayat, April 11, 1994.
46. Details of Khayrat's death from Al Hayat, April 11, 1994; Al Ahram, April 12, 1994. Contents of Islamic Group fax in Kim Murphy, "The Battle for Egypt," Los Angeles Times Sunday Magazine, November 27, 1994.
47. Cherif Cordahi, "Crackdown on 'Dangerous Terrorist Cell,' " Inter Press Service, April 13, 1994.
48. Jonathan Wright, "Egypt Says Bank Bomb Group Broken Up," Reuters, March 8, 1994.
49. The official account of Hammam's death comes from the Interior Ministry's statement of April 25, 1994; Al Ahram, April 26 and 27, 1994; Middle East Times, May 2, 1994; and Middle East News Agency reports of April 25, 1994.
50. Hammam's central role in the insurgency is not in dispute and was shared by such informed observers as Hisham Mubarak. "What I know well," Mubarak said in an interview in April 1996, "is that all acts of violence which took place in Egypt starting in 1989 until Hammam's death in 1994, he was responsible for the planning."
51. The "Confrontation Fox," said Al Ahram on April 27, 1994, "sits day and night in his office following all the details of the [extremist religious] groups with his men, who don't see their children."
52. Rizk, "Decline of Terrorism." Hammam had rented the two apartments from Esmat Abdel Raouf Awad, who was sometimes described in press reports as Hammam's aunt and at other times as his wife's aunt. After his death, police confiscated the flat in which he had been killed.
53. Interior Minister Alfi told parliament that 120 of Hammam's men had been arrested, according to BBC Summary of World Broadcasts on June 15, 1994, quoting Middle East News Agency reports of June 13, 1994.
54. Al Ahram, April 27, 1994.
55. Hammam married Ragaa Younis from the village of Nagah Al Nagar, near Assiut, in 1990, according to Rizk, "Decline of Terrorism." The Egyptian Organization for Human Rights (EOHR) said his wife's name was Ragaa Yousef and that she came from a village called Nazlet Abdalla, near Assiut. The EOHR said she was detained for two months before being sent to Sohag. Some accounts of Hammam's death said his wife

was not present in the same apartment when he was killed. More reliable accounts, however, indicate she was present. It may have been her screams that were heard by the man I interviewed who lived three floors above Hammam's apartment.

56. *Al Ahram* on April 28, 1994, quoted security sources as saying Hammam had received $480,000 from abroad by cashing money orders at six different Cairo banks under false names. The paper did not specify over what time period Hammam got this amount of money and officials never substantiated these assertions publicly with documents.

57. Mubarak was among those who believed that the police had successfully placed a mole inside Hammam's operation. Hamdi Rizk's "The Decline of Terrorism" article said police had grown suspicious of a man living in Hada'ak Al Kubbah two months before the April 1994 raid on his apartment. "The information stated that a young man elegantly dressed as a business man appeared suddenly in one of the . . . apartments," Rizk wrote. It was noted that his wife wore the full-face veil and that the man "tended to move at night" going to a second apartment in a nearby building of the same complex. Despite his "well-polished shoes and avant garde ties," police confirmed it was Hammam. The article did not answer the obvious question: Why police did not immediately arrest, or at least question Hammam? The delay may have cost them dearly in the death of Khayrat.

58. Other major attacks attributed to Islamic Group after Hammam's death included the October 1994 stabbing of eighty-two-year-old Naguib Mahfouz, the Arab world's only Nobel Laureate in literature; the November 1995 murder in Geneva of an Egyptian "commercial" attaché (believed to have been a security official responsible for tracking exiled Egyptian Islamists); the April 1996 slaying of seventeen Greek tourists outside a Cairo hotel and the September 1997 killing of nine German tourists outside the Egyptian Museum in Tahrir Square. The 1997 Luxor massacre appears to have been the initiative of a small, local band of militants either acting on their own or under instructions from Islamic Group's more radical leadership-in-exile. The movement's internal leaders were embarrassed by the slaughter, though the attack was a foreseeable outcome of their antitourism strategy. Another incident, the November 1995 suicide car-bombing of Egypt's embassy in Islamabad, which killed seventeen and wounded sixty people, was carried out by Zawahiri's Islamic Jihad.

59. In June 2000, Abdel Rahman's American lawyer, Lynne Stewart, issued a press statement quoting him as saying that he was "withdrawing support for the cease-fire that currently exists." In April 2002, Stewart was indicted on charges of helping pass unlawful messages from Abdel Rahman to his followers in Egypt. The New York indictment, which grew out of U.S. government clandestine monitoring of Abdel Rahman's conversations with Stewart, alleges that Stewart, by speaking loudly in English, appeared to be trying to conceal from prison guards a conversation about the cease-fire in Arabic between Abdel Rahman and a visitor in May 2000. Stewart pleaded not guilty. Steve Fainaru and Brooke A. Masters, "Attorney Accused of Passing Terrorist Messages," *Washington Post*, April 10, 2002.

60. Other Egyptians who played key roles in the 1990s insurgency and later joined Bin Laden's network included Mustafa Hamza, Mohammed Atef (who was killed during the U.S. war in Afghanistan), Mohammed Islambouli, (brother of Sadat assassin Khalid Islambouli), and two sons of Sheikh Omar Abdel Rahman, all of Islamic Group. Also Mohammed Mekkawi, Tariq Anwar Sayyid Ahmad and Muhammad Salah of Islamic Jihad.

6. DEATH OF A LAWYER

1. Mubarak comment from Mary Anne Weaver, "The Novelist and the Sheikh," *The New Yorker.* January 30, 1995, p. 69.

2. Torture's radicalizing effect on Egypt's Islamist opposition has been documented by Egyptians knowledgeable about earlier periods of Islamist militancy. While studying the radicals who killed Sadat, Nemat Guenena had a conversation with an elderly Mus-

lim Brother imprisoned under Nasser. Some of his fellow detainees, he told her, concluded that "rulers who had inflicted such torture on fellow Muslims could not be Muslims." Nemat Guenena, *The "Jihad," an "Islamic Alternative" in Egypt* (Cairo: American University in Cairo Press, Summer 1986), Cairo Papers in Social Science 9, monograph 2, p. 37.

This abuse influenced Qutb, the radical Islamist ideologue, who witnessed some of it firsthand, including the killing of twenty-three fellow Muslim Brothers in 1957 when prison guards opened fire on them because they had staged a sit-in, refusing to work in quarries. Hisham Mubarak, "A Tragedy of Errors," *Cairo Times*, January 22, 1998.

Gilles Kepel wrote that "the martyrology of the Nasser period is of the utmost importance for the subsequent Islamicist movement. The halo of persecution suffered in defence of a faith and a social ideal confers a status of absolute truth upon Islamicist discourse." Kepel, *The Prophet and Pharaoh*, trans. by Jon Rothschild (London: Al Saqi Books, 1985), p. 35.

In late 2001, Ayman Zawahiri, the Egyptian aide of Osama Bin Laden, issued his biography, "Knights Under the Banner of the Prophet." He wrote: "After Sadat's assassination the torture started again, to write a new bloody chapter of the history of the Islamic movement in Egypt. The torture was brutal this time. Bones were broken, skin was removed, bodies were electrocuted and souls were killed. . . . And still this wheel is still turning until today. . . . The Egyptian army turned its back toward Israel and started fighting its own people." Excerpted in "Beware of Hidden Enemies and Their Wolves and Foxes," *New York Times*, December 9, 2001.

Muslim Brother Moukhtar Nouh told me in an interview that when police began routinely torturing Islamic Group detainees in the late 1980s, he went to Egypt's interior minister Zaki Badr and warned that this tactic would boomerang. "It will produce a phenomenon called social revenge, according to which a citizen will take his rights into his own hand and you'll see the blood of both citizens and officials running on the ground," Nouh said he told Badr in 1989. Eight years later, the terrorists who killed fifty-eight foreign tourists at Luxor in November 1997 left a pamphlet at the scene. It said, in part, "We shall take revenge for our brothers who have died on the gallows. The depths of the earth are better for us than the surface . . . since we have seen . . . our brothers and families tortured in their jails." "Bloodbath at Luxor," *Economist*, November 22, 1997.

3. On Israel's use of torture, see Stephen S. Rosenfeld, "Coming to Terms with Torture," *Washington Post*, November 22, 1996; "U.N. Questions Israeli Ruling," *Washington Post*, November 16, 1996; "Israeli Court Allows Coercion of Detainee," *Washington Post*, November 15, 1996; Glenn Frankel, *Beyond the Promised Land, Jews and Arabs on a Hard Road to a New Israel* (New York: Simon & Schuster, 1994), pp. 257–262.

4. John Pomfret, "Inside the Taliban's Torture Chambers," *Washington Post*, December 17, 2001.

5. Yusuf Idris, "The Black Policeman," in *Rings of Burnished Brass*, trans. by Catherine Cobham (Cairo: American University in Cairo Press, 1990), pp. 73 and 78. The fictional torturer of Idris's story purportedly was based on a real person written about in Cairo's opposition press in the late 1940s. The articles described the torturer as a top aide to a politician named Ibrahim Abd Al Hadi, according to Idris's translator, Catherine Cobham. Cairo journalist Mohammed Sid Ahmed also recalled these press accounts of a torturer but added that it was never entirely clear that such a person really existed. Nonetheless, the "Black Policeman," so called because of his dark skin, became a potent symbol of government terror after Idris's story appeared. It was published when Egypt was ruled by Gamal Abdel Nasser, who used torture extensively against political opponents, in particular Muslim Brothers. Under his successor, Anwar Sadat, torture was not a major weapon of the state. It made a comeback in the late 1980s under Mubarak.

6. *Behind Closed Doors, Torture and Detention in Egypt* (New York: Human Rights Watch/Middle East, July 1992), pp. 61–68, and "Human Rights Practices in Egypt" (Washington, D.C.: U.S. State Department. 1996), Sec. 1b.

7. The Egyptian Organization for Human Rights [EOHR] issued a December 10, 1993, report stating that in 1991, nineteen citizens were subjected to torture in special detention camps for "persons suspected of belonging to Islamist groups." That number shot up to 315 by October 1992.

   As for *deaths* from torture, it is difficult to obtain accurate data. But such deaths tend to rise as political violence rises. In an April 1996 interview in Cairo, EOHR official Mahmoud Kandil said his organization had counted twenty deaths from torture from 1990 to 1996. The U.S. State Department's 1996 report on human rights practices in Egypt (Sec. 1a) stated that, according to the Egyptian government, ninety-seven people died in custody in 1993; eighty-two in 1994; and seventy-one in 1995. The government said these deaths were from natural causes or sickness. By 1998, as Islamic Group's campaign of violence diminished, so did deaths attributed by human rights groups to torture. In that year, according to the U.S. State Department's 1999 human rights report (Sec. 1a), torture led to three deaths in detention.

   In recent years, human rights groups have called attention to the use of torture by police investigating ordinary criminal cases. In a February 1999 report on torture, EOHR documented two deaths in 1998. The report also detailed thirty instances of torture in fifteen different police stations during criminal investigations. Each of the thirty cases, it noted, involved "ordinary citizens who do not belong to any political trend and are not accused in political cases."

8. Mubarak interview, Cairo, May 1994.

9. Egypt's SSI gained such a reputation for "expertise" in making detainees "sing" that Kuwait sought Egypt's help in interrogating Arabs suspected of collaborating with Iraq during its 1990–1991 occupation of Kuwait. Caryle Murphy, "Kuwait Reported Moving to Curb Human Rights Abuses," *Washington Post*, October 2, 1991.

10. The 1992 incident was related by Bahey Eddin Hassan, then secretary-general of EOHR, in a May 1993 interview in Cairo.

11. *Behind Closed Doors*, pp. 9–10. Amnesty International concluded that "political detainees are routinely tortured" in *Egypt Indefinite Detention and Systematic Torture: The Forgotten Victims* (London: Amnesty International, July 1996), p. 1. In May 1996, the U.N. Committee Against Torture stated that "torture is systematically practiced by the Security Forces in Egypt, in particular by [SSI], since in spite of the denials of the Government, the allegations of torture submitted by reliable non-governmental organizations consistently indicate that reported cases of torture are seen to be habitual, widespread and deliberate in at least a considerable part of the country." Cited in *Egypt Indefinite Detention and Systematic Torture*, p. 1.

    The U.S. State Department's 2002 report "Human Rights Practices in Egypt" (Intro; Sec. 1c) stated that the Egyptian government's "record improved somewhat over the previous year in such areas as . . . death from torture." However, the report stated, "torture . . . by police, security personnel, and prison guards is common." It added that torture "takes place in" SSI offices.

12. Alfi's first remark was reported by Reuters, October 16, 1993. His second quote comes from an August 1995 interview with *Al Ahram*, cited in *Human Rights Watch's World Report, 1996*, p. 274. On another occasion, Interior Ministry spokesman, Major General Raouf Al Mannawi declared: "Egypt respects human rights. There are no violations of such rights be it in prisons or elsewhere, due to the complete freedom and democracy that Egypt enjoys under the leadership of President Hosni Mubarak. . . . The government system highly respects human rights. Any person can express himself freely. Torture is utterly rejected. It does not exist and is not part of the government's policy." *Cairo Press Review*, November 22, 1993, p. 3.

13. Mubarak comment from *Middle East Times*, May 27, 1996. In its 2002 report on Egypt (Intro; Sec. 1c), the U.S. State Department said the Egyptian government had improved somewhat in disciplining officers involved in deaths from torture, but added that "the punishments at times do not conform to the seriousness of the offense."

    In a March 12, 2002, release, the Human Rights Center for the Assistance of Prisoners (HRCAP) expressed satisfaction that the government prosecutor had ordered several policemen detained and a police doctor interrogated in connection with the alleged torture death of an Egyptian earlier that year. However, HRCAP said it was "deeply concerned" that the prosecutor does not move more aggressively against torture and only gets serious when "the victim of torture expires."

Prior to these improvements, however, policemen and security personnel enjoyed virtual immunity from punishment for torturing detainees. EOHR noted in an October 24, 1993, press release that "since 1986 not a single official or police officer was presented for trial over torture charges." The U.S. State Department observed in its 1995 report on human rights in Egypt (Sec. 1c) that for the previous ten years, "there is no evidence that officers implicated in such cases have been prosecuted or punished."

And in May 1996, the U.N. Committee Against Torture reported that "no investigation has ever been made and no legal action been brought against members of [SSI] since the entry into force of the Convention [Against Torture] for Egypt in June 1987." The Committee urged Egypt to "make particular efforts to prevent its security forces from acting as a state within a State, for they seem to escape control by superior authorities." Cited in *Egypt Indefinite Detention and Systematic Torture*, p. 12.

14. The most recent presidential decree extending emergency law until June 2003 was rubber-stamped by parliament in February 2000. In fact, twentieth-century Egypt has more often been ruled by emergency law than not. Between 1914 and 1996, Egypt had 55½ years of rule by emergency law and 26½ years of normal constitutional rule. This, despite the fact that emergency laws are to be invoked only when "security or public order are jeopardized" due to "war . . . national unrest, general disasters or . . . an epidemic." Mohammad Ghamry, "Know Your Rights, a Study of the Constitutional and Legal System of Detention," Center for Human Rights Legal Aid [CHRLA], Cairo, September 1995, pp. 13–14.

15. Ghamry, "Know Your Rights," p. 36, and Amnesty's *Egypt Indefinite Detention and Systematic Torture*, p. 2, which states: "In practice . . . detainees [ordered released] are, most of the time, secretly transferred to local police stations . . . [and other places] . . . for a few days before they are issued with new detention orders and taken back to prison."

In September 1995, CHRLA reported that as of May 1995, only 2 of 158 defendants acquitted by military tribunals since December 1992 had been released from detention. It noted that their postacquittal detention "is a crime punishable by law." In this case, however, it blamed the military courts, not SSI.

HRCAP in Cairo reported in 1997 that sixty of the sixty-one prisoners it examined in one prison had not been freed despite release orders from court. Richard Engel, "Report Exposes Disease and Abuse in Prisons," *Middle East Times*, November 2, 1997.

The U.S. State Department 2002 report on "Human Rights Practices in Egypt," stated that "Human rights groups reported that hundreds, perhaps thousands, of persons detained under the Emergency Law have been incarcerated for several years without charge. The courts have ordered the release of several of these detainees, but prison officials have reportedly ignored the orders. The Ministry of Interior frequently reissues detention orders to return detainees to prison" (Sec. 1d).

The government has released more than 7,000 persons from detention since 1998, according to the U.S. State Department's 2000 report on Egypt (Sec. 1d). But thousands more are still being held without charge. Its 2002 report stated that "estimates by local human rights organizations indicate that there are approximately 13,000–16,000 detained administratively on suspicion of terrorist or political activity" (Sec. 1d).

Mohammed Ghanem, a retired Egyptian police colonel and professor of criminal law at the police academy, wrote an article for the *Middle East Times* in mid-1999 saying that "tens of thousands of Egyptians languish in jails for indefinite periods without the knowledge of the courts . . . or charged with any offense." He said the number of detainees "is more than double" the fourteen thousand held under Nasser's regime. Ghanem blamed "the tragedy of administrative detention," which he said "has reached dangerous proportions." The government forbade the paper from publishing Ghanem's article but it is available at http//dfn.org/index.htm. Ghanem left Egypt in May after he was granted political asylum by Switzerland.

Hassan Al Gharabawi is a notorious example of someone held for long periods without being charged or after being acquitted. An Islamic Group activist, Gharabawi was arrested in January 1989 with twelve other men for allegedly participating in violence against policemen during several days of unrest in Ain Shams, a low-income district of Cairo. They were all acquitted at a May 1990 trial after the judge concluded they had been tortured to extract "confessions." Six years later, Gharabawi was still in prison. In that time, the courts ordered him released at least thirty times. Each time, SSI wrote out a new thirty-day detention order. By 1996, he held the dubious distinction of being the longest-held out of more than forty lawyers detained without charges in the early 1990s.

While in prison, he finished his coursework for a law degree and became a member of the Egyptian Bar Association. From 1993 to 1995, he was denied visitors. In early 1995, he was transferred from Cairo to a desert detention camp in southern Egypt. One of his friends, attorney Shadly Al Sahrir, visited him at that camp. Like other prisoners, Gharabawi was forced to crawl into the visiting room. The prisoners could stand only after the guards gave a signal by clapping. When Sahrir asked Gharabawi if he needed anything, he replied: "I don't want anything. I don't want anything. I'm dying in here." At the time, Gharabawi was thirty-four years old. Sahrir was interviewed in Cairo, April 1996.

When Amnesty International asked the Egyptian government about Gharabawi's detention in 1993, it responded by saying that he "is a leading member of a secret terrorist organization using violence and terrorism to achieve its unlawful aims. . . . He is currently being held in detention . . . in light of the criminal and terrorist danger he represents, issuing directives and orders to elements of a secret terrorist organization to undertake acts of violence and terrorism." The government made no mention of the fact that Gharabawi had been acquitted at his 1990 trial. See Amnesty's *Egypt Indefinite Detention and Systematic Torture*, p. 5, and Human Rights Watch's *Behind Closed Doors*, pp. 119–120. In its annual report on Egypt in 2000, Amnesty said, "at least 90 lawyers arrested in previous years remained in administrative detention."

In March 2002, Human Rights Watch confirmed that Gharabawi was still held in administrative detention.

16. Refai interview, Cairo, January 1990.
17. An example of how even senior officials disregard the courts came in April 1994. A court agreed with Madani and other Islamist attorneys that Interior Minister Alfi's ban on visits by relatives and lawyers to political detainees in "The Scorpion," a notorious maximum-security prison, was unconstitutional. It ordered Alfi to rescind the ban. Prison officials ignored the court order while the government appealed and to show who was boss, Alfi extended the ban to other prisons. Eight years later, the ban was still in force despite 112 court orders that it should be reversed. HRCAP press release, February 13, 2002.
18. Details of Madani's early life were supplied by his wife, Wafaa Mohammed Ahmed, in an interview, Cairo, April 1996.
19. Madani's organizing work "was the first time Islamic Group had a presence in Isna," Hisham Mubarak said in an interview, Cairo, May 1994. Madani's first arrest in Isna was in 1990, when he was detained for stopping people from visiting shrines of local saints—a practice that Islamic Group regarded as un-Islamic. A year later he was arrested for distributing leaflets with militant language. He was not officially charged in either case.
20. Citations from Ibrahim's August 1993 verdict come from "Human Rights Abuses Mount in 1993," *Human Rights Watch* 5, no. 8 (October 22, 1993): 4, and "Civil Society," Ibn Khaldoun Center for Development Studies, Cairo, September 1993, p. 16. The civilian judges found ten of the defendants guilty of lesser charges and gave them prison terms. Their trial in a civilian court began before Mubarak decided to send insurgency-related cases to military courts in late 1992.
21. Khalid challenged the election law as unconstitutional because it infringed the right of independent candidates like himself to run for office. His greatest victory came after his

death when the Supreme Constitutional Court, in July 2000, ruled in another case initiated by Khalid that the government had to allow judicial oversight at election polling stations. Because of this, many observers said, the 2000 elections were much fairer than those in the past.

22. Khalid was interviewed in Cairo, April 1996.

Madani's concern to avoid having it appear that Islamic Group had struck a deal with the government may have reflected a desire by Islamic Group leaders inside Egypt to deflect accusations from their more hard-line colleagues abroad that they were selling out. They may also have feared that the exiled leadership would try to sabotage the cease-fire effort. This split between the internal and external leaderships was evident when I asked Madani's friend, attorney Ali Ismail Hussein, about Madani's misgivings about the attacks on tourists. Hussein said in a 1996 interview that both he and Madani disapproved of them. "It's not acceptable to . . . Islam," he said. "It's also alien to the methods of 'Islamic Group.' I understand that it could be understood that it's a method of 'Islamic Group' [because of] some announcements of leaders who are abroad. But it's not the method of 'Islamic Group.' "

23. Wafaa interview, Cairo, April, 1996.

24. Hussein interview, Cairo, April 1996. Amnesty International confirmed that Ibrahim was sentenced to death on July 16, 1994, for his role in the August 1993 assassination attempt on Interior Minister Alfi and was hanged on August 22, 1994.

25. Kandil interview, Cairo, April 1996.

26. The account of Madani's trip home to Isna and the fight over his body was provided by Wafaa.

27. Reuters, May 11, 1994.

28. More than a month after Madani's death, Interior Minister Alfi was still elaborating on his links to terrorists. Responding to questions in parliament from then-member Kamal Khalid, Alfi said "information" about bombs outside banks in Cairo had "proved" Madani had played a major role in these incidents and had received instructions directly from Hammam. Alfi added that militants in police custody had admitted to the "organizational role" of Madani. The government-run Middle East News Agency (MENA) reported that Alfi declared Madani to be "the direct link with Hammam for transmitting orders among the leaders of the organization from inside and outside prison." MENA, June 13, 1994, monitored by the BBC Summary of World Broadcasts, June 15, 1993.

29. The Associated Press report by James Martone, quoting Aida Wassifa, supervisory doctor at Qasr Al 'Aini Hospital, and the New York Times report were published May 17, 1994; the Washington Post report was published May 18, 1994.

30. "Unanswered Questions in Events Surrounding the Death of Lawyer, Abdel Harith Madani," Lawyers' Committee for Human Rights, New York, June 1, 1994, p. 3. The seventeen injury marks were reported by Agence France Presse, June 28, 1994, cited in "Egypt: Hostage-Taking and Intimidation by Security Forces," Human Rights Watch/Middle East, January 1995, pp. 27–28 note 64. Also Human Rights Watch World Report, 1995, pp. 263–264.

The existence of the internal May 7 memo was disclosed by the Cairo-based Arab Center for the Independence of the Judiciary and the Legal Profession, after the document surfaced in an unrelated 1997 military court trial. Three years earlier, in an October 1994 letter to Amnesty International, the Egyptian government had confirmed that a postmortem was carried out April 28, 1994, but it did not disclose its findings. That letter was attached as an appendix to Egypt Indefinite Detention and Systematic Torture.

31. A copy of Madani's death certificate was obtained from Human Rights Watch/Middle East.

32. The government's October 1994 letter is an appendix to Amnesty's Egypt Indefinite Detention and Systematic Torture. The U.S. State Department's 1996 "Human Rights Practices In Egypt" (Sec. 1a) noted that the Egyptian government had finished its probe into the circumstances of Madani's death but "declined to publicize the results."

33. "Unanswered Questions," p. 5.

34. Idris, "Black Policeman," p. 96.

7. EDUCATION, NOT REVOLUTION

1. Kandil's quotes in this and other chapters are from interview in Cairo, April 1996.
2. The Brotherhood's membership is difficult, if not impossible, to know given the group's tenuous legal status and secrecy. The highest estimate I am aware of was in a Pentagon study, which mentioned two million. "Strategic Assessment 1995," Institute for National Strategic Studies National Defense University, Washington, D.C., 1995, p. 72.
3. Details of Erian's life are from my interviews and correspondence with him from 1992 to 1996; interviews with his associates and a 1996 interview in Cairo with his wife.
4. See Chapter 4, note 44.
5. Robert Springborg discusses the "embourgeoisment" of the Brotherhood with its stress on private property and abandonment of earlier, populist economic positions. He also notes the establishment by some Brothers of Bank Al Taqwa (Devoutness Bank), a Bahamas-registered investment bank headquartered in Geneva and capitalized at $30 million. Springborg, *Mubarak's Egypt: Fragmentation of the Political Order* (Boulder, Colo.: Westview Press, 1989), pp. 232 and 60.

    Perhaps the best analysis of what he calls the 1970s "neo-Muslim Brethren" is in Gilles Kepel's *The Prophet and Pharaoh*, trans. by Jon Rothschild (London: Al Saqi Books, 1985).

    In a February 1993 interview in Cairo, human rights activist and writer Hisham Mubarak noted: "Most Muslim Brotherhood leaders are businessmen, owners of companies and clinics, lawyers. They are well-off socially and economically. I don't see any reason for them to give up all this for revolutionary work. The Muslim Brotherhood is no longer the Muslim Brotherhood of Banna. At that time, it was a radical movement of the economically oppressed. But with money . . . it became a different organization."

    Abd Al Moneim Said Aly, a scholar at Cairo's Al Ahram Center for Political and Strategic Studies, wrote that after returning to Egypt in the late 1970s, exiled Muslim Brothers invested "their newly acquired wealth through 'Islamic' corporations which, in turn, made them a socioeconomic force with which to reckon. By 1987, the Muslim Brothers had become owners of several giant financial institutions with multinational interests. Their dealings spread from New York to Tokyo. Three huge Islamic finance houses—Al Sharif, Al Raiyan, and Al Saad—were said to have backed the political campaigns of the Muslim Brothers." Aly, "Democratization in Egypt," *American-Arab Affairs*, no. 22 (Fall 1987): 21.
6. Kepel, *Prophet and Pharaoh*, p. 110.

    The Brotherhood describes its economic program as an "Islamic" one situated "between capitalism and socialism." Generally, they endorse private property rights and see the private sector as the main engine of economic development. They do not favor radical land reform or nationalization. They would like the Islamic alms tax, or *zakat*, which all Muslims are supposed to pay annually for the poor, made a legal obligation. (The *zakat* is set at 2.5 percent of one's net worth.) They would also like Egypt's banking system to stop paying interest, which they believe is banned by *shari'a*, and instead pay dividends, which are permissible. The Brotherhood generally favors some state intervention in the economy and a state-owned public sector, though one much smaller than now exists in Egypt. In the past, they argued for Egypt to be more economically independent from the West by restricting imports and maintaining protective tariffs for domestic industries. They favor trading with other Arab states rather than Western ones. For more on the Brotherhood economic policies: Bjorn Olav Utvik, "Filling the Vacant Throne of Nasser," *Middle East Insight*, January-February 1995, pp. 24–28, and Sana Abed-Kotob, "The Accommodationists Speak: Goals and Strategies of the Muslim Brotherhood of Egypt," *International Journal of Middle East Studies* 27, (1995): 321–339.
7. Hodeiby interview, Cairo, February 1992.
8. The uneasy relationship between the Brotherhood and the more militant students in the 1970s is addressed in Abdel Azim Ramadan, "Fundamentalist Influence in Egypt," in

Fundamentalisms and the State, eds. Martin E. Marty and R. Scott Appleby (Chicago: University of Chicago Press, 1993), pp. 152–183. Also, during Hisham Mubarak's 1993 interview with Islamic Group leader Talaat Fouad Kassim, he said that in 1978 when the Brotherhood approached student leaders of the Islamic Associations and asked them to join the Brotherhood, he and others, mostly from southern Egypt, "refused because of the differences in our agenda." But, Kassim added, the Brotherhood "succeeded in influencing" others, including Erian, Abdul Moneim Abdul-Futuh, Abou Elela Mady, Hilmi El Jazzar, Ahmad Omar and Ibrahim El Za'farani—all of whom became major figures in the younger generation of Brotherhood activists. Transcript of interview supplied by Mubarak.

9. Erian comments from a 1996 letter he wrote to the author from prison in Cairo.
10. Kepel, *Prophet and Pharaoh*, pp. 154 and 152–153.
11. Omar interview, Cairo, April 1996.
12. Ibrahim interview, New York, December 1995.
13. Erian's quotes are from his 1996 letter from prison. His wife told me about their child's death.
14. Islamists' control of six of twenty-four associations is from Kandil interview. Other facts on their electoral progress is from Carrie Rosefsky Wickham, "Islamic Mobilization and Political Change: The Islamist Trend in Egypt's Professional Associations," in *Political Islam*, eds. Joel Beinin and Joe Stork (Berkeley: University of California Press, 1997), pp. 120–135.

    Wickham, assistant professor of political science at Emory University, examined the activities of the younger generation of Muslim Brothers in the professional associations. She writes that the Islamic trend tried to "deliver something qualitatively different from the factional infighting and competition which long preoccupied old guard secular politicians. By initiating new programs to address the grievances of members, taking a public stand in support of democracy and human rights and in some associations actively seeking the cooperation of secular opponents, the young Islamist leaders have attempted to portray themselves as representatives of a broad consensus for reform rather than a narrow set of political objectives."

    The Islamist movement, she added, was "fostering a new ethic of participation among the younger members of Egypt's educated middle class, one which entails increasing disengagement from or confrontation with the present regime. In this way it has begun to isolate the regime from a strategic sector of the public . . . [and] to erode Egypt's authoritarian order from below." By "indoctrinating youth with the idea that the reform of society is a religious duty incumbent on every Muslim, Islamist activists have begun to erode long-entrenched patterns of popular non-participation and to foster an activist subculture rooted in Islamic symbols and ideals." *Political Islam*, pp. 130, 133, 124, and 125.

    For discussions of the bar association election see Wickham and Nabil Abdel Fattah's *Veiled Violence* (Cairo: Khattab Press, 1994), p. 44. Fattah states the 1992 vote suggested "a sharp change in the political mood of the middle and lower middle class who form the social backbone of the Egyptian legal community." But once again the Islamist victory had a lot to do with their superior organizational skills since only 10 percent of the association's 140,000 members actually voted.

    Islamists being only 20 percent is from Said Eddin Ibrahim interview, Cairo, April 1992.
15. In one famous episode, volunteers from the Islamist-led medical syndicate quickly converged on poor neighborhoods hit hard by the 1992 earthquake. They were handing out money, food, medical care, and tents to residents while government officials were nowhere in sight. Embarrassed by the Islamists' quick response, the government ordered the syndicate to stop collecting money for the quake's victims.
16. The two parties the Brotherhood joined were the Socialist Labor Party and Liberal Party. *The New York Times* reported that "the Islamic sector put as much as $6 million into the Brotherhood's electoral campaign" of 1987. Cited in Springborg, *Mubarak's Egypt*, p. 250. Egyptian law prohibits political parties with religious ideologies. Though

the Brotherhood complains about its status, it has never formally requested registration as a legal party, largely because its leadership sees itself as above partisan politics. Although individual Brotherhood candidates occasionally ran in local elections as far back as the 1940s, they generally remained aloof from electoral politics until the mid-1980s. Even President Mubarak's ruling National Democratic Party began adopting Islamic symbols in election campaigns by the late 1980s. Its election posters were printed in green, the color of Islam, and carried the Islamic icon, a crescent moon.

17. Springborg, *Mubarak's Egypt*, pp. 201, 216, and 218.
18. Sayed interview, Cairo, April 1996.
19. Other Brotherhood legislative proposals included the imposition of hand-cutting for theft, required memorization of the Qur'an in all government bodies, and a dress code for women. Abd Al Moneim Said Aly and Manfred Wenner, "Modern Islamic Reform Movements: The Muslim Brotherhood in Contemporary Egypt," *Middle East Journal* 36, no.3 (1982): 349–350. Most of these parliamentary initiatives, however, were shuffled into the slow-death purgatory of "committee study." In May 1985, parliament endorsed a recommendation of its religious affairs committee for the gradual application of *shari'a* through a two-step procedure: preparation of public attitudes and then purification of existing laws of material incompatible with *shari'a*. Springborg, *Mubarak's Egypt*, p. 249 note 81.
20. Islamist Ismail Raji Al Faruqi defined *tawhid* as "the conviction and witnessing that 'there is no God but God' " and the recognition that at "the core of the Islamic religious experience, therefore, stands God Who is unique and Whose will is the initiative and guide for all men's lives.' " John L. Esposito and John O. Voll, *Islam and Democracy* (New York: Oxford University Press, 1996), p. 23. Also see "*Tawhid*" in *Oxford Encyclopedia of the Modern Islamic World*, ed. John L. Esposito (New York: Oxford University Press, 1995).

The concept of *tawhid* can be better understood by recalling that the Western idea of religion as a private matter is a relatively recent phenomenon in history. The "modern notion of religion" as a system of personal belief, rather than a comprehensive way of living providing the basis for political arrangements as well as individual conscience, "has its origins in the post-Enlightenment West," writes John J. Esposito in *Islamic Threat, Myth or Reality?* (New York: Oxford University Press, 1992), pp. 198–199. Karen Armstrong also notes that in the context of man's history as a conscious being, "our current secularism is an entirely new experiment, unprecedented in human history. We have yet to see how it will work." Armstrong, *A History of God* (New York: Knopf, 1994), p. xix.

Kepel noted that Islam "is marked by *tawhid*, or fundamental unity. The distinction between din and dawla, the spiritual and the temporal, is meaningless in Muslim doctrine, since . . . the Koran . . . contains both the rules regulating relations between man and God and the principles governing social life. No system of secular law was ever articulated with Islam as Roman law was with Christian doctrine. . . . If *tawhid* is to be realized, the commander of the faithful, the caliph, must see to the application of the Koranic imperatives. In particular, he must permit the smooth functioning of justice and must safeguard Muslim ethics." Kepel, *Prophet and Pharaoh*, p. 228.
21. The "semisecular" label is from Springborg, *Mubarak's Egypt*, p. 219. The tacit, and unacknowledged, separation of religious and temporal spheres was also noted by Madawi Al Rasheed, who wrote: "Although there is no de jure separation of religion and politics in [Saudi Arabia], there has been a de facto acceptance of separate spheres of influence represented in the division of labor between the government and the religious authorities. . . . Against this background, the [Islamist] opposition wants to reinstate religion in . . . state politics." Rasheed, "Saudi Arabia's Islamic Opposition," *Current History*, January 1996, p. 21.

This reality was also noted by Kepel, who wrote: "All Egyptian Islamicists insist that Islam is a total and complete system . . . their problem is to get this across to Muslims whose conduct is now motivated by considerations drawn from other systems of thought (whether the socialistic or liberal jargon of successive governments or more simply the hustles of day-to-day survival)." *Prophet and Pharaoh*, p. 186.

22. "Islamic obligation" is from a Brotherhood policy statement issued April 4, 1995. The "unity of life" is in Richard P. Mitchell, *The Society of Muslim Brothers* (London: Oxford University Press, 1969), p. 245.

    For Brotherhood founder Banna, John O. Voll writes, the "emphasis on the doctrine of the unity of God (*tawhid*) carried with it implications for actual life in human society. More than an important tenet in a creed, 'the oneness of God' served as the foundation for a program in which Islam is the proper point of reference for all aspects of life. If there is only one sovereign for humanity, it is not possible to separate religion from politics." Voll, "Fundamentalism in the Sunni Arab World: Egypt and the Sudan," in *Fundamentalisms Observed*, eds. Martin E. Marty and R. Scott Appleby (Chicago: University of Chicago Press, 1991), p. 364. After Banna, Sayyid Qutb and other radical Islamist thinkers made even more explicit arguments demonstrating how *tawhid* requires that Muslims be ruled by Islamic law, or *shari'a*. See "*Tawhid*" in *Oxford Encyclopedia*.

23. Muslim scholar Fazlur Rahman defined *shari'a* as "the path or the road leading to the water, i.e., a way to the very source of life." It is "the assembly of Divine imperatives to man, imperatives which are frankly admitted to be primarily of a moral character. Shari'a is thus not an actual code of particular and specific enactments but is coterminous with the 'good.' " Thomas W. Lippman, *Understanding Islam* (New York: Mentor, 1990), p. 71.

24. Tahseen Basheer called *shari'a* "an ocean of knowledge and contradictions just like the real ocean." This "ocean," however, has been codified into schools of legal thought. Shiite Islam has one main school and Sunnis have four: Hanbali, Shafi'i, Hanafi and Maliki.

    Abdullahi A. An-Na'im, a law professor at Emory University, notes the diversity of *fiqh* rulings: "Although Shari'a professes to be a single logical whole, there is significant diversity of opinion not only between the schools but also among different jurists of the same school," he wrote, adding that "to speak in categorical terms of Shari'a as a definite and well-settled code of law ... is grossly misleading." Na'im, *Toward an Islamic Reformation* (New York: Syracuse University Press, 1990), pp, 33 and 40.

    Sheikh Hassan Al Saffar, a prominent Shiite Muslim scholar in Saudi Arabia, noted that Islam implicitly recognizes freedom of opinion because *shari'a* is open to many different interpretations. Saffar quoted Imam Malik Ibn Anas, a famous early Islamic jurist, who said: "There are many sound interpretations of the *shari'a* and mine is merely one of them." Mamoun Fandy, "From Confrontation to Creative Resistance: The Shia's Oppositional Discourse in Saudi Arabia," *Critique*, Fall 1996, p. 16.

25. A couple of examples illustrate this. In 1992, the head of Al Azhar University, the late Sheikh Gad Al Haq Ali Gad Al Haq declared the rhythm method as the only permissible form of birth control in Islam. But forty years before, a Muslim Brotherhood study on women had concluded that contraceptives, withdrawal, and sterilization were Islamically acceptable methods of birth control when good reasons existed to prevent pregnancy. Those reasons included the health of the mother and the financial burden of another child.

    Or take the issue of female genital mutilation. Gad Al Haq warned that "girls who are not circumcised when young have a sharp temperament and bad habits. . . . If girls are not circumcised as the Prophet said, they will be subjected to situations which will lead them to immorality and corruption." But Egypt's then mufti, the state's top legal authority, said he could find no mention of female circumcision in the Qur'an and only vague references to it in Prophet Muhammed's sayings. He neither endorsed nor condemned the practice.

    Yet another sheikh disagreed with both. The clitoris "must remain intact and not be cut," said Abdel Gaffar Mansour, adding that "as someone who has studied religion I think we should make society happy. . . . Circumcision removes from her the ability . . . to be happy because this part was created by God to make a woman happy with her husband." A gentle man in his early sixties, Mansour graduated from Al Azhar and is a consultant on Islamic education. He began exploring what Islam's holy texts said about this issue after a relative bled to death from a botched circumcision operation. "I was sure that God could not tell people to do things which make them so unhappy," he said. Under Islamic law, "the human body should be kept whole and respected. . . . There is not one verse, there's nothing, which talks about circumcision despite the fact that the Qur'an talked about everything else even marriage and sexual ethics between a man and his wife."

Mansour, noting that Prophet Muhammed, who had four daughters and no sons, did not circumcise his girls, added, "You always find the Qur'an pushes for a higher status for the woman."

Brotherhood study is in Mitchell, *Society of Muslim Brothers*, p, 283. Gad Al Haq on FGM in John Lancaster, "Top Islamic University Gains Influence in Cairo; Al Azhar Reflects Revival of Fundamentalism," *Washington Post*, April 11, 1995. My interview with Mansour was in Cairo, June 1994.

26. Na'im said he found it "remarkable . . . how misinformed Islamists themselves are about *Shari'a*. They really do not understand what they are talking about when they are calling for implementation of *Shari'a*." *Islam and Justice* (New York: Lawyers Committee for Human Rights, January 1997), p. 104.

Distinguishing between *shari'a* and *fiqh* is crucial to proper understanding of Islam, according to Muhammad Nowaihi of American University in Cairo. Lippman, *Understanding Islam*, pp. 102–103. Yet they have often been conflated. "*Fiqh* is the vast body of religious and legal rulings, often quite incomprehensible and meaningless in contemporary circumstances, given by the jurists of classical Islam," wrote Ziauddin Sardar. "In time, *fiqh* itself acquired a sacred identity, first by being associated with the *Shari'ah* or 'Islamic law' and then by becoming the *Shari'ah*. What goes under the rubric of *Shari'ah* in the contemporary Muslim world is little more than classical jurisprudence; it has little to do with the teaching of the Qur'an or the Prophet Muhammad himself." Sardar, "Paper, Printing and Compact Disks: The Making and Unmaking of Islamic Culture," *Media, Culture and Society* (London: SAGE), 15 (1993): 53.

27. Brotherhood spokesman Hodeiby told me all women, even Christians, would be required to veil. Interview in Cairo, February 1992. Brotherhood scholars and other Islamic jurists have argued that the cutting off of thieves' hands is only permissible if the theft takes place after a totally just society, which meets the basic needs of all citizens, has been achieved. As for adultery, they argue that capital punishment could only be imposed in two unlikely scenarios: The couple confessed to their crime or the required four witnesses testified they saw the sexual act in progress.

28. Author interviews with Mashur, Cairo, March and July 1993 and April 1996.

29. For the Brotherhood generation gap, see Diaa Rashwan, "Islamism in Transition," *Al Ahram Weekly*, March 11–17, 1999. Members are reluctant to talk about the group's internal structure, but it is believed to be headed by a policy-making Guidance Council that supposedly consults with a larger body beneath it called the Shura Council. How individuals get seated on either body is unclear.

30. James Pittaway, "A Benign Brotherhood?" *Harpers*, January 1989, p. 32.

31. The report was summarized in *Al Ahram Weekly*, November 18, 1993. Islamists were also making gains in university student elections. In 1990–1991, at Cairo University, Islamists won forty-seven of forty-eight seats on the Faculty of Science's student union, all seventy-two seats on the Faculty of Medicine's, and all sixty seats in the Faculty of Engineering's, according to Wickham. The Egyptian army's officer corps was also presumably affected by an increasingly Islamicized society. But they are coddled with financial favors by the state and carefully scrutinized by Egyptian intelligence for any displays of Islamist sympathies that go beyond normal religious practices.

32. Dessouky interview, Cairo, July 1993. Bahaeddin's "tip of the iceberg" quote is from Reuters, December 21, 1994. His other comments came in a 1993 interview in Cairo with me.

33. Reuters, May 6, 1993

34. Four years after Mahgoub's 1992 initiative, parliament passed a law requiring all preachers to obtain permits from the ministry with fines and a month in jail for non-

compliance. *Human Rights Watch World Report, 1998*, p. 326. By June 1997, fifteen thousand permits had been issued. The new minister of religious affairs Mohammad Hamdi Zaqzouq said the measure was to protect Islamic preaching from "being penetrated by parasites, ignorant and semieducated people." *Mideast Mirror*, January 29, 1997.

As on previous occasions when the government registered its intent to control sermons from Egypt's pulpits, its latest effort foundered on the reality that it lacked the funds and manpower to cover Egypt's plethora of mosques. For a history of how the government has unsuccessfully tried to control mosque preaching since the early 1900s, see Patrick D. Gaffney, "The Changing Voices of Islam: The Emergence of Professional Preachers in Contemporary Egypt," *Muslim World* 81, no. 1 (January 1991).

By law, all mosques in Egypt are to be licensed by the state. But most experts agree that the majority—somewhere between two-thirds and three-quarters—were not controlled by the government. Rather, they were supported by private funds and run by the individuals or community groups that built them. See Andrea B. Rugh's "Reshaping Personal Relations in Egypt," in Marty and Appleby, *Fundamentalisms and Society*, p. 164.

One explanation for the explosive growth of privately maintained mosques since the 1970s is that the government gives a tax break to builders who incorporate a mosque into their premises. Another reason is the increase in religious devotion and in population. As for the total number of mosques in Egypt, estimates vary greatly from around 50,000 to 170,000. One reason for this wide range is the elastic definition of mosque. The higher estimates apparently include *zawaya*, tiny rooms within larger buildings that are set aside for worship.

35. *Human Rights Watch World Report, 1996*, p. 272. On its face, the bill's passage appears illegal since Article 107 of Egypt's constitution states that meetings of parliament "shall be considered invalid unless the majority of its members are present." However, the article also states that resolutions can be adopted "by an absolute majority of its attending members." Whether this is a valid legal loophole or worse, a poorly written constitutional provision, it is clearly another example of how "democratic" institutions are subverted by the government to maintain control.

36. "Human Rights Practices in Egypt," U.S. State Department 1996 (Sec. 2a). "Saying What We Think," Center for Human Rights Legal Aid (CHRLA), February 1996, p. 27.

37. Islamic Group leader Talaat Fuad Kassim told Hisham Mubarak in 1993 that "the Muslim Brothers today have abandoned the ideas of Sayyid Qutb." Transcript provided by Mubarak, p. 4. Ayman Zawahiri, exiled leader of Islamic Jihad and future aide to Osama Bin Laden, wrote that the Brotherhood "continues to adhere to its failed and deviant methods." He urged it to stop "appeasing" the government and take the "correct decision" of declaring *jihad*. "When that happens, they will find that we are the closest and most supportive of people to them." Zawahiri's article in Islamic Jihad's magazine *Al Mujahidoon* was reported in *Mideast Mirror*, September 18, 1995.

Islamic Group's spiritual mentor Sheikh Omar Abdel Rahman had earlier castigated the Brotherhood. "The Muslim Brotherhood had their *jihad* at the beginning, at the time of their founder and leader Sheikh Hassan Al Banna. Then days passed and there were those who abandoned *jihad* or compromised it in order to lean toward the government. Now they do not speak of *jihad*, and they turn people away from *jihad* and accuse those who speak of *jihad* or who struggle as extremist and radical, like the words of the regime. . . . " Maha Azzam, "Islamic Oriented Protest Groups in Egypt, 1971–1981: Politics and Dogma," Ph.D. thesis, Faculty of Social Studies, University of Oxford, 1989, pp. 282–283.

At a 1993 press conference in Cairo, Brotherhood spokesman Hodeiby was asked about the Brotherhood's differences with Abdel Rahman. "The real difference between us," he replied, "is that we don't believe in force. We don't believe, even if we are against the political system now . . . and even if we don't trust that this government will change voluntarily, we are convinced that force will never get the objectives we want. We will never be able to change by force. That will not be good for our nation or for our activities . . . and it's not permitted in our beliefs."

The Brotherhood always insisted that if the government allowed it to operate normally and have access to the state-run media, they would be able to sway the younger, radical rebels to "true Islam." But many Egyptians, even some close to the Brotherhood, doubted the militants could be swayed by people they regarded as sell-outs. "If they take over," a moderate Islamist lawyer said of the rebels, "the first ones they will kill are us. I hope they don't take over." For more evidence of attacks on the Brotherhood by young militants, see the questions posed to a Brotherhood spokesman on this Web site: www.ummah.org.uk/ikhwan/questions.html.

Muslim Brother Mohammad Sayed Habib, a geology professor at Assiut University, told me in a 1993 interview in Assiut that he and other Brothers had had little success in persuading Islamic Group militants to halt their violent campaign. "We said 'You must try to change through constitutional laws,' " Habib said. But after the government imposed new restrictions on elections in professional associations, Habib said, "the youth of Islamic Group started to laugh at us, asking 'This is the road you want?' "

8. GUILTY OF PRACTICING DEMOCRACY

1. "Civil Society," Ibn Khaldoun Center, January 1993, p. 12.
2. Montassir interview, Cairo, September 1993.
3. These court-ordered changes were the result of the lawsuits filed by Kamal Khalid, the lawyer visited by Madani a week before his death.
4. "Military Courts in Egypt," Center for Human Rights Legal Aid (CHRLA), September 1995, p. 1.
5. Charges against the thirty-three are from an English translation of the October 24, 1995, indictment provided by Penny Parker of the Minnesota Advocates for Human Rights, an American lawyer who observed the trial.
6. Attorney Parker was interviewed by telephone, December 1995. A September 7, 1995, letter to Mubarak from the New York–based Lawyers Committee for Human Rights stated: "[D]espite months of investigations, prosecutors have apparently been unable to assemble a case that would stand up in a civilian court linking any individual defendant to specific acts of political violence." See also *Human Rights Watch World Report, 1996*, New York, December 1995, pp. 271–272.
7. CHRLA, "Military Courts in Egypt," p. 2. "Human Rights Practices in Egypt," U.S. State Department, 1996 (Sec. 1e): "These trials expanded the jurisdiction of the military courts beyond terrorism-related offenses . . . [and] . . . mark the first time since the mid-1960's that the government has tried civilian defendants in a military court on political charges." The Lawyers Committee letter to Mubarak stated: "The fact that your government is using exceptional powers to imprison and prosecute its political opponents during the run-up to parliamentary elections . . . suggests that the fundamental human rights of these defendants are being violated for political reasons."
8. Interview with "high judicial source" in *Al Ahram*, September 17, 1995.
9. *Mideast Mirror*, September 18, 1995.
10. Abdul 'Aal's testimony was recounted by Mohamed Salim El Awa and Moukhtar Nouh, attorneys who were on the defense team, in separate interviews, Cairo, April 1996.
11. The defendants' claim that they were on their way to buy cows was related by attorney Parker. Awa described the SSI's inability to detail the incident in court, which was also described in Fatemah Farag, "54 Guilty in First Brotherhood Verdict," *Middle East Times*, December 26, 1995.
12. Alfi interview with Al Hayat in *Mideast Mirror*, November 24, 1995.
13. Around the time of the Brotherhood's August indictments, exiled militants apparently associated with Islamic Group issued a statement in London mocking the Brotherhood for condemning the terrorists' violence and presuming that it was the unique voice of Islamist reform in Egypt. "The Muslim Brotherhood wants to prove that the other groups are illegitimate, especially 'Islamic Group,' in accordance [with] the Muslim

Brotherhood's belief that it alone has the sole right to Islamic action. . . . This is a good joke for which the Muslim Brotherhood should be held accountable," said the statement, which was signed by the "Islamic League of Upholders of the Book and the *Sunna*."

"What has the Muslim Brotherhood achieved since its inception relative to the meaning and aims of Islam, the hopes and aspirations of Muslim people, and the duties and necessities of the times?" it continued. The Brotherhood "is suffering from a serious disease" because it "embraces the legality of" Arab secular governments and doesn't learn from the past, it charged. Foreign Broadcast Information Service (FBIS), August 11, 1995.

For other evidence of differences, see Chapter 7, note 37. This moderate-radical competition even extended beyond Egypt to the New Jersey shores. According to Hisham Mubarak, who met many Egyptian militants living in and around New York in the early 1990s, one of the radicals' goals was to form "an international organization for *jihad* in competition with the Muslim Brotherhood network. The *jihad* trend and Brotherhood trend are in conflict in New York and New Jersey. It's as if they are in Upper Egypt," Mubarak told me in a Cairo interview, April 1993. Subsequent events showed that Mubarak had noticed the beginning of something important.

14. Farag, "54 Guilty," The others given five-year sentences included Erian's close friend and medical school colleague Abdel Moneim Abdul-Futuh, then a top official of the Arab Physicians Federation; Mohammad Khairat Al Shater, head of Salsabeel, a computer firm the government alleges is a Brotherhood front; Mohammad Sayed Habib, geology professor and head of Assiut University's faculty association; and Sayyed Mahmoud Ezzat, professor of medicine at Zagazig University. One of the eighty-two defendents was not sentenced because he was a fugitive.

According to defense attorney Awa, Omram, the man who had claimed he was on his way to buy cows, was convicted of being a Brotherhood member and given three years at hard labor. The three other Brothers who were also in the car when he was detained were acquitted.

15. A handwritten copy of Erian's statement was obtained by the author.

16. Sayed interview, Cairo, April 1996.

Human Rights Watch/Middle East, in a November 27, 1995, letter to Mubarak, called the trials "a blatant move to disenfranchise key members of the country's largest political opposition movement, closing the door to their peaceful participation in electoral politics." *Mideast Mirror,* November 28, 1995.

Amnesty International called the defendants "prisoners of conscience," and noted that their trials were unfair because civilians are not tried by military courts; the judges were not independent; there was no appeals process and the terrorism law under which they were tried was too broadly worded. Report of December 16, 1995, by Amnesty observer at the trial, provided to author by Amnesty.

The lack of evidence that the Brotherhood had supported or encouraged violence was noted by several sources. Amnesty's report related how, during a November 5, 1995, meeting with Judge Abdullah, the military officer "agreed that [the defendants] had not used violence—yet—but that the Brotherhood was dissolved by a political decree in 1954 and that therefore this group was meeting in secret. He went on to say that in Egypt there is freedom of expression and meeting secretly suggests that they had the intent to overthrow the government and nullify the constitution."

Shortly after the verdicts, senior SSI officer Mansour Al Esawi told *The Wall Street Journal*: "At present, we admit, the Brotherhood are not engaged in violence." But "even though we have no concrete evidence for a court, I have to move. The security of the state is at risk." Peter Waldman, "Unrest on the Nile," *Wall Street Journal*, December 8, 1995. In a March 1996 interview in Washington, D.C., a senior U.S. official who followed Egypt said he had not seen "a smidgen of evidence" at the trials of violent activity by the Brothers.

17. Interview with Fatma Fadl Sayed, Cairo, April 1996.

18. "Final Report on the Legislative Elections in Egypt 1995," CHRLA, December 1995, p. 25; Human Rights Watch/Middle East, November 27, 1995, letter to Mubarak, pp.

12–13; *Mideast Mirror,* November 29, 1995, p. 18; CHRLA report, p. 28; *Mideast Mirror,* November 27, 1995, p. 10.

19. Ezzat interview, Cairo, April 1996.
20. Some seven hundred Islamists were arrested in the run-up to the election. John Lancaster, "Egyptian Vote Draws Complaints," *Washington Post,* November 30, 1995 p. A31. From November 15 to December 6, 1995—the electoral period—1,392 Islamist campaign workers, supporters, and poll-watchers were arrested, according to Joel Campagna, "From Accommodation to Confrontation: The Muslim Brotherhood in the Mubarak Years," *Journal of International Affairs* 50, no. 1 (Summer 1996): 10. *Mideast Mirror,* December 11, 1995, p. 19; *Mideast Mirror,* November 28, 1995, p. 10; CHRLA report, p. 35; and U.S. State Department "Human Rights Practices in Egypt," 1996 (Sec.3).

    The property damage was reported by Interior Minister Alfi in *Al Ahram,* December 22, 1995. He also said 36 people were killed and 411 injured in election-related violence. Independent monitoring groups reported higher figures. "Independent Commission for Electoral Review (ICER)" report on January 10, 1996, said 51 people died and "ten times more" were injured. It said National Democratic Party apparatchiks were the worst perpetrators of what it called "unprecedented" election-related violence (pp. 19–20). A CHRLA report said "at least 51 persons" died and "at least 878" were injured during both rounds of elections (p. 45). Only the U.S. State Department's 1996 human rights report on Egypt (Sec.3) cited lower figures, saying "about 20" people were killed.
21. Jon B. Alterman," Middle East Leadership Succession," *Washington Quarterly* 23, no. 4, (Autumn 2000).

    After the first round of voting, courts suspended election results in over 100 of Egypt's 222 constituencies in response to complaints of vote-rigging and other irregularities from candidates. But the government proceeded with the second round of voting in districts where close races required run-offs. It quickly swore in the new parliament. The Court of Cassation eventually nullified results in 66 of the country's 222 constituencies because of irregularities. But the government asserted "parliamentary sovereignty," meaning that only parliament itself, and not the courts, can remove an elected member. In other words, parliament does not have to abide by court rulings.

    The government claimed turnout was 50 percent. But this turnout does not come near the participation in elections at the private sporting and social clubs that are fixtures of middle- and upper-class living in Egypt. *Al Ahram* senior editor Salama Ahmed Salama once noted in a column that club elections are heated contests often drawing 80 percent of a club's membership. The reason for this turnout, wrote Salama, is that people know the voting is fair.
22. ICER report, p. 22. According to ICER chairman Saad Eddin Ibrahim, the government's manipulation of the election was not even necessary. He reckoned that the ruling National Democratic Party would still have gotten around 70 percent of the vote in a fair election due to its vast resources, including the state treasury, the media, and the internal security forces. During a seminar in Washington, D.C., in November 1997, he made "the biggest rigging ever" comment.
23. Every year from 1993 through 2002, the annual U.S. State Department report on human rights in Egypt has observed that the NDP "dominates the political scene to such an extent that, as a practical matter, Egyptians do not have a meaningful ability to change their government."
24. The Trojan Horse allusion comes from Egyptian journalist Mohammed Sid Ahmed during a speech in New York, March 1996. The general was interviewed on a not-for-attribution basis. Amin quotes from interviews with him, Cairo, February 1992 and April 1996.
25. *Mideast Mirror,* December 8, 1995.
26. Kandil interview, Cairo, April 1996. Ghassan Salame added, "It should never be forgotten that most governments and even many secular opposition groups have not shown themselves to be any more committed to democracy than are the Islamists." Salame, "Islam and the West," *Foreign Policy,* Spring 1993 (p. 34).
27. In February 2000, an appeals court ordered a retrial of Ibrahim and his former employ-

ees. "Local observers believe that Ibrahim was prosecuted because of public remarks . . . regarding high-ranking officials . . ." said the U.S. State Department 2001 "Human Rights Practices in Egypt" report (Sec. 2a).

28. On June 3, 2000, the Supreme Constitutional Court declared the law unconstitutional on a technicality: it had not been presented to the upper parliamentary body (the Shura) for consideration. Prior to its 1999 enactment, Human Rights Watch/Middle East did an analysis in June 1998 of the proposed bill and found that it prohibited groups of citizens from carrying out "any political activities regardless of their nature," as well as any activities that threatened "the security of society," "public order," "national unity," or "morality." The proposed law allowed the government to reject candidates standing for elections to a group's board of directors; dissolve any group that had failed to accomplish its stated purpose; require notification within fifteen days of all decisions made by a group's officers; bar groups from soliciting funds from Egyptian or foreign sources; require advance approval for receiving or sending funds abroad; appoint government representatives to a group's board of directors and require advance permission to join an international association. Penalties for violations included closure of the organization and/or imprisonment for up to two years and fines up to $3,000 for individual officers.

When the law was nullified by the court, the government fell back on the 1964 "Law of Associations" to control NGOs. Enacted by Nasser's regime, the law requires every citizen-run organization, even soccer clubs and artist workshops, to obtain permission to operate from the Ministry of Social Affairs. That authorization is not granted until the group's leaders have been vetted by security police.

The groundswell of activism that arose in the post–Cold War years clearly worried the government. "At least three Cabinet meetings during the summer and fall of 1995 were devoted to discussions on how to curb, control or co-opt certain sectors of Egypt's sprouting civil society organizations," wrote Saad Eddin Ibrahim in his unpublished paper "Civil Society and Electoral Politics in Egypt," December 1995. As one Cairo resident once noted, "for the Egyptian government, everything that moves is a threat."

The government was most vexed by citizen groups created to monitor human rights abuses. One of the bright spots in the Arab world's political life of the 1990s was the slow but steady emergence of an indigenous, independent human rights movement. When I arrived in Cairo in 1989, there were only two human rights groups, the Arab Organization for Human Rights (AOHR) and the Egyptian Organization for Human Rights (EOHR). Six years later, there were more than a dozen such groups challenging the government in ways that the feeble secular political parties never could. Many of these human rights groups were assisted by funding from Western organizations interested in helping Arabs build grassroots awareness of human rights. It was this overseas funding—a good example of global integration outside the commercial sphere—that the Cairo government wanted to curb.

When that proved difficult, the government responded with official harassment. For several years, it blocked local groups from holding training seminars, often attended by foreign human rights workers. The 1996 U.S. State Department report on human rights in Egypt (Sec. 4) said that "on at least six occasions during [1995] the Government banned meetings of human rights groups or denied permits for them to hold conferences."

In December 1998, EOHR head Hafez Abu Seada was charged with disseminating false information harmful to Egypt's national interests; accepting foreign funds to carry out acts harmful to Egypt; and receiving donations without government permission. The charges came a month after an EOHR report on police brutality, including torture, in the Christian villlage of Al Kosheh. Seada was detained for about two weeks. It turned out that the $25,000 in foreign funds had come from the British House of Commons to support a women's legal aid project. The charges were eventually dropped.

By 2000, the government was relenting some. Three human rights groups were given legal status though others, including EOHR, were not. The government also began allowing human rights groups to hold some training seminars.

29. By November 2001, according to EOHR, 118 Muslim Brothers had been tried before military courts; 79 were convicted and given prison sentences; 39 were acquitted.

30. Richard P. Mitchell, *The Society of Muslim Brothers* (London: Oxford University Press, 1969), pp. 326–327.

For a detailed rendering of power struggles within the Brotherhood in the 1980s see Robert Springborg's *Mubarak's Egypt: Fragmentation of the Political Order* (Boulder, Colo.: Westview Press, 1989), pp. 233–238. Springborg has a slightly different description of the Brotherhood's senior councils, describing a "Founding Organization," composed of one-hundred-plus men, as the main decision-making body, though its role has been usurped by the fifteen-member Guidance Council. The author also said no new members have been added to the Founding Organization since 1954, making it literally a dying group.

31. The Qur'anic verse 2:143 states, "Thus have We made of you an *Ummat* justly balanced. That ye might be witnesses over the nations."

32. Omayma Abdel Latif, "The Hardest Choice Is Moderation," *Al Ahram Weekly*, December 12–22, 1999.

33. Mashur's remark is from an interview in Cairo, April 1996. For a good recounting of the Brotherhood's anger with Wasat and what Wasat means for Islamist politics, see Anthony Shadid, *Legacy of the Prophet* (Boulder, Colo.: Westview Press, 2001), esp. pp. 254–255.

34. "Abu Leila Magd, Founder of Al Wasat, Talks to the *Independent*," *Al Musakillah (The Independent)* newspaper, London, November 3, 1997. In another interview, Mady said, "The old guard is hung up on secretive work and are holding on to antiquated ideas on women, Copts and pluralism." Hamza Hendawi, "Muslim Brotherhood vies with Mubarak's Government for Hearts of Egyptians," Associated Press, January 5, 2002.

35. Mady comment in Khaled Dawoud, "Islamism in Crisis," *Al Ahram Weekly*, December 31, 1998. Three years after Wasat, two more Islamist political parties were formed in Cairo. Kamal Habib's Reform Party and the Islamic Law Party. Both were denied legal status in 1999.

36. Details on Erian after his release are from Mona El Ghobashy, "The Doctor Is Out," *Cairo Times*, November 9–12, 2000. While in prison, Erian told Ghobashy, besides the Qur'an, he read Charles Dickens, Naguib Mahfouz, and *King Lear*.

37. Ayman Zawahiri warned that the aborted 1992 Algerian election was proof that "Western powers" and "their clients" would never permit Islamist parties to come to power through the ballot box. His article in Islamic Jihad's magazine *Al Mujahidoon* was reported in *Mideast Mirror*, September 18, 1995.

38. Basheer's comment came during a seminar on Egypt at Columbia University, New York, October 1995. Nabil Abdel Fattah, "The Story of the Decade," *Al Ahram Weekly*, September 17–23, 1992.

39. Islamist parties have openly participated in elections in the past decade in Kuwait, Lebanon, Jordan, Morocco, Yemen, and Turkey. Often, they took a large share of the vote, but not a majority. While this made them powerful blocs in their legislatures, they still had to deal with established, secular-oriented political and military leaders in their respective states. Also, they often did not do as well in a second election as they did in the first. These experiences demonstrate that when Islamist parties are permitted to compete in elections, they do not necessarily obtain a permanent hold on power. See Jillian Schwedler, "A Paradox of Democracy? Islamist Participation in Elections," *Middle East Report*, no. 209 (Winter 1998).

On the other hand, Islamist electoral gains tend to provoke severe reactions from secular military regimes, as in Algeria and Turkey. Barely a month after Egypt's 1995 elections, Turkish voters shocked their secular establishment by giving 21 percent of their votes to the Islamist Welfare Party. A moderate movement some describe as "Islamist-lite," Welfare got more votes than the two main secular parties that had dominated Turkish politics for decades. Welfare formed a coalition with one of those parties and became the first Islamist movement to govern a Middle East country as the result of elections. By mid-1997, however, Turkey's powerful, secular military had forced Prime Minister Necmettin Erbakan, head of the Welfare Party, out of office.

9. MIDDLE GROUND

1. The Qur'an's eightieth chapter, entitled "Abasa, or "He Frowned," relates that while Prophet Muhammad was explaining the Qur'an to a group of people, he was interrupted by a poor, blind man who also wanted to know about it. Annoyed at the interruption, the Prophet "frowned and turned away," the chapter states. It goes on to say that he was later instructed by a revelation from God that he had a duty to explain His message to everyone and was sorry about the way he had treated the man.

2. There was also a difference in price. Nahla's delivery cost 800 Egyptian pounds, then about $236. His sister paid next to nothing because fees at government hospitals are minimal.

3. See Hazem Saghiya, "The Problems of Egypt's Political Culture," *Middle East Times*, August 25–31, 2001.

4. When the Political Parties Committee denies an application, its decision can be appealed to the courts, which have approved some party applications. But this legal battle is time-consuming and unpredictable for those seeking to form new parties. U.S. State Department 1998 report "Human Rights Practices in Egypt" (Sec. 3). The Center for Human Rights Legal Aid, in an August 15, 1996, report, noted that the Committee, set up in 1977, had denied the applications of thirty-two political groups seeking legal status as parties.

5. The Wafd Party was led by Fouad Serageddin until his death in 2001 at the age of eighty-nine.

6. Mostafa interview, Cairo, November 1993

7. Amin interview, Cairo, April 1996

8. Gihad Audeh interview, New York, 1995. In another example of the secular opposition's spinelessness, they called for a silent march on the U.S. embassy to protest a 1996 Israeli bombardment in south Lebanon that killed over two hundred civilians. Such a march would have violated the Emergency Laws and been promptly routed by police. "At the last moment, however," a newspaper reported, "the heads of the political parties decided to cancel [the march] in favor of attending the speech being given at the same time by the President." *Middle East Times*, April 28, 1996

9. Ahmed made this observation in an address in New York, February 1996. The Arabic word for secularism is *ilmaniyah*, whose root word, *ilm*, means "science" or "knowledge." However, some Islamists insist that a better word for secularism is *almaniyah*, derived from *alam*, which means "the world." The preferred provenance of the word usually depends on one's attitude toward secularism.

10. Alfred Farag's column appeared in *Al Ahram Weekly*, October 17, 1991, p. 5. Farag is not alone in his complaint about Arab political culture. Ali Oumleil, a Moroccan human rights activist, observed, "In the Arab world there is a political culture which is susceptible to the emergence of dictators and dictatorship. . . . For me, the problem is the nature of the political culture, and how we can change that." *Islam and Justice* (New York: Lawyers Committee for Human Rights, January 1997), p. 72. And Tunisian Islamist leader Rashed Al Gannouchi noted, "There is a cultural problem in the lives of the Muslims . . . and that is despotism. Despotism is inherent in the prevalent culture. You find it in the schools, in the family, in the street, everywhere." *Islam and Justice*, p. 40.

11. Free-flowing public debate is essential for political development and the suppression of political violence. As Islamist scholar Abdelwahab El Affendi noted: "Before we can have *ijtihad*, before we can criticize other groups, we have to have a society and a community in which to do it. We do not have this at the moment; we have the law of the jungle. And in the law of the jungle, the only language we have is that of beasts, which is violence." *Islam and Justice*, p. 82. Ironically, it is in the Islamic Republic of Iran where public debate over Islam's relationship to government is currently most robust and parliament is most independent.

 In recent years, satellite TV stations, including three newly licensed ones in Egypt, have added to the pressure for more open debate in Arab countries. State-owned stations have found it necessary to keep up with the competition and have thus been more open to on-air discussions of sensitive political topics.

10. A Culture of Our Own

1. Caryle Murphy, "When Kiss Comes to Shove in Jordan," *Washington Post*, October 23, 1991.
2. François Burgat and William Dowell, *The Islamic Movement in North Africa* (Austin: Center for Middle Eastern Studies at University of Texas, 1993), p. 53.
3. Mohammad Khatami, "Our Culture Belongs to a Bygone Civilisation," in *ISLAM21* (London: The International Forum for Islamic Dialogue, July 1997), p. 2.
4. Khaled Salah Hassanein's quotes come from two interviews in Cairo, April 1996.
5. "In the Muslim world, the profound process of reconnecting with the 'pre-colonial' symbolic universe, which is the essence of the Islamist resurgence, will more and more affect the entire political chess board," wrote François Burgat. "[I]t is the cultural impact of the recourse to Islam that engages the adherents of its 'return.' " Burgat and Dowell, *Islamic Movement*, pp. 309 and 68. Burgat sees this cultural "reconnecting" as a further step in Egypt's continuing emergence from colonialism. First came political independence in the 1920s, then economic independence, epitomized in Nasser's "Arab socialism" of the 1950s, and the nationalization of the Suez Canal operations. Egypt's Islamists, Burgat contended in an interview in Cairo in April 1993, are "doing on a cultural level what their fathers did on a political and economic level.... The main door" into Islamist politics, he added "is identity. It's not being poor."

    A Tunisian agronomist, speaking of Arab countries, said the following: "There is an attitude that you find in all politicians and in all the intelligentsia.... The point of reference is always the West. So the problem is, to put it simply, one of decolonizing the elites, decolonizing their psychology. It seems to me that this is a very important notion.... But this problem of psychological independence, of freeing the mind—well, a lot of people have alluded to it, but it hasn't been tackled as the real problem that it is. ... This is why the question of identity, of authenticity, is now at the forefront." Kevin Dwyer, *Arab Voices, The Human Rights Debate in the Middle East* (London: Routledge, 1991), p. 23.
6. Writing of the headscarf, Ibrahim B. Syed, a professor at the University of Louisville, Kentucky, and president of the Islamic Research Foundation, said that it "has come to signify the sum total of traditional institutions governing women's role in Islamic society. Thus, in the ideological struggles surrounding the definition of Islam's nature and role in the modern world, the [headscarf] has acquired the status of 'cultural symbol.' " Syed's "Women in Islam: Hijab," posted at Web site: www.geocities.com/~almanraj/Topics.
7. Richard P. Mitchell, *The Society of Muslim Brothers* (London: Oxford University Press, 1969), pp. 230 and 242. Resentment at the idea that Egypt's Muslim culture was seen as inferior by the British and their local allies was an important factor in Banna's founding of the Brotherhood in 1928 (p. 222).

    Mitchell observed that Banna saw a threat not only to Islam but to Islamic civilization. "What is at stake is not the advance of the religion of Christianity at the expense of Islam, but the retreat of Muslim civilization before Western civilization" (p. 230). This is still strongly felt today. "Muslims wish to live in the modern world but without simply imitating blindly the ways followed by the West," according to "Islam a Global Civilization," a booklet published by the Embassy of Saudi Arabia, Washington, D.C. (undated). "The Islamic world wishes to live at peace with the West as well as the East but at the same time not to be dominated by them.... It seeks finally to be create better understanding with the West and to be better understood by the West" (p. 40).
8. Caryle Murphy, "Iran: Reconciling Ideology and a Modern State," *Washington Post*, April 28, 1992.
9. "Westoxification" was coined in the 1960s by Iranian intellectual Jalal Al-e Ahmad. Roy Mottahedeh, *The Mantle of the Prophet* (New York: Pantheon Books, 1985), p. 296.
10. The Egyptian government discourages elementary school girls from wearing scarves and bans the full-face veils at universities. It believes that teachers who were imposing the headscarf on eight-year-olds and the university students covering their faces were making political statements in solidarity with the radical Islamist opposition. The full-

face veil, or *niqab*, is not traditionally worn in Egypt. It is much more common in the Gulf.

11. In 1997, Egyptian security police arrested around eighty young men and women whom they accused of devil worship and Satanism during open-air rock concerts featuring heavy metal music of such Western bands as Metallica and Megadeth. The youths were all eventually released and a police official said that they were "just a group of spoiled teenagers who suffer from lack of parental control." Some Egyptians believed the arrests were made to fend off Islamist complaints that the government tolerated such concerts. That such music had a following in Egypt shocked many people because it showed "the degree of Westernization in our society," one person told *The Guardian* newspaper. Janine Di Giovanni, "A Deadly Divide," *The Guardian*, October 4, 1997; Azza Khattab, "The Devil They Know," *Egypt Today*, May 1, 1997.

12. Burgat and Dowell, *Islamic Movement*, pp. 107–108. The response of Islamic scholars is not unlike that of the Christian right in the United States, whose literal interpretations of scripture and conservative dogmas are reactions in part to fears that America's traditional moral order is threatened by a godless and secular pop culture laden with nudity, profanity, and violence.

13. Hassan Hanafi, "Not into Salvation," *Al Ahram Weekly*, April 18, 1996; Hassan Hanafi, "The Relevance of the Islamic Alternative in Egypt," *Arab Studies Quarterly* 4, nos. 1 and 2 (1982): 71. An interesting insight into how Muslims view themselves came after September 11, 2001. Many disputed the U.S. government's assertion that Osama Bin Laden was responsible for the terrorist attacks in New York and Washington, saying they didn't believe Muslims had the expertise to organize such a synchronized attack involving four different airplanes. Laurie Goodstein, "Some Muslims Say Tape Removes Previous Doubt," *New York Times*, December 15, 2001.

14. Oshin quote from Susan Sachs, "Egypt Hooked on U.S. Soap Opera," *Newsday*, November 28, 1993. House of Donuts is a Saudi-owned franchise, but its style and ethos are overtly American.

15. Mustafa Mahmoud, "A Campaign Against Islam," *Al Ahram Weekly*, November 1993.

16. Some American Christians hold similar views to Egypt's Islamists. The Southern Baptist Convention launched a boycott of the Walt Disney Corporation in 1997 to protest its alleged disrespect for "family values" and its acceptance of homosexual employees. Shortly after the September 2001 terrorist attacks in New York and Washington, Baptist preacher Jerry Falwell said God had given America "probably what we deserve" because of "the pagans and the abortionists and the feminists and the gays and lesbians . . . all of them who have tried to secularize" American society.

17. Salah Eldin Hafiz, "A Wasted 50-Year Life," *Mideast Mirror*, March 22, 1995. All other quotes from Hafiz are from an interview in Cairo, April 1996.

18. Nabil Abdel Fattah, *Veiled Violence* (Cairo: Khattab Press Cairo, 1994), p. 86. Fattah goes on to say: "Regardless of how objective the problematic is of the Egyptian national identity, we do nevertheless have groups who feel, rightly or wrongly, that their identity is threatened, and we have to take their anxieties and fears seriously because these groups and the social forces behind them perceive the issue as a crisis."

    Richard W. Bulliet adds, "[C]onvinced that Islam is all that can preserve their identity from being submerged by the tidal wave of Western culture circling the globe, a generation of students is providing an eager audience for a new breed of religious leader, often only half educated in conventional Islamic teachings, but determined to interpret the faith in ways that make sense to people with modern educations." *Islam: The View from the Edge* (New York: Columbia University Press, 1994), p. 205.

19. Quote is from Tahseen Basheer. Andrea Rugh wrote of the young Islamists she studied in Cairo: "There is an element of generational rebellion in the removal from family, whether spiritual or actual. Rebellious young people have the choice of carrying out in secret activities disapproved by their parents, or they can openly pursue a religious life as a sign of their disapproval of the secular lives of their parents." Rugh, "Reshaping Personal Relations in Egypt," in *Fundamentalisms and Society*, eds. Martin E. Marty and R. Scott Appleby (Chicago: University of Chicago Press, 1993), p. 163.

20. Youssra's quotes are from a 1996 Cable News Network interview. The suit against her was dismissed by an appeals court in 1999 and the lawyers who brought the case were fined.

21. Saif Al Islam Al Banna, as quoted in "Banquet of Confusion in Egypt," *Mideast Mirror*, May 19, 2000.

22. Chahine said this in a documentary shown in New York at a February 1996 workshop on Egyptian film. In the end, the Islamists lost their case against him. Secular Egyptians were constantly urging the government to "grasp the religious nettle," as one writer put it, and stand up to the Islamists. But that was hard to do for a government long addicted to censorship for other reasons, usually to suppress politically embarrassing information. Also, the government was sensitive to the Islamist charge that it was not applying *shari'a*. So instead of confronting the Islamists on the cultural front, the government usually gave in. In the case of *A Banquet for Seaweed*, for example, it recalled all copies of the book and charged two Ministry of Culture employees with allowing publication of a blasphemous publication. The irony is that in using state censorship to quell Islamist complaints, the government abetted the Islamist assault on free expression. The "religious nettle" is from Cherif Cordahi, "No Sex Please, We're Egyptian," *The Guardian*, May 31, 1995.

23. Cartoons are an especially dangerous area because Islamists have little patience with satire or humor when it comes to religion. In a 1993 incident in Saudi Arabia, the comics editor at *Arab News*, an English-language newspaper, was thrown into jail and deported to his native India after running a "BC" comic strip humorously questioning the existence of God. In the two-frame strip, the famous pelt-clad prototype man said, "God, if you're up there give me a sign." He next appears in downpour of rain. "Well, we know two things," "BC" muses, "He's up there and he's got a sense of humor." As one Saudi said afterward, "The point is, if He's up there, there is no questioning of this. In an Islamic state, you cannot doubt if God is there." Caryle Murphy, "To Some, This Comic Is No Joke; Gentle Jest Involving God Lands Saudi Editor in Jail," *Washington Post*, July 24, 1993.

24. Burgat interview, Cairo, April 1993.

25. "Islam and Equality" (New York: Lawyers Committee for Human Rights, 1999), pp. 181–182.

26. Ezzat, telephone interview, January 2002.

27. Rafik Habib's quotes are from an interview in Cairo, April 1996. Wasat is currently promoting its ideas through a cultural organization called Egyptian Society for Dialogue and Culture. Habib said in a February 2002 e-mail that he is working on a "vision of the so-called culture project" that he will eventually present to the Islamist movement. Habib's father, the Reverend Samuel Habib, was president of the Protestant Churches of Egypt and a leader of the Evangelical (Protestant) Church of Egypt. He died one year after my conversation with his son.

28. Ezzat, telephone interview, January 2002.

29. This is a recurring theme in discussions about democracy in Islamic countries. Gassan Salame wrote: "Western states ought to acknowledge that democracy is not necessarily built upon a one-person, one-vote system. . . . Individualism is not a universal, nor a morally superior philosophy; communitarianism is still valid as a shield against authoritarianism and arbitrary rule." Salame further argues that "the West has to learn that its model of the secular nation-state is not as universal as it presumes. . . . Too often, the Western triumph in the Cold War is mistakenly equated with a triumph of Western political and intellectual models. Gassan Salame, "Islam and the West," *Foreign Policy*, Spring 1993, pp. 34–35; 32–33.

Mark Juergensmeyer noted that religious nationalism differs from the West's secular nationalism in its "exaltation of communitarian values over individual ones." The "logic of religious nationalism [is] that a nation should reflect the collective values of the moral community that constitutes it. Modern secular nationalism starts from the opposite premise. It sees individuals . . . as the basis for political order."

Like Salame, Juergensmeyer also questions the universal appeal of secular nationalism. He argues that in many parts of the developing world that have not accepted a fully secular orientation toward life, religious nationalists are attempting to create a new synthesis between traditional religions and the modern secular state. "[W]ithout the legitimacy conferred by religion, the democratic process does not seem to work in some parts of the world. In these places, it may be necessary for the essential elements of democracy to be conveyed in the vessels of new religious states," he wrote. Mark Juergensmeyer, *The New Cold War? Religious Nationalism Confronts the Secular State* (Berkeley: University of California Press, 1993), pp. 196–197 and 202.

For an explanation of the flaws that many Arabs see in the U.S. democratic model, Mohamed Elhachmi Hamdi, "The Limits of the Western Model," *Journal of Democracy* 7, no. 2 (April 1996): 81–85. On why Islamic democratic system are unlikely to look exactly like the West's, Frank E. Vogel, "Is Islam Compatible with Democracy?" in *Under Siege: Islam and Democracy*, ed. Richard W. Bulliet (New York: The Middle East Institute Columbia University, 1993), pp. 93–105.

30. *Islam and Justice* (New York: Lawyers Committee for Human Rights, January 1997), pp. 59–60; Louay M. Safi, "Towards an Islamic Tradition of Human Rights," and Omar Siddiqui, "Relativism vs. Universalism: Islam and the Human Rights Debate," both in *American Journal of Islamic Social Sciences* 18, no. 1 (Winter 2001). Abdullahi An Na'im, "The Synergy and Interdependence of Human Rights, Religion and Secularism," posted at Web site: www.polylog.org.

31. Yahya H. S. Farghal, as quoted in Bassam Tibi, "The Worldview of Sunni Arab Fundamentalists: Attitudes Toward Science and Technology," in *Fundamentalisms and Society*, p. 87. In the same essay, Tibi wrote, "While the Western mind splits the view of the world, Islamic *tawhid* (theocentrism) restores in the Islamic worldview the unity of the world as governed by God."

32. Hanafi interview, Cairo, April 1996.

Vatikiotis observes that "Islamic nationalism" may prove an alternative to nation-state because its appeal is indigenous. "We saw how previous adoption of a liberal ideology by the intellectuals deepened the chasm between them and the masses. It produced a two-level society without contact, sympathy, or understanding between them. The social-political consciousness of the few was unable to produce a new order, because it was counteracted by the traditional conservatism and inertia of the many. The masses, with their devotion to the past, were beyond the reach of the intellectuals. . . . Islamic nationalism [on the other hand] asserts the sentiment of religious-communal solidarity—a vague, yet emotionally acceptable concept." P. J. Vatikiotis, *Arab and Regional Politics in the Middle East* (New York: St. Martin's Press, 1984), p. 27.

33. "To practice *shari'a* is not only religion. It is also our national culture and national identity," said the late Adel Hussein, who, like Bishri, was once a leftist and became an Islamist thinker. "That's why even secular people if they are nationalists, it's quite logical for them to respect *shari'a* as our tradition." Hussein interview, Cairo, April 1993.

34. Burgat and Dowell, *Islamic Movement*, p. 51. When he retired, Bishri was a vice president of the Council of State, a judicial body that arbitrates administrative disputes within the court system. Former Egyptian diplomat Hussein Amin, who has known Bishri for fifty years, said of his former schoolmate, "He strongly feels that our traditions, culture, and way of life are being threatened by Western civilization and that our attachment to Islam is our only defense against this invasion."

35. Burgat and Dowell, *Islamic Movement*, pp. 52 and 51.

36. Bishri interview, Cairo, April 1996. Emphasis mine.

37. "Islam's 'Cairo Declaration,' " *Mideast Mirror*, January 22, 1993. To curb this "split personality," participants at the 1993 conference of the Higher Council of Islamic Affairs recommended that their governments "preserve Islamic social principles and values and the elements of Islamic culture" by subjecting all print and audiovisual media to strict controls, carefully selecting what their citizens see, "in order to accentuate the values of an Islamic society."

38. Khatami, *ISLAM21*, p. 2.

39. The hoax was reported in an August 30, 1989, Reuters dispatch from Cairo, which said that British Airways flight 156 departed for London hours later than scheduled after a search of the Tristar jet found no explosives.

11. New Thinking in Islam

1. Mohamed Salim El Awa, *On the Political System of the Islamic State* (Indianapolis, Ind.: American Trust Publications,1980), p. 76.
2. In this chapter, unless otherwise indicated, Abu Zaid's comments are from a July 1993 interview with the author in Cairo; a June 1996 discussion he led at the Council on Foreign Relations in New York, and a November 1998 seminar he gave at Johns Hopkins School of Advanced International Studies in Washington, D.C. Awa was interviewed in Cairo, April 1996. Hanafi interviews in Cairo, April 1996, and Washington, D.C., April 2000.
3. "We are currently living through one of the greatest periods of intellectual and religious creativity in Islamic—and human—history," wrote Richard W. Bulliet, *Islam, the View from the Edge* (New York: Columbia University Press, 1994), p. 207.
4. Laith Kubba, ed., *ISLAM21* (London: The International Forum for Islamic Dialogue, August 1996), pp. 3 and 8.
5. *Ijtihad*, writes Abdullahi A. An-Na'im, "literally means hard striving or strenuousness, but technically it means exercising independent juristic reasoning to provide answers when the Qur'an and Sunna are silent." Na'im, *Toward an Islamic Reformation* (Syracuse, N.Y.: Syracuse University Press, 1990), p. 27. See also "Law " in *Oxford Encyclopedia of the Modern Islamic World*, ed. John L. Esposito (New York: Oxford University Press, 1995): "As a juristic term, [*ijtihad*] means the exertion of the utmost possible effort to discover, on the basis of revelation interpreted in the light of all the rules, the ruling on a particular juristic question."
6. As Muqtedar Khan, an Islamic scholar at Michigan's Adrian College, wrote on his Web site (www.ijtihad.org): "The present rigid and inflexible approach to Islamic legal opinions of the past must be discarded and replaced with a more open and compassionate understanding of Islam. . . . The practice of hero-worship of past scholars determines which interpretation is accepted. I believe that this traditionalist approach is counterproductive. It merely recycles past opinions without actually making Islam relevant to specific times and circumstances." Similar sentiments are found in the Islamist newsletter *ISLAM21*. "The expanding boundaries of human perception of the Qur'an must not be limited to the static boundaries of the previous generations," it said (June 1996, p. 3).
7. Community acceptance to legitimize an individual's analysis of a problem as genuine *ijtihad* was stressed at a conference on Islam and technology by the Oxford Center for Islamic Studies at Ditchley Park, October 4–6, 1996. Its final report, entitled "The Islamic World and the Third Industrial Revolution: The Political, Economic and Cultural Implications of Changes in Information Technology," noted: "Any individual may exercise conscience and reason to interpret the Qur'an and Hadith, but it would be meaningless to give this activity the title of *ijtihad*, unless and until that individual's authority is recognized by a sufficient community of believers and then accepted by that community as law" (p. 15).
8. Ziauddin Sardar, "Paper, Printing and Compact Disks: The Making and Unmaking of Islamic Culture," *Media, Culture and Society* (London: SAGE) 15 (1993): 43. Imad-ad-Dean Ahmad, *Signs in the Heavens: A Muslim Astronomer's Perspective on Religion and Science* (Beltsville, Md.: Writer's Inc.-International, 1992), p. 21.
9. Ahmad, *Signs in the Heavens*, p. 149. Ahmad and Sardar noted that early Muslims were among the first to perfect the practice of rigorous citation so indispensable to modern scientific research. After Prophet Muhammad died, Muslims collected stories of what he said and did. These anecdotes, or *hadith*, are complements to the Qur'an and scriptural sources for Muslims. In order to make sure *hadiths* were accurate, and not embellished by imagination, scholars began tracing back who told whom each story. The aim was to verify the accuracy of every story about the Prophet. These who-said-what-to-whom reports were then attached to each *hadith* so people could know which might be bogus and which genuine. This was an early model for verifying transmitted data in the natural sciences. Sardar, "Paper, Printing and Compact Disks," p. 46; Ahmad, *Signs in the Heavens*, pp. 42–43.

10. Quote is from Sardar, "Paper, Printing and Compact Disks," p. 53. The transformation of religious knowledge into legal expertise is described by Bulliet, *Islam*, pp. 181–182; Sardar, pp. 52–53. Bulliet also discusses the *ulama*'s efforts toward uniformity, p. 195. Frank E. Vogel describes how the *ulama* acquired and maintained their position as interpreters of Islamic law in "Is Islam Compatible with Democracy?" in *Under Siege: Islam and Democracy*, Richard W. Bulliet ed. (New York: The Middle East Institute, Columbia University, 1993), pp. 93–105. And Bassam Tibi noted the "classical well-known enmity in Islam between the text-oriented *fiqh* (sacred jurisprudence) and *falasafa* (philosophy) [which] reveals that inductive reasoning has always been denounced in Islam as a source of heresy." Bassam Tibi, "The Worldview of Sunni Arab Fundamentalists: Attitudes Toward Science and Technology," in *Fundamentalisms and Society*, Martin E. Marty and R. Scott Appleby, eds. (Chicago: University of Chicago Press, 1993), p. 99 note 65.

One of the most influential Muslim personalities in "closing the gates" of *ijtihad* was the twelfth century's Abu Hamid Al Ghazali. Ghazali took on the question of whether God's existence could be proved empirically or through metaphysics. After years of wrestling with the problem—to the point of having a nervous breakdown—he concluded that God's existence could not be proved through logic and rational thought. He attacked Muslim philosophers for attempting to do so. The only way to know God, he wrote, was through a personal, mystical experience achieved by asceticism and imitation of tradition as practiced by Sufis, or Muslim mystics. He also attacked physics for contradicting *shari'a* and religion. By elevating Sufi mysticism and asceticism over rigorous intellectual debate and inquiry, Ghazali left a legacy that dampened *ijtihad* and boosted Islam as a closed system with its eyes ever backward on the past as the ideal. See Ahmad, *Signs in the Heavens*, pp. 139–143; Hassan Hanafi, "Two Victims," in Muslim Politics Reports, Council on Foreign Relations, Summer 1995, p. 1; and Karen Armstrong, *A History of God* (New York: Knopf, 1994), pp. 188–191.

11. For the view that the gates of *ijtihad* were not shut, or at least not as much as has been said, see "*Ijtihad*," in *Oxford Encyclopedia*; Albert Hourani, *A History of the Arab People* (Cambridge: Belknap Press of Harvard University Press, 1991), p. 160; and especially, Wael B. Hallaq, "Was the Gate of Ijtihad Closed?," *International Journal of Middle East Studies* 16, no. 1 (1984): 3–41. It does seem true, however, that by the tenth century, "Islamic law did tend to become more fixed as many jurists concluded that the essentials of God's law had been adequately delineated in legal texts. Thus there was a tendency to restrict substantive interpretation [*ijtihad*] and instead emphasize the obligation to simply follow or imitate [*taqlid*] Islamic legal texts," wrote John L. Esposito, *The Islamic Threat, Myth or Reality?* (New York: Oxford University Press, 1992), p. 36.

"Political backwardness" quote is Ahmad in December 1997 interview with author, Washington, D.C. Ahmad added in his book: "The decline of Islamic science can be associated with the 'closing of the door to *ijtihad*' by the Muslim establishment.... *Ijtihad*, the individual struggle for understanding, was replaced by *taqlid*, blind imitation of the past." Ahmad,136,143. For an overview of changing attitudes toward knowledge and *ijtihad*'s decline, see also Sardar, "Paper, Printing and Compact Disks," pp. 43–59.

The revival of *ijtihad* in order to reconcile Islam with modernity has been gaining steam for a century. In Egypt, scholars who followed Abduh diverged into two separate trends. Proponents of both considered themselves reformers. One trend dates to Abduh's disciple Rashid Rida, who stressed the need to go back to the original sources of the religion for guidance in developing a social morality. This return to a "pure Islam" involved reinterpreting the Qur'an through *ijtihad*, thus rejecting *taqlid*. But its *ijtihad* emphasized a return to orthodoxy with the early days of Islam as the model. Rida's most noted disciple was Hasan Al Banna of the Muslim Brotherhood. The ideas of Sayyid Qutb also grew out of this trend.

The other trend that claims Abduh as its founder is the modernist one. It adopts Abduh's benign attitude toward Western civilization, seeing no harm in adopting its best ideas into an Islamic context. In its *ijtihad*, this trend seeks to demonstrate the compatibility of Islam with modern life. It is more open to the secularist option and to modern scientific knowledge. Among its proponents was the Egyptian judge and religious scholar Ali Abd Al Raziq, whose 1925 book *Islam and the Fundamentals of Government* caused a furor in the Muslim world. Raziq wrote that Prophet Muhammad had not founded a political state, that religion and politics should be separate, and that *shari'a* should only govern religious matters. For these ideas, the *ulama* expelled Raziq from their ranks. A year later, the blind poet and educator Taha Husayn questioned the *ulama*'s traditional interpretation of the Qur'an and called for the use of modern philosophical methods in literary criticism. He was branded an apostate and dismissed from his job at Cairo University. For a general discussion of Abduh's double-barreled legacy, see Hourani, *History of the Arab People*, pp. 307–308 and 346–347. Also, "Modernism," in *Oxford Encyclopedia*.

12. Ezzat's written quote comes from her essay "Women and the Interpretation of Islamic Sources," at www.islam21.net. Her next quote is from a telephone interview, January 2002. In that interview, Ezzat added that she does not see "political positions" as "the measure of women empowerment . . . so it is not really the main issue of women equality from my point of view."

13. Mustafa Malik, a journalism scholar with the German Marshall Fund of the United States who is studying Muslims in Western Europe, estimates that its Muslim population is between 10 and 12 million. The number of Muslims in the United States is disputed, with estimates ranging from 1.5 million to 7 million. Bill Broadway, "Number of U.S. Muslims Depends on Who's Counting," *Washington Post*, November 24, 2001. Most likely, Muslims in America are somewhere between those two extremes, numbering three to four million.

14. Nyang, who teaches at Washington, D.C.'s Howard University, was quoted in Ira Rifkin, "Islam's Outlook Brighter," *Ventura County Star*, December 12, 1999, as cited in the November 2001 report of the Carnegie Corporation of New York, "Muslims in America: Identity, Diversity and the Challenge of Understanding." "Today," that report added, "it could be said that American Muslims are undertaking their own unique journey to forge 'e pluribus ummah' " (p. 4).

15. Bulliet, *Islam*, pp. 206–207. Bulliet added that "any lights that we see in the tunnel do not come from the end . . . the ideas that will be taken as the most authoritative synthesis of Islam and modern conditions fifty years from now have not yet been thought and are not on the current agenda." Bulliet, *Under Siege*, pp. 11–12.

Bulliet sees a likelihood of conflicts during this period of renewed *ijtihad*, writing that a "harmonious *umma* . . . seems to me improbable." The current divide between secular and religious Muslims will be complemented by "deep conflicts of interpretation" among the latter group "as to how Islam should be articulated as a social and political system in a modern world." Bulliet, *Under Siege*, p. 10.

In the Middle East, Islamist moderates such as Tariq Al-Bishri and Hassan Hanafi of Egypt, Mohammad Abid Al-Jabri of Morocco, Abdalla Al-Nafisi of Kuwait, Muhammad Al-Talbi and Abdel Majid Al-Sharfi of Tunisia are "working from an explicitly Islamic perspective in their respective fields of law, philosophy, history, politics, and sociology," wrote Abdullahi A. An-Na'im, and "attempting to modernize interpretations of Islam both in the academy and in areas of practical concern like development, constitutionalism, and the protection of human rights." Na'im, "A New Islamic Politics," *Foreign Affairs* 75, no. 3 (May/June 1996): 125. See also Dale F. Eickelman, "Inside the Islamic Reformation," *Wilson Quarterly*, Winter 1998.

Other prominent thinkers injecting new ideas into Islam include Muhammad Shahrur in Syria, Ali Bulac and Fethullah Gullen in Turkey, Sa'id Binsa'id in Morocco, Abdolkarim Soroush in Iran, and Nazir Ahmad in Pakistan.

16. Sardar, "Paper, Printing and Compact Disks," pp. 55–57. I am grateful to James Piscatori, lecturer in Islamic Politics at the Oxford Center for Islamic Studies, and author of many books on Islam, for his insights into the fragmentation of authority in contemporary Islam. A good discussion of what Egyptian-American Muslim Khaled Abou El Fadl called the "vacuum of authoritativeness in contemporary Islam," is in Douglas McCollam, "Annotating Islam," *The American Lawyer*, December 6, 2001. Dale F. Eickelman has examined the information revolution's effect on Islamic authority. See his "Islamic

Reformation." Bulliet looks at why the *ulama*'s religious authority in early Islam collapsed in *Islam*, chap. 11.

For some Muslims, the splintering of religious authority represents a threat to Islam. To counter it, they maintain that authority rests in the very words of Islam's sacred scriptures. But this stance tends to lead to literalist readings of the Qur'an and Sunna, and thus to outdated, inflexible interpretations of these sacred texts. Others say the problem of authority in Islam can be resolved by having an Islamic state ruled by *shari'a*. Since they view *shari'a* as God's law, it is the basis of authority. But this is really not a remedy because it puts religious authority into the hands of whoever controls the coercive power of the state. Sudan, Iran, and Afghanistan come to mind. Clearly, neither a literal approach to sacred texts nor a *shari'a*-based Islamic state will resolve the problem of fragmented authority in a religion undergoing a global reawakening.

17. Affendi's comment is in *Islam and Justice* (New York: Lawyers Committee for Human Rights, January 1997), p. 99. Laith Kubba wrote that "in order to accommodate the diversity of opinion among Muslims, the Islamists will have to learn to accept a system based on pluralism." Kubba, "Recognizing Pluralism," *Journal of Democracy* 7, no. 2 (April 1996): 86–89.

18. Kubba, citing the problems of Muslim societies, asks, "Why is it happening to the best '*Umma*' known to people while the 'nonbelievers' continue to thrive?" *ISLAM21*, p. 1.

Bassam Tibi wrote that Islamic fundamentalists in Egypt were reacting "to the crisis of modern Islam brought about by the discrepancy between the claim of Islam to be in possession of the perfect and final knowledge (revelation) and the concrete reality of the 'backward' abode of Islam as existentially challenged by the modern and militarily superior Euro-American powers." Tibi, "Worldview of Sunni and Arab Fundamentalists," pp. 81–82.

19. Sardar described the "continuous interpretative relationship with their sacred text" in discussing the implications of new communications technology for contemporary *ijtihad*. Sardar, "Paper, Printing and Compact Disks," p. 56.

20. Younes's remarks are from a July 1993 interview in Cairo, except for her last comment, which came from Mona Eltahawy, " 'Separated' Wife Claims Psychological Abuse," *Middle East Times*, July 9–15, 1995, p. 9. Unless otherwise indicated, quotes from Abu Zaid and his wife are from interviews in Cairo, 1993, and New York, 1996.

Abu Zaid's biographical details come from New York 1996 interview; Mona Anis and Amira Howeidy's "The Madding Crowd," *Al Ahram Weekly* June 22–28, 1995, p. 5, and "People's Rights," a publication of the Legal Research and Resource Center for Human Rights in Cairo, August 1995, p. 2.

21. "Silencing Is at the Heart of My Case," *Middle East Report*, November-December 1993, pp. 27–28.

22. Abu Zaid quoted in "A Case of Academic Freedom," a November 5, 1994, lecture by Fred Leemhuis of the Netherlands' Groningen University, Department of Middle East Languages and Culture. Abu Zaid's approach to reading the Qur'an was reflected in the work of the late Pakistani scholar Fazlur Rahman. See Hourani, *A History*, p. 447.

23. "Abu Zaid did not discuss the religious text itself, but rather people's readings of the text," observed Hassan Hanafi. "He was trying to show how people hid behind Islam to achieve their own political and social goals." "People's Rights," August 1995, p. 5.

24. "A Rigorous Reading of Metaphor?," *Al Ahram Weekly*, June 22–28, 1995.

25. For Shahine's relationship to Islamic investment companies, see "The Case of Abu Zaid," *Index on Censorship* 4 (1996): 36–37, and Loutfi Al Khouli, "University and Academic Freedom," *Al Ahram Weekly*, April 8–14, 1993.

26. Quotes from Shahine's report are from Al Khouli, "University and Academic Freedom, A Rigorous Reading of Metaphor?" and Caryle Murphy, "Egypt's 'Intellectual Civil War,' " *Washington Post*, July 22, 1993.

Shahine's literalist views were not an anomaly in Egypt's academic community. Mohamed Al Beltagi, professor of Islamic jurisprudence and dean of the science faculty at Cairo University, and Ismail Salem Abdel 'Aal, assistant professor in Islamic studies, deemed Abu Zaid's work heresy, according to court papers. Mustafa Al Shaq'aa, dean of

Ain Shams University's arts faculty, branded Abu Zaid an "infidel," according to Amira Howeidy, "A Man for All Reason," *Al Ahram Weekly*, June 22–28 1995, p. 4.

27. The 7–6 vote is in *Index on Censorship*, p. 36. The Council's March 1993 vote is in "From Confiscation to Charges of Apostasy," Center for Human Rights Legal Aid, July 1995, p. 5.

28. Steve Negus, "Professor Charged with Apostasy," *Middle East Times*, July 6–12, 1993, p. 1.

29. "Islamic Banner" quotes from editions of April 15 and 22, 1993 are in *Index on Censorship*, p. 39.

30. "A Man for All Reason," *Al Ahram Weekly*, June 22, 1995, p. 5.

31. *Human Rights Watch World Report, 1997*, p. 279, citing the Egyptian Organization for Human Rights (EOHR). A similar case occurred in 1917 when a man was ordered to divorce after a court found him an apostate for declaring that Noah, not Adam, was the first prophet of Islam. An appeals court overturned that decision, lamenting that "while the West concerned itself with progress, Egyptians preoccupied themselves with trivialities." See "A Man for All Reason."

32. Excerpts from the appeals court ruling come from a translation in "People's Rights," June 1995, pp. 4–5.

The judges' comments on *jizya*, however, come from "Confiscation to Charges of Apostasy," p. 11. A *jinn* [or *jinni*], is the origin of the English word *genie* and means a supernatural being who can take human form and influence human events.

A month after the ruling, Judge Abdel Alim told an Egyptian magazine that Muslims must believe in spirits, devils, and the throne of God. He also said that even if Abu Zaid repented, it would not automatically undo the separation ruling. The couple would have to remarry. "If an apostate repents, then after repenting he must sign a new marriage contract with his wife and give her a new dowry," Abdel Alim said. Reuters, Cairo, July 13, 1995.

33. I am grateful to M. Cherif Bassiouni, professor of law at DePaul University in Chicago, for his insights on this issue in a 1996 interview. "The bottom line is that the constitution looks at *shari'a* as the principle source of legislation," which is equivalent to regarding *shari'a* as a "constitutional framework," Bassiouni said. But Islamists seek to introduce "details of *shari'a*" into Egypt's court system and legal rulings in order to move *shari'a* beyond a "constitutional framework" so it becomes the only basis for all judicial decisions. In Abu Zaid's case, the rulings of the appeals court and the Court of Cassation [which affirmed the appeals court's use of *shari'a*] reinforced this trend, Bassiouni explained. Further, apostasy from Islam had historically meant withdrawing from the *umma* to join the enemies of Islam, so "it was treason more than a matter of conscience," Bassiouni added. Traditionally, apostasy had "never applied to utterances." All told, he concluded, the Abu Zaid case set "a terrible precedent."

34. "Medieval nonsense," is in *Human Rights Watch World Report, 1996*, p. 274; Shukri quote is from "A Man for All Reason"; Zakariya quote is from "People's Rights," June 1995, p. 3. "Abu Zaid isn't against Islam," Egyptian journalist Mohammed Sid Ahmed told me. "Abu Zaid is against medievalism. He is against not having had our Luther and Calvins who want Islam to be ready to deal with problems of genetical engineering."

35. Shahine's and Berri's comments come from "A Man for All Reason" and Dina Ezzat, "Islamists Divided over Abu Zeid Case," *Al Ahram Weekly*, July 5–12, 1995. Berri was then deputy chairman of the ultraconservative Al Azhar Scholars Front. A year later, when the appeals court ruling was upheld by the higher Court of Cassation, Al Azhar's Grand Sheikh Mohammed Sayed Tantawi said that the "judiciary in this case followed the rules of Islamic law. The verdict is now binding and the case is closed . . . and the couple must separate." Abu Zaid's only option, Tantawi added, was to publicly renounce his writings. "Sheikh Supports Egyptian Apostasy Divorce Ruling," Reuters, Cairo, August 22, 1996, quoting from an interview Tantawi gave *Al Hayat* newspaper.

36. Islamic Jihad faxed its statement to *Al Hayat*, Reuters reported June 22, 1995. The death threat was also in Jihad's newspaper *Mujahidoon*, then being published in Switzerland. See "People's Rights," June, 1995, p. 7.

37. "Confiscation to Charges of Apostasy," p. 5. Abu Zaid continued his legal fight from

abroad for several years, first appealing to the Court of Cassation, which reviews appeals of court decisions for technical deficiencies but not substantive errors. After more than a year of deliberation, it found no legal grounds for overturning the 1995 ruling. (A few months later, in December 1996, a lower court indefinitely suspended implementation of the divorce ruling but this had little practical effect since Abu Zaid and his wife were no longer in Egypt.) Abu Zaid then challenged the constitutionality of the Court of Cassation's 1996 affirmation of the apostasy ruling to the Supreme Constitutional Court. In August 2000, that court rejected his appeal.

38. Cable News Network, October 20, 1995.

39. For the restrictions on *hisba*, see "Human Rights Practices in Egypt," U.S. State Department, 1997 (Sec. 2a). Conservative Islamists had been aggressively using *hisba* to sue writers and journalists, alleging that they were denigrating Islam or Muslims. Many Egyptians saw this legal harassment as a threat to freedom of speech.

Shahine's losses are recounted in Mary Ann Weaver, "Revolution by Stealth," *The New Yorker*, June 8, 1998, p. 46. In an ironic footnote, Shahine later was accused of "blasphemy" and of being an "infidel" by Sheikh Badri, his erstwhile confederate in the suit against Abu Zaid. Badri objected to Shahine's 1998 book in which he analyzed the Qur'an's story of man's creation. He asked Shahine "to declare his repentance" because his book "supports Darwin's theory." Defending himself, Shahine sounded much like Abu Zaid. "All I did was attempt to remove from the Muslim mind certain naive and backward myths about the creation of mankind," he said. As for the "ignorant" Badri, Shahine added, he is "the very model of Islamic fanaticism." Amira Howeidy, "Out of Eden," *Al Ahram Weekly*, January 21–28, 1999.

40. "People's Rights," August 1995, p. 5. Hanafi added that the state has "allowed fundamentalist sheikhs to infiltrate the media, accusing people and intellectuals of heresies" and "fundamentalist groups" have infiltrated "state institutions including the security, the police and more recently the judiciary."

41. The Qur'anic verse 2:256 is the basis for freedom of religious conscience. Two other relevant verses are 10:99–100 and 18:29. The conflict between these verses and some Sunna passages, as well as the prevailing view among Muslim jurists that death is the punishment for apostasy, are discussed in Malika Zeghal, *Gardiens De L'Islam* (Paris: Presses de la Fondation Nationale des Sciences Politiques, 1996), p. 336, and Na'im, *Toward an Islamic Reformation*, pp. 109 and 183. Other Sunna passages say it is unacceptable for a Muslim to declare another an unbeliever, a practice called *takfir*. See "*Kufr*," *Oxford Encyclopedia*.

The Abu Zaid controversy was intensified by an unrelated but extraordinary event during a murder trial occurring at the same time. Charged with the 1992 slaying of secular writer Farag Foda, thirteen Islamic Group extremists claimed that it was their "Islamic duty" to kill Foda because he rejected implementing *shari'a* and this made him an apostate. The defendants called Muslim scholar Muhammad Al Ghazali as an expert witness. Ghazali, who died in 1996, was then in his late seventies. He was highly regarded in the Arab world as a learned interpreter of *shari'a*. He had a doctorate from Al Azhar and for many years had worked as the government's religious representative abroad. He also had a lifelong association with the Muslim Brotherhood. Though no longer an official member, he was regarded as one of the organization's leading theoreticians.

The bearded, white-turbaned scholar wanted Egypt to be an Islamic state ruled by *shari'a*. But his rulings on women and technology had often been forward-looking and he'd once scored the Islamist rebels for their "infantile" understanding of the Qur'an. Ghazali certainly had more widespread respect among devout Egyptians than radical sheikhs like Islamic Group's Omar Abdel Rahman.

But Ghazali's trial testimony turned out to be a shocker for secular Egyptians.

"There are many people who do not want *shari'a*, debate its applicability and endorse its 'death sentence' issued by foreign governments and international imperialism," said Ghazali. "They take us lightly when we say that God's law must rule.... [But] refusing to implement *shari'a* is apostasy."

Most Muslim scholars say apostates should be given time to repent and killed if they refuse to do so, Ghazali continued, adding that he was more lenient. "I personally believe they should be given a life sentence."

"Who," the defense lawyers asked Ghazali, "has the right to kill an apostate?"

"Supposedly the judicial system and not the mass of people in order to avoid anarchy."

"But what if the law does not condemn apostates?"

"Then the law is flawed and there is anarchy in society."

"What if an individual kills an apostate?"

"Then he is considered to have overstepped the government."

"And is there a penalty for overstepping the government in killing an apostate?"

"I remember no such penalty in Islam." (Testimony as reported in *Al Shaab*, June 25, 1993, p. 3.)

Ghazali's remarks set off a firestorm. One human rights group said they were "tantamount to the excommunication of a large section of Muslim society, as well as being a clear invitation to murder." By suggesting that individuals who murdered alleged apostates were not liable to any punishment, he legitimized "the various acts of terrorism and violence that have afflicted this country in recent times" and gave "a clear invitation to any Muslim to usurp the legal role of their courts" (EOHR statement, June 29, 1993).

In the weeks that followed, Ghazali did not claim he'd been misquoted or misunderstood. An apostate, he told reporters, is "anyone who derides religion or mocks *shari'a*." He suggested the government appoint a committee of Al Azhar scholars to judge suspected apostates. And contradicting his earlier testimony that unrepentant apostates should get life sentences, Ghazali said the government should execute them. "Egypt Sheikh Wants State to Kill Heretics," Reuters, July 16, 1993.

Other religious conservatives supported his view that apostates should be killed but questioned whether individuals acting on their own could do so with impunity. "No one can claim that someone is apostate or punish him unless it is confirmed through proper regulations and then he must be punished by the leader," said a statement from Al Azhar. "Those who overstep this will be severely punished in the afterlife." *Al Ahram*, July 9, 1993.

Muslim Brotherhood leader Mustafa Mashur said he found Ghazali's statement "strange" because it could "result in anarchy in society if anybody can go ahead and kill" an apostate. "The government should do this. An Islamic government." Caryle Murphy, "Killing Apostates Condoned," *Washington Post*, July 22, 1993.

The government tried to ignore Ghazali's remarks. But pressed by reporters, Osama Al Baz, President Mubarak's senior foreign policy adviser, finally said, "I believe the consensus of scholars on this point is as follows: That no citizen can take the law into his own hands, for any purpose." And if Ghazali's statements are "interpreted by some people here to condone the killing, even the hurting of anybody . . . this I would consider a regression and a negative development." Murphy, "Killing Apostates Condoned."

42. "People's Rights," June 1995, p. 7.

43. Awa's first remarks are from *Al Shaab*, July 21, 1995, and the others from an interview in Cairo, April 1996. Bishri interview, April 1996. Imara comments were in Ezzat, "Islamists Divided over Abu Zaid Case."

44. R. Stephen Humphreys called the Qur'an "the charter" for the Islamic community in Toby Lester, "What Is the Koran?" *Atlantic Monthly*, January 1999, p. 45.

45. "After the 9th century A.D. the dominant theological view in Sunni Islam became that the [Qur'an] is the uncreated Word of God and an eternal and immutable attribute of His nature," noted Fred Leemhuis, "A Case of Academic Freedom." See also Lester, "What Is the Koran?," p. 54.

All Muslims read some Qur'anic passages metaphorically while other passages, usually called "clear" or "unambiguous," are read more literally. But there is disagreement among Muslims about which passages are allegorical and are literal, Abu Zaid said. "The Madding Crowd," p. 5.

Early Christians had similar disputes. More than three centuries before the Mu'-tazilites, St. Augustine published a commentary on Genesis (*De Genesi ad Litteram*, 401–415 C.E.) in which he discussed the contrast between how he and his contemporaries viewed the natural world and how the authors of Genesis understood it. He concluded there was a need to deal critically with the earlier biblical worldview. See "Biblical Scholarship," *Microsoft Encarta Encyclopedia* 1999.

46. The case of Taha Husayn, for example. See note 11 above. Egyptian historian Sayed Al Qimany has also come under fire from fellow Muslims for his views on how to read the Qur'an. He has said, "The Quran has two aspects—facts which deal with realistic things that could have happened in any age, such as the battle of Badr, difficulties with the Jews of Medina, and so on. But there are some incidents that could not have happened and these are mythology. . . . We need to say what is symbolic, and avoid things that are not rational or logical. . . . We need to lead the ordinary people to a better understanding of what went on." "In Search of What Went Wrong," *Middle East Times*. Egyptian government censors forbade publication of this 1996 article but it can be read at www.metimes.com/cens/c3.htm.

Fred Leemhuis, the Dutch scholar, noted that attempts to examine the Qur'an's origins are controversial because if people accept that its text is "situationally determined," then the "consequence of this conclusion is that the text . . . as we have it cannot be the eternal unchangeable word of God and there's the rub. . . ." Leemhuis, "A Case of Academic Freedom."

In 1996, Mohammed Arkoun, professor of the history of Islamic thought at the Sorbonne, called it "unfortunate that the philosophical critique of sacred texts—which has been applied to the Hebrew Bible and the New Testament without engendering negative consequences for the notion of revelation—continues to be rejected by Muslim scholarly opinion." "Islam and Toleration. Writers' Block," *The Economist*, January 27, 1996.

47. Abu Zaid used the "devil question" phrase in his 1998 Hopkins seminar. The "cognitive certainty" phrase is S. Parvez Manzoor's, cited by Lester, "What Is the Koran?," p. 48. Lester's article is an excellent explanation of the obstacles facing modern Qur'anic exegesis and the impact of the 1972 Yemen discovery. See also Abul Taher, "Querying the Koran," *The Guardian*, August 8, 2000. Abu Zaid's "essential" quote is in Lester, p. 50.

48. Two examples of this argument are Tibi, "Worldview of Sunni and Arab Fundamentalists," pp. 74, 92–93, and Nadav Safran, who discussed what he called "the epistemological significance of the problem of the dogma of the Qur'an." Safran wrote that Abduh and other early Islamist reformers underestimated how much insistence that the Qur'an is the literal Word of God would hamper a new "intellectual reorientation" in Islam for modern times. As long as the reformers hewed to "the traditional view of its content as objective divine truth" there was a conflict between revelation and reason and "the ideological readjustment could never be complete and permanent," Safran wrote.

"With Abduh," Safran wrote, "Islamic Reformism faced the problem of the relation between reason and revelation consciously and deliberately." But he concluded that Abduh's contribution, though great, fell short. "He accomplished the necessary step of reopening the traditional doctrine for fresh inquiry and inspired confidence in the vitality and liberality of Islam, but he failed to reconcile *concretely* and objectively the content of revelation with the driving forces of modern life." As a result, the "Islamic Reformist alternative . . . has been severely handicapped in its aim of adjusting Islam to modern life by the dogma of the Qur'an as the integral and perfect revelation of God's word." Safran, *Egypt in Search of Political Community* (Cambridge: Harvard University Press, 1961), pp. 179–180 and 247–249.

49. Shahrur comments come from Dale F. Eickelman, "Islamic Liberalism Strikes Back," *Middle East Studies Association Bulletin* 27, no. 2 (December 1993): 163–168, and Michael Jansen, "Syria's Islamic Reformer Outsells Mullahs," *The Irish Times*, August 13, 1993. See also Eickelman, "Inside the Islamic Reformation."

The importance and urgency that many modern Muslims attach to the issue of how to read the Qur'an is addressed in a series of essays by American Muslims in the

December 2001 and January 2002 issues of *Boston Review*, a publication of the Massachusetts Institute of Technology.

Iranian Islamist philosopher Abdolkarim Soroush has noted that religious knowledge "is, like other forms of knowledge, subject to all the attributes of knowledge. It is human, fallible, evolving, and most important of all, it is constantly in the process of exchange with other forms of knowledge. As such, its inevitable transformations mirror the transformation of science and other domains of human knowledge." His remarks are from an interview by Mahmoud Sadri and Ahmad Sadri posted on www.iranian.com in May 1999.

Even Iran's president Mohammad Khatemi noted the importance of distinguishing religion and religious knowledge. "Faith is best served," he wrote, "by differentiating— bravely—between the essence of faith as a holy and divine affair, and people's impression of faith which is relative, limited and alterable." *ISLAM21*, July 1997, p. 3.

Meanwhile, American Muslim scholar Amina Wadud-Muhsin, borrowing from the late Muslim scholar Fazlur Rahman, who had a Mu'tazilite orientation, argues for a distinction between the Qur'an's "prior text" set in a specific cultural and historical context and its "metatext," which conveys a more tolerant and universalistic worldview. "Qur'an," *Oxford Encyclopedia*.

50. Lester notes how some Muslims believe that critical exegesis of the Qur'an "will provide fuel for an Islamic revival of sorts—a reappropriation of tradition, a going forward by looking back . . . [which] as the histories of the Renaissance and Reformation demonstrate—can lead to major social change." Lester, "What Is the Koran?," p. 44.

51. Mohamed Salim El Awa, *On the Political System of the Islamic State*, pp. 75, 76, and 80–81. Awa rejects, as do most Islamists, the ideas of Egyptian religious scholar Ali Abd Al Raziq who argued in a controversial 1925 book that religion and politics should be separate and *shari'a* should govern only religious matters. See note 11 above.

52. Awa, *On the Political System of the Islamic State*, pp. 64, 68, 69, 74, 85, 35, and 90. Islamic states ruled by *shari'a* include Iran, Sudan, Pakistan, and Saudi Arabia. While Iran's top official, the so-called Supreme Guide, is an unelected clergyman, the country has universal suffrage, the region's freest elections, and its most rambunctious, independent parliament. In 1997, long-shot reformist candidate Mohammad Khatemi won the presidential election and took office in a mostly peaceful transition. He was peacefully reelected despite robust opposition from conservative forces in 2001. Iranian women hold top government jobs.

By contrast, Saudi Arabia, a hereditary monarchy, is the only country in the world where women cannot drive and beheading is the state-approved form of capital punishment. In the early 1990s, the Saudi king proclaimed that elections are not part of the Islamic system, provoking hoots of ridicule from Egyptians, including Islamists. The monarchy finally made a bow to *shura* by appointing an all-male advisory body to review government policies. Its deliberations are secret.

53. Awa, *On the Political System of the Islamic State*, p. 107.

54. Awa states in his book (ibid., p. 76) that "the Muslim *Jama'ah*, which in its political association constitutes the state . . ." Elsewhere, the book's glossary (pp. 124 and 126) defines *Jama'ah* as "the community (of Muslims)" and the *umma* as "the community of Muslims," making them seemingly interchangeable terms. Even apart from this confusion, it would appear that the *umma* could only become a legitimate democratic body politic if its definition under *shari'a* is revised. Abdullahi A. An-Na'im observes that "the conception of the *Umma* as the collective original agent of the divine sovereign, and as such the only human sovereign, can provide a viable foundation of constitutionalism only if the composition of the *Umma* under *Shari'a* is revised to include all citizens on the basis of complete equality, with no discrimination on grounds of religion or gender." Na'im, *Toward an Islamic Reformation*, p. 85.

55. Awa pluralism quote is from Mohamed Salim El Awa, "Political Pluralism from an Islamic Perspective," in *Power-Sharing Islam?* ed. Azzam Tamimi (London: Liberty for Muslim World Publications, 1993), pp. 74 and 75.

Islam's historic pluralism is noted by Bernard Lewis. "Almost from the beginning the Islamic world has shown an astonishing diversity. . . . Sectarian strife and religious persecution are not unknown in Islamic history, but they are rare and atypical, and never reached the level of intensity of the great religious wars and persecutions in Christendom." Lewis, "Islam and Liberal Democracy," *Atlantic Monthly*, February 1993, p. 98. Also, P. J. Vatikiotis wrote that Islam's "history abounds with a diversity of religious, social and political adaptive experience. In fact, its political pluralism has been its most salient feature." Vatikiotis, *Arab and Regional Politics in the Middle East* (New York: St. Martin's Press, 1984), p. 66. This book contains many helpful insights on Egypt, and its modern intellectual development.

Islamist political theorists generally have failed to offer practical ideas on several aspects of an Islamic state, including the mechanics of the political process, what checks and balances would exist, and how its political institutions would cope with conflicting opinions. The role of women, pluralism, and the state's role in overseeing personal morality are other issues that they have not yet fully tackled. For critiques of current conceptions of an Islamist state see Na'im, *Toward an Islamic Reformation*, pp. 69–100, 75–85, and 209. "Islamic State," *Oxford Encyclopedia*, criticizes some notions of an Islamist state for being "ideological" and promoting a "militant cultural mission." A similar critique is made by Daniel Brumberg, "Islamists and Power Sharing," a paper presented at the U.S. Institute of Peace, July 15, 1999.

56. *Umma* as authority is from Wasat party program, p. 17. Habib's comments are from an April 1996 interview in Cairo and Karim El Gawhary, "We Are a Civil Party with an Islamic Identity—An Interview with Abu 'Ila Madi Abu 'Ila and Rafik Habib," *Middle East Report*, April–June 1996, pp. 30–32. In that article, Habib stated: "The Muslim Brotherhood has yet to elaborate a specific political program. Our thinking is more social than political. . . . *Umma* is for us as civil society is for the West . . . [it] has a very important role to play in bringing about our renaissance. The *umma*, not the state, will be the catalyst of progress. The function of the state must be restricted, while civil society must play a much more important role."

57. Ezzat, telephone interview January 2002.

Seeing civil society rather than the state as the repository of political responsibility appears to be a growing trend within contemporary Islamist political thought. Iran's Soroush made the same point in a 1995 seminar at Georgetown University when speaking about new interpretations of Islamic scriptures. "The locus of interpretation is civil society not the state. . . . The state has got nothing to do with it." Author's notes.

The idea of working for a strong, vibrant civil society based on Islamic values rather than struggling to establish an Islamic state is even more advanced in non-Arab Muslim societies like Indonesia. Robin Wright, "Islam's New Face Visible in Indonesia," *Los Angeles Times*, December 27, 2000.

58. François Burgat, the French scholar of Islamists, wrote that "the two major processes under way" in the Middle East are "reconnecting the political discourse with the pre-colonial symbolic system on the one hand, and the developing of political attitudes respectful of a pluralistic culture on the other." François Burgat and William Dowell, *The Islamic Movement in North Africa* (Austin: Center for Middle Eastern Studies at University of Texas, 1993), pp. 309–310.

59. Charles Kurzman places Hanafi among a small group of liberal Islamists who believe that diversity is inevitable in interpretations of Islam's scriptures. He quotes Hanafi as writing, "There is no one interpretation of a text, but there are many interpretations given the difference in understanding between various interpreters. An interpretation of a text is essentially pluralistic. The text is only a vehicle for human interests and even passions. . . . The conflict of interpretation is essentially a socio-political conflict, not a theoretical one. Theory indeed is only an epistemological cover-up. Each interpretation expresses the socio-political commitment of the interpreter." Kurzman, "Liberal Islam: Prospects and Challenges," *Middle East Review of International Affairs* 3, no. 3 (September 1999).

Citing the appeal of other Islamist thinkers like Hanafi, notably Syria's Muhammad Shahrur, Dale F. Eickelman writes that it illustrates "that 'political Islam' is not exclusively radical and intolerant" and that "Islamic liberalism is alive and well, and perhaps even on the verge of effectively asserting its voice." "Islamic Liberalism Strikes Back," pp. 163–168.

60. Years later, Hanafi elaborated on why he came to believe the Brotherhood had abandoned its original mission. "The themes of social justice in Islam, the battle between capitalism and Islam, world peace and Islam, were dropped from the Brethren's thought and were carried on by the [Nasser's socialist] revolution of the sixties. The more open and wide conception of Islam, that of the founder Hasan al-Banna, turned into a more closed and fanatic view of the world." Hassan Hanafi, "The Relevance of the Islamic Alternative in Egypt," *Arab Studies Quarterly* 4, nos. 1–2 (1982): 61.

61. "Ideas imported from the West," Hanafi wrote, "have consistently met with staunch resistance from the defenders of traditional culture. No attempts at nurturing their growth on Arab soil have succeeded: neither Arab liberalism, nor Arab socialism or Marxism. Religious reform remains the only channel through which to effect change." Hassan Hanafi, "Not into Salvation," *Al Ahram Weekly*, April 18, 1996.

62. Like some Christian thinkers, Hanafi speaks of a "liberation theology" whose purpose is "to change the status quo, not to defend it. . . . It takes the side of the oppressed against the oppressors, of the poor against the rich . . . and of the third world against the first world. It does not matter in which name this is done, in the name of God, in the name of salvation or in the name of mankind." He regards "liberation theology" as "the most viable paradigm" for ecumenical dialogue. Hassan Hanafi, *Islam in the Modern World*, vol. 2: *Tradition, Revolution and Culture* (Cairo: Anglo-Egyptian Bookshop, 1995), pp. 195–196.

63. Hanafi's quote is from Tibi, "Worldview of Sunni and Arab Fundamentalists," p. 90. "Hanafi sees himself as bearing the torch unto a new age of Enlightenment (*tanwir*), using rationalism . . . [and] as a spearhead of a new Islamic Left aiming at improving the life of the crushed Arab masses by making them regain their identity . . . while developing a new Islamic theology of man." Issa J. Boulatta, *Trends and Issues in Contemporary Arab Thought* (Albany: State University of New York Press, 1990) pp. 44–45.

64. Hanafi complained in a 1996 newspaper article that Arab religious officials "continue to teach Islamic jurisprudence with regard to spoils of war, slaves, chattel, women and the people of the book. But the world has changed. There are no longer spoils of war, slavery has been abolished and all citizens are equal regardless of race, ethnic origin, creed or gender." Islamic theology and jurisprudence, he added, "have not undergone the slightest transformation, while the natural and applied sciences have no place in our consciousness whatsoever. The crisis of Arab culture is that our spirit is in one era while our body lives in another." Hanafi, "Not into Salvation."

65. Hanafi, "Relevance of the Islamic Alternative in Egypt," p. 74 and Hanafi, *Tradition, Revolution and Culture*, p. 62.

66. Hanafi admits his "Islamic Left" is currently "not a real alternative in Egypt" as an organized political force. See his "Relevance of the Islamic Alternative in Egypt," p. 74. Boulatta notes that Hanafi's work is "too theoretical to be practical in the real world." Boulatta, *Trends and Issues in Contemporary Arab Thought*, p. 45.

Others agree with Hanafi that the ideas of moderate and liberal Islamists will fare better in the long term than they do now. "The increasing numbers of Islamists who adhere to a modern interpretation of Islam form a loose-knit group with little chance of making an impact in the short term. The long term is a different matter, however," wrote Laith Kubba. "Given time, these Islamists could become a stabilizing and constructive force with great capacities for developing public institutions and modernizing Muslim societies. Although liberal Islamists are part of the mainstream of the Islamic movement, their presence has not yet been institutionalized. . . . Traditionalists see them as 'Westernized,' radicals see them as 'compromised,' and authoritarian rulers see them as 'dangerous.' " Kubba, "Recognizing Pluralism," *Journal of Democracy* 7, no. 2 (April 1996): 88.

67. "Egypt's Apostasy Debate Rears Its Ugly Head Once Again," *Mideast Mirror*, May 13, 1997; "Muslim Scholars Say Professor's Work Questions Islam," Associated Press,

Cairo, May 1, 1997; "Another University Professor Branded an Apostate," EOHR, May 15, 1997.

Although Ismail claimed to be speaking for Al Azhar Scholars Front, its chairman said the group had nothing to do with Ismail's statement. But another Front official, board member Abdelmahi Abdelqader, told *Al Wasat* magazine that "Yahya Ismail is a courageous scholar who has spoken the truth and we must help him confront the secularists and make the people's errors clear to them." A former Al Azhar dean, Abdelmu'ti Bayoumi, countered that most Front members were "extremists in thought and behavior" and incapable of understanding Hanafi's thinking. See "Egypt's Apostasy Debate Rears Its Ugly Head Once Again," *Mideast Mirror,* May 13, 1997.

68. Daniel Crecelius, "Nonideological Responses of the Egyptian Ulama to Modernization," in *Scholars, Saints, and Sufis,* ed. Nikki R. Keddie (Berkeley: University of California Press, 1972), p. 190. Crecelius noted that "modernization has meant for the *ulama* an agonizing and constant retreat from political power and social preeminence." And while they have "successfully delayed" modernization in Egypt, this has been achieved "at a terrible price for Islam and the *ulama.* The sheikhs have become completely isolated from the modernizing segment of society and their traditional views almost totally rejected" (pp. 185 and 208).

69. Patrick A. Gaffney of University of Notre Dame, in a February 22, 1999, address at Georgetown University. The *ulama* resisted modern changes in Egypt, Gaffney observed, because of "inherited attitudes of righteous certainty flowing largely from a naive confidence that prompted them to identify their own interests with those of heaven." These attitudes led them to express their opposition "principally by withdrawal behind the cracking walls of their own aging, grand institutions." As a result, he added, the "descendants of this scholarly class, although having the same name, hardly occupy the same historical niche."

70. One professor once said that "Al Azhar has the right to hegemony over anything revealed in Islam," and added that a well-known secular writer "has no right to publish any statement on Islam except with the permission of Al Azhar." "Al Azhar Protests State Propaganda," *Middle East Times,* May 1994, p. 1.

Al Azhar's testiness about its subservient role vis-à-vis the state was illustrated when a reporter referred to its Grand Sheikh Mohamed Sayed Tantawi as "a government employee." An indignant Tantawi replied, "Who told you this nonsense? The Sheikh of Al Azhar's position is on a par with the prime minister's." "Al Azhar Chief: Syrian Author of Cairo Riot Book is a 'Blasphemer,' " *Mideast Mirror,* June 5, 2000.

71. John Lancaster, "Top Islamic University Gains Influence in Cairo: Al Azhar Reflects Revival of Fundamentalism," *Washington Post,* April 11, 1995.

72. The university's internal divisions intensified after Tantawi succeeded the late Sheikh Gad Al Haq Ali Gad Al Haq, who was theologically closer to the orthodox dissidents. In 1996, after some *ulama* called Palestinian suicide-bombers "the best of martyrs," Tantawi disagreed saying, "I cannot equate someone who blows himself up to kill enemies who have declared war on us, with someone who blows himself up to kill Muslims, non-Muslims, children, and women." "Tantawi Reaffirms Liberal View," *Al Ahram Weekly,* April 18–24, 1996, p. 3. A year later, the Front blasted Tantawi for receiving Israel's chief rabbi Yisrael Meir Lau in his Cairo office. It also objected to his effort to modernize the Al Azhar curriculum by increasing scientific and secular subjects and decreasing religious instruction. For more on infighting within Al Azhar, see articles in *Mideast Mirror,* May 13, 1997, March 13, 1997, and June 5, 1998.

An excellent and illuminating study of Al Azhar, to which I am indebted, is Malika Zeghal's *Gardiens De L'Islam.* Zeghal examines the growing diversity of views among Azhar's *ulama* and the emergence of factions that use religious rhetoric similar to radical Islamists. *Gardiens De L'Islam,* pp. 47–48, 304, 334, 337, and 366.

73. Raymond Stock, "How Islamist Militants Put Egypt on Trial," *Financial Times,* March 4, 1995. Stock was quoting Tantawi's predecessor, Gad Al Haq Ali Gad Al Haq.

74. Karim Alrawi, "University of the Extreme," *The Guardian* (London), June 23, 1992, and Zeghal, *Gardiens De L'Islam,* pp. 327–332. Zeghal called Al Azhar "the silent ally of

Islamism" because of its orthodox approach to interpreting religious texts (pp. 324–325). She relates the story of Ahmad Subhi Mansur, who was sent to prison for a month for advocating a new approach to interpretation in his dissertation at Al Azhar (pp. 140–141 and 322–325).

75. Tantawi interview Cairo, April 1996. On another occasion, Tantawi offered this view of permissible innovation in Islamic theology: "If someone came and said that the sun rises in the West rather than the East, we wouldn't call this new interpretation," he said. "There can be innovation only in peripheral matters, not in aspects of religion which are necessarily permanent." "Sheikh Supports Egyptian Apostasy Divorce Ruling," Reuters, August 22, 1996.

76. As Zeghal writes, Al Azhar today is "a controlled and rebellious institution" and its attachment to a fixed Islamic heritage "makes very unlikely a reform of the religious patrimony from the official institution." Zeghal, *Gardiens De L'Islam*, pp. 367 and 371–372.

77. *ISLAM21*, July 1997, p. 12.

78. Abdelwahab El Affendi, *Who Needs an Islamic State?* (London: Grey Seal Books, 1991), pp. 36–39, 94, and 57. Affendi is senior research fellow and coordinator of a project on Democracy in the Muslim World at the Center for the Study of Democracy, University of Westminster, London. Sardar also criticizes the "totalitarian" aspect of some Islamist states as being "quite divorced from the spirit of the Qur'an and the teachings of the Prophet Muhammad." "It represents Islam not as a total system of knowing, being and doing, but as a totalitarian moral order presided over by a group with exclusive access to religious knowledge, the truncated perversion of '*ilm*.' " Sardar, "Paper, Printing and Compact Disks," p. 55.

79. Affendi, *Who Needs an Islamic State?*, pp. 88, 93, and 96–97.

80. Ibid., pp. 90 and 94–95.

81. Na'im noted that decrees authorizing Muslims to spread Islam by force violate international law, in particular the United Nations Charter. Similarly, *shari'a* regulations governing marriage, divorce, and inheritance, though progressive in Prophet Muhammad's time, are discriminatory by today's standards. And the *shari'a* mandate to punish unrepentant apostates, Na'im wrote, violates international guarantees of freedom of conscience. Obviously, most Muslim states generally obey international laws when dealings with other states. But Na'im contends it is unacceptable to allow problematic *shari'a* rulings to go unchallenged because *shari'a* has an emotional pull on Muslims and therefore influences their views on international affairs. It is not surprising, Na'im noted, that a draft Islamic constitution for Egypt drawn up by Al Azhar in 1978 did not have one word about the status and rights of non-Muslims even though the country has millions of Christian citizens. Na'im, *Toward an Islamic Reformation*, pp. 55, 151, 8, and 94–97.

Indeed, the contrast between what *shari'a* and international norms demand is not a new conundrum. As Richard P. Mitchell wrote, it has been "the ideological issue for Islam in the twentieth century." For "to insist on the *shari'a* was to insist on a complex of corollaries which appeared . . . anachronistic; but to insist on less would have been to repudiate what was regarded as the 'essence' of Islam." Mitchell, *The Society of Muslim Brothers* (London: Oxford University Press, 1969), p. 243.

82. Na'im, *Toward an Islamic Reformation*, pp. 34, 67–68, 185, and 187.

83. Ibid., pp. 49 and 28–29. Na'im uses a "paradigm shift" in "Islam and Justice" (p. 124). For centuries, *ijtihad* has been discouraged in matters already covered by *shari'a* rulings accepted by most Islamic scholars. Also out of bounds for *ijtihad* are matters covered by rulings based on clear, or explicit, passages in the Qur'an or Sunna. Na'im reasons that if *ijtihad* remains forbidden in such matters, then *shari'a* cannot be modernized. He is basically challenging the traditional methodology for performing *ijtihad* in Islamic jurisprudence, or *fiqh*. This methodology is called *usul al fiqh*, which mean "roots (or foundations) of law." It uses four main sources for developing legal rulings: the Qur'an, the Sunna, the consensus of other scholars, and reasoning by analogy. See *"Usul Al Fiqh," Oxford Encyclopedia.*

84. Na'im, *Toward an Islamic Reformation*, pp. 99 and 44.

85. Iran's Soroush noted that "secularism is a subtle notion that cannot be summarized in the principle of the separation of the church and state. It has deeper philosophical implications." Interview posted on www.iranian.com in May 1999.

In his study of fundamentalist Muslim views toward science, Tibi wrote that "secularism, as an attitude of mind, cannot thrive if unaccompanied by the secularization of societal structures and institutions." In places like Egypt, Tibi added, "secular-modern education was imposed within which Western values and norms were transmitted but not institutionalized due to the lack of structures for their appropriation. This penetration did not therefore result in cultural uniformity consonant with modernity. It rather contributed to further cultural fragmentation, of which current varieties of Islamic fundamentalists are a distinctive outgrowth." Tibi added that "Muslims import techno-scientific products from the West; they hire scientists and technologists and even send their children to study in the West. But . . . they are hostile to adopting the worldview related to these products and achievements." Tibi, "Worldview of Sunni and Arab Fundamentalists," pp. 79 and 84–85.

American Muslim astronomer Imad-ad-Dean Ahmad wrote that "any renaissance of Islamic science will require the critical incorporation of modern Western knowledge into the new Islamic knowledge. . . . Today's Muslims have not yet demonstrated that they accept this. Instead, there is still an undertone of feeling that everything in the West is bad and must be rejected in toto." Ahmad added, "I have met many students from Muslim countries and their attitude is too often a desire to learn engineering and urban planning but to avoid getting contaminated by any notions of independent or original thought. This will not do. Scientific progress does not consist of mere imitation of the products of technology. Learning and study must include a reopening of *ijtihad*. Scientific research will require total freedom of thought, experiment and discussion: all of the elements of induction." Ahmad, *Signs in the Heavens*, pp. 144 and 146.

86. The poll results appeared on the front page of *Al Ahram*, May 23, 1991. "The actual dichotomy in the Muslim world between secular ruling elite and Muslim masses makes the political power always a minority ruling on a majority," Hassan Hanafi wrote in *Islam in the Modern World*, p. 70.

87. Some analysts believe such a convergence is impossible. "[T]here can ultimately be no true convergence between religious and secular political ideologies," wrote Mark Juergensmeyer. "On the level of ideology, the new cold war will persist." However, he sees religious nationalists, including those in faiths besides Islam, creating "a synthesis between religion and the secular state." Juergensmeyer, *The New Cold War? Religious Nationalism Confronts the Secular State* (Berkeley: University of California Press, 1993) pp. 197 and 201.

88. "People's Rights," August 1995, p. 5. Like Hanafi, Affendi also speaks about a long time frame for reform in the Muslim world. Islamic nations, he wrote, are faced with a "grave responsibility . . . [to] first put their houses in order and then see that justice and equity rule in the international order. Therefore, the Muslim world must undergo a prolonged period of internal change before it can assume its international role." Affendi, *Who Needs an Islamic State?*, p. 73.

12. WE WERE HERE FIRST

1. Lucie Duff Gordon, *Letters from Egypt* (London: Virago Press, 1986).
2. Abdel Rahman interview, Musha, November 1993.
3. Tima's sectarian violence occurred in mid-October 1992. Interview with ironer, in Tima, May 1993.
4. Events in Manshiet Nasser were chronicled in a report by the Egyptian Organization for Human Rights (EOHR), "Urgent Report on the Sectarian Massacre in Dairut," May 7, 1992. Massoud interview in Manshiet Nasser, May 1993.
5. According to U.S. State Department annual reports on "Human Rights Practices in Egypt," 127 Copts were killed by Islamist terrorists from 1992 to 1998.
6. Official government statistics from the late 1980s say Christians are about 3 million.

Coptic church and community leaders say the actual number is at least twice that. Christians appear to be decreasing as a proportion of the total population of Egypt, partly because they tend to have smaller families and partly because of emigration. The Cyprus-based Middle East Council of Churches estimates that there are 15 million Christians in the Middle East, but that figure includes Sudan and Iran. The respected demographer Philip Fargues puts the number of Christians in Arab countries much lower at 6.5 million. Fargues, "The Arab Christians of the Middle East: A Demographic Perspective," in *Christian Communities in the Arab Middle East: The Challenge of the Future*, ed. Andrea Pacini (Oxford: Clarendon Press, 1998).

Egypt's Christians also include the Armenian, Chaldean, Greek, Maronite, Roman, and Syrian Catholics; Anglicans, Seventh-Day Adventists, and members of the Coptic Evangelical Church and the Protestant Churches of Egypt.

7. An Egyptian leader is said to have sent Prophet Muhammad a Coptic slave girl named Mariam, whom he took as a concubine. She bore him a son, Ibrahim, who died in infancy. Karen Armstrong, *Islam* (New York: The Modern Library, 2000), p. 203, and Karen Armstrong, *Muhammad, a Western Attempt to Understand Islam* (London: Victor Gollancz, 1991), p. 236.

8. Makram Obeid, the former leader of Egypt's Wafd Party as cited in François Burgat and William Dowell, *The Islamic Movement in North Africa* (Austin: Center for Middle Eastern Studies at University of Texas, 1993), p. 133.

9. The Council of Chalcedon in 451 C.E. decreed that Christ had both a divine and a human nature. Many Copts refused to accept this formulation, holding instead that Christ had only one nature, though it combined both the human and divine.

10. Ira Lapidus, "The Conversion of Egypt to Islam," *Israel Oriental Studies* 2 (1972): 248–262. Lapidus argues that sometime in the tenth century Egypt had a majority Muslim population, but not until the Crusader period, when there was heavy persecution of native Christians, did the population become predominantly Muslim.

11. Wisa Wasef, a Copt from southern Egypt who ran as the Wafd candidate for a district in northern Egypt, was elected to parliament and became speaker. Such an occurrence, Milad Hanna wrote, "now could never be possible." Hanna, *The Seven Pillars of the Egyptian Identity* (Cairo: General Egyptian Book Organization, 1989), p. 57.

Hanna also notes that when a new constitution was being drafted, there were vigorous debates over whether to set aside seats in parliament for minorities. There were Christians and Muslims on both sides of the argument. One Muslim leader argued there was no need for special seats because "religious differences are diminishing" (p. 55).

12. Jews and Christians "were never called upon to suffer martyrdom or exile for their beliefs" and in general had a better status than non-Christians in Western Europe, wrote Bernard Lewis in his book *The Arabs in History* (London: Hutchinson University Library, 1966), p. 94. See also Albert Hourani, *A History of the Arab Peoples* (Cambridge: Belknap Press of Harvard University Press, 1991), pp. 117–119 and 187; Karen Armstrong, *A History of God* (New York: Alfred A.Knopf, 1994), pp. 159 and 194; Karen Armstrong, *Jerusalem, One City, Three Faiths* (New York: Alfred A. Knopf, 1996), pp. 231–232.

13. "Our Testimony by the Muslim Brotherhood," London, International Islamic Forum, April 30, 1995, p. 7.

14. "Muslim Leader Says Army Should Be Purged of Christians," Associated Press, April 13, 1997, and Khalid Daoud article, *Al Ahram Weekly* July 5–9, 1997.

15. "Beware of Hidden Enemies and Their Wolves and Foxes," *New York Times*, December 9, 2001, p. B7. When the United States attacked Afghanistan to unseat its Taliban rulers, Muslim preachers in Pakistan motivated young men to help the Taliban by telling them that it was a battle between Muslims and Christians. Edward Cody, "In an Afghan Prison, and in Limbo," *Washington Post*, January 17, 2002, p. 1.

16. Maha Azzam, "Islamic Oriented Protest Groups in Egypt, 1971–1981: Politics and Dogma," Ph.D. thesis, Faculty of Social Studies, University of Oxford, 1989, pp. 302 and 384.

17. Amin Fahim interview, Minya, February 1992. Kepel wrote that for the Islamists "to

assault the Copts is to assault the state" and its attacks "were [a] substitute for its inability to strike directly at the state." Gilles Kepel, *The Prophet and Pharaoh*, trans. Jon Rothschild (London: Al Saqi Books, 1985), p. 240. Kepel has an excellent summary of attitudes toward Christians among extremists in Egypt, see pp. 158, 160, 161, 207–209, and 237–238.

18. Islamic Group had "for a number of years been practicing systematic sectarian violence within clear sight of the local authorities." EOHR, "Urgent Report."

19. Naim Labib interview, Aswan, March 1993.

20. Priest interview, Minya, 1990.

21. Shadi George interview, Assiut, November 1993.

22. For Sadat and Shenouda quarreling, see Mohamed Heikal, *Autumn of Fury* (London: Corgi Books, 1983), pp. 170–173, 228, and 239–240; and J. D. Pennington, "The Copts in Modern Egypt," *Middle Eastern Studies* 18, no 2 (April 1982).

23. Milad Hanna, *Acceptance of the Other* (Cairo: Al Ahram Center for Political and Strategic Studies, 2001), p. 133.

24. "Hello" anecdote from Nemat Guenena interview, Cairo, July 1993. Quote about affection for non-Muslims was written by Ahmad Omar Hashim of Al Azhar in the *Islamic Banner* newspaper. As cited in "Remembering Egypt's Cassandra," *Cairo Times*, January 3–9, 2002.

25. Milad Hanna interviews in Cairo, April 1996, and Washington, D.C., January 2002.

26. Christians openly practice their faith in all Arab countries except Saudi Arabia, which has the largest Christian community in the Arabian peninsula, mainly migrant workers and diplomats. In May 2001, the U.S. Commission on International Religious Freedom recommended, after visiting Saudi Arabia, that it be designated a "country of particular concern" because of "systematic, ongoing, egregious violations of religious freedom." It found that "private worshipers have been harassed by the *mutawaa* [religious police] and forced to conduct their activities in secrecy for fear of detection and punishment. . . ."

Wahhabism does not officially denigrate Christians but there is a strong anti-Christian bias in its outlook. Abdul Rahmaan Ibn Mualaa Al Luwaihiq Al Mutairi, of Muhammad Ibn Saud Islamic University in Riyadh, wrote that Westerners blame some Muslims for mixing politics with religion. "At the same time," he added, "they do not blame the Coptic Christians, who belong to a distorted religion that has actually separated the two, for doing the same thing." Mutairi, *Religious Extremism in the Lives of Contemporary Muslims* (Denver, Colo.: Al Basheer Publications, 2001) pp. 134–135.

In Saudi high schools, religious textbooks teach that it "is compulsory for the Muslims . . . to consider the infidels their enemy" and that "one of the major requirements in hating the infidels and being hostile to them is ignoring their rituals and their festivities." There have also been reports of pamphlets handed out at malls that say it is a sin to vacation in the West. Neil MacFarquhar, "Anti-Western and Extremist Views Pervade Saudi Schools," *New York Times*, October 19, 2001.

27. Moneim interview Cairo, April 1996. At the time, he was working for the Center for Human Rights Legal Aid.

The Center, and some other human rights groups, say that official government discrimination contributes to sectarian tensions. In a February 29, 1996 release, the Center stated that "discrimination against appointing Copts to official positions, and the underrepresentation of Copts in Egypt's political system play as important a role as Islamic fundamentalists in fueling hatred, rage and sectarianism. The failure of the education system and the media to reflect the religious, cultural, social and political diversity of Egyptian society also implicitly encourages sectarianism. This is borne out by the large number of participants in the [Kafr El Demien] violence, in spite of the fact that this governorate does not have any history of strong Islamic fundamentalist groups."

28. Habib interview, Cairo, April 1996. Habib said his friends were astonished when he helped found an Islamist party because "they think that any Islamic movement is against Christianity." No one was more astonished than Habib's father, Samuel Habib, who until his death in 1997 was president of the Protestant Churches of Egypt and a

leader of the Evangelical (Protestant) Church of Egypt. The elder Habib placed an ad in the government newspaper *Al Ahram* announcing that his son had acted in his personal capacity.

29. In December 1999, President Mubarak made repairs to all places of worship subject to the 1976 civil construction code. This placed churches and mosques on an equal footing before the law. "The practical impact of the decree has been to facilitate significantly church repairs," according to U.S. State Department report on "Human Rights Practices in Egypt" 2001 (Sec. 2c). The report added that in 2000 more than 350 permits for repairs were issued. But these regulations are time-consuming and "insufficiently responsive to the wishes of the Christian community," the report said. Applications for new churches and for church repairs are often delayed or blocked by security officials, it added.

30. Summaries of discrimination against Copts and recent government improvements are found in the U.S. State Department's annual "Human Rights Practices in Egypt" report and its "International Religious Freedom" reports. Also see reports of U.S. Commission on Religious Freedom, whose latest report in May 2001 found "positive developments," in particular, permission for construction of new churches and repair of older ones is given "far more frequently than was previously the case." But, it added, "religiously based discrimination, particularly in government employment, the military, and security services, remains a pervasive problem." Christians also are frequently discriminated against by private employers in hiring and promotion, the report said. Also, "Egypt's Endangered Christians," Center for Religious Freedom, Freedom House, Washington, D.C., 1999.

31. Coptic church sources have estimated that over a million Copts have left Egypt in the past thirty years. "Egypt's Endangered Christians," p. 9.

32. Shenouda quote is in "Egypt: Violations of Freedom of Religious Belief and Expression of the Christian Minority," Human Rights Watch, New York, November 1994, p. 5 note 15.

33. "I have endless examples" quote from a source interviewed in Cairo in 1992. Milad Hanna said many conversions to Islam "are the result of the Islamicization of society. . . . We are breathing Islam and therefore young people . . . at the age of adolescence . . . could easily be carried away with the wave of Islamic revival." A large part of it, he added, is poverty. See also Human Rights Watch, "Egypt: Violations of Freedom," p. 6.

34. Instances of security police abuse of converts and threats against Christian proselytizers in Human Rights Watch, "Egypt: Violations of Freedom," pp. 2 and 20.

35. The U.S. Copts Association in Falls Church, Virginia, operates the Web site.

36. In 1998, the U.S. Congress passed the Freedom from Religious Persecution Act, which mandates sanctions against countries found to be violating freedom of religion.

37. EOHR report on the massacre at Abu Qurqas, February 1997.

13. ONE DREAM FULFILLED, ANOTHER DENIED

1. Abba Eban, *My People, The Story of the Jews* (New York: Random House, 1968), Dan Kurzman, *Ben-Gurion: Prophet of Fire* (New York: Simon and Schuster, 1983), and Bernard Postal and Henry W. Levy, *And the Hills Shouted for Joy* (New York: David McKay, 1973). Tel Aviv Museum is now the Museum of the Bible.

2. *Al Nakba* is also used by Arabs to describe their devastating military defeat by Israel in 1967, though Egyptians generally used the word *Al Naqsa*, "setback," for the latter.

3. Israeli historian Benny Morris, an expert on the Palestinian refugee issue, cites between 600,000 and 760,000 as the best estimate for the number of Palestinians made homeless between 1947 and 1949. Morris found multiple causes for the Palestinian exodus. They included a lack of leadership and help from Arab leaders, economic problems, breakdowns in law and order, and fears of Jewish attacks and atrocities. He wrote that there was no blanket call by Arab states for Palestinians to leave and neither was there a call for them to stay. He added, "in most cases, the final and decisive precipitant to flight" was attacks by Jewish forces or fears of such attacks." He concluded: "The memory or vicarious mem-

ory of 1948 and the subsequent decades of humiliation and deprivation in the refugee camps would ultimately turn generations of Palestinians into potential or active terrorists and the 'Palestinian problem' into one of the world's most intractable." Benny Morris, *The Birth of the Palestinian Refugee Problem 1947–49* (New York: Cambridge University Press, 1987), pp. 298 and 294–296.

In a more recent work, Morris wrote, "In retrospect, it is clear that what occurred in 1948 in Palestine was a variety of ethnic cleansing of Arab areas by Jews. It is impossible to say how many of the 700,000 or so Palestinians who became refugees in 1948 were physically expelled, as distinct from simply fleeing a combat zone. What is certain is that almost all were barred by the Israeli government decision of June 1948 and, consequently, by IDF fire, from returning to their homes or areas." Morris added that "upward of fifty thousand people" were forced out of the Arab villages of Lydda and Ramle alone on July 12/13, 1948, and that Israeli forces razed almost 400 depopulated Arab villages in part to prevent residents from returning. Arabs expelled Jewish communities from less than a dozen sites and the number of Jewish expellees were far fewer than Arab expellees, he wrote. Benny Morris, "Case Study: Arab-Israeli War" in *Crimes of War: What the Public Should Know*, eds. Roy Gutman and David Rieff (New York: W. W. Norton, 1999), p. 32.

4. The 2001 poll by Zogby International also surveyed opinion in Saudi Arabia, Kuwait, the United Arab Emirates, and Lebanon. The survey "reflects a serious psychological mood that no Arab government can ignore," wrote Shibley Telhami, "Sympathy for the Palestinians," *Washington Post*, July 25, 2001. "To the Arab world," said American pollster John Zogby, "the lack of a Palestinian state in 2001 is what taxation without representation was to us in 1776." In Charles Pappas, "Should American Values Be Marketed to Muslim Nations?" at AdAge.com Web site, December 17, 2001.

An earlier poll of Egyptians by *Al Ahram* in December 1994 found that fifteen years after Egypt's peace treaty with Israel, 71 percent said they would not buy Israeli goods and 63 percent said they would not visit Israel. Fawaz A. Gerges, "The Crisis in Egyptian-Israeli Relations," *Foreign Affairs*, May/June 1995, p. 7.

5. "I don't see the sense of justice and the sense of righteousness ordained by God Almighty in what is happening in the territories," Saudi Arabia's Crown Prince Abdullah said. "We see children being shot at, buildings being destroyed, trees uprooted, people encircled, territories closed and women killed. The reasons that lead people to become suicide bombers, these are the reasons they do so." Elaine Sciolino, "Saudi Affirms U.S. Ties But Says Bush Ignores Palestinians' Cause" and accompanying, "In the Prince's Words: Excerpts from Talk," *New York Times*, January 29, 2002.

Some Israelis also recognize the need to right the wrongs that accompanied the birth of Israel. "The moral case for the establishment of an independent Jewish state was strong, especially in the aftermath of the Holocaust," wrote Israeli historian Avi Shlaim. "But there is no denying that the establishment of the State of Israel involved a massive injustice to the Palestinians. Half a century on, Israel still had to arrive at the reckoning of its own sins against the Palestinians, a recognition that it owed the Palestinians a debt that must at some point be repaid." Shlaim, *The Iron Wall: Israel and the Arab World* (New York: W. W. Norton, 2000), p. 598.

There are 3.7 million Palestinians registered as refugees with the United Nations Relief and Works Agency as of December 2000. At least 2.6 million other Palestinians not registered as refugees live scattered around the Middle East (see Web site badil.org). Gaza's total population is over 1 million; in December 2000, 824,622 of them were registered with UNRWA. The global Palestinian population was estimated in 1998 at 7.7 million. Clyde R. Mark, *Palestinians and Middle East Peace: Issues for the United States*, Congressional Research Service, Library of Congress, Washington, D.C., updated January 25, 2002, p. 15.

6. Jeffrey Goldberg, "Behind Mubarak, Egyptian Clerics and Intellectuals Respond to Terrorism," *The New Yorker*, October 8, 2001.

7. Ibid.; "Tantawi Reaffirms Liberal View," *Al Ahram Weekly*, April 18–24, 1996, p. 3; Joseph Lelyveld, "All Suicide Bombers Are Not Alike," *New York Times Magazine*, October 28, 2001.

8. Caryle Murphy and Nora Boustany, "Arabs and Israelis Now Getting Down to Business," *Washington Post*, May 23, 1994; Caryle Murphy "Egyptians Bullish About Israeli Contacts," *Washington Post*, October 19, 1993.

9. Palestinian-American Edward Said has written in favor of a binational, secular democracy. For an Islamist perspective, Ahmed Yousef, "The Bi-National State: Toward a Peaceful Solution in the Holy Land," United Association for Studies and Research, Annandale, Va., Occasional Paper Series, no. 21, February 2001. Egyptian Islamist attorney Mohamed S. El Awa envisions for Palestine "a democratic state . . . in the most comprehensive sense of democracy where citizens should have equal rights at all levels." E-mail to author, February 13, 2002.

10. Mashur interview, Cairo, September 1993.

11. Andrew Gowers and Tony Walker, *Behind the Myth, Yasser Arafat and the Palestinian Revolution* (London: W. H. Allen, 1990) pp. 44–45; David Hirst, *The Gun and the Olive Branch* (New York: Harcourt Brace and Jovanovich, 1977), pp. 277–278.

12. Daniel Williams, "Where Palestinian Martyrs Are Groomed," *Washington Post*, August 15, 2001.

13. Ze'ev Schiff and Edud Ya'ari, *Intifada, The Palestinian Uprising—Israel's Third Front* (New York: Simon & Schuster, 1989), p. 223.

14. Azzam Sultan Tamimi, "The Legitimacy of Palestinian Resistance: An Islamist Perspective," published by the Center for Policy Analysis on Palestine, Washington, D.C., December 1998.

    John L. Esposito has noted that in Christianity, a similar view of spiritual reward marked the Crusades, whose participants "drew inspiration from two Christian institutions, pilgrimage and holy war. . . . Warriors were victorious whether they won their earthly battles or not . . . the indulgences earned by all who fought in the Crusades guaranteed the remission of sins and entrance into paradise. To fall in battle was to die a martyr for the faith and gain immediate access to heaven despite past sins." Esposito, *The Islamic Threat, Myth or Reality?* (New York: Oxford University Press, 1992), p. 41.

15. Mousa Abu Marzuk, Hamas official, interviewed on CBS's "60 Minutes," January 27, 2002. During the second Palestinian intifada, 2000–2002, some suicide bombers were sponsored by other Palestinian nationalist groups, including one linked to Arafat's Fatah.

16. Charles A. Radin, "Hamas Children Raised to Fight, Die," *Boston Globe*, December 26, 2001; Lelyveld, "All Suicide Bombers Are Not Alike."

17. "Abou Elela Mady, Founder of Al Wasat, Talks to the *Independent*," *Al Musakillah* (*The Independent*) (London), November 3, 1997.

18. Ian S. Lustick, *For the Land and the Lord: Jewish Fundamentalism in Israel* (New York: Council on Foreign Relations, 1988) pp. 35 and 74–84; Gershom Gorenberg, *The End of Days* (New York: The Free Press, 2000), pp. 112–114.

19. "Fundamentalist thinking also provided a systematic and evocative symbol system for rising Likud politicians . . . to endow their ambitions with an aura of Jewish authenticity and Zionist idealism." Lustick, *For the Land and the Lord*, p. 9. Soon after Begin was elected, he paid a visit to Rabbi Kook and knelt before him. Begin also dropped in at a Gush Emunim settlement on the West Bank and, holding a Torah scroll, vowed to build many more such communities. Lustick, *For the Land and the Lord*, pp. 37 and 40.

20. Shamir and "holy work" is in Donald Neff's *Fallen Pillars* (Washington, D.C.: Institute for Palestine Studies, 1995), p. 159. Several months after attending the 1991 Madrid Peace Conference, which led to the first face-to-face talks between Israelis and Palestinians, Israeli prime minister Yitzhak Shamir disclosed that his intention was to "have conducted negotiations for ten years" until "half a million" Jews were settled in the West Bank, making a Palestinian state impossible. David Makovsky, "Talks Team Feels 'Deceived' by Shamir," *Jerusalem Post*, June 29, 1992. In May 2002, the Likud Party voted for a resolution saying there should never be a Palestinian state in the West Bank and Gaza Strip.

21. "Report on Israeli Settlement in the Occupied Territories," Foundation for Middle East Peace, Washington, D.C., vol. 11, no. 6 (November-December 2001): 4–5.

22. Judith Miller, "Israel's Fundamentalist Thing," *New York Times*, June 9, 1996; John Kifner, "Belief to Blood: The Making of Rabin's Killer," *New York Times*, November 19, 1995.

23. Amir quote from Kifner, "Belief to Blood."

According to the Israeli Committee Against House Demolitions, a movement of Israelis opposed to Palestinian home demolitions, "since 1967 some 7,000 Palestinian homes have been destroyed on the West Bank, in Gaza and in Arab East Jerusalem, more than 2,000 since 1987, leaving 30,000 people homeless." It said that "in 1999, 'only' about 100 homes were demolished, down from 277 in 1998. Yet 2,000 demolition orders remain outstanding in the West Bank, another 2,000 for East Jerusalem." Summary available at Web site: Mennonitechurch.ca/peace.

24. William Claiborne and Edward Cody, "The West Bank, Hostage of History," Foundation for Middle East Peace, Washington, D.C., 1980, p. i.

25. "America is a democracy . . . but when it comes to Israel, then there is a real inhibition about standing up and criticizing Israel openly," said Israeli historian Avi Shlaim in an interview with Terry Gross on "Fresh Air," broadcast on March 13, 2001, by WHYY-FM in Philadelphia.

26. President Harry S Truman's decision to recognize Israel was a difficult one because his advisers strongly disagreed over whether it was a good idea. Some, including Secretary of State George Marshall, opposed recognition fearing that it would doom the U.N. partition plan. Others, including Clark Clifford, wanted Truman to recognize Israel because they believed it would bring him political support in the upcoming U.S. presidential election of 1948. David McCullough, *Truman* (New York: Simon & Schuster, 1992), pp. 600–620.

27. AIPAC, as the pro-Israel lobbying organization is called, was rated by *Fortune* magazine as number four on a list of the twenty-five most effective lobbying groups in Washington. It came after the National Rifle Association, the American Association of Retired Persons, and the National Federation of Independent Business. *Fortune*, May 28, 2001.

28. Clyde R. Mark, *Israel: U.S. Foreign Assistance*, Congressional Research Service, Library of Congress, Washington, D.C., updated January 14, 2002. The Israeli per capita GDP is from the *CIA World Factbook*. In addition to economic assistance, the United States has provided Israel with $625 million to develop and deploy the Arrow antimissile missile; $1.3 billion to develop the Lavi aircraft, $200 million to develop the Merkava tank, and $130 million to develop a high-energy laser antimissile system. Mark, *Israel: U.S. Foreign Assistance*, p. 1.

Egypt is the second largest recipient of both annual foreign U.S. aid and of cumulative U.S. aid since 1948, having received $55.8 billion as of 2002. Clyde R. Mark, *Egypt–United States Relations*, Congressional Research Service, Library of Congress, Washington, D.C., updated January 17, 2002, p. 12. The United States has provided Palestinians with about $780 million in U.S. assistance since 1993. Clyde R. Mark, *Middle East: U.S. Foreign Assistance, FY2000, FY2201, and FY2002 Request*, May 2, 2001, p. 3.

29. "Report on Israeli Settlement," p. 5.

30. "Money is fungible" quote is from Mark, *Israel: U.S. Foreign Assistance*, p. 7. The same report states, "The United States did withhold aid to Israel in 1953, during the Eisenhower Administration, until Israel stopped a water diversion project in a U.N. demilitarized zone along the Israeli-Syrian border," but between "Presidents Eisenhower and Bush, as far as is known, no Administration applied conditions to U.S. aid to Israel." Mark, *Israel: U.S. Foreign Assistance*, p. 5. Glenn Frankel, *Beyond the Promised Land* (New York: Simon & Schuster, 1994), p. 307.

31. Bush comment in Walid Khalidi, "Islam, the West and Jerusalem," Center for Contemporary Arab Studies and Center for Muslim-Christian Understanding, Georgetown University, 1996, p. 24. Baker quote in Neff, *Fallen Pillars*, p. 159.

32. Under the Rabin-Bush agreement, which does not affect the amount of bilateral aid Israel receives, the U.S. reduces the amount of guaranteed loan money by whatever amount the U.S. estimates Israel has spent on settlement building in the occupied territories. It is not clear if the U.S. makes deductions equivalent to what Israel spends to build Jewish housing in East Jerusalem. Since 1993, the U.S. has deducted $773.8 mil-

lion from loan guarantees worth $10 billion. By 2002, Israel had only used $6.6 billion of the original $10 billion. Mark, *Israel: U.S. Foreign Assistance*, p. 4.

After the Oslo Accords the Israeli government continued to build settlements and confiscate Palestinian property in the West Bank for highways for exclusive use by Israelis. In East Jerusalem, it built an apartment settlement of 6,500 units for 30,000 Israelis in southeast Jerusalem at Jabal Abu Ghanaim (Har Homa in Hebrew). In April 2001, Israel announced plans for 700 more home sites in the West Bank. The U.S. issued a statement calling the expansions "provocative." Clyde R. Mark, *Palestinians and Middle East Peace: Issues for the United States*, Congressional Research Service, updated January 25, 2002, p. 10; Caryle Murphy, "Israel Girdling Jerusalem with New Jewish Housing," *Washington Post*, December 13, 1994; "Report on Israeli Settlement," pp. 4–5.

These post-Oslo Israeli actions contributed to Palestinian frustration and anger, which helped spark the second Palestinian intifada of 2000–2002, as Jeff Halper, professor of anthropology at Israel's Ben Gurion University, laid out in a biting essay entitled "How to Start an Intifada," and published at ramallahonline.com, April 21, 2001.

33. The United States also halted a shipment of cluster bombs to Israel in July 1982 after reports that Israel had used the antipersonnel weapon in Lebanon, contravening U.S. restrictions that they should only be used for defensive purposes. *Facts on File 1982*, pp. 432 and 528.

34. Khalidi, "Islam, the West and Jerusalem," p. 20.

35. For the Camp David and Taba talk summary, I have used these sources: Deborah Sontag, "And Yet So Far: Quest for Mideast Peace: How and Why It Failed," *New York Times*, July 26, 2001; Akiva Eldar, "The Peace that Nearly Was at Taba," *Ha'aretz*, Special Report, February 14, 2002; Sara Leibovich-Dar, "What Else Is New?" *Ha'aretz*, on-line edition, January 4, 2002; Robert Malley and Hussein 'Agha, "Camp David: The Tragedy of Errors," *New York Review of Books*, August 9, 2001; and the European Union (Ambassador Miguel Moratinos) "Non-Paper" on Taba talks available online at badil.org and "Report on Israeli Settlement in the Occupied Territories," Foundation for Middle East Peace, Washington, D.C., vol. 11, no. 2 (March-April 2001).

36. Israeli historian Shlaim said in an interview that Sharon's "cruelty is very consistent," noting that he had ordered a 1953 raid on a Palestinian village in which sixty-nine civilians were killed and "perceived his job in the reprisal raids to be to kill as many Arabs as possible." *Ha'aretz* on-line interview, "What Else Is New?"

The 1983 Kahan Commission of Inquiry into the 1982 slaughter of hundreds of Palestinian refugees in the Lebanese refugee camps of Sabra and Shatila found that Sharon as defense minister had been negligent in not foreseeing the potential for a massacre when his Christian Phalangist allies were allowed into the camps. The Commission's report found that Sharon bore indirect responsibility and recommended he be removed from office, saying in its closing comments that he "bears personal responsibility" for the massacre. "It is impossible to justify the Minister of Defense's disregard of the danger of a massacre," the report stated, adding that "responsibility is to be imputed to the Minister of Defense for having disregarded" that danger. The Kahan Commission said seven hundred to eight hundred Palestinians—mostly all civilians— were killed. The exact number is disputed. Final report of Kahan Commission, *The Jerusalem Post*, February 9, 1983.

Ellen Siegel, an American nurse working in the refugee camps during the massacre, has given one of the most moving firsthand accounts of what happened. "After Nineteen Years: Sabra and Shatila Remembered," *Middle East Policy Council Journal* 8, no. 4 (December 2001). Siegel testified before the Kahane Commission.

More than a score of survivors of the Sabra and Shatila massacre charged Sharon with crimes against humanity in Belgian courts under a controversial Belgian law claiming universal jurisdiction over human rights cases. But the International Court at the Hague ruled in February 2002 that serving ministers have immunity from prosecution in such cases. And in June 2002, a Belgian appeals court dismissed the charges because Sharon was not on Belgian territory.

37. In January 2002, a group of Israeli Army reservists refused to serve in the West Bank

and Gaza Strip saying they did not want to be part of a "mission of occupation and repression." Joel Greenberg, "Israeli Group Declares Limit in Making War on Palestinians," *New York Times*, January 29, 2002. Over the next few months, the number of reservists who refused to serve grew to nearly five hundred. As of June 2002, after disciplinary hearings before their military commanders, nearly ninety of them had been sentenced to military jail for thirty-five days. But none received lengthy prison terms.

38. "An Unconditional Withdrawal from the Territories Is Urgently Needed," *Le Monde*, December 22, 2001. Ayalon headed Shin Bet, the agency responsible for Israeli internal security, from February 1996 to May 2000. In the interview, he added that he favored "unconditional withdrawal from the territories, a true withdrawal, which gives the Palestinians territorial continuity." If they proclaim a state, he said, "Israel should be the first to recognize it."

14. The Promise and the Passion

1. The phase was used by Amina Wadud, "Beyond Interpretation," *Boston Review*, a publication of Massachusetts Institute of Technology, January 2002.

GLOSSARY

alim; ulama (pl.)—a Muslim religious scholar

dhimmi—"protected minority," status accorded to Jews and Christians in Islamic law

fatwa; fatawa (pl.)—religious opinion by a recognized scholar in Islamic law, usually given in response to a question

fiqh—Islamic jurisprudence; a body of legal rulings

hadith—a story or anecdote about the life or thought of Prophet Muhammad, usually quoting him

hajj—pilgrimage to Mecca, Islam's holiest city, which is a once-in-a-lifetime obligation for a Muslim if physically and financially able

haraam—religiously forbidden

hijab—literally, curtain or barrier; also Islamic dress for women, usually the headscarf or veil

hisba—ancient Islamic legal principle permitting Muslims to be taken to court for doing something that harmed Islam

ijtihad—exerting one's utmost to understand

imam—a prayer leader

jihad—exertion or struggle of any kind, can be interior and spiritual or exterior and physical

jizya—poll tax once paid by Jews and Christians, "People of the Book," to Muslim governments

kafir—an unbeliever, infidel

kufr—the act of unbelief

Qur'an—book of 114 chapters containing God's revelation to humankind, transmitted through Prophet Muhammad

Ramadan—holy month of fasting for Muslims

shahada—the Muslim profession of faith (and first requirement of Muslims) that states: "There is no god but God, and Muhammad is His messenger"

shari'a—Islamic law; more broadly, principles for moral conduct

shura—consultation

Sunna—the written collection of customs, precedents, and traditions dating from Prophet Muhammad's time, passed down through generations of Muslims and regarded as the second scriptural source of their faith after the Qur'an. The Sunna is composed in part of *hadith*, the stories or anecdotes about the life or thought of Prophet Muhammad, usually with a quote from him.

taqlid—blind imitation or following of past legal rulings

tawhid—the unity or oneness of God

umma—community of believers in Islam

zakat—obligatory donation to charity required of Muslims, usually 2.5 percent of one's net worth

ACKNOWLEDGMENTS

If ever a book could be compared to a community garden it is this one. *Passion for Islam* is the result of an effort nurtured by many hands, some sowing, some pruning, some watering. So many people have kindly and generously helped bring it to fruition that I am unable to adequately thank them all. But let me try. I first want to thank the Graham family, particularly Don Graham and his mother, the late Katharine Graham, for keeping aglow the bright light of dedicated journalism in a newspaper that has been my professional home for more than twenty years. I thank them for the reporting opportunities I had at *The Washington Post*, which were the roots of this book.

Among the many wonderful editors at the paper that I have been blessed to work with, I want to thank in particular Michael Getler, who provided the prologue by having faith in me and sending me off to Cairo, and to Jo-Ann Armao, who provided the epilogue years later by giving me the time to finish the manuscript.

I also want to thank Les Gelb of the Council on Foreign Relations, where I was an Edward R. Murrow Fellow from 1994 to 1995, for giving me a cubbyhole to work in at East Sixty-eighth Street in New York. My appreciation, too, to Leigh Gusts of the Council's library and her staff for their help. It was also at the Council that I met James Piscatori, to whom I am most grateful for patiently listening and leading me to a deeper understanding of Islam today.

To my agent, Gail Ross, goes thanks for taking a leap of faith with my proposal. And to Lisa Drew, my editor, and Erin Curler, her assistant, more thanks for their patient and encouraging shepherding that made the book a reality.

Throughout the Middle East, scores of people have my gratitude for helping me understand their world. Whether translating, driving, feeding, listening, or answering my questions, they were always gracious and generous. I had some special friends in Cairo who were indispensable to giving this book life. They include the late Tahseen Basheer, who was always there with sound counsel; the late Hisham Mubarak, who willingly shared his insights and research; Mohamed Kamal Shahda, who translated many key documents; and last but not least, the Shariah Sri Lanka Crew, without whom I could not have done my job: James Martone, Fatemah Farag, and Mohamed Abdel Salam. I also want to thank all the Egyptians you met in these pages for sharing their ideas and lives with me.

Many people generously took time to read my manuscript, clearing it of the debris of extraneous words and factual inaccuracies. For this, my thanks go to Geoffrey Aronson, Carl Ek, Mamoun Fandy, Jean Hudson, Laith Kubba, Molly and Jim McCartney, Augustus Richard Norton, Houeida Saad, Susan Saccoccia, Ellen Siegel, Christopher Taylor, Mona Yacoubian, and an Iraqi friend who wishes to remain unnamed. I also want to thank Charles E. Butterworth and John O. Voll for their help.

No garden prospers without sunshine and that was supplied by many friends, some old, some new, who gave encouragement and help at crucial times. For that, I thank Lois Alsop, Karlyn Barker, Annie Dant, Raghida Dergham, Pamela McClintock, Carol Morello, Sylvia Moreno, Ellen Nakashima, Elizabeth Neuffer, Carmen Nicholson, Ladislas Orsy, Bobbye Pratt, Dana Priest, Lisa Rein, Mary Beth Sheridan, Virginia Sherry, Alan Sipress, Margot Williams, and for her support, lo these many years, Robin Wright.

Finally, I especially thank my mother, Muriel, who taught me the most important lessons in life, and the rest of my family—Kerry, Jerry, Colin, Nina, Kevin, Laura, Kenan, Erin, Colleen, and David. All sustained me with their love and support throughout this project, for which I am grateful, even if it did come packaged in their own Celtic version of encouragement, as in: "So, are you on chapter two yet?"

INDEX